The Environmental Policy Paradox

second edition

The Environmental Policy Paradox

ZACHARY A. SMITH

Northern Arizona University

PRENTICE HALL, Englewood Cliffs, New Jersey 07632

Library of Congress Cataloging-in-Publication Data

SMITH, ZACHARY A. (ZACHARY ALDEN)
    The environmental policy paradox/Zachary A. Smith—2nd ed.
      p. cm.
    Includes index.
    ISBN 0-13-081606-X
    1. Environmental policy—United States. 2. Environmental policy.
I. Title.
GE180.S45 1994
363.7′00973—dc20   94-6532
                                      CIP

Acquisitions editor: Charlyce Jones Owen
Assistant editor: Jennie Katsaros
Copy editor: Anne Lesser
Cover designer: Bruce Kenselaar
Production coordinator: Mary Ann Gloriande
Editorial assistant: Nicole Signoretti
Editorial/production supervision
   and interior design: Rob DeGeorge

 © 1995, 1992 by Prentice-Hall, Inc.
A Simon & Schuster Company
Englewood Cliffs, New Jersey 07632

Printed in the United States of America

10 9 8 7 6 5 4 3 2 1

ISBN 0-13-081606-X

PRENTICE-HALL INTERNATIONAL (UK) LIMITED, *London*
PRENTICE-HALL OF AUSTRALIA PTY. LIMITED, *Sydney*
PRENTICE-HALL CANADA INC., *Toronto*
PRENTICE-HALL HISPANOAMERICANA, S.A., *Mexico*
PRENTICE-HALL OF INDIA PRIVATE LIMITED, *New Delhi*
PRENTICE-HALL OF JAPAN, INC., *Tokyo*
SIMON & SCHUSTER ASIA PTE. LTD., *Singapore*
EDITORA PRENTICE-HALL DO BRASIL, LTDA., *Rio de Janeiro*

for Lisa

Contents

Preface

The policy-making process described in many public policy and American government texts shows just the tip of the iceberg. This book, designed for courses on environmental policy, environmental studies, and public policy, and as supplemental reading in American government and public administration courses, exposes the rest of the iceberg: the workings of government that are rarely visible but necessary for an appreciation of the formation of environmental policy. It examines environmental policy in the United States in air, water, land use, agriculture, energy, waste disposal, and other areas, and, in so doing, provides an introduction to the policy-making process in the United States.

A paradox is an apparently contradictory combination of opposing ideas. The paradox of environmental policy is that we often understand what the best short- and long-term solutions to environmental problems are, yet the task of implementing these solutions is either left undone or is completed too late. Although this is a general characteristic of policy formation in the United States, it is particularly true of environmental policy. The explanation lies in the nature of the policy-making process. A few broad examples will illustrate the nature of the environmental policy paradox.

Problems in regard to farming and food production in the United States include the loss of topsoil due to soil erosion, the loss of soil productivity, and the overuse of pesticides and fertilizers. Although opinions vary, there is strong evidence that a shift to organic farming would increase farm income and reduce soil erosion and nutrient depletion while meeting American food needs and reducing oil imports. However, regardless of the potential benefits of organic farming, the incentives operating on policy-makers in the policy-making process make it very unlikely that any significant changes will be made in the foreseeable future in U.S. farm policy. That is the paradox.

Energy provides another good example. Although estimates vary as to how long fossil fuels will last, there is widespread agreement that a transition must be made from fossil to renewable fuels. This transition will have a significant impact on our economic, social, cultural, and political lives. This paradox is that, in the 1990s, little is being done in the public sector to prepare for this change.

Finally, one of the most dramatic examples of the paradox is in the management of solid waste. The total amount of solid waste produced in the United States from all sources amounts to an average of 21 tons a year or 115 pounds a day for each American. Roughly 80 percent of the solid waste generated in the United States is deposited in sanitary landfills; only 10 percent is recycled. For several decades we have understood and could have anticipated most of our solid waste problems. Paradoxically, largely because of political considerations, little has been done to address the problem. More than half of the cities in the United States either have exhausted, or are very close to exhausting, their landfill capacity.

Any examination of environmental policy must begin with a discussion of the setting in which policy is formulated. No simple explanations or definitions can completely convey why or why not a given policy comes into being. Limitations on human comprehension, as well as in the quality and extent of information available, make it difficult to understand the cause-and-effect relationships in public policy formation.

This book, nevertheless, provides a basic understanding of why some environmental ideas shape policy while others do not. We describe the formal institutional setting in which environmental policy is developed, the major participants involved, and the political and institutional incentives that motivate those attempting to influence the policy-formation system. Through an understanding of the informal political and institutional incentives that influence policy formation, the reader will be able to see that the system, though complex and uncertain, does respond to appropriate inputs. People can make changes when they understand the game.

ORGANIZATION

The book is divided into two parts. Part One, The Policy-Making Process, provides an overview of how governmental policy is made in the United States. It emphasizes informal and noninstitutional aspects of the process and the incentives in the policy-making process that direct participant behavior.

Before delving into the policy-making process in environmental policy, however, Chapter 1 introduces ecosystems and the study of ecology, thus setting the stage for the chapters that follow. Good environmental policy is based on an understanding of how the physical environment works. Chapter 1 also provides a general discussion of the interdependence of ecosystems and explains the need to evaluate environmental policy from a multidisciplinary perspective. The complexity of ecosystem interdependence requires, in many cases, an international or global perspective.

Chapter 2 explores the relationship of our dominant social paradigm (those clusters of Western cultural beliefs, values, and ideals that influence our thinking about society, government, and individual responsibility) to environmental policy formation. The chapter also summarizes the history of the environmental movement and public opinion about environmental problems—two important components of the Western industrial dominant social paradigm.

Chapter 3 examines the regulatory environment in the environmental policy area. This discussion includes an examination of the current regulatory framework in the United States, various regulatory alternatives that have been suggested, and some of the assumptions that underlie current thinking about appropriate environmental regulations.

Chapter 4 examines the institutional setting of the policy-making process. The incentives operating on participants in the process and the role of interest groups are discussed along with advantages certain policy-making participants enjoy when influencing environmental policy. These incentives include the short-term incentives available to policymakers for evaluating policy options; incentives or disincentives in dealing with externalities (i.e., those costs or benefits of a course of action not directly involved in the policy); the status quo orientation of the system; the role of subgovernments or "iron triangles" in certain policy areas; and the incremental nature, in most cases, of policy formation in the United States. Chapter 4 also describes more formal means of environmental control, such as the requirement of an environmental impact statement, or EIS, and introduces the administrative agencies most involved in environmental administration in the United States.

In Part Two we examine environmental policy in seven chapters that discuss air pollution, energy policy, solid and hazardous waste policy, land management, international environmental problems, and international environmental management. In each area there are current policies that do not effectively address the problems with which they were meant to deal. This is true even though experts are often in agreement about what needs to be done. The paradox of environmental policy is that the system does not produce policies that will get it done.

The impact we are having on our environment calls into serious question whether or not humans will survive many more generations. It is my hope that after reading this book you will have a better understanding of environmental problems, the system that produced these problems, and what you can do to help produce a better future.

ACKNOWLEDGMENTS

Many people provided guidance and support for this project, for both the first and second editions. Early on I asked for input on the topics to be covered and the treatment afforded each topic. I want to thank Richard C. Allison, Richard N.L. Andrews, Mary Timney Bailey, C. Richard Bath, James S. Bowman, M. Paul Brown, Gary Bryner, Susan J. Buck, John A. Busterud, Jerry W. Calvert, Henry P. Caulfield, Jr., Jeanne Nienaber Clarke, Bruce Clary, Barbara Coe, Hanna J. Cortner, W. Douglas Costain, John Crow, Paul J. Culhane, Kenneth A. Dahlberg, Ralph C. D'Arge, Clarence J. Davies, David Howard, Davis, Riley E. Dunlap, Robert E. Eagle, Sheldon M. Edner, Ward E. Elliott, John G. Francis, John C. Freemuth, William Green, Forest Grieves, George M. Guess, Marjorie Randon Hershey, Sandra K. Hinchman, William W. Hogan, John D. Hutcheson, Jr., Susan Hunter, Harold C. Jordahl, Jr., Lauriston R. King, John Kingdon, Michael E. Kraft, Henry Krisch, Berton L. Lamb, Kai N. Lee, James P. Lester, Harvery Lieber, Daniel R. Mandelker, Dean E. Mann, David L. Martin, Albert R. Matheny, Daniel McCool, Stephen P. Mumme, Tom Payette, Charles S. Pearson, John Duncan Powell, Barry G. Rabe, James L. Regens, Mark E. Rushefsky, William Russell, Dean Schooler, Ronald G. Shaiko, Gilbert B. Siegel, J. Allen Singleton, Henry B. Sirgo, Nancy Paige Smith, Dennis L. Soden, Marvin S. Soroos, Peter G. Stillman, Lawrence Susskind, Dennis Thompson, Richard Tobin, Evert Vedung, Norman J. Vig, Lettie M. Wenner, and Clifton E. Wilson for their valuable suggestions. Several others, notably government officials, desired anonymity. Since they know who they are, I thank them just the same.

For research and editorial assistance I would like to thank Mary Brentwood, Connie Brooks, Sandra Demoruelle, Kathleen Dorn, Lucinda John, and Sharon Ridgeway. Their input was crucial.

The following reviewers provided helpful suggestions and useful insights: Lowell Dittmer, University of California at Berkeley, and Peter Kim, Westminster College.

I of course, hold all of the above blameless for the results.

Abbreviations

AEC	Atomic Energy Commission
AQCRs	Air Quality Control Regions
BIA	Bureau of Indian Affairs
BLM	Bureau of Land Management
CAA	Clean Air Act
CEQ	Council on Environmental Quality
CFCs	Chlorofluorocarbons
CNEPA	Comprehensive National Energy Policy Act
COET	Crude Oil and Equalization Tax
CWA	Clean Water Act
DOE	Department of Energy
DOI	Department of Interior
DSP	Dominant social paradigm
EA	Environmental Assessment
ECE	United Nations Economic Commission for Europe
EEC	European Economic Community
EIS	Environmental Impact Statement
EPA	Environmental Protection Agency
ERC	Emission Reduction Credit
ERDA	Energy Research and Development Administration
FERC	Federal Energy Regulatory Commission
FIPS	Federal Implementation Plans

FLPMA	Federal Land Policy and Land Management Act
FONSI	Finding of No Significant Impact
FPC	Federal Power Commission
GAO	General Accounting Office
IAEA	International Atomic Energy Commission
IGO	International Government Organization
JCAE	Joint Committee on Atomic Energy
LCEP	Least Cost Energy Planning
LDC	Less Developed Countries
LEAF	Legal Environmental Assistance Foundation
LNG	Liquid Natural Gas
LULU	Locally Unwanted Land Use
LWR	Light water reactor
MOIP	Mandatory Oil Import Program
MU	Multiple use
NAAQS	National Ambient Air Quality Standards
NARUC	National Association of Regulatory Utility Commissioners
NASA	National Aeronautics and Space Administration
NEP	National Energy Plan
NEPA	National Environmental Policy Act
NO_x	Nitrogen oxides
NPDES	National Pollution Discharge Elimination System
NRC	Nuclear Regulatory Commission
NRDC	Natural Resources Defense Council
NSPS	New source performance standards
OPEC	Organization of Petroleum Exporting Countries
OSHA	Occupational Safety and Health Administration
ppm	Parts per million
PURPA	Public Utilities Regulatory Policies Act
PV	Photovoltaic
R&D	Research and development
RARE	Roadless Area Review and Evaluation
RCRA	Resource Conservation and Recovery Act
REA	Rural Electrification Act
SDWA	Safe Drinking Water Act
SIP	State Implementation Plan
SO_2	Sulfur dioxide
SO_3	Sulfur trioxide
TCE	Trichloroethylene
TMI	Three Mile Island
TVA	Tennessee Valley Authority
USDA	United States Department of Agriculture

The Environmental
Policy Paradox

chapter 1

Ecosystem Interdependence

No examination of environmental policy can be complete without an understanding of the laws and forces that drive the natural world. In this chapter we explore ecology, the subfield of biology that strives to explain the relationship of people and other living things to their natural environment. Only through an understanding of how a natural environment works can we understand the impact of policies designed to regulate that environment.

An ecosystem is any group of plants, animals, and nonliving things interacting within their external environment. Typically ecologists study individual organisms (the life cycle of the individual, requirements, functioning in the environment); populations of organisms (including questions such as stability, decline, or growth in populations); communities of organisms; or the ecosystem as a whole (including the biogeochemical cycles of carbon, oxygen, hydrogen, soil minerals, and energy).[1]

Ecosystems may seem to be independent units that interact very little with their external environment. Some ecologists describe them as "a watershed in New Hampshire, a Syrian desert, the Arctic icecap, or Lake Michigan."[2] Yet ecosystems are "open," in the sense that they interact with everything else in the environment. In fact, the earth itself is an ecosystem commonly referred to as the ecosphere or biosphere.[3]

Earth, like all ecosystems, receives energy from the sun. Otherwise, there is very little interaction between the earth and the external environment. Consequently, with the exception of energy from the sun, the resources that the planet started with are the same as those that exist today (although constantly changing form). This is why some use the term *Spaceship earth* to describe the earth's relationship with the external environment. Like a spaceship the planet must work with what it has. When certain resources are exhausted, or converted into a form in which they are no longer useful to humans, they are lost forever.

To better understand how an ecosystem functions, let's use the oversimplified example of a freshwater ecological cycle. Fish, in a river or a lake, produce organic waste that settles to the bottom, nourishing bacteria and creating inorganic products from which algae feed. The fish in turn feed off the algae. This example suggests that the interrelationships within an ecosystem are relatively simple. But in fact, as Edward Kormondy, a leading ecologist, wrote, "The ecologist, in studying natural systems, is confronted by the complexities of almost unlimited variables."[4] Barry Commoner, in his book *The Closing Circle*, identifies four "laws of ecology" that are based on accepted norms in the science of ecology. These laws are useful in understanding how ecosystems function and the limits to humankind's ability to manipulate them.[5]

The first law of ecology is that everything is connected to everything else. "An ecosystem consists of multiple interconnective parts, which act on one another."[6] The interconnectedness of ecosystems suggest it is difficult, if not impossible, to manipulate one aspect of an ecosystem without having impacts, often unintentional, on other aspects of it. The first law of ecology "reflects the existence of the elaborate network of interconnections in the ecosphere: among different living organisms, and between populations, species, and individual organisms in their physicochemical surroundings."[7]

When an ecosystem is disrupted by the introduction of a foreign element, for example, changes occur in the relationship between organisms within the system. However, they can often adjust and regain their balance. For example, in the case of drought in a grassland, lack of food will result in malnutrition of mice, which will eventually lead to their hibernation. During hibernation they are, of course, eating less, allowing the grasses to rejuvenate and protecting their own numbers by being less exposed to predators.[8]

When an ecosystem is disrupted, that system may not always go back into balance. For example, in the case of a freshwater lake, the organic waste that appears in the lake naturally plays an important role in the food chain, affecting the growth of algae. If, however, a foreign source of nutrient is introduced to the lake, it can lead to the rapid growth of algae, resulting in eutrophication. In this example the nutrient might be septic tank sewage. The bacteria from a septic tank stimulates the growth of algae, which consumes available oxygen. The lack of oxygen eventually kills other life-forms in the lake.

The second law of ecology is that everything must go somewhere. Commoner uses the example of the mercury in a dry cell battery to illustrate this point.

First it is placed in a container of rubbish; this is collected and taken to an incinerator. Here the mercury is heated; this produces mercury vapor which is emitted by the incinerator stack, and mercury vapor is toxic. Mercury vapor is carried by the wind, eventually brought to earth in rain or snow. Entering a mountain lake, let us say, the mercury condenses and sinks to the bottom. Here it is acted on by bacteria which convert it to methyl mercury. This is soluble and taken up by fish; since it is not metabolized, the mercury accumulates in the organs and flesh of the fish. The fish is caught and eaten by a man and the mercury becomes deposited in his organs, where it might be harmful. And so on.[9]

This second law of ecology is applicable when thinking of the earth. It is an enclosed unit, like a spaceship. Nothing is just thrown away. The fossil fuels when they burn release sulfur dioxide and nitrogen oxides that must go somewhere—and as we have learned, it often may be into our rivers and lakes as acid rain, or into the upper atmosphere contributing to the greenhouse effect, or global warming. As we see later, some environmental policies, such as solid waste disposal, seem to ignore the second law of ecology.

The third law of ecology is that nature knows best. Throughout most of human history, at least in the West, there has been an assumption that humans can, or perhaps should, conquer nature. This third law of ecology suggests that when it comes to manipulating relationships in nature humankind is at best a poor judge of how their manipulations of the environment will impact nature. Commoner uses the analogy of the watch to explain the third law of ecology.

Suppose you were to open the back of your watch, close your eyes, and poke a pencil into the exposed works. The almost certain result would be to damage the watch. . . . Over the years numerous watchmakers, each taught by a predecessor, have tried out a huge variety of detailed arrangements of how a watch works, have discarded those that are not compatible with the overall operation of the system and retain the better features. . . . Any random change made in the watch is likely to fall into a very large class of inconsistent, or harmful, arrangements which have been tried out in past watchmaking experience and discarded.[10]

The third law of ecology suggests that humans' tinkering with natural systems, like the random poke of your watch with a pencil, will, ultimately, prove detrimental to those systems.

To understand the importance of the third law of ecology, we must remember that ecosystems have developed through natural selection over billions of years. The interactions within natural systems sometimes present a very delicate balance, and interfering can disrupt that system. Nature is usually a better judge of what is good for the long-term viability of any given system. Commoner goes on to note, "The artificial introduction of an organic compound that does not occur in nature, but is man-made and is nevertheless active in a living system, is very likely to be harmful."[11]

The fourth law of ecology is that there is no such thing as a free lunch. Simply stated, this law provides that any interaction with nature, any extraction, use, or disruption, carries with it some cost. That cost may be in the form of the conversion of resources to a form in which they are no longer of use to humans, or the disruption of an ecosystem that renders it unstable. Commoner notes, "Because the global ecosystem is a connected whole, in which nothing can be gained or lost and which is not subject to overall improvement, anything extracted from it by human effort must be replaced. Payment of this price cannot be avoided; it can only be delayed."[12]

THE STEADY STATE

While Commoner's four laws of ecology provide a useful orientation for our thinking about humankind's interaction with its environment, there are two additional components of our relationship with nature that need to be expounded on: the notion of a steady state and the common pool nature of resources.

A *steady state* refers to that level of activity within an ecosystem that can be maintained over a long period of time. For example, given the limitations on arable land and water resources, there is some upper limit of human population that the world can sustain. Given the finite nature of the earth's resources, the exhaustion of resources has an impact on the form a steady state on earth will take.

All ecosystems have some point at which they reach a steady state. This is not to suggest that resource utilization cannot be greater than that necessary for sustaining the steady state, but only that resources used today impact the nature and circumstances of the balance necessary to create a steady state within an ecosystem in the future. The steady state idea—as applied to environmental policy—is problematic, as you will see later, where there is disagreement about what the upper limit or carrying capacity of an ecosystem is.

COMMON POOL RESOURCES

Garrett Hardin, in his influential essay "The Tragedy of the Commons,"[13] drew the attention to the problems associated with common pool resources. He uses the analogy of a common green, or the sharing of a common pasture, where the rational individual will seek to maximize his or her returns from that pasture by putting as many additional cattle as he or she can afford onto the commons. This rational individual behavior, however, will result in destruction through overgrazing of the common pasture. No individual in this situation has an incentive to protect the pasture. In fact, the incentives operating on individuals are to increase their return from the pasture, the result being the destruction of the pasture for everyone.

Common pool property problems are very much a part of environmental policy. The groundwater in an aquifer underlying several farms, for example, may be a common pool resource. Farmers located above the property have no incentive to save the groundwater for a future use. In fact, if adjacent landowners are pumping the water rapidly, they may have an incentive to pull as much out of the ground as possible as soon as possible, there being no incentive to manage the resource for the long-term beneficial use of all.

Air is also a common pool resource. Each individual polluter has no incentive to protect the common pool resource of clean air. In fact, the individual has every incentive to continue polluting. The cost of air pollution is not borne by the polluter but rather by the community as a whole.

Polluters on a body of water are in a similar situation, as are users of any resource who are not responsible and have no incentive to ensure the use and management of that resource over the long term. The oceans are a classic example of common pool resource problems. Nations have little or no incentive to restrict their harvesting of fish when they are competing with other nations that are not willing to similarly restrict their fishing activities. The result is the depletion, and possibly the eventual destruction, of the common pool fisheries. Likewise in ocean pollution, because there is no international body governing pollution discharges into the ocean, individual nations have little or no incentive to regulate their polluting activities in a way that will provide for a clean ocean environment for all the inhabitants of the earth. Again, what makes sense for the individual, that is, the nations that are polluting, will ultimately lead to the destruction of the overall resource. As you will see later, common pool problems are often involved in environmental policy implementation.

SUMMARY

Understanding ecological relationships, common pool problems, and the notion of the steady state provides the background necessary for appreciating the complexities involved in environmental policy formation and implementation. An understanding of the values that drive the policy-making process is an important component of this appreciation. This is the subject of the next chapter.

NOTES

1. Thomas C. Emmel, *Ecology & Population Biology* (New York: Norton, 1973), pp. 3,13.
2. Jonathan Turk, *Introduction to Environmental Studies* (2nd Ed.) (Philadelphia: Saunders, 1985), p. 26.
3. Edward J. Kormondy, *Concepts of Ecology* (3rd ed.) (Englewood Cliffs, NJ: Prentice-Hall, 1984), p. 8.
4. Ibid., p. 9.
5. Barry Commoner, *The Closing Circle* (New York: Knopf, 1971).

6. Ibid., p. 33.
7. Ibid.
8. This example was taken from Turk, *Introduction to Environmental Studies*, p. 39.
9. Commoner, *The Closing Circle*, p. 40.
10. Ibid., p. 42.
11. Ibid., p. 43.
12. Ibid., p. 46.
13. Garrett Hardin, "The Tragedy of the Commons," *Science*, 162 (1968), pp. 1243–1248.

chapter 2

The Public
and Environmental
Awareness

DOMINANT SOCIAL PARADIGM

Many argue that environmental problems and the policies that have been adopted to deal with them are a direct result of our dominant social paradigm (DSP). The DSP constitutes those clusters of beliefs, values, and ideals that influence our thinking about society, government, and individual responsibility. The DSP can be defined in various ways but includes acceptance of laissez-faire capitalism, individualism, growth and progress, and a faith in science and technology. Our DSP has influenced the history of environmental policy, public attitudes toward the environment, and environmental regulations. The most important components of the DSP are free market economics, faith in science and technology, and the growth orientation common in Western democracies.

In the United States, the DSP is rooted in the early history of the country—a period when individualism and growth did not seem to conflict with sound resource management. Political philosophers such as John Locke, Emmerich von Vattel, and Jean-Jacques Rousseau, had an important influence on the framers of the U.S. Constitution. These and other philosophers held that humans had certain natural rights, rights we were born with, including the right to life, liberty, and private property. As the Declaration of Independence proclaims, "[W]e hold these truths to be self-evident, that all men are created equal, that they are endowed by their Creator with certain unalienable Rights, that among these are Life, Liberty and the pursuit of Happiness." The idea of individual freedom and the right to hold and use one's property is and always has been fundamental to our DSP and our understanding of what American democracy is all about.[1] For most of our history this has meant a freedom to pollute the environment. Today these freedoms, particularly private property rights, may be inconsistent with sound environmental management.

Continued dominance of the DSP today contributes to environmental problems in a variety of ways. Studies have shown that individual commitment to the DSP is directly connected to lower levels of environmental concern.[2] Furthermore, many scholars have argued that the DSP has a direct relationship to public policy responses to environmental problems.[3]

Economics and Growth

Economic growth, meaning the production of goods and services, to the extent it is dependent on inputs from the environment, has some limitations. The resources for additional automobiles, washing machines, and toasters cannot continue forever—even with highly efficient recycling.[4] Yet it is an assumption of industrial societies, as well as socialist and communist societies, that growth will and should continue. In capitalist countries the profit motive to produce, and induce consumption, drives the economy. As William Ophuls wrote, "[A]ll the incentives of producers are towards growth. . . . [I]t is in the interest of producers to have a high throughput economy characterized by high consumption through product proliferation and promotion, rapid obsolescence, and the like."[5]

Economists study the distribution, production, exchange, and consumption of goods and services. Examining supply and demand in markets that consist of mutual voluntary exchanges where both parties hope to gain is, in large part, the study of economics. Economists assume that consumers attempt to maximize utility, or to spend their money in ways that will give them as much pleasure as possible. They assume consumers pursuing their own self-interest in the marketplace will seek out those goods and services that provide them with the most comfort. Producers, responding to or anticipating consumer demand, provide the goods and services as efficiently as possible, thereby maximizing their profits. All participants in the process, pursuing their own interests, contribute to national income and contribute, it is argued, to the betterment of society. This is the mechanism of the "hidden hand" that Adam Smith referred to in his early economic theory. Market mechanisms such as self-interest, supply and demand, and others are seen to provide not only the maximum available benefits for individuals, but also for society as a whole.

Only in the last few decades have economists turned their attention to environmental issues. The field of economics has long recognized there are certain public goods (such as defense) that private markets do not adequately provide for or provide for at all; therefore economists accept a role for government in the provision of such goods. Only recently, however, have economists addressed themselves to the environmental problems that private markets sometimes ignore. What follows are some criticisms of the assumptions of classic economics as it relates to environmental problems.

Economic transactions do not always incorporate the full range of costs and benefits associated with the production or distribution of goods. For example, when you purchase a set of tires for your car, you anticipate that the cost includes the price of materials, labor, and a reasonable profit for the producer. The cost of those tires may or may not include the cost of cleaning up the pollution that was associated with their production. Yet the air pollution coming from the tire manufacturing plant, if unregulated, presents a real cost to society in terms of contributing to respiratory illness or damage to fish and wildlife through acid rain. This additional cost is referred to as an *externality*. There are both positive and negative externalities. Air pollution is a negative externality. An example of a positive externality would be the benefits one receives by building one's home adjacent to a public park. Theoretically, if the cost of a negative externality is internalized into the cost of a product, then the product's price will reflect its true cost to society. Unfortunately, oftentimes the environmental costs of goods are not internalized.

Two additional criticisms sometimes leveled at market mechanisms for the distribution of goods and services involve information and participation. A perfect market would operate with perfect knowledge of the participants concerning the cost and benefits of their transactions. Oftentimes, however, consumers lack even rudimentary knowledge of those costs and benefits. With respect to benefits, most economists argue that if the consumer perceives the exchanges as beneficial, then for that consumer the exchange is worthwhile. Concerning the true cost of a transaction, often the information, such as the amount of unregulated polluted air that resulted in the manufacturing process, is not available. Under those circumstances, critics argue, even environmentally aware consumers find it difficult, if not impossible, to make environmentally responsible market decisions.

In this author's opinion, perhaps the most fundamental criticism of market mechanisms for distributing goods and services is the failure to consider all the participants affected by market transactions. Assuming that markets maximize benefits for the individuals who participate in them and even accepting that the sum total of all those transactions contributes to the betterment of society, there are affected parties whose interests are not represented in the marketplace. Interests of nonhuman participants, such as plants and animals or ecosystems, and human participants, such as future generations, are not reflected in market transactions. For example, my decision to clear-cut the timber from the slopes of my property may maximize my benefits and produce income for both myself and the lumber company to which the timber is sold today. But it is my children and grandchildren who will have to live with the cost associated with the soil erosion that may result from the removal of the watershed. Similarly, the rapid development of fossil fuels in the twentieth century heavily discounts if not ignores the potential benefits those fuels could have for future generations.

Market systems often pay little attention to the future values of natural resources and little if any attention to values that are not measurable in monetary terms. For example, if a developing country has hardwood stocks that are worth $100 million on the open market today which, if sold, can be put in a bank to earn 10 percent interest a year, then it pays to harvest the trees now *unless* the rate of growth is more than 10 percent a year. As Colin Clark, a professor of applied mathematics at the University of British Columbia explained, "If dollars in banks are growing faster than a timber company's forests, it is more profitable (indeed, more economical) to chop down the trees, sell them, and invest the proceeds elsewhere."[6] Under those conditions clear-cutting a forest or harvesting whales to extinction makes economic sense.

The theory of substitution in economics, that is, that when the price of a good becomes too high consumers will substitute other goods or producers will develop alternative goods, also presents problems for some critics of market economies. Substitution may work quite well in many simple transactions. For example, when the price of a box of cornflakes goes beyond an acceptable threshold set by the consumer, substitution can easily be made to a more economical alternative, such as puffed rice. However, markets are less adept at dealing with absolute scarcity. In a famine situation markets for food collapse.[7] A related problem is that in response to increased prices, consumer preferences do not always lead to substitution. For example, after the 1973 Arab oil embargo, small cars enjoyed a boom in the automobile market but manufacturers soon discovered that even with the increased cost of gas, consumers wanted large cars and hence car manufacturers continued to produce them.[8]

Finally economists view their science as "value free." As Richard McKenzie and Gordon Tullock put it, "[T]he approach of economics is amoral. . . . [A]s economists we cannot say what is just or fair."[9] Yet it seems that the commitment to markets or efficiency or the maximization of utility are in themselves values—and they may be values that preclude other values such as equity, beauty, or the preservation of nature for its own sake.

Whatever the flaws of market mechanisms, there is no denying the growth of orientation of markets and the DSP that embraces them. Given the ultimate limits to economic growth, at *some point* the growth orientation of market economies and our DSP will have to give way to a sustainable societal orientation. In this sense, capitalism may not be consistent with sound long-term environmental management. Again quoting William Ophuls, "[E]cological scarcity undercuts the basic laissez-faire, individualistic premises of the American political economy, so that current institutions are incapable of meeting the challenges of scarcity; what is needed is a new paradigm of politics."[10] Ophuls may be right. However, as we see later, communist and socialist systems have fared no better in protecting the environment.

Science and Technology:
Our Views of Nature

Modern science and technology has its roots in Western civilization and has always had, as a major driving force, the purpose of conquering nature for utilitarian ends.[11] Faith in science and technology and the idea that science will provide solutions for our problems with nature is an important component of our dominant social paradigm.

The twentieth century has seen a number of developments that could lead the casual observer to conclude little in nature is beyond the capacity of people to manipulate. Our grandparents and great-grandparents lived in a world without the polio vaccine, jet travel, the development of antibiotics, or the computer.

In environmental policy, faith in science and technology, and technological breakthroughs which will make everything okay, can be found everywhere. For example, both the Clean Air and Clean Water acts, as we will see later, contain "technology forcing" aspects, in the sense that, when initiated, these acts were based on the assumption that technological breakthroughs would make their requirements possible to implement. In a similar vein, during the nuclear age, many assumed that technological developments would produce ways to neutralize the hazards of radioactive waste. That, of course, never happened.

Faith in science and technology and humankind's ability to manipulate nature also permeates popular and governmental thinking about how to approach environmental problems. For example, as we see later, traditional wastewater treatment involves the removal of solids, floating matter, along with aeration and possibly some level of chemical treatment. Chemicals used in the treatment process may have negative impacts on the ecosystems in which wastewater has been discharged. In contrast, water that does not contain toxic waste can largely be recycled producing fertilizer, nutrients that may be used in aquaculture, and plant matter that may be used as animal feed. The former method is potentially disruptive of ecosystems whereas the latter, which simulates nature, is designed to work with natural systems.

Our faith in science as a cure for environmental problems and the science-based civilization that has dominated the twentieth century has produced dramatic environmental changes, both in quantity and quality. Forests that aboriginal humans would have taken centuries to slash and burn are deforested with bulldozers and chain saws in weeks or days.

Faith in science has, for many, replaced other values (God, family, unity of purpose). Many nations have adopted a blind faith in science as a cure-all for our environmental problems. If it is the "scientific" solution to a problem, it is believed to be automatically the best one. Actually, there are no absolute scientific answers to many questions. Science offers no technological quick fix to ecological problems. In fact, in the enthusiastic flush of scientific do-gooding, much environmental harm can and has been done.

Indeed, it is often said by social commentators that Western society is addicted to technology.[12] Like other addicts, Westerners look to science with the expectation of the "technological fix" or "magic bullet" without a change in human values or morality.[13] Examples of the negative impacts from these technological fixes abound. Modern medicine offers the cure of antibiotics for many fatal infectious diseases of childhood, but this has also contributed to overpopulation. Pesticides, the technological fix that helps to feed the burgeoning global populations, also cause numerous cancers.

The Role of Religion

Religion has played a crucial role in the development of our DSP and defining perceptions of the relationship of humans to their physical environment. The primacy of humans in nature—a central tenet in Judeo-Christian thought—and relatedly, the acceptance of the exploitation of nature for human purposes, has provided a moral justification for the development of the environment in ways that pay little heed to, or ignore, ecosystem balance. At its extreme our religious beliefs may dictate an orientation toward a specific type of environmental management. James Watt, President Reagan's first secretary of the interior, exemplified this when he testified before Congress in 1981 that long-term management of natural resources was not problematic because he did not "know how many future generations we can count on before the Lord returns."[14]

Although religions differ in their formal theories of the relationship of people to the natural world, in practice none of the world's major religious belief systems have motivated their adherents to exercise sound environmental practices.

At societal levels, religion has been used in most cultures to uphold the status quo with minimal turmoil.[15] Religious beliefs are often a critical element in defining and upholding a culture. Many tribal peoples have enjoyed prosperity and unity under the auspices of a successful shaman or other such holy personage who acted as a mediator between the gods and the community.

In more supposedly advanced civilizations, religion historically often acted to sanction the state by authorizing rulers to govern, sharing in the wealth and power amassed through this governance and restraining the masses from objecting when corruption occurred during these liaisons. Examples of church-state collaborations abound, and many are unsavory. The Russian Revolution involved the overthrow of greedy priests along with the conspiring nobles; similarly, Martin Luther joined forces with German princes against the then all-powerful Roman Catholic church and the Holy Roman Emperor; as well, the Buddhists, after a thousand years of assimilation, have engaged in a centuries-old struggle for secular control of Japan with the endemic Shinto religion.

The role of religion in shaping modern industrial societies that value change is generally less identifiable than in traditional societies. Western civilization in the past three centuries has experienced and welcomed ongoing changes accompanied by a decline in the blending of religion and state. Prior to the secularizing progress of the Enlightenment, a moral consensus was seen to arise out of Christendom, with traditional values dominating the populace.[16] During the Age of Enlightenment a shift occurred from belief in the myth and tradition of Christianity to belief in reason and empiricism. The increase in reliance on human experiences as the basis for judging morality in place of divine decrees led to the acceptance of the ethical dichotomy of "pleasure" as righteous and "pain" as evil. It was a short step to the acceptance of the sensualist "pleasure principle" that has fostered the craving for materialistic consumption so prominent in many more developed countries today. Along with the constant materialistic demand for new items to consume that proceeded from the era of the Enlightenment was the concept of the "perfectibility of man," the Victorian ideal of the perpetual improvement of the human race.

This human-centered moral view permeates Western society. Humans, not God, determine destiny through progressive improvements. Increasing secularism placed value on material abundance and loathed poverty. At least since the Industrial Revolution, the only value placed on natural objects, such as trees and rivers, has been their usefulness to humans, especially in regard to applications in industry. Economic concerns were paramount without consideration for the environmental costs.

The drive for material possessions is not the sole explanation for the ecological problems in the West. Our supposedly more spiritually attuned brethren in the East have had their own escalating environmental degradation dilemmas. In Japan, a person has customarily been Shinto simply by virtue of birth. Although the Shinto belief values cleanliness and purity, abhorring pollutants, Japan has had terrible environmental problems such as the mercury poisoning that went on for 20 years at Minamata Bay.[17] Meanwhile, in Hindu India and Pakistan, the reverence for life has resulted in burgeoning populations, struggling merely to survive and unintentionally abusing their environment in the process.[18]

HISTORY OF THE ENVIRONMENTAL MOVEMENT

Historical as well as modern thinking about environmental policy has been shaped by our DSP. Historically, environmental awareness has influenced how environmental policy has developed. The history of the environmental movement may be best understood as having evolved through seven, often overlapping, phases: the period of dominance, the early awakening, early conservationist, later conservationist, the reawakening, complacency, and what we term the little Reagan revolution.

Dominance

Throughout most of American history the environment has been viewed as hostile. Appreciation of the environment for its own sake was rare early in our history. Wilderness was to be conquered and used. Anything of no direct utility to humans was thought to be of little value.[19] This attitude dominated public perceptions of the environment and natural resources throughout the seventeenth, eighteenth, and most of the nineteenth centuries. However, beginning in the second half of the eighteenth century, American writers began to expound on nonutilitarian relationships with nature.

Early Awakening

In the age before mass communication, ideas circulated much more slowly. Important communicators of thought were, to a much greater extent than today, artists and writers who appealed to mass audiences. Nature writers, artists, and poets assisted the early environmental movement by drawing attention to natural areas and environmental problems. The drawings of George Catlin, and the writings of Henry David Thoreau and Ralph Waldo Emerson, were an important catalyst in getting people to think differently about their relationship with nature. Also during the mid-1800s public reaction to the slaughter of bison on the great plains provided the impetus for the beginning of national concern with wildlife preservation.

One of the most influential writers of the period, George Perkins Marsh, published *Man and Nature* in 1864. This work brought to the public's attention environmental degradation and the impact of humans on the environment.

Early Conservationist

The later nineteenth century saw the emergence of the country's first environmentalists—those who, in addition to being concerned about environmental degradation, took up political action. These conservationists, as they called themselves, the most notable of which was John Muir, a founder of the Sierra Club, would now more properly be labeled preservationists. The crusades of these conservationists to establish Yellowstone, Yosemite, and other parks were aimed at severely limiting, if not eliminating, human impact on the natural areas they sought to protect.

The early conservationists had a number of victories. By the time the National Park Service was created in 1916, 37 parks were included under its jurisdiction. Significantly, the early battles between conservationists and those that desired to hold the land open for further development were won in great measure because the future national parks were often viewed as being worthless for anything other than sightseeing.[20] Hence the dominant view in government, if not society, was still one of conquering nature for resource use and exploitation.

By the end of the nineteenth century, conservationists could be divided into those who favored the planned use of natural resources and those who were interested in preserving them in an unspoiled state. We have labeled these individuals early conservationists and later conservationists, respectively.

Later Conservationists

Influenced by the work of George Perkins Marsh, President Theodore Roosevelt became an ardent proponent of resource conservation. However, unlike the earlier conservationists, conservation meant something different to Roosevelt and the first head of the U.S. Forest Service, Gifford Pinchot. Conservation was redefined to mean multiple use or the management of resources so as to return the maximum benefits for people, for example by maximizing the production of water and timber.

In 1898 Pinchot was named the head of the Forestry Division of the Department of Agriculture, and in 1905 after a bitter struggle between the Department of Agriculture and the Department of Interior, Congress placed all forest reserves under the jurisdiction of the Department of Agriculture. Conservation, according to Pinchot, meant the use of natural resources for the benefit of humans. "The object of our forest policy is not to preserve the forests because they are beautiful . . . or because they are refuges for the wild creatures of the wilderness . . . but . . . the making of prosperous homes . . . every other consideration becomes secondary."[21] This attitude was both anthropocentric (the centering of one's views of everything around humans—still a common criticism of environmental policy) and utilitarian (concerned with the utility and practical uses of resources). Should values and uses other than those associated with humans be considered in the management of natural resources? These later conservationists thought not. This utilitarianism was in stark contrast to Muir's and the other preservationists' views of nature. "The frustrated advocates of wilderness preservation had no choice but to call Pinchot a 'deconservationist.'"[22] In 1908 when Pinchot organized a governor's conference on conservation of the natural resources, Muir, along with other spokespersons for the preservation of nature, was not invited.[23]

The new conservationists and their resource policies dominated natural resource policy through most of the twentieth century. The influence of nature societies and clubs such as the Sierra Club and the Audubon Society was little felt until the late 1960s.

The Reawakening

A series of events in the 1960s brought environmental issues to the attention of the public and, eventually, policymakers. Rachel Carson published *Silent Spring* in 1962, focusing public attention, some say for the first time, on pollution with its eye-opening descriptions of the impact of chemicals, primarily pesticides, on the environment.

A number of sensational events also increased public awareness of environmental matters. In the summer of 1969 when a sailor threw a cigarette into Cleveland's Cyahoga River, the river burst into flames. And on January 28, 1969, a Union Oil Company oil platform in the Santa Barbara Channel ruptured, sending hundreds of thousands of gallons of crude oil onto the beaches of Santa Barbara and adjacent communities.

By the late 1960s and early 1970s the environment had become a hot political issue. Politicians from every political persuasion claimed to be in favor of protecting the environment. On January 1, 1970, President Richard Nixon signed the National Environmental Policy Act, stating, "The 1970s absolutely must be the years when America pays its debt to the past by reclaiming the purity of its air, its water, and our living environment. It is literally now or never."[24]

On April 22, 1970, the country observed the first Earth Day. Twenty-two U.S. senators, thousands of students on college campuses, and millions of other people joined in the activities. The goal of Dennis Hayes, founder and organizer of Earth Day, was to keep environmentalism attractive to a broad spectrum of society. "There was a conscious decision in organizing Earth Day that 'environmentalism' would not be posited in a fashion that was ideologically exclusive; there was room for middle-class housewives, business executives, and radical college kids."[25]

From 1968 to 1972 the membership in many organizations including the Sierra Club, the National Audubon Society, the Wilderness Society, and the National Wildlife Federation, increased dramatically, doubling and in some cases tripling.[26]

Thus for the first time it appeared environmentalism was developing a broad base that cut across political ideology, and to a lesser extent, classes. This was in contrast to the earlier conservation movements, which were "hardly a popular movement. The achievements were made by the fortunate influence of a handful of thoughtful men upon a few receptive presidents . . . [It was] . . . the work of an elite—of a few particularly well-placed and influential individuals and small groups."[27]

As we see later, it was during this period that the major environmental regulations dealing with air and water pollution were passed.

Complacency

Through the 1970s public concern about environmental issues leveled and slowly declined, as did the membership in many environmental organizations. But the decade also saw the establishment of new environmental organizations such as the Environmental Defense Fund and the Natural Resources Defense Council, with more specialized objectives—in these cases litigation. Even though President Jimmy Carter was considered a strong environmentalist, who appointed representatives from environmental interest groups to positions of power in the Department of Interior, Environmental Protection Agency, and U.S. Forest Service, some pundits in the late 1970s predicted that the environment as a driving issue in American politics was dead.

The Little Reagan Revolution

Ronald Reagan was elected president with what he claimed was a mandate to "get regulators off our backs." The administration's early appointments made it clear that environmental regulations were a prime target. Although we deal with the policies of the Reagan administration in subsequent chapters, it is important to note here that beginning in 1981, there was a public backlash to what was perceived as the administration's anti-environmentalism. Within a few years after the 1980 election, membership in major environmental organizations skyrocketed—in some cases doubling and tripling.[28]

The 1980s also saw further splintering and growth of new types of environmental groups. For example so-called radical action groups developed such as Earth First! and the Sea Shepherd Conservation Society. These groups engaged in activities such as spiking trees (driving steel spikes into trees, making their harvesting extremely dangerous), lying down in front of bulldozers, and sinking whaling ships.[29]

The 1980s also saw the change in the makeup, organization, and tactics of some of the more traditional environmental organizations. The growth of major environmental organizations had, in some cases, made coordination of efforts on all levels problematic. This growth led to decentralization, so that some organizations, such as the Sierra Club and the Audubon Society, operate semiautonomously, with central offices mainly providing information and services. The strategies of some mainline groups also shifted subtly. Many groups began to feel little could be gained from obstructionism and to have a long-term impact, in addition to pointing out environmental problems, they must provide practical solutions that address the concerns of government and polluters. This approach has been referred to as the new environmentalism.[30]

Why did the membership of environmental interest groups grow in the 1980s and why did additional groups form? Political scientists have developed a number of theories. David Truman in *The Governmental Process* argued that group formation was the result of two related factors: the growing complexity of society and political and economic "disturbances."[31] Complexity or growth and change in society results in some groups or interests becoming more powerful and others less powerful. Technological developments, such as the ability to extract inexpensive fossil fuels from the earth, have in large part been responsible for the environmental problems we face today. Groups are created or grow in response to these developments. The second idea, that of disturbances, refers to political, social, or economic disruptions that upset the equilibrium in some sector of society and bring together the previously unorganized into an interest group whose goals are to deal with the problem that caused the disturbance.

Truman's theory would seem to explain why environmental interest groups were created and grew in the 1970s and 1980s. Technology and society changed, creating more environmental degradation and a series of disturbances such as Love Canal and the Santa Barbara oil spill. These events, and others, provided the catalyst for groups to form and people to join them. The theory has some problems, however. As Jeffrey Berry has pointed out, Truman's theory "is based on optimistic and unjustified assumptions about all people's ability to organize. . . . Equally damning . . . is that many groups have formed without a distinct, identifiable disturbance."[32]

Robert Salisbury has developed what he calls "an exchange theory of interest groups," which attributes group organization and growth to group leadership ability and the delivery of one of three types of benefits to group members. Salisbury argues there are three types of benefits group leaders can use to get members to join groups: *purposive benefits* associated with ideological goals without individual material reward; *material benefits* such as an expected increase in income that induces many to join professional associations such as the American Medical Association; and *solidarity benefits*, or the social rewards one can expect from interacting with a group of people with whom one shares interests.[33] According to this theory the rise in environmental interest group membership and the creation of new groups would have been in large part a function of the activities of group leadership in presenting to potential members the benefits that could come from group membership (primarily purposive benefits). Although environmental groups did seek publicity and try to attract new members during the 1970s and 1980s, much of the growth in many groups was not the result of recruiting but due to external factors (some groups didn't do any advertising or recruiting and still grew).

It would seem that both Truman and Salisbury have contributed to our understanding of why groups form, but that neither alone can account for the formation and growth of environmental groups.

It is interesting to note that during the two periods in American history of greatest natural resource/environmental concern, the early conservation movement and the late 1960s and early 1970s, the issues that were first raised by people who, at the time, were considered to be "radicals," later came to be accepted and adopted by the political mainstream, including, to varying degrees, the business community.

What form will the next phase of the environmental movement take in the United States? Surely a series of environmental disasters such as another Three Mile Island nuclear incident or the accidental pollution of a major source of drinking water for a metropolitan area could trigger widespread demands by the public for increased environmental action. Consequently, it is difficult to predict with any certainty what future environmental policies may develop. However, an examination of public opinion, and particularly how public opinion has changed since the early 1970s, is illuminating for what it says about the depth and importance that environmental issues have for the public.

PUBLIC OPINION AND THE ENVIRONMENT

One of the most important indicators of the salience of environmental issues to the public has been the shift of the public's attitudes toward environmental regulations from the late 1970s to the 1990s. In 1979 when the Roper Organization polled the general public, only 5 percent would agree that environmental regulations had "not gone far enough" to protect the environment. By 1983 the percentage of the public agreeing with that statement had increased to 48.[34]

A series of Cambridge reports taken in the late 1970s and 1980s found similar results. When asked whether or not we should "sacrifice economic growth for environmental protection" in 1979, 37 percent of the population were in favor of sacrificing environmental protection whereas 23 percent were in favor of sacrificing economic growth for the benefit of environmental protection. When asked again in 1988, 19 percent of the public were in favor of sacrificing environmental protection and 58 percent were in favor of sacrificing economic growth. The Cambridge survey also asked respondents if they think "there is too much, too little, or about the right amount of government regulations and involvement in the area of environmental protection." In 1982 35 percent of the public indicated there was too little environmental protection, and in 1986 the percentage indicating there was too little protection had climbed to 59. In 1987, 1988, and 1989 Cambridge Reports asked a national survey to identify the "two most important problems facing the United States today." Only 2 percent named the environment as one of the two most important problems in 1987. By 1988 the number of people identifying the environment had increased to 6 percent and in 1989 this jumped to 16 percent.[35] A CBS News/New York Times Poll asked the public to agree or disagree with the statement that environmental protection "cannot be too high" and should be pursued "regardless of the cost." In 1981 the public was nearly evenly divided with 45 percent agreeing that environmental standards cannot be too high and should be pursued regardless of cost and 42 percent disagreeing with this statement. By 1984 66 percent were in agreement and 27 percent were in disagreement.

What makes these poll results interesting is that social scientists generally are in agreement that public opinion does not often change much in the short term. As Robert Erikson, Norman Luttbeg, and Kent Tedin wrote, "[O]ur review of the results of opinion surveys has disclosed a few instances in which the distribution of opinion on an issue has changed somewhat over time. But these shifts ... can best be seen over a span of many years. In the short run, opinion distribution on long standing issues is generally quite stable."[36]

How can we explain these shifts in public attitude toward the environment? As we see later there were a number of highly publicized environmental problems in the 1980s. Acid rain received more attention during the decade than it had previously. The disaster at Chernobyl certainly alerted many to potential drawbacks of nuclear power, and every few months in the 1980s it seemed there were new revelations about hazardous or toxic waste and the pollution of water resources.

Another reason for the shift in public attitude could be attributed to the perceived anti-environmentalism of the Reagan administration. Reagan's first secretary of the interior, James Watt, was openly hostile toward environmentalists, reportedly refusing phone calls, and repeatedly referring to environmentalists as "extremists." The first administrator of the Environmental Protection Agency (EPA) in the Reagan administration, Anne Burford, was openly and repeatedly criticized for ignoring environmental concerns and currying favor with industrial polluters in the administration and implementation of EPA regulations. Although backlash to the Reagan administration policies surely played some role in the percentage shifts just noted along with the reports of environmental disasters, it is not entirely clear why public attitudes shifted so dramatically.

A closer examination of public opinion with respect to environmental issues reveals several interesting trends. First most analysts thought, until the 1980s, that environmentalism was an upper-middle-class or elite issue. A number of studies conducted during the 1980s found, however, that although the membership of environmental *organizations* is drawn disproportionately from the upper middle class (members of the environmental organizations are likely to have higher educations, incomes, and greater occupational prestige than the general public), that same upper-middle-class bias does not extend to environmental concern in the public at large.[37]

In a thorough review of studies that dealt with environmental concern, Kent D. Van Liere and Riley Dunlap found that the correlations between environmental concern and income, education, and occupation were very weak. The strongest correlations were with education and environmental concern, but even these were inconclusive.[38]

Van Liere and Dunlap also found that among the public there was very little relationship between environmental concern and political party; however among elites, who also happen to be policymakers, and among the college-educated public, Democrats were found to be significantly more environmentally concerned than Republicans. Self-identified liberals were also found to be more environmentally concerned than conservatives.

When comparing the environmental concerns of urban residents with rural residents, with some exceptions, urban residents are generally found to be more concerned than rural residents.[39]

An individual's age is a good indicator of environmental concern. People between the ages of 20 and 24 years old register the greatest concern over environmental issues of any age group. However, environmental activism and participation, as measured by involvement in environmental organizations, is not the highest among 20 to 24 year olds—the most active group is in its early 40s.[40]

What impact do environmental attitudes have on elections? This is a difficult question to answer. Judging from public attitudes in the early 1980s as to their concern for the environment and the dramatic increase in the percentage of the public that was perturbed about the amount of environmental regulation, one might expect that environmental issues would play a major role in national elections. President Reagan's landslide victory in 1984 over Walter Mondale suggests otherwise. This seeming inconsistency is probably best explained by examining the salience of environmental issues vis-à-vis other issues. Simply stated, although the public registers high levels of environmental concern, there are other issues, such as unemployment and inflation, that, when it comes time to vote, are more important. Evidence of this was found in a CBS News/New York Times exit poll taken after the November 1982 election that asked voters "Which of these issues were most important in deciding how you voted for the U.S. House?" The voters were handed a checklist that contained nine issues but were only allowed to check two of them. Only 3 percent of those polled checked "the environment," making it the least often decided item in the list.[41]

This is not to suggest that environmental issues are not important in elections. During the 1988 presidential elections both candidates George Bush and Michael Dukakis thought it prudent to incorporate environmentalism in their platforms and campaigns. President Bush used the backdrop of polluted Boston harbor in Dukakis's home state of Massachusetts to announce he wanted to be the "environment president." Similarly, during the 1992 presidential elections both President Bush and Bill Clinton professed to be "environmentalists," although as an issue the environment appeared to play a minimal role in the election.

As we see later, the Reagan revolution in environmental regulation was largely unsuccessful and—receiving no immediate threat to existing regulations—many of those concerned with the environment may feel free to vote on other issues. Also environmental issues frequently play an important role in state and local elections. For example, zoning controversies and waste disposal selection issues are primarily local concerns that frequently play an important role in local elections.[42]

SUMMARY

As you have seen, the dominant social paradigm, which has itself been shaped by historical influences, in turn affects the electoral choices made by the American public. More broadly, the DSP in the United States has driven our history, our attitudes toward environmental regulation, and will continue to shape public policy responses to environmental problems in the future. The question for students of environmental policy is what limitations will our DSP have on our ability to respond appropriately to future environmental problems?

In this chapter we have examined the nature of our DSP. Historical attitudes toward individual liberty, property rights, economics, religion, and other values have impacted the history of our policy relationship to the environment as well as contemporary public opinion on environmental issues. The regulatory constraints and assumptions in the environmental policy-making process also have a significant impact on environmental policy outcomes. That regulatory environment is the subject of the next chapter.

NOTES

1. If you are confused about how these ideals fit with a U.S. history that includes slavery and the treatment of blacks and women as personal property, remember that the founding fathers, and many of the political philosophers who influenced them, had somewhat different notions of equality than we do today. For John Locke, governments were established by the rich and serve the interests of the rich. As French philosopher Paul d'Holbach wrote at about the time our government was being formed, "[B]y the word people I do not mean the stupid populace. . . . Every man who can live respectably from the income of his property and every head of a family who owns land ought to be regarded as a citizen." Quoted in George H. Sabine, *A History of Political Theory* (New York: Holt, Rinehart and Winston, 1961), p. 570.

2. Riley E. Dunlap and Kent D. Van Liere, "Commitment to the Dominant Social Paradigm in Concern for Environmental Quality," *Social Science Quarterly*, 65 (4) (December 1984), pp. 1014–1028.

3. See, for example, William R. Catton, Jr., *Overshoot: The Ecological Basis of Revolutionary Change* (Urbana: University of Illinois Press, 1980); Alan R. Drengson, "Shifting Paradigms: From the Technocratic to the Person-Planetary," *Environmental Ethics* (Fall 1980), pp. 221–240; Dennis Clarke Pirages, *Sustainable Society* (New York: Praeger, 1977); and Jeremy Rifkin, *Entropy: A New World View* (New York: Viking, 1980).

4. Fifty percent recycling is considered an optimistic goal and even then recycling is not 100 percent efficient. Sme resources—such as the iron loss to rust prior to recycling—are not recoverable.

5. William Ophuls, *Ecology and the Politics of Scarcity* (San Francisco: Freeman, 1977), p. 170.

6. Quoted in Sandra Postel, "Toward a New 'Eco'-Nomics," *World Watch*, 3 (5) (Sept./Oct. 1990), p. 20.

7. Ophuls, *Ecology and the Politics of Scarcity*, p. 169.

8. The final problem with the market distribution of goods and services raised by some critics concerns efficiency in the marketplace. Efficiency for economists is usually described in terms of "pareto-optimality." A pareto improvement can be made when a voluntary exchange results in one party being better off and no party being worse off. A situation is pareto optimal when it is impossible to enact an exchange that will not make some party worse off. As philosophers Donald Van De Veer and Christine Pierce point out, "We may have some serious moral reservations about even maximally efficient situations. For example, suppose I am your master and you are my slave. There may be no way to alter this arrangement so that one of us can be better off and no one worse off. That is, it may be pareto optimal or maximally efficient." Donald Van De Veer and Christine Pierce (ed.), *People, Penguins, and Plastic Trees: Basic Issues in Environmental Ethics* (Belmont, CA: Wadsworth, 1986), p. 211. The same point can be made about any social organization (country, corporation, etc.) in which all rights and privileges are held by a ruling elite.

9. Richard B. McKenzie and Gordon Tullock, *The New World of Economics* (Homewood, IL: Irwin, 1978), p. 7.

10. Ophuls, *Ecology and the Politics of Scarcity*, p. 167.
11. Lynn White, Jr., "The Historical Roots of Our Ecologic Crisis," *Science*, 155 (March 10, 1967), pp. 1203–1207.
12. See, for example, Robert Sinsheimer, "The Presumptions of Science," in Herman E. Daly (ed.), *Economics, Ecology and Ethics: Essays Toward a Steady State Economy* (San Francisco: Freemen, 1980), p. 159.
13. Ibid., p. 159.
14. Anne and Paul Ehrlich, "Ecoscience," *Mother Earth News*, 72 (Nov./Dec. 1981), p. 198.
15. E.J. Mishan, "The Growth of Affluence and the Decline of Welfare," in Herman E. Daly (ed.), *Economics, Ecology, and Ethics: Essays Toward a Steady State Economy* (San Francisco: Freeman, 1980), p. 281.
16. Ibid., p. 277.
17. For a further discussion of Minamata Bay and other environmental problems in Japan, see Norie Huddle, Michael Reich, and Nahum Stiskin, *Island of Dreams: Environmental Crisis in Japan* (Rochester, VT: Schenkman Books, 1987).
18. Joseph W. Meeker, "The Assisi Connection," *Wilderness*, 51 (180) (Spring 1988), p. 63.
19. Hans Hughs, "The Aesthetic Emphasis," in Roderick Nash, (ed.), *Environment and Americans: The Problem of Priorities* (New York: Holt, Rinehart and Winston, 1972), pp. 24–31.
20. Alfred Runte, *National Parks: The American Experience*, unpublished Ph.D. dissertation, 1976, University of California, Santa Barbara.
21. Grant McConnell, "The Failures and Success of Organized Conservation," in Nash, *Environment and Americans*, p. 49.
22. Roderick Nash, "The Conservation Schism," in Nash, *Environment and Americans*, p. 71.
23. Ibid.
24. Robert L. Sansom, *The New American Dream Machine* (New York: Anchor Books, 1976), p. 4.
25. Peter Borrelli, "Environmentalism at the Crossroads," *The Amicus Journal* (Summer 1987), p. 28.
26. Riley E. Dunlap, "Public Opinion on the Environment in the Reagan Era," *Environment*, 29 (July-August 1987), p. 35.
27. Grant McConnell, "The Failures and Successes of Organized Conservation," *Environment and Americans*, in Nash, p. 47.
28. Riley E. Dunlap, "Public Opinion on the Environment in the Reagan Era," *Environment*, 29 (July-August 1987), p. 35. Membership in the major national environmental organizations rose significantly from 1980 to 1989. Defenders of Wildlife membership went from 44,000 to 80,000 (average annual increase of 9 percent). The Environmental Defense Fund from 45,000 to 100,000 (average annual increase of 14 percent); National Audubon Society from 412,000 to 575,000 (average annual increase of 4 percent); Natural Resources Defense Council from 42,000 to 117,000 (average annual increase of 20 percent); Sierra Club from 180,000 to 496,000 (average annual increase of 20 percent); and the Wilderness Society saw a membership increase in the 1980s from 45,000 to 317,000 (an average annual increase of 67 percent). See Robert Cameron Mitchell, "Public Opinion and the Green Lobby: Poised for the 1990s?" in Norman J. Vig and Michael E. Kraft (eds.), *Environmental Policy in the 1990s* (Washington DC: Congressional Quarterly Press, 1990), p. 92.
29. Borrelli, "Environmentalism at the Crossroads," p. 35.
30. Frederick D. Crupp, "The Third Stage of Environmentalist," *EDF (Environmental Defense Fund) Newsletter*, 17 (3) (August 1986), p. 4.
31. David B. Truman, *The Governmental Process* (New York: Knopf, 1951).
32. Jeffrey M. Berry, *The Interest Group Society* (Boston: Little, Brown, 1984), p. 69.

33. Robert H. Salisbury, "An Exchange Theory of Interest Groups," *Midwest Journal of Political Science*, 13 (February 1968), pp. 1–32.
34. Riley E. Dunlap. The information reported from these polls was taken from "Public Opinion on the Environment in the Reagan Era," *Environment*, 29 (July-August 1987).
35. Mitchell, "Public Opinion and the Green Lobby: Poised for the 1990s?", p. 84.
36. Robert S. Erikson, Norman R. Luttbeg, and Kent L. Tedin, *American Public Opinion* (3rd ed.) (New York: Macmillan, 1988), p. 67.
37. See, for example, Paul Mohai, "Public Concern and Elite Involvement in Environmental-Conservation Issues," *Social Sciences Quarterly*, 66 (4) (December 1985), p. A20; Robert Cameron Mitchell, "Public Opinion and Environmental Politics in the 1970s and 1980s," in N. G. Vig and M. E. Craft (eds.), *Environmental Policy in the 80s: Reagan's New Agenda* (Washington, DC: Congressional Quarterly, 1984), pp. 51–73; Kent D. Van Liere and Riley Dunlap, "The Social Basis of Environmental Concern," *The Public Opinion Quarterly*, 44 (2) (Summer 1980), pp. 183–197; and Denton E. Morrison and Riley E. Dunlap, "Environmentalism and Elitism: A Conceptual and Empirical Analysis," *Environmental Management* 10 (5) (1986), pp. 581–589.
38. Kent D. Van Liere and Riley Dunlap, "The Social Basis of Environmental Concern," *The Public Opinion Quarterly* 44 (2) (Summer 1980), pp. 183–197. See also Paul Mohai, "Public Concern and Elite Involvement in Environmental-Conservation Issues," *Social Sciences Quarterly* 66 (4) (December 1985), p. A20; and Robert Cameron Mitchell, "Public Opinion and Environmental Politics in the 1970s and 1980s," in N. G. Vig and M. E. Craft (eds.), *Environmental Policy in the 80s: Reagan's New Agenda* (Washington, DC: Congressional Quarterly, 1984), pp. 51–73.
39. Ibid.
40. Paul Mohai and Ben W. Twight, "Age in Environmentalism: An Elaboration of the Buttel Model Using National Survey Evidence," *Social Sciences Quarterly*, 68 (4) (December 1987), pp. 789–815.
41. Dunlap, "Public Opinion on the Environment in the Reagan Era," p. 35.
42. For example, the politics of water importation dominated water control board and county elections in Santa Barbara County in the late 1970s and early 1980s; an initiative petition that would have prohibited the building of a luxury hotel on the Big Island in Hawaii played an important role in the 1988 County of Hawaii elections; and the location of a permanent nuclear waste repository was an important issue in the Washington State 1986 U.S. Senate elections.

chapter 3

The Regulatory Environment

THE REGULATORY CONTEXT

Our dominant social paradigm has a significant impact on the scope and force of regulations that have been devised to deal with environmental problems. In this chapter we explore varying approaches to environmental regulation, including the impact of the assumptions of science and risk analysis, and examine the accepted role of government regulation on environmental policy.

Scholars of regulatory theory use several models to explain when and under what conditions government regulates business. The *economic theory of regulation*, exemplified by the work of George Stigler, holds that regulations are driven by the needs of business and are acquired, designed, and operated primarily for the benefit of business in a manner, not surprisingly, that protects the profits and competitive environment of regulated business.[1] (This is also called the "self-interest" theory of regulation.) In contrast, other scholars, notably James Q. Wilson, have argued that regulations are best understood as arising out of the *political incentives* that operate on policymakers. Examining the "costs" and "benefits" associated with different regulations and their distribution, we can determine under which conditions government is more likely to regulate industry. For example, if benefits are concentrated and costs diffused, then organized groups are likely to persuade policymakers to regulate and thereby institutionalize the benefit. Usually, in this example, there will be little political opposition to the regulation.[2] Finally, adherents of the *public interest theory of regulation* hold that policymakers regulate in response to broad social movements or crisis situations and act to protect the public from undesirable business practices. The public interest theory is most often used by policymakers to explain the introduction of environmental regulations.

Each of the theories just described contain some truth, but all fail to explain the emergence of environmental regulations. Certainly, some environmental regulations have been developed by public-spirited policymakers in response to constituent demands that undesirable business practices be curtailed, as the public interest theory holds. On the other hand, other environmental regulations, such as uniform auto emission standards or energy efficiency ratings for appliances, have been sought by industries to stabilize markets and protect themselves from a variety of state regulations or from regional competitors operating under more lax state laws. The most appropriate regulatory theory for environmental regulations would seem to depend on the politics surrounding a given regulation. With this in mind, let us move on to looking at the role of science and risk analysis and the accepted role of government in environmental policy, for both of these are fused with politics.

Science and Risk Analysis

Regardless of the specific environmental policy or regulation, an assessment must be made of the environmental impacts of human activities. All the major health and environmental agencies in the United States engage in some kind of risk analysis or risk assessment.[3] Risk is inherent in any activity. The question of acceptable risk involves the personal decisions and trade-offs that individuals are willing to make in their own lives. However, in environmental management, there may be what are called *involuntary risks*, risks over which the individual has no control. In these situations, government organizations or other third parties make the assessment of risk for society as a whole.

For practical, political, and economic reasons, it would be impossible to eliminate all forms of pollution from the environment. Therefore, acceptable levels of pollution and the risks to human health contained therein are required for any form of environmental management. For example, a flowing river has a natural capacity to cleanse itself and hence can absorb a certain level of nontoxic pollutants. The determination of that level is part of what we mean by acceptable risks.

What is an acceptable level of risk? For some substances, for example carcinogens (cancer-causing agents), it is widely accepted there is no safe threshold level of exposure. Reflecting this, the Delaney clause of the U.S. Food, Drug and Cosmetic Act stipulates that no substances found to be carcinogenic will be allowed in food, drugs, or cosmetics in the United States. However, risk analysis is fraught with uncertainty and experts disagree on the appropriate level of exposure to many substances.

Three points are important to remember when examining risk analysis and environmental policy: (1) analysis is as political as it is scientific; a conflict of values must be considered over and above scientific information; (2) because of a lack of data or the appropriate methodology, science often lacks information to make risk assessments with any degree of certainty; (3) there is often disagreement within the scientific community itself as to the harm or risk involved in a given level of pollution or exposure to a chemical substance.

Ronald Brickman, Sheila Jasanoff, and Thomas Ilgen, in a four-country comparison of the regulation of the herbicide 2,4,5-T, concluded that the experience in the four nations

[I]llustrates how regulatory procedure interacts with science to produce different assessments of risk. Yet it also suggests that, in the case of genuinely controversial products, political pressure ultimately overwhelms scientific evaluations and forces similar outcomes in very different policy making environments.[4]

Although the layperson might assume that objective scientific analysis would determine acceptable levels of risk, such is not the case. In another study of environmental risk assessment, Larry Silver concluded, "[R]isk selection and resolution is not objective, but inevitably is subject to the result of the political process. It is policy making at its essence."[5]

The political nature of risk analysis is inherently tied to the uncertainty involved in the process. "Sufficient information will rarely be available to permit an accurate assessment of environmental health risks. Generally, the uncertainties as to the degree of risk are substantial, and many issues in assessing the risk can be estimated only judgmentally. ... Uncertainties arise at all stages of risk assessment."[6] This uncertainty means risk assessment is naturally both a scientific and a political process.

Attempts by the Occupational Safety and Health Administration (OSHA) to set workplace exposure levels for benzene illustrate both the political aspects of risk assessment and the scientific uncertainty involved. OSHA developed regulations lowering the maximum workplace exposure level for benzene from 10 parts per million to 1 part per million. In a U.S. Supreme Court case involving a challenge to the new regulation, *Industrial Union Department, AFL-CIO v. American Petroleum Institute*,[7] the Court found that OSHA had no direct evidence of a link between benzene exposure at 10 parts per million and adverse health effects. OSHA did know, however, that benzene could cause leukemia in humans at high levels of exposure, that it was absorbed rapidly into the human body through inhalation, and that other toxins were carcinogenic at low levels of exposure. Lacking more solid data on which to make a decision, the choice of setting the exposure level at 10 or 1 part per million was a matter of judgment. In this kind of a decision-making environment, we would anticipate that the actors who have a stake in risk assessment will actively attempt to influence the assessment process through the courts, legislators, or administrative agencies. Uncertainty in and of itself has not been found to be grounds for invalidating regulations.[8]

Faced with uncertainty, environmental regulators have an incentive to guess on the side of safety.[9] However, the regulated industries would naturally prefer risk assessments that maximized their options by setting more lenient exposure levels.

Related to issues of uncertainty is the question of unanticipated consequences. As we see later, many environmental policies have had results that were both unanticipated and sometimes undesirable. For example, federal regulations that required minimum fleet averages for gasoline mileage in automobiles had the impact of stimulating automobile manufacturers to build lighter and more fuel-efficient cars. A study by the Harvard School of Public Health and a Brookings Institute economist found that as a result, many American and Japanese cars were 500 pounds lighter than they would have been without federal regulations. The study concluded that fatalities would increase due to the decreased safety factor of the lighter cars, and estimated the increase in fatalities would total 20,000 by the year 1998.[10] This is a serious unanticipated consequence of this policy.

Uncertainty naturally leads to disagreement within the scientific community over what is acceptable environmental risk. For example, in 1985 the Universities Associated for Research and Education in Pathology published a report on an 18-month study of health effects related to exposure from chemicals in toxic waste dumps. They found, among other things, that "[T]here's little scientific evidence that chemical disposal sites have had serious impacts on the health of populations residing near them."[11] A year earlier, a study of a chemical waste disposal plant in Wales found that the number of babies born with abnormalities in the vicinity of the disposal plant was significantly higher than the average for the rest of the country.[12] In 1978 a report released by a group of well known scientists representing three U.S. federal research institutions estimated that 20 percent of all cancer was caused by occupational exposure and that this figure "may even be conservative."[13] Although Samuel Epstein in *Politics of Cancer* endorsed the 1985 report and President Carter's Toxic Substances Strategy Committee accepted these estimations with minor qualification,[14] this study was denounced in an editorial in the magazine *Science* as being "flimsy" and reviewed in the British medical journal *Lancet* with the comment, "[I]t is sad to see such a fragile report under such distinguished names."[15]

For a more detailed examination of problems in risk assessment you are referred elsewhere.[16] For the purpose of understanding environmental policy and the regulatory process, it is important to remember that a faith in science and technology is a part of our dominant social paradigm: A survey of the U.S. public undertaken in 1986 found that 72 percent felt that science and technology will do more good than harm in the future.[17] Risk assessment is not, however, an objective science, and determining acceptable levels of pollution or exposure to potentially dangerous chemicals involves as much politics as science. Subsequent chapters dealing with air and water pollution control measures illustrate this interaction of science and politics.

The Role of Government

Although the dominant social paradigm plays an important role in the form and content of environmental policy, there are important differences in the approach government takes to environmental regulations. These differences may be best understood as the orientation of a policymaker to the role of government (including the level of government activity, that is, national, state, or local) and the role and use of market forces in the implementation of environmental policy.

For purposes of analysis, it is useful to describe policy orientation toward the role of government as lying on a continuum. At one end there is no government involvement, that is, total free-market control, and, at the other end, total national government control over environmental policy. In between the complete free-market approach and total national control are the various combinations of market forces and government controls (see Figure 3.1).

None of these policy orientations characterized American environmental policy until the mid-nineteenth century.[18] As we saw in our summary of the history of environmental policy in the United States, pollution was not perceived as a problem early in American history; nature was a force to be conquered without concern for the environmental consequences. The establishment of Yellowstone National Park in 1872 is early evidence of the acceptance of a role for government in our control over the environment in the United States.

Today, for all practical purposes, much of international environmental management, notably management of ocean pollution, is essentially free-market management. But most countries are engaged to some degree in the management of the environment to prevent pollution.

Although it is not a popular position, those in the United States who advocate no role for government in environmental protection often use the

Figure 3.1

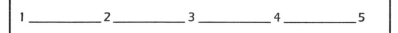

1 _____ 2 _____ 3 _____ 4 _____ 5

1. Free market.
2. Use of market forces with some government controls.
3. Government controls on the state and local level (which may or may not utilize market or marketlike mechanisms).
4. Government controls developed on the national level and implemented on the state and local level.
5. Controls developed and implemented on the national level—total national control.

argument that corporate self-interest provides the necessary environmental safeguards. The Reagan and Bush administrations, as we see in our discussion of energy, came close to a totally free-market approach to energy policy.

The second step on the continuum of the role of government and environmental policy is the utilization of market forces. As we see later, some environmental policies are designed to limit government involvement in implementing controls by using market mechanisms to produce desired outcomes. One way this has been done is through tax incentives or pollution charges. This category includes a number of quasi-market arrangements with varying degrees of governmental influence. For example, the EPA through the use of a bubble concept (see Chapter 5) allowed manufacturing plants to determine their own mix of pollutants admitted into the atmosphere from a given plant. Although not a market mechanism, the bubble concept allows polluters to choose the areas within a plant on which to concentrate their pollution control efforts. This is in contrast to a regulatory scheme in which government regulators make those determinations.

Government intervention in the form of state and local control over environmental regulations, both in the formulation and implementation process, was the primary form of environmental regulation in the United States up to the early 1970s. In 1964 California was the first government in the United States to begin regulating automobile emissions. Solid waste management and land-use planning continue to be primarily a local government concern. In some other countries, for example Canada, the national government's role is severely limited, leaving primary responsibility for pollution control with the provinces. Beginning in the early 1970s, environmental regulations in the United States were formulated by the national government and implemented primarily by state and local governments. This pattern of regulatory control has been adopted by many other countries as well. Total national control over the formulation of environmental regulations and their implementation has only been attempted on a very limited basis in the United States, for example in regulating nuclear power.

These descriptions of varying types of governmental control and the use of market forces in environmental regulations provide the framework for understanding differences in the types of environmental regulations that we will discuss later. Clearly no correct formula is best in all circumstances. Combinations of national, state, and local control, and market forces may be used in different situations, and often different combinations work better in some cases than in others.

Approaches to Regulation

Our orientation toward the proper role of government in the free market colors our perception of what is good or bad environmental regulation. The common pool nature of environmental problems tells us that without some type of regulation or self-control we will, in pursuing our own interests, destroy common pool resources—the air, water, or land.

There are four general approaches to dealing with common pool problems, each of which to varying degrees relate to the role of government in environmental management as we discussed earlier. The first approach is essentially the free-market option, a reliance on self-interest and volunteerism with no government intervention to correct for common pool resource problems. Decades of human experience, as well as much current practice, tells us that volunteerism is not a reliable solution to common pool problems.

The second means of dealing with common pool problems is a "standards and enforcement" or "command and control" system of environmental regulation. Essentially, some governmental unit determines what the appropriate level of a given pollutant or activity is, sets the standards, and establishes a way to enforce adherence to these standards. This is the primary means of environmental regulation in the United States and includes permitting, setting standards for discharges (and other types of rule making), and requiring that information on discharges be reported. In addition, in the United States pollution is regulated by banning certain activities, zoning to isolate undesirable activities, and, when necessary, adjudication.

There have been a number of criticisms of the command and control system of environmental regulation including the following: (1) uniform national standards ignore varying local conditions; (2) national standards may or may not provide an incentive to find the least costly method of pollution control; (3) once a standard is set, there is no incentive for pollution discharges less than the established amount; and (4) standards limit the flexibility that might allow polluters to reduce the total amount of emissions at the lowest cost.

In defense of the command and control system of regulation, it has been argued that (1) a uniform standard produces equity in implementation, since all polluters are, theoretically, treated alike; (2) it is less expensive to administer because time and energy are not necessary to investigate individual cases; and (3) it is less susceptible to political influence and manipulation.

A third approach to dealing with common pool problems, and an alternative often suggested to command and control strategies, is the use of taxes or effluent charges or some other type of monetary measure that would provide polluters with an incentive to find the most cost-efficient means of limiting their pollution.

As an example of how an effluent charge might work, imagine a lake surrounded by three manufacturing plants. All of the plants wish to discharge their waste into the lake. Assuming none of the potential discharges was toxic, the government could estimate the total amount of discharge that could be accepted by the lake without causing unwanted damage. For example, let's set that amount at 3 million gallons a day. Under these circumstances, each of the manufacturing plants might be given a permit to discharge 1 million gallons a day into the lake with the stipulation that every additional gallon would be charged a fee. If the fee was high enough, this would theoretically prevent any of the plants from discharging above the limit that would damage the lake. On the other hand, if the fee was too low, the plant might find little incentive to hold discharge below the limit and merely pay the tax. The primary benefit of an effluent tax regulatory system would be that the polluter, the manufacturer in this example, would have an incentive to find the least costly way within the plant to limit discharges. In addition, if the effluent tax started at a relatively low rate on the first unit of pollution and then gradually increased to a high rate on units of pollution above a standard acceptable for the lake, then the polluter would have an incentive to reduce discharges even further than the acceptable standard.

Finally, another way to deal with the common pool problem is through establishing property rights in the commons. The essential idea here is to divide the commons, giving individuals a stake in the appropriate use and management of their now private resources. In short, it would no longer be common property. This is obviously not possible for many common pool resources such as air, but it is frequently advanced as a means of managing forests. A *Wall Street Journal* editorial on private ownership of U.S. forests illustrates this perspective: "[I]t would be in the timber companies' natural interest to properly harvest, reseed and nourish the lands they manage."[19] Some argue, however, that the drive for short-term profits to satisfy stockholders, pay off bonds used to finance corporate acquisitions, or to enhance the careers of upwardly mobile executives outweigh long-term profit and loss considerations.

Related to the privatization of common pool resources is the idea of creating private enforceable rights to a clean environment. In common law, the "nuisance" doctrine has been available to varying degrees when the activities of one individual cause harm or damage to another. For example, if your neighbor decided to put a hog farm in his backyard, which resulted in a stench that caused you personal discomfort and reduced your property value, you might have a cause of action under the nuisance doctrine. In modern environmental law, nuisance suits have been replaced by regulations that limit such activity, such as agricultural zoning regulations. Other regulations, such as the Clean Water Act, have provisions that allow individuals to sue polluters or force EPA to sue for compliance with existing regulations.

It would be possible to establish enforceable rights to clean air and water whereby citizens might use the courts to protect themselves for many infringements upon those rights. One potential problem with this approach is that an individual might have little incentive to pursue an action on his or her own. The cost of a lawsuit is high, and an individual, when calculating personal cost and benefits, may find the expense is not worth it. In such situations, the common legal remedy is the class action suit wherein a group of individuals, each of whose personal injuries may be relatively small, can represent a whole class of persons that have been damaged. Unfortunately, for a variety of reasons, the federal courts, and many state courts, have procedural requirements that make the bringing of such suits very expensive.[20]

SUMMARY

Clearly, not all regulatory systems are created equal. Different regulatory systems affect different interests or groups in different ways. The type of regulatory system adopted to deal with environmental problems depends, to a great extent, on the influence of affected interests on the policy-making process. In this chapter we have seen some of the problems associated with developing environmental regulations. Science is not always exact (or as we often say, "hard"); hence determining acceptable levels of risk is difficult. In addition, the need for and type of regulation, including appropriate levels of market control, are matters for political debate. The type of regulation developed for an environmental problem and the interests that are benefited by the regulation are, to a large extent, determined by the ability of participants to exercise influence on the policy-making process. Many of what we call the paradoxes of environmental policy are the result of political outcomes, or regulations, which are not the best suited for dealing with an environmental problem. This is because influential political actors can influence the process in ways that produce policies that are to their benefit, but may not be the most environmentally desirable. The ability to exercise influence on the policy-making process is the subject of the next chapter.

NOTES

1. George J. Stigler, "The Theory of Economic Regulation," *The Bell Journal of Economics and Management Science*, 2 (1) (Spring 1971), pp. 3–21.
2. See James Q. Wilson, "The Politics of Regulation," *Social Responsibility and the Business Predicament* (Washington, DC: Brookings Institution, 1974), pp. 135–168.
3. Ronald Brickman, Sheila Jasanoff, and Thomas Ilgen, *Controlling Chemicals: Politics of Regulation in Europe and the United States* (Ithaca: Cornell University Press, 1985), p. 41.
4. Ibid., p. 212.
5. Larry D. Silver, "The Common Law of Environmental Risk and Some Recent Applications," *Harvard Environmental Law Review*, 10 (61) (1986), p. 96.
6. Chris G. Whipple, "Fundamentals of Risk Assessment," *Environmental Law Reporter*, 16 (August 1986), pp. 10192–10193.
7. 448 U.S. 607, 100 S.Ct. 2844, 65 L.E.2nd 1010 (1980).
8. See generally Silver, "The Common Law of Environmental Risk and Some Recent Applications."
9. Whipple, "Fundamentals of Risk Assessment," p. 10191.
10. "High Fuel Mileage Requirement for Autos Is Tragic Mistake, Researchers Report," *Houston Chronicle*, March 27, 1988, p. 14, sec. 1.

11. Cited in David J. Hanson, "Little Serious Health Damage Linked to Waste Sites," *Chemical and Engineering News*, 63 (March 25, 1985), p. 29. This research was funded, incidentally, by a consortium that included the Chemical Manufacturers Association, U.S. Chamber of Commerce, National Agricultural Chemicals Association, National Association of Printing Ink Manufacturers, and the National Paint and Coatings Association. Ibid., p. 30.
12. "Birth Defects Up Near Waste Unit," *European Chemical News*, 43 (October 15, 1984), p. 27.
13. Cited in Brickman, Jasanoff, and Ilgen, *Controlling Chemicals: Politics of Regulation in Europe and the United States*, p. 190.
14. Samuel S. Epstein, *The Politics of Cancer* (rev. ed.) (New York: Anchor Press, 1981), p. 18, in Ibid.
15. Brickman, Jasanoff, and Ilgen, *Controlling Chemicals: Politics of Regulation in Europe and the United States*, p. 191.
16. See generally, Whipple, "Fundamentals of Risk Assessment."
17. "Living dangerously," *U.S. News and World Report*, May 19, 1986, p. 19.
18. One could argue that American environmental policy until the mid-nineteenth century was one of a free-market approach. My point here is that there was no governmental policy per se.
19. "Burning Yellowstone," *Wall Street Journal*, August 30, 1988, p. 18.
20. Zachary A. Smith, "Class Action: State Notification Requirements After Eisen," *Western State University Law Review*, 8 (1) (Fall 1980), pp. 1–20.

chapter 4

The Political
and Institutional
Setting

PLURALISM

The United States is a pluralist democracy. Pluralism means that public policy is determined, in large part, through the bargaining, compromise, and negotiating of various interest groups in society. Although group activity is not the only explanatory variable in determining public policy, according to most scholars who have studied the policy-making process it is a very important part. As V.O. Key wrote, "[A]t bottom, group interests are the animating forces in the political process; an understanding of American politics requires a knowledge of the chief interests and their stake in public policy."[1]

The notion that groups compete over the nature of public policy is as old as the republic. James Madison's analysis of interest groups (which he called "factions") in essay 10 of *The Federalist* remains, in the words of political scientist Jeffrey Berry, "the foundation of American political theory on interest groups."[2] Madison defined a faction as "a number of citizens, whether amounting to a majority or minority of the whole, who are united and actuated by some common impulse of passion, or of interest, adverse to the rights of other citizens, or to the permanent and aggregate interests of the community."[3] The tendency toward faction, according to Madison, was "in the nature of man" and would lead people, when possible, "much more disposed to vex and oppress each other than to co-operate for the common good."[4] Madison feared that a tyrannical faction would come to dominate others in society but felt a republic form of government (incorporating checks and balances), combined with the many and diverse interests competing with each other in a large country such as the United States, was good insurance against the dominance of one faction.[5]

The contemporary focus of study on interest groups was first emphasized by sociologist Arthur Bentley in *The Process of Government*, published in 1908.[6] Bentley argued that "there are no political phenomena except group phenomena" and that politics "reflects, represents, the underlying groups."[7]

Bentley's work appeared at a time when the study of government was oriented toward formal institutions; hence scholars were not quick to adopt a group approach to politics. During the 1920s and 1930s, several important works contributed to the development of pluralist theory. These were primarily case studies providing insights into interest group activity.[8] However, perhaps the biggest boost for pluralist theory was the publication of *The Governmental Process* by David Truman in 1951.[9] Group activity for Truman, particularly interest groups, had a significant impact on policy. "[Interest groups] are so intimately related to the daily functioning of those constitutionalized groups—legislature, chief executives, administrative agencies, and even courts—that make up the institution of government that the latter cannot adequately be described if these relationships are not recognized as the weft of the fabric."[10]

Since the publication of *The Governmental Process* a number of political scientists have expanded on, defended, and criticized pluralist theory. Robert Dahl, in *Who Governs?*, a study of political influence in New Haven, Connecticut, confirmed and gave a boost to pluralist theory by finding that policies in New Haven were influenced by different groups of people acting in different policy areas.[11] Other scholars, such as Terry Moe and Zachary Smith, have examined the organization, incentives, and behavior of interest groups.[12] Among the critics, Jack Walker and Theodore Lowi have argued that pluralism maintains the status quo by making it more difficult for newer organized groups to influence the policy-making process.[13] The greatest weakness of pluralism, as a *normative* theory of politics, is in the failure of all groups and interests to be represented in the bargaining and policy-making process. In environmental policy, for example, how are the interests of your grandchildren represented in the process? Or the interests of inanimate objects such as trees? And even when these interests are represented by "public interest" groups, these groups are, as we soon see, at a serious disadvantage vis-à-vis economic interests when competing in the policy formation and implementation arena. But just because pluralism is not useful as a normative blueprint for the policy-making process does not mean it is not valuable as a descriptive tool. Although the behavior of interest groups is not the sole force influencing the policy-making process, groups and group activity, according to most scholars of American politics, do have a significant impact on the policy outputs of American democracy.

Group Types

A distinction can be made between types of interest groups by examining their goals and the resources they have available to achieve these goals. Although not all interest groups fall into one of the two following categories, the distinction sharpens our analysis and enables us to better understand the advantages of some groups in participating in the policy-making process.

The first type of group are the "private-economic" interest groups. This is the type of organization we typically think of when we hear the term *interest group*. Characteristically, private-economic interest groups pursue noncollective benefits, or benefits the group seeks for its membership but that are not available to society at large. Examples of private-economic interest groups would include associations of oil and gas producers, fishers, cattle or timber producers, or any organization that regulates a business or profession and simultaneously attempts to influence government policy.

The second type of group is the "public noneconomic" interest groups that pursue collective benefits which cannot be withheld from society at large. Examples of such benefits include clean air, clean water, and a strong national defense. Examples of such groups include most environmental and conservation organizations, consumer organizations, and associations that are involved in nonspecific foreign policy or defense issues.

In contrast to the private-economic interest group leader, the leader of a public noneconomic interest group, when soliciting contributions, is unable to hold out any specific individual advantage for members who participate through their contributions. Some have argued, therefore, that it is illogical for members of such groups to contribute or participate in the activities of noncollective groups.[14] When soliciting contributions for a public noneconomic interest group, the group leader might hold out the benefits of an expanded national park system or a coastline free of oil platforms; however, the rational member of a public noneconomic interest group quickly realizes that these potential benefits may be available whether or not he or she decides to contribute to the group. This is a major fund-raising disadvantage for public noneconomic interest groups.

By virtue of their organization and the incentives operating on members and leadership, private-economic interest groups have several advantages when attempting to influence the policy-making process compared to public noneconomic interest groups. First, private-economic interest groups are advantaged in their fund-raising ability. Given the noncollective nature of their benefits, private-economic interest groups can offer benefits to members in return for their support. For example, the head of a state oil and gas association can solicit contributions from their membership with promises the money will be used to lobby for additional taxes on imported oil. The relationship between the contribution and the potential benefit is straightforward.

The difference between public and private interest groups in their ability to raise money is important. As we soon see, although groups have many different types of resources and these resources have varying utility for influencing the policy-making process, money is a very important part of the process, due primarily to the role it can play in campaign contributions and public relations.

Interest Groups and the Policy Cycle

In describing the policy-making process, a number of scholars have identified stages through which policies pass. Characterizations of the policy-making process almost always describe the process as (1) agenda setting, or having an item up for the serious consideration of policymakers; (2) policy making, or having action taken on the item; and (3) implementation, or the carrying out of a given policy.

The "agenda" is commonly defined as the listing of items for governmental action. Agenda setting is obviously a prerequisite to any policy action. Proficiency at agenda setting means the ability to get your issue on the list of items to be taken up by policymakers.

Policy-making in government involves the desired action or nonaction on an item that has been placed on the public agenda. It can take place in any one of the three branches of government. It is important to know that inaction, or the continuation of the status quo, is also a form of policy making. As we see later, proficiency at policy making requires different skills and resources depending on the type of policy involved and the location of decision-making authority over the policy issue.

Policy implementation is, in large part, the purview of the bureaucracy. Administrators have discretion in implementing programs. Discretion is power. Even seemingly minor administrative decisions can have a significant impact on how a general legislative mandate is translated into governmental action. For example, the decision about when and where to hold public hearings can have a significant impact on who participates in those hearings. Hearings conducted by the U.S. Forest Service for its first Roadless Area Review and Evaluation (RARE 1) to determine, among other things, the extent and location of wilderness areas on Forest Service lands, were held in the Pacific Northwest. The hearings were often held close or adjacent to logging communities, and large numbers of loggers participated in the hearing process. This was significant in that the RARE 1 hearings in the region generated an abundance of testimony against establishing additional wilderness areas.

Agenda setting, policy making, and implementation are all important in different ways. For a major public policy such as the Clean Water Act to be successful there must be success at each stage of the policy process. For example, water must become an issue that policymakers, in this case the U.S. Congress, are interested in addressing; the interested parties and their representatives in Congress must be able to agree on a policy; and some organization, such as the Environmental Protection Agency, must have the incentives and resources to carry out the policy. Failure at any one of these stages in the policy-making process will prevent the objectives of the policy from being enacted.

Like any organization, interest groups vary significantly in terms of their size, organization, assets, and other measures. Some groups have combinations of attributes or resources that enable them to participate effectively in any stage of the policy-making process. For example, the oil industry in the United States in the 1950s and 1960s and their associated groups and supporters were influential enough to have most of their policy objectives dealt with favorably in the U.S. Congress.[15]

The resources that are useful for influencing a particular stage of the policy-making process vary. For example, bringing an issue to the attention of policymakers and thereby getting it on the public agenda requires a different set of resources than having the issue acted upon favorably. Hence different groups, based on the types of resources they possess, have different levels of strength and influence when attempting to have an impact on a particular stage of the policy process.

The ability to attract media attention is one important preliminary step in the agenda-setting process. By virtue of their strategy, tactics, or their available resources, some groups are more likely to use the media for getting their items on the public agenda. Media managers, particularly of broadcast media, have incentives to produce salable, interesting, attention-attracting news. Some groups pursue policy goals that are better suited for satisfying that need. For example, the news that drinking water supplies are threatened by toxic substances is much more likely to be reported than the release of a study showing that toxic residues in water are below U.S. Public Health standards.

Tactics that are conducive to attracting media attention include disclosure of the unusual, frightening, or bizarre. A case in point was when an antinuclear activist jumped into Hilo Bay in front of a U.S. Navy nuclear destroyer to protest nuclear weaponry in the early 1980s. Another attention-attracting tactic is protest activities, such as demonstrations or picketing. Also, the perception that a group is an "underdog" fighting the "big boys" or the establishment will attract attention.

In each of these cases the group using a particular media-attracting tactic is likely to lack resources necessary for more conventional means of getting their policy issue on the public agenda. An example of conventional agenda setting in the U.S. Congress would be having a sympathetic congressperson introduce a bill and lobby on the bill's behalf in the hope that it is passed by Congress and signed by the president.

Accordingly, groups that are influential and are able to get their items on the public agenda are either those groups that can attract the attention of the media or that possess the conventional resources necessary for influencing the policy-making stage of the policy formation process. Environmental organizations are more likely to use media-grabbing tactics than are organizations that have the resources for influencing the other stages of the policy-making process.[16] As we see, if an organization is successful in influencing the policy-making stage of the process, then the group is also likely to have the resources necessary for influencing the agenda-setting stage of the process.

Group Resources and Policy Making

The relationship between group resources and interest group influence is important within each of the three branches of government and at every stage of the policy process. Policy making means many different things to different people and can be difficult to define. To illustrate, when the Organization of Petroleum Exporting Countries (OPEC) decides to raise the target price for its oil, there may be a variety of related consequences that affect the world's economy and environment. Consequently, it is often difficult to distinguish between what is strictly public policy making and what is private sector policy making. Here, however, we limit our discussion to policy making traditionally defined as the activity that takes place in legislative bodies, the executive branch, and the judicial systems. It will be useful for you to remember, however, that there is a close relationship between what goes on in the private sector and what ultimately happens in the public policy-making arena.

The Judicial System Environmental battles are often fought in the courts. This is particularly true of interest groups lacking the resources necessary to fight in more traditional arenas, such as legislative bodies. There are a number of long-standing common law judicial remedies for those concerned with the environment, including the public nuisance doctrine. But since the early 1970s, the most common legal challenge used by environmental organizations has been to enforce the environmental impact statement requirements of the National Environmental Policy Act (NEPA). Most often, environmental impact statements are challenged on the grounds that they do not sufficiently assess environmental impacts or their alternatives.

As we see in Part Two, a number of environmental statutes, notably the National Environmental Policy Act and the Clean Water Act, have provided environmentalists with opportunities to use the judicial branch of government to enforce environmental laws. Early in the history of the contemporary environmental movement, access to court systems was limited somewhat by questions of legal standing. *Standing* means a party has a right to represent an interest in court. For example, to bring a lawsuit, a person or organization must show (1) that it suffered an injury; and (2) that the injury can be remedied. Standing has not been a major obstacle to use of the judicial system by environmentalists since the early 1970s, when the Supreme Court began taking a somewhat more liberal view of standing in environmental cases.[17]

The use of the courts in environmental matters and the benefit to be derived from pursuing a court action vary depending on the interests involved. For instance, if a lengthy lawsuit will allow the maintenance of the status quo (such as continuing to pollute), then clearly the benefited party is advantaged by pursuing its interest in the courts at length. Thus the utility of initiating court action will vary depending on a group's objectives and the resources available to a group.

There are a number of considerations that make the use of the judicial system an attractive alternative which are different from those considered in dealing with the other branches of government. For example, there is the question of time. Lawsuits take time. Relatively new interest groups might be concerned with simple organizational maintenance and hence would avoid undertaking commitments of resources to lawsuits when the benefits to be achieved are long term and uncertain. Moreover, groups with few monetary resources would avoid lawsuits for fear of not being able to see them through to their conclusion. The decision by an interest group to pursue its environmental policy goals through the judicial system then will be influenced by a number of variables. These include the group's relative strength in other stages of the policy-making process, the desirability of seeking a short- or long-term solution to the problem, and the nature of the dispute. For example, if the court is the only forum available this may play a part in the decision of group leaders to use the courts.

Also, the decision by environmental organizations to use the courts may be affected by which court has jurisdiction over a case. The courts in some states are much less likely to find in favor of environmental interests than are the courts of other states. On the federal level, Lettie Wenner, an expert on environmental litigation, found that federal courts in the Northeast, Midwest, and on the West Coast have, since the 1970s, been favorably disposed toward environmental litigants, whereas federal courts in the Southeast, Southwest, and Rocky Mountains have been more likely to favor economic and development interests.[18]

The Legislative Branch   Generally, environmental groups continue to find legal systems useful in pursuing their policy interests. This is partly because some environmental statutes provide for judicial remedies. Perhaps more importantly, environmental organizations traditionally have lacked the political resources useful for exercising influence in the legislative or executive branches of government.

It is important to remember that legislatures are, for the most part, decentralized in their organization and operation. In the U.S. Congress, for example, the major work is done by committees and subcommittees. As we see, decentralization has a number of effects on the policy-making process. The committee system and the bicameral nature of legislatures in all the states except Nebraska make it much more difficult to pass legislation than to block it. Consequently, those interests that are benefited by the status quo have an advantage in the policy-making process in the United States. Because there are so many different points in the legislative process where a bill can be defeated, those attempting to influence legislation must follow it closely through each stage. Some groups have the resources to closely monitor legislation, such as attending hearings, whereas other groups do not.

One of the most important aspects to consider when examining the policy-making process in legislatures is that legislators are, in large part, motivated by a desire for reelection.[19] Although there are a number of different demands on the attention of a legislator and a variety of incentives not directly related to reelection that are important to legislators, most analysts have concluded reelection is a primary motive for legislative behavior. Thus legislators are likely to be influenced by the forces that impact on their ability to be reelected. Basically, legislators will respond to the demands of their constituents, vote as their constituents desire, and thereby be rewarded with a return to office.

The late Jesse Unruh, who was speaker of the California Assembly and state treasurer, once remarked, "[M]oney is the mother's milk of politics."[20] In practical terms, this means money is necessary for reelection and that groups with the money to support politicians in their bid for reelection are most likely to have influence in the legislative process. Although it is difficult to show a direct causal relationship, empirically, between contributions and influence, there is widespread agreement that campaign contributions buy access to the legislative policy-making process. Access is a very valuable commodity. Because of limitations on a legislator's time, and given the large number of issues a legislator must address, access provides a crucial opportunity to influence.

Although money is important, a large membership can be a source of influence as well. Interest groups with a large and motivated membership are likely to be more influential in the legislative policy-making process than groups without these resources. Members vote, campaign, and can be enlisted to attend hearings.

The Executive Branch   The executive branch of government on the federal level is responsible for administering federal environmental regulations through a variety of federal agencies. The Environmental Protection Agency (EPA) is perhaps the most important regulatory agency concerned with environmental matters. The EPA was established in 1970 through a reorganization that consolidated pollution regulatory activities from a variety of different departments into a single agency. The EPA is responsible for a wide variety of environmental regulations, including the Clean Air Act, the Clean Water Act, the Toxic Substances Control Act, the Safe Drinking Water Act, the Resource Conservation Recovery Act, and the Federal Insecticide, Fungicide and Rodenticide Act.

Another federal agency involved in environmental matters is the Interior Department. Under the Interior Department is the Bureau of Land Management, the National Park Service, the U.S. Fish and Wildlife Service, and the Office of Surface Mining. Another agency is the Agriculture Department, which houses the U.S. Forest Service and the Soil and Conservation Service.

The resources that help provide access to the chief executive of a governmental body are similar to those resources needed by groups working with the legislative branch, such as a large or motivated membership or any resources conducive to providing electoral support. The needs of career bureaucrats, the individuals primarily responsible for the implementation of policy, are, however, somewhat different than those of the chief executive. Public administrators, particularly those working in state or local governments with poor support staff, have limited resources for acquiring information. Interest groups provide that needed information.

Administrators also need political support from interest groups. They are often concerned with maintaining organizational autonomy and integrity. This is accomplished, among other ways, by developing networks of support within the legislature and among the public. Public support is most often cultivated among the individuals or groups in the public that the administrative organization serves. It is often developed by the provision of a particular service. We might expect, therefore, administrative organizations to be most responsive to these groups that are the beneficiaries of whatever service or function the organization performs and that these groups will have more access and influence than other groups. To illustrate, the National Park Service enjoys the support of the National Parks and Recreation Association and other supporters of the National Park System during its budget hearings. In return these organizations enjoy increased access to the agency and prompt responses to their inquiries.

An important resource for influence in the administrative process is familiarity with the implementation process and the informational needs of the organization. Paul Culhane, in a study of interest group influence in the Forest Service and Bureau of Land Management, found that "[Forest Service administrators] expected public participation to be professional; that is, they expected comments and public participation forums to present new information about the subject under consideration that they had overlooked."[21] Those participants in implementation that have backgrounds and training similar to organizational members will be advantaged in interaction with the organization, as opposed to participants that do not have such experience.

Finally, implementation is a long-term process. Battles won today in the legislature may be lost in the implementation process if mandates are ignored or misinterpreted. Consequently, to influence the implementation process it is necessary to have the resources to monitor the process on a continuous and long-term basis. This is particularly important in environmental policy where in many areas once the environmental side loses the battle it has lost the war. Accordingly, groups lacking the resources to send well-prepared spokespersons to agency hearings and to follow up agency action are disadvantaged.

In summary, resources most useful for influencing the implementation stages of the policy-making process are the traditional resources of money, political support, and information and expertise that are useful to promote interaction with bureaucrats. Finally, these resources must be adequate and channeled in such a way that groups can stay involved in the implementation process for the long term.

Although different groups may choose to exercise their influence at different stages of the policy-making process, it is clear in all cases that monetary resources are very beneficial either for initiation or follow-through of a group's policy goals. Given the inherent advantages private economic interest groups have in fund-raising, it should not be surprising to find that in all stages of the policy-making process these groups have a certain advantage. This is not to suggest, of course, that private economic interest groups always win out in environmental battles with public noneconomic interest groups. However, it is clear that in policy formation they start with an advantage. As we see next, the policy process is not only driven by the concerns that have been detailed in this section. There are numerous examples in American history where, because of the volatile or intense nature of a policy debate, the incentives that traditionally operate on policymakers have, so to speak, gone out the window. Indeed, much of the major U.S. environmental legislation that was passed in the early 1970s provide examples of how the status quo and traditional incremental forms of influence can give way in the face of widespread public support for environmental regulations. Nevertheless, in the day-to-day operation of government, nonincremental change is the exception rather than the rule.

Incrementalism

It is widely accepted among scholars of the American policy process that policy is made incrementally. Incremental theory, or simply incrementalism, may be summarized in the following manner:

1. Only some of the possible alternatives for dealing with a problem are considered by the decision maker. Either by virtue of limitations on information, ability, time, or because of the desire to achieve a consensus, a comprehensive evaluation of all alternatives is not undertaken.
2. The alternatives considered and the option ultimately selected will differ only slightly or incrementally from existing policy.
3. Only a limited number of consequences for each alternative are evaluated.
4. The problem being evaluated is continually redefined with adjustments being made to make the problem more manageable.[22]

There are practical and political reasons why policy is made incrementally in the United States. Practically, it would be impossible to consider all the numerous alternatives to a decision and the consequences of each alternative. Given the nature of pluralism, the numerous parties that are involved in the policy-making process, and the inherent limits on human ability to comprehensively analyze all the alternatives and the ramifications of policy options, it may be that incremental decision making is inevitable. Given limited capacity and information, it makes sense to simplify decision making to facilitate some kind of action. In political terms, incrementalism makes sense because it allows participants in the battle over policy in a given area the advantage of being able to work from past policy agreements and shared assumptions. Since politics inherently involves trade-offs, bargaining, and compromise, we should not be surprised to find decisions are often made in relatively small increments that do not differ greatly from past decisions. It is easier to reach agreement on matters when the modifications being discussed in a given policy vary only slightly from prior agreements.

Whether incrementalism is inevitable or desirable, it is a fact that many environmental policy decisions are made on an incremental basis. To cite one example, which we discuss in more detail later, the national debate on the appropriate means of protecting water quality has always centered on evaluation of existing standards, procedures, and means of enforcement. Rarely have federal policymakers seriously considered simply eliminating the entire "standards and enforcement" approach to water quality and substituting, for example, some kind of market-incentive mechanism. Incrementalism means that new, unique, or seemingly radical policy alternatives are rarely, if ever, given serious consideration.

The incremental nature of the policy-making process in the United States has important consequences for environmental policy. First, policies are rarely comprehensive in the sense that they thoroughly evaluate, question, and analyze all the possible options available to decision makers. During the policy process, it is likely to be assumed that past decisions and policies were fundamentally correct and, if anything, may only need fine tuning. Given the interrelated and interdependent nature of many environmental problems, the incremental approach increases the likelihood that a solution will address only part of the problem. Second, the incremental nature of the policy-making process virtually assures the established relationships and alliances that enabled programs to develop, remain, and guide subsequent policy adjustments.

In many policy areas, the attributes of incrementalism give stability to the process. Although stability is clearly a benefit for political systems, at times it may be necessary to take quick and decisive action inconsistent with past policy decisions. As we see later, sometimes the system has been able to respond quickly to an environmental emergency. But unfortunately, a majority of the time, constraints inherent in the policy-formation system, including incrementalism, prevent the development of policy to address short- and long-term problems.

Decentralization

Policy making and implementation in the United States are decentralized. Many policy decisions are made at the state and local level. Within governments, at all levels, decision making and influence are divided up among committees, commissions, boards, and various executive branches.

For example, environmental regulatory standards are established by the federal government and enforced by state and local governments according to federal regulations. This can make management of environmental programs problematic. David Brian Robertson and Dennis R. Judd have traced the development of political conflicts over the establishment of a national environmental policy within a federal structure. They point out that states and local governments charged with enforcement of federal regulations face many obstacles, including the following: (1) limited resources (especially since the 1980s when federal grants-in-aid for pollution control were reduced); (2) the need for cooperation among various state and local agencies that deal with such diverse areas as highways, land use, natural resources, and economic development—all of which have environmental impacts; (3) direct economic dependence on local industries to be regulated; and (4) interstate cooperation on environmental problems that cross state boundaries.[23]

In a variety of ways the decentralized nature of policy formation affects which groups will be successful in pursuing their policy goals. Decentralization helps or hurts some organizations and their interests. For example, it is helpful to those with influence in a state legislature but not in the U.S. Congress.

Short-Term Bias

If given a choice between two policy options that will both accomplish the same goals over the same period of time, rational political actors will select the option with the lowest short-term cost. To illustrate, imagine you are a congressperson considering two competing bills designed to deal with the problem of acid rain. The first bill, which we will call the Anderson bill, is estimated to cost approximately $5 billion a year for each of the first 5 years and then $25 billion for each of the next 20 years. The total cost of the Anderson bill is $525 billion. The competing bill, which we will call the Jones bill, has an initial cost of $25 billion for each of the first 5 years with subsequent costs of $5 billion for each of the following 20 years. The total cost of the Jones bill over the 25-year life of the program is estimated at $225 billion. Which bill would you support?

Although such a decision might seem relatively easy, if you were a member of Congress faced with a decision between these two policy actions, the rational and the logical choice for society may not be the rational choice for you. Election cycles, those 2-, 4-, or 6-year periods in which politicians must run for reelection, require that politicians be responsive to constituent demands in the short term. When deciding between two competing programs, one with low short-term costs and high long-term costs and another with high short-term costs and low long-term costs, it is easier for politicians to select the program that is less costly over the short term. The average voter may not follow particular votes closely, but voters are sensitive to tax increases. The electoral cycle and the pressures of reelection do not always function to push policymakers toward policy options that are attractive only in the short term, but, as we see in Part Two, this has often been the case in environmental policy.

Related to the short-term bias of the policy-making process is the tendency of both policymakers and individuals to discount the future in their calculations of the options to select. In individual behavior this is evidenced by those who smoke cigarettes or purchase on credit, to give only two examples. Collectively, in the policy-making process it is evidenced by making decisions that defer costs into the future or assume that technological advances or other changes will mitigate any undesired future consequences of decisions made today. Hence the short-term bias in the system is driven not only by the politicians' attention to the electoral cycle but also by shared cultural assumptions about a society's and the scientific community's ability to cope with future problems.

Ideological Bias

Throughout most of America's history, an ideological bias in the system has favored growth and development, an important part of our dominant social paradigm. Assumptions that are considered normal in a capitalist system about production and consumption may or may not be consistent with the rational stewardship of natural resources and the environment. Without passing judgment on the appropriateness or necessity of such assumptions, it is important to remember that an orientation toward growth and development underlies much of the policy-making process in the United States.

For example, when communities plan for future development, rarely is zero growth a serious option. Instead, the question is the acceptable percentage of growth. But for any community, and ultimately for the planet, there has to come a time when the development of new housing tracts on agricultural land, for instance, comes to a halt, thereby limiting growth significantly. This is rarely one of the seriously considered options.

The same orientation was evident in energy planning through the 1950s and 1960s. In making their projections of demand, utilities frequently employed linear projections based on past and current usage and ignored variables that might affect future demand. During the same period, many municipalities employed the same type of projections in their planning for future water resource needs.

Politicians have a number of incentives to heed the call for increased growth. For one, the businesspeople who make up the local chamber of commerce, who want to sell more newspapers, cars, or whatever the product or service, naturally see an expanding market as directly related to their future well-being. These local businesspeople are the people who are most often in contact with elected officials, and make campaign contributions, and they share similar backgrounds and are most likely to interact socially and officially, formally and informally, with elected officials. Labor unions and, to a certain extent, representatives of minority groups are also often proponents of economic expansion. Both groups understandably perceive economic growth as the way to provide additional employment. It should not be surprising, therefore, to find that many policymakers share an orientation toward expanding production, increasing development, and expanding economic opportunity.

Finally, there's strong evidence throughout the twentieth century of an ideological bias toward increased energy consumption. Often it has been assumed that increased energy consumption is necessary for maintaining or expanding the country's gross national product and the overall quality of life. Although strong evidence indicates little relationship between prosperity and energy consumption,[24] as we see in Chapter 7, the debate over energy development has often been reduced to simply how to produce more energy.

Private Nature of Public Policy Making

Most of what elected officials do escapes public attention. Although major issues may generate headlines, the details related to these issues are largely ignored by the public. Furthermore, although we may know how elected officials vote from roll call and recorded vote figures, we know much less about what motivates them to vote one way or the other. Many decisions are made outside of the public spotlight. Much new legislation and many refinements in existing legislation receive very little, if any, attention from anyone other than the parties directly involved in the legislation.

Considering the resource-raising advantages of private economic interest groups and the resource and organizational disadvantages of public noneconomic interest groups, these facts skew the less controversial or less visible decisions to the advantage of private economic interests. It is estimated that in excess of 70 percent of the bills Congress votes on are not contested by two parties or interests on opposite sides of the issue.[25]

Crisis Planning

Although policy, for the most part, is developed and redeveloped in an incremental fashion, the system does seem to respond reasonably well to a crisis or an emergency. The bargaining, compromise, and give-and-take that characterize the policy-making process during normal times can be suspended during times of crisis. A notable example in recent U.S. history is the Great Depression. During Franklin Roosevelt's first 100 days in office, the policy process was streamlined both by a sense of urgency and through the force of Roosevelt's personality. In more recent times, due largely to congressional fears that U.S. forces had been attacked in Vietnam, President Lyndon Johnson was able to secure swift passage of the Tonkin Gulf Resolution.

We have every reason to believe the policy-making system will respond to urgent environmental problems perceived to require immediate action. The Three Mile Island nuclear reactor accident resulted in relatively swift change in the policies of the Nuclear Regulatory Commission. Much of the major environmental legislation passed in the early 1970s in the United States represented a significant departure from past environmental policies.

Although the system can and does react to crisis or emergency situations, most environmental problems do not present themselves as urgent. The discovery of the toxic dump in Love Canal, New York, and related health effects in that community surely added impetus to the passage of the Comprehensive Environmental Response, Compensation, and Liability Act, otherwise known as the Superfund, in 1980. Nevertheless, the Superfund, in its passage and undoubtedly in its implementation, has followed the incremental process that typifies the policy formation process.

Many environmental problems, such as global warming or the greenhouse effect, the discovery of polluted groundwater, the depletion of fossil fuel resources, and the pollution of an air or river basin, progress slowly without noticeable or dramatic change from one month to the next. This slow progression is ideally suited to incremental decision making and also does not disrupt or challenge the short-term bias of elected policymakers or the ideological bias toward growth and development. In short, environmental problems often lend themselves to incremental solutions.

Unfortunately, the slow, cumulative nature of many environmental problems means these issues are not perceived as urgent by the public or policymakers. Hydrologists and water resource managers, for example, may be concerned about declining groundwater levels and that farmers are ceasing to irrigate in parts of the Southwest, but to many in the public and to many policymakers these are viewed as unfortunate yet isolated or unrelated incidents. And the news that another lake in Canada has been found to be devoid of life may spark concern among the public as well as policymakers, but such news is unlikely to provide the necessary incentive for effective action to deal with acid rain.

As we see later, nonincremental policy options are available today that may provide long-term and inexpensive solutions to many environmental problems. These options may not be available in the future when it becomes politically feasible to act on environmental issues in a comprehensive manner. It may be that environmental policy is doomed to failure if the system is unable to respond appropriately or in time.

THE REGULATORS

Although the laws and agencies that govern environmental management are discussed throughout the text, we identify here the major participants in the process and present an overview of one of the most significant environmental laws in the United States: the National Environmental Policy Act (NEPA).

National Environmental Policy Act

In 1969 Congress passed the National Environmental Policy Act (NEPA). Although relatively simple and straightforward, NEPA eventually became the most litigated of all federal environmental statutes. Unlike other federal legislation in the environmental area, NEPA exerted control on federal agencies themselves in an attempt to make them more responsive to environmental concerns and values.

In the opening section of the act, NEPA declares its purpose as follows:

> [T]he Congress, recognizing the profound impact of man's activity on the interrelationships of all components of the natural environment, particularly the profound influence of population growth ... industrial expansion, resource exploitation, and new and expanding technological advances, and recognizing further the importance of restoring and maintaining environmental quality to the overall welfare and development of man, declares it is the continuing policy of the federal government ... to use all practicable means and measures ... in a manner calculated to foster and promote the general welfare, to create and maintain conditions under which man and nature can exist in productive harmony, and fulfill the social, economic, and other requirements of present and future generations of Americans.[26]

To back up these lofty goals, "action forcing" procedures were developed in Section 102 of the act.[27] The most important requirement of NEPA was that an "environmental impact statement," or EIS, accompany "major federal actions significantly affecting the human environment."[28] NEPA directed that an EIS contain the environmental impact of a proposed federal action, any adverse environmental effects that cannot be avoided should the federal action proposed be implemented, any alternative to the proposed action, and any irreversible commitments of resources that an action would involve should it be implemented.[29]

NEPA also established the Council on Environmental Quality (CEQ) within the executive branch. Although the primary purpose of the CEQ was to advise the president about environmental matters, the CEQ became influential by developing regulations governing the EIS process and its implementation by federal agencies. The U.S. Supreme Court has recognized the authority of the CEQ in developing regulations for the implementation of NEPA.[30] During the administrations of Ronald Reagan and George Bush, environmentalists charged that the CEQ had been stripped of its power. President Reagan wanted to eliminate the CEQ, and during both the Reagan and Bush administrations funding for CEQ operations was significantly reduced. In response, President Bill Clinton, in the first month of his presidency, announced his intention to abolish the CEQ and create the White House Office on Environmental Policy. The new office is designed to strengthen the hand of Vice President Al Gore in shaping environmental policy, thus signaling the Clinton administration's intentions to give environmental issues priority in the executive branch.[31]

The EIS provisions of NEPA are binding on all federal agencies. Early agency reactions to these provisions were mixed. Some agencies were quick to adopt a thorough environmental impact statement process, whereas others were slow to respond, as evidenced by numerous lawsuits forcing agency action. Consequently, much of what NEPA has come to mean in practical terms has been decided by the courts.

NEPA requires that an EIS be circulated among state, local, and federal agencies as well as the public. The act itself has no enforcement provisions; however, the courts, through a number of decisions, have provided enforcement mechanisms.[32]

Two bills introduced in 1969, House Resolution 6750, introduced by Congressman John D. Dingell, and Senate Bill 1075, introduced by Senator Henry Jackson, became the basis of NEPA. In a House-Senate conference committee, the final version of NEPA emerged with an important component deleted. The Senate bill had provided that "[E]ach person has a fundamental and inalienable right to a healthful environment. . . ."[33] In the final version, these words were changed to, "[E]ach person should enjoy a healthful environment." inclusion of the original language might have given citizens legally enforceable environmental rights.

The conference report on NEPA indicated the intent of Congress when it stated, "[A]ll federal agencies shall comply with the provisions of Section 102 to the fullest extent possible, . . . [T]hus it is the intent of the conferees that the provision, to the fullest extent possible, shall not be used by any federal agency as a means of avoiding compliance with the directives set out in Section 102."[34] This report suggests that Congress had intended NEPA to be interpreted as an act which could affect the *substance* of agency decisions and was not intended to be only a procedural requirement.

Three major questions have been before the courts in NEPA litigation: (1) the determination of whether an EIS is necessary, (2) finding that it is, what the EIS should contain, and (3) when it should be prepared. Concerning the first issue, according to NEPA, an EIS is required when a federal action is major and has a significant environmental impact. The cases revolve around determining what constitutes "major" and what is a "significant environmental impact." An action is a federal action if a federal agency has some control over that action or if the action is carried out by the agency itself. For example, since the federal government is involved in licensing nuclear power plants, an EIS is required for their construction. The determination of whether or not an act is "major" generally involves any substantial commitment by the government of money or other resources.

While Supreme Court decisions over the nature of major federal actions have been fairly clear, more activity has focused on determining what constitutes "significant environmental impact." First, according to NEPA, the environment does not refer to just woods and streams. The language of NEPA requires that the public in all locations be provided "safe, healthful, productive, and aesthetically and culturally pleasing surroundings."[35]

To illustrate, a New York federal court found that the construction of a new jail in downtown New York involved an impact significant enough to require an EIS.[36] In another case, the Supreme Court found that "[E]ffects on human health can be recognizable under NEPA, and that human health may include psychological health."[37]

To determine whether or not an impact is "significant," a two-step process has been developed that involves assessing the degree of change from the current use of land and the total quantity of the impact involved.[38] The EIS process starts at the time of a proposal for a federal action. In 1975 the U.S. Supreme Court found that "[W]here an agency initiates federal action by publishing a proposal and then holding hearings on the proposal, the statute would appear to require that an impact statement be included in the proposal and to be considered at the hearing."[39]

The first step in the EIS process is the preparation of an "environmental assessment," or EA. If no significant impact is found, then the agency is required to make a "finding of no significant impact," or FONSI. In the cases where the impact is found to be significant, the second step is taken—the preparation of an EIS.

When an EIS is prepared, it must take into consideration the environmental impacts of the total project, not just one particular component of that project. For example, an Atomic Energy Commission EIS for a single breeder reactor was found to be inadequate, and a federal circuit court held that an EIS was necessary to cover the entire breeder reactor program.[40]

Although NEPA contains both procedural requirements (for example, the EIS), and a number of substantive recommendations (for example, to maintain a clean and healthy environment for all Americans), the courts have not enforced any of the substantive language. In effect this means that once the procedures have been followed and the EIS prepared, an agency may then go forward with its plans regardless of the negative impacts these plans may actually have on the environment. This is not to suggest the EIS process is pointless. The mere identification of environmental problems, sometimes coupled with public reaction to these problems, has caused many government plans to be changed or dropped.

Environmental Administration

In the United States, all three levels of government, national, state, and local, are involved in some capacity in environmental management. Most states have several agencies that are involved in environmental protection. State agencies may go under the name of the environmental protection agency or may be identified by function such as Department of Health, Department of Water Resources, or Water Quality Control. At the local level, there are a variety of air and water quality management districts in cities and counties. Larger cities often have environmental quality control departments or, more often, cities have health or public service agencies that have some responsibility for environmental quality control. Also on the local level, there are various special districts or single-purpose districts that have responsibility over environmental quality control. Special districts are local government units organized to perform one or a limited number of functions, such as park and recreation development or mosquito abatement.

Preferences differ as to the appropriate level of government for the development and implementation of environmental regulations. There is no "correct" level of government for environmental regulation, and the appropriate regulatory authority may vary depending on the issue and the problem. However, certain interests have preferences for the location of regulatory authority. In addition, certain environmental problems have traditionally been handled in one level of government. For example, land-use planning, with minor exceptions, has been a local government concern in the United States. On the national level, nuclear power, again with minor exceptions, has primarily been the responsibility of the federal government.

Interest groups prefer that decision making over public policy be made in an arena where they feel they have the most influence. For example, in a state like Hawaii, in which a particular agricultural activity plays a dominant role in the state's economy, agricultural interests might prefer that pesticide regulation over pineapple and sugar cane be centered in the state government. In another example, the coal mining industry in West Virginia prefers strip mine reclamation to be on the state level.

On the other hand, major manufacturing companies with nationwide distribution systems often prefer environmental regulations to be implemented on the national level. The consistency and uniformity possible through national regulation costs the companies less than several different types of regulation in different states. In the face of multiple and sometimes conflicting state auto emission requirements, the automobile industry preferred the establishment of national standards to avoid the necessity of producing numerous types of cars for sale in states with differing air pollution control laws. In the late 1980s, refrigerator manufacturers lobbied for national energy efficiency guidelines to head off numerous and potentially conflicting guidelines being considered in state legislatures.

The Environmental Protection Agency

The Environmental Protection Agency (EPA) was established to have the primary responsibility for enforcing environmental regulations in the United States. President Richard Nixon, through an executive order in 1970, reorganized environmental administration in the United States, grouping together numerous programs throughout the federal bureaucracy under the direction of the EPA. "[The EPA is] designed to serve as the public's advocate for a livable environment."[41] The agency engages in research, the setting of standards, and monitoring and supporting similar activities on the state and local level.

The EPA is basically organized around programs over which Congress has given it enforcement authority. The agency is headed by an administrator with nine assistant administrators. There is also a general counsel, an inspector general, and ten regional offices. The regional offices are the primary contact points for the agency with state and local officials. Administrative units with substantive policy responsibilities include divisions of water, solid waste, air and radiation, pesticides and toxic substances, and research and development.

One of the potential problems with this type of organization is that it ignores the interrelationship of environmental problems. For example, the water division might not interrelate with the solid waste division. The agency refers to the overlapping of related problems as "multimedia" management. Although the term *media* correctly refers to the affected environmental media such as air, water, and land, the agency uses the term to refer to "media programs" or the major statutory programs under the administration's jurisdiction. As former EPA administrator Lee Thomas described multimedia solutions, "[Y]ou look at a problem on a geographic basis instead of pollution and air, water, or land. That way, you don't just pull the pollution out of the air and flush it into the water, or pull it out of the water and dump it out onto the land."[42]

Enforcement of environmental regulations within the EPA is the responsibility of the assistant administrator for enforcement and compliance, which includes an office of criminal enforcement; each of the major program areas, for example, water, pesticides, toxic substances, also has an enforcement office and/or an office of compliance monitoring. The EPA has special agents who work within the agency's Office of Criminal Enforcement. These agents are required to have at least six years of experience investigating organized crime, white-collar crime, or major felonies. Coming to the agency from police departments, the FBI, and the Treasury Department, EPA agents have jobs very much like the law enforcement agencies from which they come—serving warrants, collecting evidence, and occasionally getting shot at.[43]

The EPA was criticized for being lax in its enforcement efforts during the Reagan administration. For example, the Federal Water Pollution Control Act Amendments of 1972 directed the EPA to develop regulations to prohibit the discharge of toxic pollutants. During the three years that followed passage of the 1972 Act, the EPA developed effluent standards for only six pollutants. By November 1987, the EPA had published standards for 63 toxic pollutants discharged by organic chemical plants, but it was not anticipated that standards for the pesticide industry would be developed until sometime into the 1990s.[44] In 1986 a U.S. General Accounting Office (GAO) report criticized EPA enforcement of the Superfund as being unsystematic and uncoordinated, and stated that enforcement decisions were not uniform between the EPA regions or even within the same region. Representative James Florio, who requested the GAO report, remarked that EPA management of the Superfund was characterized by "delay after delay with no effective enforcement."[45] Another GAO study found in 1983 that 3,400, or about half, of the nation's major manufacturing plants had broken the law for discharging pollutants into water for at least six months of the previous year.[46]

EPA enforcement of its regulations has at times in the past been motivated as much by political considerations as by any real intention to elicit compliance. For instance, in 1987 the EPA imposed construction limits on major new sources of pollution in 10 areas that were not in compliance with the Clean Air Act. EPA administrator Lee Thomas, anticipating the public reaction, commented at the time, "I think there will be a real uproar."[47] The EPA's action was seen as an attempt to put pressure on Congress to amend the law. Representative Henry Waxman from Los Angeles, one of the affected areas, remarked, "I think what the EPA is doing is trying to shift the burden to Congress to deal with the Clean Air Act. I find this somewhat unfortunate because for the last six years they've failed to use the law to force the kind of reductions in air pollution that might have been achieved."[48]

The politics of enforcement has always been an issue in EPA management. The EPA has enjoyed the support of both political parties. As an attorney with extensive experience representing clients before the EPA wrote, "[B]oth Republicans and Democrats have enforced the environmental statutes, requested and obtained additional statutory authority, and issued new regulatory controls to improve the environment. . . . [T]he differences between administrations in the environmental enforcement area are merely of degree."[49] And as the former EPA administrator during the Carter administration remarked, the Environmental Protection Agency has "always enjoyed a strong degree of bi-partisan support."[50]

The first administrator of the EPA was William Ruckelshaus, a former Indiana politician and attorney for the U.S. Justice Department. Ruckelshaus quickly built a reputation for himself and the EPA as being aggressive in the enforcement of environmental statutes. Although often at odds with the EPA, President Nixon wanted to draw attention to the environmental activities of his administration in an effort to prevent potential Democratic presidential nominee Edmund Muskie from using the issue in the 1972 elections. Within weeks after assuming the administrator's job, Ruckelshaus moved against Atlanta, Detroit, and Cleveland, threatening federal court action to prevent the discharge of untreated sewage. These cities all had Democratic mayors. It was part of Ruckelshaus's early strategy, and the EPA's strategy through most of its institutional history, to go after highly visible polluters in an effort to generate publicity. Early in his term, Ruckelshaus took action against Republic Steel, Jones and Laughlin, and the Kennebec River Pulp and Paper Company.[51] As a press officer for the EPA at the time of Ruckelshaus's tenure remarked, "[Ruckelshaus was] anxious to bring the big polluters into line, [so] he used the press to instill fear in their hearts by holding up a few of them as bad examples."[52]

Throughout the 1970s, the EPA continued to enjoy bipartisan support and a reputation for strong enforcement of environmental statutes. The Reagan administration brought a new approach to the management of the EPA. Reagan's first EPA administrator, Anne Burford, sought to ease the enforcement of environmental laws and place more emphasis on voluntary compliance. Uncharacteristic of typical agency behavior, Burford sought smaller, not larger appropriations for her agency and, atypically for EPA administrators, her main priority was relief for regulated industries. During the first two years of the Reagan administration, the EPA's enforcement budget was cut by 45 percent. The number of cases referred by the EPA to the Department of Justice for prosecution had hovered at about 200 per year prior to the Reagan administration, dropping to 50 during the first year of his administration.

The journal of the Natural Resources Defense Council editorialized that "[A]bout all that has mattered has been the sight, smell, and taste of politics. Although the President failed in his promise to weaken environmental laws, through rhetoric, appointments, and budget constraints, his administration has succeeded in blunting their effectiveness."[53]

Appointments to major offices within the EPA, like other environmental appointments during the Reagan administration, often came directly from the regulated industries. For example, the first general counsel of the EPA was formerly a lawyer for Exxon Corporation. Burford's chief of staff was formerly with Johns-Manville Corporation, and the assistant administrator in charge of air quality was the former lobbyist for Crown Zellerbach Corporation.[54]

The emphasis on voluntary compliance and the primacy of politics in the EPA created an atmosphere within the agency that apparently was conducive to political abuses of environmental administration. The head of the Superfund during Burford's tenure at the EPA was Rita Lavalle, a former campaign worker for President Reagan when he was running for governor of California. In 1983 Lavalle was discovered to have used her office to further the chances of Republican Congressional candidates in the 1982 elections. Lavalle was distributing Superfund cleanup monies in ways that might be seen as politically advantageous for Republicans.[55]

The combination of Lavalle's problems and accusations of politicized environmental enforcement leveled against Burford and the EPA generally led to a great deal of turmoil within the agency early in 1983. According to agency officials, the EPA was "demoralized and virtually inert."[56] Both administrator Burford and Superfund administrator Lavalle were forced to leave the EPA in March 1983.[57] Lavalle was accused of perjury and obstructing a congressional investigation of EPA management of the Superfund. The charge concerned at what point she learned her former employer, Aerojet General Corporation, had been a user of the Stringfellow Dump in California. When dismissed from office, Lavalle's staff "went into a flurry of removing sensitive documents from her office."[58] In December 1983, Lavalle was convicted of perjury and sentenced to prison.

To the delight of environmentalists, Anne Burford was replaced by William Ruckelshaus. Though he had spent the previous eight years as an executive for Weyerhaeuser Corporation, environmentalists remembered the assertive action Ruckelshaus had taken as the first EPA administrator and were optimistic he would continue with that style of management. Many of the hopes of environmentalists were realized. Ruckelshaus replaced most of the EPA's top administrators with people who had wide experience in environmental policy and science. This was in contrast to many of Burford's inexperienced appointees.[59]

The EPA administrator who succeeded Ruckelshaus when he resigned in 1985 was Lee Thomas, formerly the head of the Federal Emergency Management Agency. Earlier he had assumed control of the toxic waste division of the EPA from Rita Lavalle at the time of her departure. On most issues, Thomas was much more aggressive in implementing EPA's mandate than was administrator Burford. An article in *Business Week* magazine reported:

> "[U]nder Rita Lavalle's stewardship, environmentalists charge, the Toxic Waste Cleanup Program was rife with political favoritism and soft on polluters. After her ouster, business leaders say the agency compensated by taking too hard a line, forcing some companies to pay the full cost of cleanups even when they were responsible for only a portion of the waste."[60]

A change in management strategy in the EPA was evident by the increased number of enforcement actions referred from the agency to the Department of Justice for prosecution.[61]

During the election of 1988, George Bush promised to be the "environmental president." His EPA administrator, William K. Reilly, a professionally trained environmentalist, pushed through the 1990 amendments to the Clean Air Act. However, at the same time, Vice President Dan Quayle's Council on Competitiveness and the Office of Management and Budget were working to weaken implementation of the 1990 amendments as well as other environmental regulations, in the name of economic efficiency. While the Council had no statutory authority, it did have the ear of President Bush, and, as such, provided a format for businesses seeking regulatory relief. The *Sierra* magazine characterized the council's attack on the 1990 Clean Air Act Amendments as follows: "[T]he Competitiveness Council has pecked at the act ever since its passage, handing out exemptions like candy to power plant operators, automobile manufacturers, and newspaper publishers, among others."[62]

Early in the Clinton administration the president moved to abolish the Council on Competitiveness. Clinton appointed Carol Browner as the new EPA administrator. Browner is a former member of Vice President Gore's Senate staff and head of the Florida Department of Environmental Regulation. Environmental organizations generally applauded her appointment.[63]

In summary, the politics of the Environmental Protection Agency may best be described as bipartisan, and, depending on the issue and the administration in power, aggressive on enforcement. The early Reagan administration and the EPA administration of Burford was an exception to this trend; and, once the political liabilities of a politicized EPA soft on enforcement became apparent, was short lived.

Being a relatively new agency, the EPA has not had as much of an opportunity as other federal agencies to develop strong and lasting relations with interest groups. Such relationships would assist the agency in its battles with polluters or an unfriendly administration. A natural constituency for the agency would be the environmental organizations that support the programs within the agency's jurisdiction. Unfortunately for the long-term political health of the agency, the early actions of the Reagan administration made environmental organizations leery of the agency. It remains to be seen if this hesitation to support the EPA will be reversed in the Clinton administration.

Department of Interior

The Department of the Interior was established in 1849 by combining the Treasury Department's General Land Office, the War Department's Office of Indian Affairs, which later became the Bureau of Indian Affairs, the Patent Office, the Pension Office, and the Census Office. In its first year of operation, the department had a permanent work force of 10 people and a budget of $14,200.[64] Today the Department of Interior has extensive responsibility over environmental and land management. The Department of Interior houses the National Park Service, the U.S. Fish and Wildlife Service, the Bureau of Land Management, the Minerals Management Service, the Office of Surface Mining, the U.S. Geological Survey, the Bureau of Reclamation, and the Bureau of Mines. The department is organized with a secretary and five assistant secretaries covering each of the major substantive areas within the department's jurisdiction.

Traditionally, major Interior Department appointees, which include the secretary and the assistant secretaries, have had ties to the West and, to a lesser extent, the Midwest.[65] Although the agency has known its share of scandal, the Department of the Interior and many of its component agencies, such as the National Park Service, enjoy a long institutional history and tradition and a well-developed interest group support system.[66]

Consistent with their western roots and the conservation goals of many of the agencies within the Department of Interior, secretaries of the interior have, for the most part, been conservationists themselves. However the management pattern we saw in the EPA early in the Reagan administration also occurred in the management of the Department of Interior. President Reagan's first secretary of the interior, James Watt, came to the department from the Mountain States Legal Defense Fund, an organization that had been active in suing the Interior Department over the management of western lands. As Patricia and Robert Cahn, contributing editors to *National Parks Magazine*, wrote, "[W]ith the advent of James Watt and the Reagan administration in 1981, came the attempt to make drastic changes. The Watt team brought an anti-government 'sagebrush rebellion' philosophy to the department and a tilt toward development and privatization, which they aggressively sought to impose. . . ."[67]

Secretary Watt put the Interior Department on a path away from conservation and toward greater development of federal resources. These activities included the opening of the outer continental shelf to additional oil company bidding; the rapid acceleration of coal, oil, and gas leasing, including the opening of wilderness areas for mineral exploration; and an end to spending for the acquisition of additional park lands.[68] Watt immediately drew criticism from environmental organizations for both his actions and attitudes. The secretary did not shy away from controversy nor was he willing to appease environmentalists. Watt regularly referred to environmentalists as "radicals" and compared those in the environmental movement to "communists" and "Nazis."[69] A staunch conservative, Watt, in his own words, felt "[T]he contest between liberals and conservatives . . . is a moral battle. It is a contest over who's right and who's wrong."[70]

Watt's outspokenness eventually led to his resignation. The secretary had become a political liability for Republicans in the 1984 elections, and on October 10, 1983, President Reagan accepted the secretary's resignation.[71] In addition to attacks on environmentalists, Watt alienated other Interior Department constituent groups. For example, the secretary had called the department's Bureau of Indian Affairs an example of the "failure of socialism," and when characterizing the makeup of an Interior Department's coal advisory board, described the board as being "well balanced," including "a woman, a black, a Jew, and a cripple."[72] This comment turned out to be the fatal blow to his Interior Department career.

Ironically, many in the environmental movement as well as some Democratic party leaders did not welcome Watt's resignation. The controversy caused by Watt's tenure helped fuel the rapid rise of membership in environmental organizations and, undoubtedly, was a catalyst for increased public support for environmental regulation. There is also some irony in the fact that Watt actually accomplished very little, in spite of his rhetoric. By drawing attention to his actions, he undermined the resource development and privatization goals he sought to achieve.

Watt was replaced by Interior Secretary William Clark, who was replaced in 1985 by Donald Hodel. Both Clark and Hodel assumed relatively low profiles and attempted, publicly at least, a more moderate form of management. Hodel, in what was seen variously as an attempt to either appease or divide environmentalists, suggested in 1987 that the Hetch Hetchy Dam in Yosemite National Park be torn down and the valley be allowed to revert to its natural state. The drive in the Interior Department for privatization and increased development on federal lands continued throughout the Reagan and Bush administrations.

President Clinton appointed former Arizona governor Bruce Babbitt as his secretary of the interior. The Babbitt appointment was widely praised by environmental organizations. During the spring of 1993 when Babbitt was rumored to be under consideration for appointment to the U.S. Supreme Court, environmental organizations lobbied the White House to keep the interior secretary at Interior, which is what happened.[73]

Bureau of Land Management

The Bureau of Land Management (BLM), created in 1946 through the consolidation of the general land office and grazing services, manages 27 million acres of public lands primarily in the Far West and Alaska, as well as 300 million acres where mineral rights are owned by the federal government.[74] After farmers had taken those federal lands they wanted for farming, prime forests were reserved in the U.S. Forest System, and the most spectacular or unique land was preserved in the National Park Service. What was left, those lands that no one wanted, became the responsibility of the Bureau of Land Management. Ironically, those "unwanted" lands are now the focus of much controversy in federal land management.

For most of the bureau's history, the agency has been criticized, correctly most analysts feel, for serving the interest of the ranchers that depend on bureau grazing permits to the exclusion of other interests. As one author wrote, "[F]or the first three decades after its creation in 1946 ... BLM did essentially what its parent bureaucracies had done: handed down land parcels, grazing leases, and mineral claims. It became a standard joke that BLM actually stood for Bureau of Livestocking and Mining."[75]

In 1976 passage of the Federal Land Policy and Land Management Act (or FLPMA) led to a change in BLM land management practices. FLPMA required the BLM to adopt the management principles of multiple use and sustained yield that were the mandate of the Forest Service. FLPMA also directed the BLM to examine its holdings to determine which were suitable for wilderness designation, giving the agency 15 years, until 1991, to complete the task. The early history of the BLM had consisted largely of agency validation of the existing arrangements and preferences of established local groups.[76]

After 1976 this was less the case, and in fact BLM offices both in Washington and in the field are staffed with professionals representing nontraditional values. Nevertheless, as one student of the BLM noted, "[P]rofessionals representing nontraditional values often complain that the values they represent are given short shrift in the planning process and that traditional values are still the dominant concern of many BLM managers."[77]

The BLM has been attempting to reach out beyond the traditional ranching and grazing interests of the past. For example, in its wilderness planning for the southern California desert, extensive efforts were made to work with individuals and organizations that were concerned with protection of the desert environment. The BLM clearly has a self-interest in involving environmentalists in the agency's decision making. The exclusion of such interests in wilderness planning could result in a backlash in Congress and potentially the removal of some lands from bureau jurisdiction. The BLM has therefore been more sensitive to the concerns of these interests since the mid-1970s.

National Park Service

The National Park Service, created in 1916, was directed to "promote and regulate the use of the federal areas known as national parks, monuments, and reservations . . . the fundamental purpose of these parks . . . is to conserve the scenery and the natural and historic objects and the wildlife therein, and to provide for the enjoyment of the same in such a manner and by such means as will leave them unimpaired for the enjoyment of future generations."[78] The inherent conflict between preservation and use is a major land-use problem for the National Park Service.

There are 367 sites within National Park Service jurisdiction, including national parks, monuments, historic sites, and recreation areas, which in total cover more than 80.6 million acres.[79] Park service holdings expanded significantly in the 1960s and 1970s, growing from 176 units in 1960 covering 26.2 million acres to 333 units covering 77 million acres by 1980. In 1980 Congress passed the Alaska National Interest Lands Conservation Act, which more than doubled the acreage of the national parks system (adding 43.6 million acres).[80]

The growth of the park system has corresponded to growth in the number of visitations to National Park units. Due undoubtedly in part to increased visitation, the Park Service, unlike the other federal land management agencies discussed in this chapter, has enjoyed a considerable amount of public approval and support. In 1978 a Gallup poll found 95 percent of those responding gave the National Park Service a favorable rating.[81] The primary constituencies of the National Park Service are environmentalist and recreationalist. Environmentalists are primarily concerned with the preservation aspects of Park Service goals, whereas recreationalists are concerned with the use and enjoyment of the parks.

The Park Service, like all the federal land management agencies studied here, has fluctuated in its management philosophies from one segment of its public constituency to another. In an effort to provide more service for the public, the Park Service has been criticized by environmentalists for having a "Disneyland" mentality. For example, in the early 1970s, the Park Service and the Music Corporation of America (the concessionaire, at that time, in Yosemite National Park) together developed a master plan for Yosemite Valley that included, among other things, a significant expansion of visitor facilities, including the building of a convention center.[82] MCA produced and distributed slick promotional brochures outlining the corporation's commitment to preserving park values. One read, "[I]t's not just another American convention hotel. ... [A]ll your worldly needs are provided for. ... [T]his isn't no man's land or primitive wilderness. This is civilization."[83]

Forest Service

The Forest Service was created in 1905 by the transference of federal forest reserves out of the Department of the Interior and into the Department of Agriculture. The Forest Service manages 156 national forests,

19 national grasslands, and 17 land utilization projects in 44 states. Forest Service holdings cover 191 million acres.

The constituent groups that have had an influence on the Forest Service may be divided into two types: resource-using and recreation groups. The resource-using groups include timber, mining, and to a lesser extent, grazing interests. The recreation groups include environmental organizations and organizations of hikers, hunters, and fishermen. The management principle of Forest Service lands, and the Bureau of Land Management lands as well, is one of multiple use and sustained yield. For the Forest Service, the guiding principle is "the greatest good to the greatest number in the long run."[84]

Traditionally and historically, resource user groups have had the most influence within the Forest Service. The national forests have been seen as a kind of agricultural product to be used for the greatest amount of production in the furtherance of economic and consumptive use goals. This traditional orientation has worked to the advantage of and led to the growth and strength within the Forest Service of resource-using constituencies. This is not to suggest the Forest Service has ignored environmental or recreation concerns. Recreationalists in particular have been an important constituency for the Forest Service, and environmentalists have been placated somewhat by efforts of the Forest Service to create wilderness areas. These outcomes are discussed in more detail later.

Although the first assistant secretary of agriculture with jurisdiction over the Forest Service during the Reagan administration was a former counsel for a lumber company, the Forest Service did not undergo the same tumultuous administrative period that the EPA and the Department of Interior went through in the early 1980s.

Forest Service management plans and problems along with those of agencies within the Department of Interior are discussed in detail in the chapters to follow.

U.S. Fish and Wildlife Service

The Department of Interior's U.S. Fish and Wildlife Service was created in 1940 by combining the Bureau of Biological Survey, established in 1885 in the Department of Agriculture, with the Bureau of Fisheries, established in 1871, first as an independent agency and then later in the Department of Commerce. The Fish and Wildlife Service oversees 493 national wildlife refuges, 166 waterfowl protection areas, 51 waterfowl coordination areas, 78 national fish hatcheries, 13 major fish and wildlife research laboratories, and centers totaling more than 93.4 million acres.[85] By acreage, most of the national wildlife refuge system, about 88 percent, is in Alaska.

SUMMARY

In this chapter we examined the regulatory process governing environmental policy in the United States. Fundamental to that process, as we have seen, is the concept of pluralism—or the bargaining that organized groups engage in when attempting to influence public policy outcomes. But all groups are not created equal. Because of differences in their ability to raise and spend money for political campaigns, as well as differences in the amount of other resources, some groups have the advantage when attempting to influence environmental policy. Generally, private economic interest groups have more and better resources for influencing the process than do public interest groups—including most environmental groups. We also saw how incrementalism, decentralization, the incentives operating on policymakers to plan for the short term instead of the long term, ideological bias, and the crisis nature of policy making all influence the policy formation process. These attributes of our political system often operate to produce policies that, as we see in greater detail in the chapters that follow, do not do the job or do not accomplish what they were intended to accomplish. In other words, they operate to help create the paradoxes of environmental policy.

We also introduced the National Environmental Policy Act and the federal agencies that have primary responsibility for implementing environmental policy. The federal agencies we discussed, the Forest Service, the Environmental Protection Agency, and the resource management agencies within the Department of the Interior, are the major governmental players in the environmental policy implementation process and are referred to throughout the book.

The remaining chapters in this book cover air, water, energy, toxic and hazardous waste, land management, international pollution problems, and international environmental management. Chapter 5, on air pollution, like most of these chapters, begins with a description of the nature of the problem of air pollution, continues with a description of laws and regulations governing it, and discusses the successes and failures of those regulatory efforts.

NOTES

1. V. O. Key, *Politics, Parties, and Pressure Groups* (5th ed.) (New York: Thomas Y. Crowell, 1964), p. 17. For a discussion of pluralism and alternative theories see Kenneth Prewitt and Alan Stone, *The Ruling Elites* (New York: Harper & Row, 1973); and Jeffrey M. Berry, *The Interest Group Society* (Boston: Little, Brown, 1984).
2. Berry, *The Interest Group Society*, p. 2.
3. *The Federalist Papers* (New York: New American Library, 1961), p. 78.

4. Ibid., p. 79.
5. It should be pointed out that Madison was not as egalitarian as the forgoing might suggest. In fact, he was suspicious of majority rule and preferred the business of government to be conducted by the elite. Pluralist theorists, including Dahl, Truman, and others, have read Madison as a forerunner of pluralist participatory democratic theory. Although this would not be an accurate portrayal of Madison, he is historically interesting in this context for he identified potential problems with interest group influence early on, which have now, in this author's opinion, come to pass.
6. Arthur Bentley, *The Process of Government* (Chicago: University of Chicago Press, 1908).
7. Bentley, *The Process of Government*, pp. 222, 210.
8. See, for example, Peter H. Odegard, *Pressure Politics: The Story of the Anti-Saloon League* (New York: Columbia University Press, 1928); E. Pendelton Herring, *Group Representation Before Congress* (Baltimore: Johns Hopkins University Press, 1929); and E. E. Schattschneider, *Politics, Pressures and the Tariff* (Englewood Cliffs, NJ: Prentice-Hall, 1935).
9. David Truman, *The Governmental Process* (New York: Knopf, 1951).
10. Ibid., p. 51.
11. Robert A. Dahl, *Who Governs?* (New Haven: Yale University Press, 1961).
12. Terry M. Moe, *The Organization of Interests* (Chicago: University of Chicago Press, 1980); Zachary A. Smith, *Interest Group Interaction and Groundwater Policy Formation in the Southwest* (Lanman, MD: University Press of America, 1985).
13. Jack L. Walker, "A Critique of the Elitist Theory of Democracy," *American Political Science Review*, 60 (June 1966), pp. 285–295; Theodore J. Lowi, *The End of Liberalism* (2nd ed.) (New York: Norton, 1979).
14. See, for example, Mancur Olsen, *The Logic of Collective Action* (Cambridge, MA: Harvard University Press, 1965).
15. See Martin V. Melosi, *Coping with Abundance: Energy and Environment in Industrial America* (New York: Knopf, 1985), Part Three.
16. Smith, *Interest Group Interaction and Groundwater Policy Formation in the Southwest*, p.26.
17. Although its impact at the time of this writing is uncertain, a 1992 U.S. Supreme Court ruling (*Lujan v. Defenders of Wildlife*) found that in order to have standing an individual must have "personally suffered a specific injury or will be harmed immediately." The case involved the Endangered Species Act. The *Wall Street Journal* reported, "Justice Harry Blackmun, in a dissent joined by Justice Sandra O'Connor, accused the splintered majority of 'what amounts to a slash-and-burn expedition through the law of environmental standing.'" See Paul M. Barrett, "Environmental Lawsuits Face Tough Standard," *Wall Street Journal*, June 15, 1992, p. A3.
18. Lettie M. Wenner, "Contextual Influences on Judicial Decision Making," *Western Political Quarterly*, 41 (March 1988), pp. 115–134; Lettie M. Wenner, "Environmental Policy in the Courts," in Norman J. Vig and Michael E. Kraft (eds.), *Environmental Policy in the 1990s* (Washington, DC: Congressional Quarterly Press, 1990), pp. 189–210.
19. Numerous scholars have addressed the importance of reelection in motivating the behavior of legislators. See, for example, David R. Mayhew, *Congress: The Electoral Connection* (New Haven: Yale University Press, 1974); and Gary C. Jacobson, *The Politics of Congressional Elections* (Boston: Little, Brown, 1987).
20. Charles G. Bell and Charles M. Price, *California Government Today* (3rd ed.) (Chicago: Dorsey, 1988), p. 69.
21. Paul J. Culhane, *Public Lands Politics* (Baltimore: Johns Hopkins University Press, 1981), p. 234.

22. Taken from James E. Anderson, *Public Policymaking* (3rd ed.) (New York: Holt, Rinehart and Winston, 1984), p. 9.
23. David Robertson and Dennis Judd, *The Development of American Public Policy: The Structure of Policy Restraint* (Boston and Glenview, IL: Scott, Foresman/Little, Brown, 1989), pp. 321–353.
24. Robert Stobaugh and Daniel Yergin (eds.), *Energy Future* (3rd ed.) (New York: Vintage Books, 1983), pp. 173–237.
25. Although this point may be found throughout the literature of political science, one of the most readable accounts may be found in Charles L. Clapp, *The Congressman* (Washington, DC: Brookings Institution, 1963).
26. National Environmental Policy Act, Section 101(a).
27. The first step in the EIS process is the preparation of an "environmental assessment" (or EA). If in the environmental assessment, which is relatively short, it is found that there is no significant impact, then the agency is required to make a "finding of no significant impact." The EIS process starts at the time of a proposal for a federal action. In 1975 the U.S. Supreme Court found that, "[W]here an agency initiates federal action by publishing a proposal and then holding hearings on the proposal, the statute would appear to require that an impact statement be included in the proposal and to be considered at the hearing." See *Aberdeen and Rockfish Railroad Company v. Students Challenging Regulatory Agency Procedures*, 422 U.S. 289 (1975).
28. National Environmental Policy Act, Section 102(c).
29. National Environmental Policy Act, Section 102(c) (i–v).
30. *Andrus v. Sierra Club*, 99 S.Ct. 2335 (1979).
31. Timothy Noah, *Wall Street Journal*, February 9, 1993, p. B6.
32. An early case, *Calvert Cliffs' Coordinating Committee, Inc. v. AEC*, found that NEPA "mandates a particular sort of careful and informed decision-making process and creates judicially enforceable rule duties." The Court went on to say that if the agency "decision was reached procedurally without individualized consideration and balancing of environmental factors—conducted fully and in good faith—it is a responsibility of the Courts to reverse." See *Calvert Cliffs' Coordinating Committee, Inc. v. AEC*, 449 F.2d 1109 (D.C. Cir. 1971).
33. U.S. Senate, Senate Report No. 91-296, 91st Congress, First Session.
34. 115 Congressional Record (Part 30) at 40417–40418.
35. National Environmental Policy Act, Section 101.
36. *Hanly v. Mitchell*, 460 F. 2d 640 (2d Cir. 1972).
37. *Metropolitan Edison Company v. People Against Nuclear Energy*, 103 S.Ct. 1556 (1983).
38. See *Hanly v. Kleindienst*, 471 F.2d 823 (2d Cir. 1972), *Cert. Denied* 412 U.S. 908 (1973); various other formulas have been adopted by other courts, but this is the one most often used.
39. *Aberdeen and Rockfish Railroad Company v. Students, Challenging Regulatory Agency Procedures*, 422 U.S. 289 (1975).
40. *Scientists' Institute for Public Information, Inc. v. AEC*, 481 F.2d 1079 (D.C. Cir. 1973).
41. *U.S. Government Manual 1987–1988* (Washington, DC: U.S. Government Printing Office, 1987), p. 525.
42. "Reagan's Policy on Pollution," Dun's Business Month, 125 (June 1985), p. 48.
43. Bill Adler, "Risky Business," *Sierra* (November/December 1985) p. 21.
44. "The Quiet Crisis II," *The Amicus Journal*, 10 (1) (Winter 1988), p. 2.
45. "EPA Assailed on Enforcing Superfund Cleanups," *Chemical and Engineering News*, 64 (May 26, 1986), p. 24.
46. "Humpty Dumpty," *The Amicus Journal*, 10 (1) (Winter 1988), p. 14.
47. Larry B. Stammer, "EPA Takes a Harder Stand on Enforcing Clean Air Act" *Los Angeles Times*, April 24, 1987, p. 3.

48. Ibid., p. 32.
49. Patrick M. Raher, "How to Get Things Done at the EPA," *The Brief*, 15 (Winter 1986), p. 23.
50. Phillip Shabecoff, "Environmental Agency: Deep and Persisting Woes," *New York Times*, March 6, 1983, p. A1.
51. Joseph Bower and Charles Christenson, *Public Management* (Homewood, IL: Irwin, 1978), pp. 101–117.
52. Jim Cibbison, "The Agency of Illusion," *Sierra* (May/June 1985) p. 19.
53. "The Quiet Crisis II," p. 2.
54. Shabecoff, "Environmental Agency: Deep and Persisting Woes," p. A1.
55. Stuart Taylor, Jr., "Dingell Says That He Has Evidence of EPA Criminal Conduct," *New York Times*, March 3, 1983, p. A1.
56. Shabecoff, "Environmental Agency: Deep and Persisting Woes," p. A1.
57. The departure of Burford was greeted with joy by longtime high-level EPA staff—they threw a party.
58. "Aides to Ex-EPA Official Testify on Removal of Document," *New York Times*, November 23, 1983, p. A16.
59. "At EPA, Two Top Scientists Come on Board," *Science*, 223 (January 20, 1984), p. 262.
60. "The EPA Is Speaking Softly and Carrying a Bigger Carrot," *Business Week*, June 16, 1986, p.42.
61. "EPA Cites Action on Enforcement in 1986," *New York Times*, Dec. 17, 1986, p. 13.
62. Reed McManus, "Ambushed from Within: The White House Tries to Smother the Clean Air Act," *Sierra* (Sept.-Oct. 1992), p. 45.
63. Curtis Lang, *The Amicus Journal* (Spring 1993), pp. 10–11.
64. T. H. Watkins, "The Terrible Tempered Mr. Ickes," *Audubon* (March 1984), pp. 94, 96.
65. Dean E. Mann and Zachary A. Smith, "The Selection of U.S. Cabinet Officers and Other Political Executives," *International Political Science Review*, 2 (2) (1981), p. 223.
66. See Watkins, "The Terrible Tempered Mr. Ickes," p. 96. An example of the department's problems: Interior Secretary Albert B. Fall was found to have secretly leased portions of U.S. naval petroleum reserves in Wyoming and California in return for bribes well in excess of $100,000.
67. Robert and Patricia Cahn, "Disputed Territory," *National Parks*, 61 (5–6) (May-June 1987), p. 30.
68. Steven Weisman, "Watt Quits Post; President Accepts with Reluctance," *New York Times*, October 9, 1983, p. A1.
69. "Words Cited by Watt Critics," *New York Times*, October 10, 1983, p. D10.
70. "Saint James," *The New Republic*, 194 (March 24, 1986), p. 30.
71. Weisman, "Watt Quits Post; President Accepts with Reluctance," p. A1.
72. "Words Cited by Watt Critics," p. D10.
73. Alexander Cockburn and Bruce Babbitt, "Compromised by Compromise," *The Washington Post National Weekly Edition*, September 6–12, 1993, p. 24.
74. *U.S. Government Manual, 1987–1988*, p. 352.
75. James Baker, "BLM Wilderness Review," *Sierra* (March-April 1983) p. 51.
76. Wesley Calef, *Private Grazing and Public Lands* (Chicago: University of Chicago Press, 1960).
77. Richard O. Miller, "Multiple Use in the Bureau of Land Management Cult: The Biases of Pluralism Revisited," in Phillip O. Foss (ed.), *Federal Lands Policy* (New York: Greenwood Press, 1987), p. 57.
78. National Parks Service Act of 1916.
79. *U.S. Government Manual, 1977–1978*, p. 1346.

80. Conservation Foundation, *State of the Environment: A View Towards the Nineties* (Washington, DC: Conservation Foundation, 1987), p. 278.
81. Alston Chase, "How to Save Our National Parks," *The Atlantic Monthly* (July 1987), p. 35.
82. U.S. House, House Committee on Appropriations, Budget Hearings, 94th Congress, First Session, p. 446.
83. *Natural History*, 86 (8) (1976), p. 59.
84. *U.S. Government Manual, 1987–1988*, p. 130.
85. Ibid., p. 344.

chapter 5

Air Pollution

Although some air pollution is generated from natural sources, such as volcanic eruptions, most air pollutants stem from human activities concentrated in urban areas. Forms of transportation, notably the automobile, are primary sources of air pollution. Other sources include power plants and factories, burning fossil fuels, and burning forests and grasslands for farming and grazing, which are common activities in the less developed world.

Although progress has been made to improve air quality in some categories of pollutants, the overall situation is not encouraging. Once thought by many to be an eye irritant at most, many feel that in the not too distant future air pollution may threaten our very existence. International common pool characteristics make the search for solutions difficult, particularly in the area of acid rain and the greenhouse effect. This chapter provides an overview of air pollution: its components, laws and regulations governing it, and its effects locally, nationally, and internationally.

SOURCES

The most common forms of air pollution are carbon monoxide, ozone, particulate matter, sulfur oxides, and nitrogen oxides. Carbon monoxide causes roughly one-half of the measurable air pollution in the United States. Sulfur oxides, nitrogen oxides, and volatile organic compounds each contribute 15 percent, with suspended particulate matter and other pollutants making up the balance. These pollutants originate from transportation (49 percent), stationary sources such as power plants (28 percent), other industrial processes (13 percent), solid waste disposal (3 percent), and various other sources (7 percent).[1]

Carbon monoxide, the most common air pollutant, is a colorless, odorless gas that forms when fossil fuels burn incompletely. In high concentrations, carbon monoxide is deadly. In lower concentrations, it can lead to drowsiness, slowed reflexes, and a reduction in the blood's ability to carry and circulate oxygen. EPA monitoring showed a decrease in the presence of carbon monoxide from the early 1970s into the mid-1980s, particularly in urban areas where the greatest carbon monoxide concentrations are found.[2] This decrease was largely attributable to the Federal Motor Vehicle Control Program for New Cars (new car standards).

The sulfur oxides include sulfur dioxide (SO_2) and sulfur trioxide (SO_3). Sulfur dioxide is a colorless gas that can aggravate respiratory diseases in humans, reduce plant growth, and corrode metal and stone. Electric utilities generate two-thirds of the SO_2 emissions in the United States, with most of that coming from coal-fired power plants.[3]

Emission levels of SO_2 in the United States decreased approximately 16 percent between 1975 and 1984 due to the burning of lower-sulfur fuels and the installation of pollution control devices.[4] Nevertheless, emissions of SO_2 in the United States are expected to increase approximately 10 percent from the 1980s to the end of this century.[5] Furthermore, SO_2 emissions in the former Soviet Union and Eastern Europe are expected to increase approximately 36 percent during the same period. Even though Eastern Europe is one-seventh the size of the United States, it is estimated that Eastern Europe's sulfur dioxide emissions will be twice that of the United States by the year 2000.[6]

Nitrogen oxides include nitric oxide and nitrogen dioxide. Like sulfur dioxide, emissions of nitrogen oxides in the United States have declined slightly from 1975 to 1984. However, total emissions of nitrogen oxides will probably increase by 25 percent from 1980 to 2000.[7] Similar increases are projected for Europe. Roughly half of all nitrogen oxides come from stationary sources, mostly utilities; the other half come from motor vehicles.[8] Both sulfur dioxide and nitrogen oxides contribute to acid rain.

Ambient suspended particulate matter, which is tiny fragments of liquid or solid matter floating in the air, has decreased 20 percent from the early 1970s into the mid-1980s, according to EPA measurements. These decreases were due in part to a reduction of industrial activities in the late 1970s and early 1980s, and the installation of pollution control equipment.

In July 1987, the EPA revised its standards to monitor only those particles designated PM-10 (particulate matter with a diameter less than or equal to a nominal 10 microns). These particles are considered small enough to pose a health risk because their size allows them to penetrate the most sensitive regions of the respiratory tract. In 1991 the EPA reported that 72 areas do not meet the standard for PM-10.[9]

Ground-level ozone (referred to by some as "smog") is not directly emitted into the air. Rather it is a poisonous form of pure oxygen that is created when sunlight reacts with nitrogen oxides and volatile organic compounds (VOCs) in the air.[10] VOCs come from three sources. Point sources or industries that use chemicals or solvents in their processing account for approximately 30 percent. Area sources that make up 20 percent of emissions are comprised of small emitters such as dry cleaners and print shops. Automobiles contribute 50 percent.[11] While many areas came close to meeting ozone standards in the mid-1980s, relaxed enforcement in the late 1980s resulted in 96 cities being categorized as nonattainment sites in 1991.

Health Effects

Although it is difficult to establish a direct causal relation between a specific pollutant when it is in the atmosphere and a particular disease or death, many studies have shown that such relationships exist. Research has found air pollution to be associated with higher mortality rates and an increase in adverse health effects.[12] Strong evidence suggests that pollution from the burning of fossil fuels leads to the premature death of between 30,000 and 35,000 Americans each year.[13] The elderly, infants, and children are particularly susceptible to harm from air pollution as are adults with respiratory problems.

The interactive effects of pollutants in the atmosphere complicate the task of establishing direct links between air pollution and human health. "Synergistic interactions between various pollutants can lead to more harm than that of one acting alone, and the multiple causes and lengthy incubation times of diseases such as emphysema, chronic bronchitis, lung cancer, and heart disease" make it extremely difficult to establish direct causal relationships.[14] However, in extreme cases of air pollution, causal relationships between pollution and human health have been clear.

Several times severe thermal inversions have trapped pollution within an area allowing pollutants that would otherwise be blown away to concentrate.[15] In December 1952 the famous London killer fog led to 1,600 more deaths than ordinarily would have occurred. Similar events occurred in the Meuse Valley in Belgium in 1930 with 63 deaths and 6,000 illnesses and in 1948 in Donora, Pennsylvania, with 20 deaths and 6,000 illnesses.[16]

These tragedies are some of the easily identifiable adverse effects of air pollution on human health. However, as the figure of 35,000 premature deaths every year suggests, many more people are affected by air pollution than we realize. Although much is known about the relationship between National Ambient Air Quality Standards (NAAQS) and human health,[17] failure to meet those standards is an indication of a lack of progress toward cleaner and presumably healthier air.

In 1991 96 cities had not attained the national standard for ground-level ozone, 41 did not meet the standard for carbon monoxide, and 72 did not meet the standard for particulate matter.[18] Thus 6 out of 10 people in the United States lived in an area which failed to meet air quality standards that had been set to protect human health.[19]

By January 1993 the situation had improved somewhat, with the EPA reporting that 41 out of the 97 areas designated as nonattainment for ozone were in compliance, and 13 of 42 areas met the standard for carbon monoxide.[20]

Internationally, the situation is much worse. In Calcutta, India, it is estimated 60 percent of the city's population suffers air pollution-related diseases. Sao Paulo, Mexico City, Cairo, and New Delhi all have serious air pollution problems that border on being hazardous. And in Athens, Greece, air pollution claims as many as 40 lives a year.[21]

The health effects of air pollution provide a good example of the paradox of environmental policy. Some argue there is a lack of scientific evidence for any link between a pollutant and a particular illness. Even in the case of killer fog in London, as an illustration, evidence of the impact on human health was derived from death rates comparing the killer fog period with other periods. The relationship was not as direct as to be absolute proof, but the degree of probability of a connection was overwhelming. While more specific evidence of the impact of air pollution on human health would lead to greater support for regulation, as a leading environmental science textbook points out, "[I]nstead of establishing absolute truth or proof, science establishes only a degree of probability or confidence in the validity of an idea, usually based on statistical or circumstantial evidence."[22]

Although health effects may be our most immediate and personal concern, air pollution can also cause significant damage to crops. Air pollution can cause a 10 to 15 percent reduction in yield, and even go so far as to cause the complete loss of crops.[23] In the United States the EPA and U.S. Department of Agriculture have estimated that air pollution has reduced crop yields from 5 to 10 percent—representing a loss of between $3.5 and $7 billion.[24]

Recall that policymakers have incentives to pursue short-term solutions with low immediate costs, without regard for the long-term costs. Since air pollution problems rarely present themselves as a "crisis," policymakers can afford politically to move slowly and incrementally. Unfortunately, some air pollution problems require immediate and costly investment, which is not likely to be made without an apparent "crisis" and will be very expensive when the problem presents itself in crisis proportions.

Many representatives of polluting industries have argued over the years that air pollution is a relatively minor problem. The Ford Motor Company, while lobbying a Los Angeles county supervisor in 1953, wrote, "[T]he Ford engineering staff, although mindful that automobile engines produce the exhaust gasses, feels that these waste vapors are dissipated in the atmosphere quickly, and do not present an air pollution problem."[25]

Although automobile companies are now willing to concede that cars contribute to air pollution, the lack of scientific certainty on the exact magnitude of the impact, which make control requirements difficult to quantify, is still used as an argument against regulation. The president of a major utility in the southern United States, when arguing for a "go slow" approach to the control of acid rain, made the point that "[T]he roster of respected scientists who have pointed out how much we don't know about acid deposition would fill at least a page of fine print."[26]

With respect to acid rain, as well as other air pollution problems, it is true scientists do not speak with a single voice. That is to be expected where science is not in the business of establishing *absolute* truth or proof but the probability of such effects. However, the negative impacts of air pollution are well established. The problem of developing policy to mitigate these negative impacts is compounded by scientific uncertainty, the nature of scientific proof, and the fact that the atmosphere does have some natural assimilative capacity. The air can accept some pollution without necessarily having a negative impact on life on earth. However, the question remains as to what is the appropriate level of air pollution control.

Motor Vehicles

Motor vehicles are a primary cause of air pollution in the United States and globally. As of 1991 the EPA estimated motor vehicles account for about one-half of all the hydrocarbon and nitrogen oxide precursor pollutants, up to 90 percent of the carbon monoxide, and over half of the toxic air pollutants in the United States.[27]

The proportionate increases in air pollutants discussed at the beginning of this chapter are surprisingly low given the increase in motor vehicle production in the United States and worldwide since the early 1970s. From 1970 to 1986, the number of passenger cars sold in the United States, for example, increased 51 percent. Sales in the then noncommunist industrial world increased by 71 percent.[28] The cost of motor vehicle emission abatement, which included the cost of equipment as well as increased fuel cost and maintenance, was estimated at approximately $8 billion a year in 1985.[29]

As great as these costs may seem, this is a fraction of the cost to society for continued air pollution from automobiles.[30] Many hidden costs (or negative externalities) exist, such as the destruction of rubber on automobiles and equipment and corrosion of stone and iron on buildings and statues. In some countries another hidden cost is the political instability that results from a dependence on foreign sources of oil. The reduction of crop yields and timber harvests, increased health costs, and the destruction of buildings are additional factors. Researchers at the University of Miami estimated the hidden cost of gasoline consumption is approximately 80 cents per gallon of gasoline burned.[31] If this is accurate, the hidden costs of gasoline consumption in the United States would have been in excess of $112 billion in 1993.[32]

These numbers are subject to interpretation based on various assumptions, but the majority of energy experts agree the current cost of gasoline does not come close to the true cost primarily because the external costs are not factored in. For example, in an Energy Project report at Harvard Business School, the researchers concluded the external cost of oil ranges from $65 to $165 a barrel.[33]

Even if these hidden costs were widely known, the obstacles to reducing pollution from moving vehicles is enormous. Automobile production plays such an important role in the economy of the United States that auto executives know any threat to the industry (real or perceived) will be taken seriously by policymakers. During the debate over passage of the 1970 Clean Air Act, auto executives used this fear to manipulate policymakers to the betterment of the auto industry. Lee Iacocca, as vice president at Ford Motor Company, warned that, were the proposed bill to become law, U.S. auto production could come to a halt after January 1, 1975. Even if production were to continue, Iacocca argued, the bill would force "huge hikes in car prices and do irreparable damage to the American economy." Iacocca continued that the act would produce "only small improvements in the quality of the air."[34]

Soon the debate focused on the capacity of auto manufacturers to meet the act's requirements. Senator Edmund Muskie, who sponsored the 1970 Clean Air Act, responded to industry charges with the argument that the auto industry already had the technology to meet the 1975 standards. "Representatives of that industry," Muskie said on the Senate floor, "whose great genius is mass production, are trying to tell us that what can be done in the laboratory cannot be converted to mass production in five years."[35] Although Muskie prevailed in 1970, the industry subsequently convinced Congress and the EPA that limits could not be met and the automakers were granted extensions. Ironically, extensions were granted to American automobile manufacturers at the same time foreign producers were meeting and exceeding the EPA's requirements.

The 1990 Clean Air Act amendments contain several measures designed to reduce motor vehicle pollutants. The phaseout of lead is scheduled for January 1, 1996. In some nonattainment areas, gasoline will have to be reformulated to contain fewer VOCs, and detergents in gasoline to prevent engine deposits will be required. During winter months, oxyfuel, which contains increased oxygen to make fuel burn more efficiently to reduce carbon monoxide release, will also be required in cities with the worst air pollution problems. Finally, the 1990 amendments also increase the number of areas that must implement inspection and maintenance programs for automobiles.

AIR POLLUTION: LAW, REGULATIONS, AND ENFORCEMENT

Air pollution regulation in the United States represents both the best and the worst of environmental policy making. On the one hand, air pollution regulation has consisted of a relatively rare nonincremental approach to a policy problem, which has represented a positive approach. For example, the Clean Air Act, passed in 1963 and amended in 1967, 1970, 1977, and 1990, has changed past practice in several ways. On the other hand, subsequent tinkering with these laws, primarily through exemptions and extensions, provide instances of incrementalism in the policy-making process, which has led to less than desirable air pollution control outcomes.

The federal response to the problem of air pollution began in 1955 with Congress offering technical expertise and financial assistance to the states. The Clean Air Act of 1963 was the first major federal involvement in air pollution. The Clean Air Act empowered federal officials to intervene in interstate air pollution matters only at the request of state governments. However, the apparatus for enforcing pollution abatement was so cumbersome as to be ineffective. Between 1965 and 1970, only 11 abatement actions had been initiated under the 1963 Clean Air Act.[36] Congress eventually amended the Clean Air Act by passing the Air Quality Act of 1967. This legislation directed the secretary of the Department of Health, Education and Welfare to establish Air Quality Control Regions (AQCRs). Within each region, states established air quality standards and emission standards for regulated pollutants. Unfortunately, by 1970, of a projected 91 ACQRs in the country, only 25 had been designated by the federal government.

These early acts deferred to state governments with respect to air pollution control enforcement. Due to the common pool nature of environmental pollution problems, deference to state government creates a special regulatory dilemma. Without federal guidelines backed by federal enforcement for uniformity, states have an incentive to compete with each other for industry by using pollution control, or a lack of pollution control, as an inducement to bring industry within its borders. Under such circumstances, all states in the region are environmental losers. A state that wishes to limit polluting activities suffers from pollution generated by its neighbors. Air pollution does not respect state borders. For this reason, some industries pushed for exclusive state pollution control. However, many other industries, particularly those doing business in several states, argued in support of federal pollution control. For example, the automobile industry initially fought strenuously against any auto emission regulation. After it became clear the states would act individually to limit automobile emissions, thus producing many separate regulations, the industry pushed for uniform national emission regulations.

The Clean Air Act of 1970 and subsequent amendments in 1977 and 1990 represented significant increases in federal involvement in air pollution regulation, addressing some of the common pool problems associated with local control of air pollution. The act directed the EPA administrator to establish "national ambient air quality standards" (NAAQS) (see Notes).[37] Primary standards represent "ambient air quality standards the attainment and maintenance of which in the judgment of the administrator, based on such criteria and allowing an adequate margin of safety are requisite to protect the public health."[38] Secondary standards are those necessary to protect the public welfare from adverse effects associated with air pollution.

Pollutants emitted directly into the atmosphere are classified as primary pollutants. Secondary pollutants are formed after emission as a result of a reaction with substances already in the atmosphere. Pollutants that consist of tiny fragments of liquid or solid matter are classified as particulates. Gaseous pollutants, which can be further divided into inorganic or organic gasses, are the final classification of pollutants.[39]

The 1970 act required uniform national standards of performance to be developed for new stationary sources of air pollution and for preexisting sources that were modified in a manner which increases the emissions of any pollutant. It also required uniform national standards for "hazardous" air pollutants, defined as "[A]ir pollution which may reasonably be anticipated to result in an increase in mortality or an increase in serious irreversible, or incapacitating irreversible, illness."[40]

The 1970 Clean Air Act originally required that primary air quality standards be met no later than December 31, 1975. This deadline, like other air quality deadlines, was extended once and then again. Nine months after the development of NAAQS, the states were required to submit to the EPA their state implementation plans (SIPs), which, when promulgated by the EPA, represent the legally binding strategies to be implemented to meet the National Ambient Air Quality Standards. The Clean Air Act requires that SIPs lead to attainment of NAAQ Standards "as expeditiously as practical but . . . in no case later than three years from the date of approval of such plan." However, a two-year extension is possible under certain circumstances. There is no specific time for the achievement of secondary standards other than a "reasonable" time. Initially, the EPA established standards for carbon monoxide, particulates, sulfur dioxide, nitrogen dioxide, hydrocarbons, and photochemical oxidants.

The Clean Air Act of 1970 also directed the EPA to establish minimum emission standards for stationary sources called "new source performance standards." These standards (the NSPS) are to be established on an industry-by-industry basis, taking cost into consideration. New source performance standards are to use the "best available control technology."

The Environmental Protection Agency uses a number of classification schemes in its implementation of the provisions of the Clean Air Act. Emission sources are divided into "major" or "minor" and are found either in "attainment areas" or in "nonattainment areas," depending on whether or not air quality goals have been met. Sources are "new" or "existing," depending on if the source of emission was in place when permits were first issued. Regulations vary depending on whether a source is major or minor, in an attainment area, or new or existing.

In 1977 amendments to the Clean Air Act divided each type of Air Quality Control Region that was attaining the standard into three classes. Class I regions include national parks, wilderness, and similar areas. Little, if any, deterioration in air quality is allowed. Class II areas are those areas where moderate increases of air pollution are allowed as long as the resulting pollution does not exceed the NAAQS. States were allowed to reclassify a class II area as a class I area or as a class III area to allow for industrial development, provided air quality standards would not be violated. Class III designation allows air quality degradation up to the NAAQS.

The 1977 Clean Air Act Amendments also established emission standards for automobiles and trucks requiring a 90 percent reduction in carbon monoxide and hydrocarbon emissions by 1975 and nitrogen oxide emissions by 1976, as measured against 1970 emission levels. The act empowered the EPA administrator with the authority to extend these deadlines, and extensions were granted by either the EPA or Congress in 1973, 1974, 1975, and 1977.

The 1977 Clean Air Act Amendments also required states to develop plans by 1982 that would bring air quality for ozone, carbon monoxide, and other pollutants up to EPA standards by December 31, 1987. When the deadline passed, approximately 60 of the 247 Air Quality Control Regions that had been established at that time within the country did not meet EPA standards. The EPA had the authority to ban construction of new major stationary sources within these 60 regions if an approved State Implementation Plan (SIP) was not submitted by 1979. In addition, those areas that had either not submitted SIPs for approval or had submitted plans that did not have inspection and maintenance plans were subject to mandatory highway sanctions. This occurred in California, Kentucky, and New Mexico. Anticipating difficulty in meeting with the standards mandated in 1977, Congress debated over amendments to the Clean Air Act to reduce the standards or grant extensions every year from 1981 to 1990.

In the event that state implementation plans were not submitted to the EPA or did not meet EPA approval, the 1970 Clean Air Act amendments provided that federal implementation plans could be imposed on a region. The EPA has been very reluctant to develop its own plans for political reasons. As a result of several lawsuits by environmental organizations, initially in Phoenix, Arizona, but also in the metropolitan Los Angeles area, Bakersfield, Sacramento, Ventura, and Fresno, California, and Chicago, Illinois, the EPA was forced to develop federal air pollution plans (FIPs).

The passage of the 1990 Clean Air Act amendments ended more than 10 years of congressional stalemate over the reauthorization of the Clean Air Act. During the 1980s, a coalition of utilities, labor unions, midwestern politicians, and auto and oil interests successfully prevented any strengthening of the Clean Air Act. President Ronald Reagan and Senate majority leader Robert Byrd (from coal-producing West Virginia) opposed new legislation to control air pollution. The election of George Mitchell of Maine as majority leader, a proponent of a stronger Clean Air Act, and President Bush led the way to tougher legislation. President Bush proposed a clean air package in 1989 that would reduce emissions of sulfur dioxide and nitrogen oxide. For the first time in 10 years the Reagan/Bush administration indicated it willingness to support tougher legislation. When the 1990

Clean Air Act amendments were being debated, midwestern politicians found themselves isolated against other sections of the country, which did not want to pay for cleaning up pollution from utilities in the Ohio Valley. These politicians had joined with the oil and auto industries and successfully prevented previous clean air bills from passing in the 1980s. However, in 1990 a combination of rising public support for environmental legislation (detailed in Chapter 2) and the perception among politicians up for reelection that it was not a good time to vote against the environment led to passage of the 1990 amendments.[41]

The 1990 Clean Air Act Amendments (CAAA) is a lengthy document of about 800 pages. It has 11 major sections, or titles, and is targeted to complete most implementation by 2005.

Title I, often referred to as the "nonattainment of ambient air standards title," deals with those states and localities that chronically exceed EPA's ground-level ozone limitation standards. As we noted previously, the 1970 Clean Air Act required the EPA to set health-based ambient air standards for certain pollutants. The 1990 CAAA revised regulations for six criteria pollutants: ground-level ozone, carbon monoxide, sulfur dioxide, nitrogen dioxide, lead, and particulate matter (PM-10). Title I designated nonattainment status for three of these criteria: ozone, particulate matter, and carbon monoxide.

For ground-level ozone, states are required to develop an ozone abatement strategy in revised SIPs based not only on ozone but on its hydrocarbon and nitrogen oxide precursors as well. Ozone pollution is not directly emitted into the air. It is created by sunlight acting on nitrogen oxides and the precursor hydrocarbons that are emitted into the air including volatile organic compounds (VOCs).

The nonattainment status for areas designated by Congress are also classified by severity. For ozone, there are five classifications, ranging from marginal to extreme. Each classification carries with it increasingly more stringent abatement measures. Carbon monoxide and particulate matter have only two classifications, moderate and serious. Title I also redefines "major" stationary sources according to the nonattainment level of their location.

Other titles of the 1990 CAAA deal with air toxics, protecting stratospheric ozone, and acid rain. We discuss them later. However, there is one new key component of the act that attempts to link all CAAA compliance programs for major sources and all other sources covered by federal regulatory programs. It was argued that SIPs were too difficult to revise or enforce because they required rule-making at both the state and federal levels. In an effort to simplify revisions and enforcement, Title V establishes an operating permit program. Based on the National Pollutant Discharge Elimination System (NPDES) of the Clean Water Act, this program requires sources to provide information on which pollutants are being released, in what quantities, and to provide plans to monitor levels of pollution. Theoretically, the permit would contain all the detailed information required by all sections of the CAAA. For instance, an electric power plant could be covered by nonattainment for the ozone, acid rain, and toxic pollutant parts of the CAAA. As of June 1993, neither the required monitoring methods nor the monitoring frequency had been specified by the EPA.

Regulatory Innovations

Since the mid-1970s, the EPA has introduced a number of innovations in the implementation of the Clean Air Act. These innovations primarily involve various types of emission-trading schemes. Trading schemes are classified as either netting, offsets, bubbles, or banking. Each of these schemes is designed to allow polluters flexibility in meeting emission limits. Trading is based on the assumption that the polluters are in the best position to understand their own sources of pollution and how to make the most cost-effective reductions in pollution.

Netting, which began in 1974, sums the total output of pollution from a given plant and allows management to reduce the output of pollution in one aspect of the plant's activities while increasing it in some other aspect or some other area.

Offsets, which have been used since 1976, allow a polluting plant to start operation in a nonattainment area. Basically, this means the new polluter must reduce pollution from existing sources within the nonattainment area. For example, an energy company desiring to build a refinery in a nonattainment area may be required to purchase and install pollution control equipment in the refineries of competitors in the region. Although the offsets are theoretically allowed only when there will be a net decrease in the amount of pollution in the nonattainment area, in practice, the reductions in pollution from offsetting, as well as from other emission-trading devices, have been minimal.[42]

Bubbles, first used in 1979, allow a polluter to total the emissions from a plant and thus allow adjustments in the source of emissions within the plant, as long as the aggregate emission levels are not exceeded. Bubbles are similar to netting except that external trading may be allowed between plants in an air quality region.

Banking, also developed in 1979, is used in conjunction with the bubble policy and allows for the saving of emission reduction "credits" for future use. Bubbles and banking have led to markets in emissions credits for particular pollutants in nonattainment areas across the United States.

The goal of emissions trading, or the buying and selling of "Emission Reduction Credits" (ERC), is to achieve cleaner air at a lower cost. Evidence suggests that emissions trading has lowered the cost of pollution control to industry, but it has had a negligible effect on air quality.[43] Theoretically, pollution reductions are achieved by the requirement that the purchase of an offset or credit from a polluting source be for a right to pollute less than the original amount of reduction. The "offset ratio" determines how much reduction in total emissions there will be as a result of an emission trade.

So, for example, an offset ratio of 1:1 would result in no net reduction in pollution, whereas a ratio of 2:1 would result in a 50 percent reduction of a particular emission from the original source when it was traded.

Although emissions trading sounds tidy and efficient in theory, there are a number of practical problems in its administration. First, emissions trading requires careful monitoring of plant emissions to determine the amount of pollution output. The states' implementation of EPA policy varies significantly in the quality of their air quality monitoring data, some requiring detailed data while others require little or none.[44] In addition, offset ratios vary significantly. For example, in California, the Bay Area Air Quality Management District requires an offset ratio of 2:1 when based on the average annual emissions of a source, provided a net air quality benefit can be demonstrated from the trade. In contrast, other jurisdictions in Connecticut, Illinois, and Virginia, for example, have offset ratios at or near 1:1, which even in the best of situations would lead to little or no net air pollution reduction.

The emissions-trading market has developed in nonattainment areas across the country. ERCs are bought, sold, and auctioned. Shopping for ERCs can be as or more important than any other aspect of a manufacturer's business. For example, the president of a spa company in Chino, California, remarked, "I spend a lot of time shopping for ERC's—for us, they are a matter of life and death."[45] Josh Margolis, an ERC broker who works for AER*X, which stands for Air Emission Reduction Exchange, based in Washington, D.C., described how the exchange process should work to reduce total air emissions. "If you have a credit of 250 tons of oxides of nitrogen per year and sell it to the plant around the corner, they can only admit 225 tons."[46] Credits are sold on the open market and consequently they can fluctuate wildly related to general economic conditions. For example, in Los Angeles hydrocarbon credits sold for around $1,000 a ton in 1984 and had more than doubled two years later.[47]

Many environmentalists are critical of emissions trading. They point out that trades do not result in reductions of emissions but rather just a shifting of emissions. One national environmental organization, the Natural Resources Defense Council (NRDC), has labeled the bubble concept "one of the most destructive impediments to the cleanup of unhealthy air."[48] The NRDC and other environmental groups have argued that emissions trading essentially allows current levels of pollution to remain the same in nonattainment areas. Some state and local officials have also been skeptical of emissions trading, repeating the concern that trading in nonattainment areas often prevents the reduction in total air pollutants within the area.[49]

The primary argument in favor of emissions trading is not that it reduces air pollution, but rather it allows corporations to determine where they can cut back internally on their polluting activities. In general, industries that are major stationary source polluters strongly favor the bubble concept. Exactly why they favor emissions trading is no mystery. Netting and offsets provide greater flexibility and allow firms to seek the least costly pollution solution available.[50] A potential problem for a firm attempting to establish a plant in a nonattainment area is that competitors may attempt to freeze new firms out of the market.[51] (The 1990 CAAA includes an emissions trading program for acid rain—discussed later in this chapter.)

Regulatory Issues

One significant problem in implementing air pollution regulations is having sufficient and accurate information. The EPA and state environmental agencies responsible for implementing air pollution regulations depend on the firms they are regulating for a great deal of information. This information is often incomplete or inaccurate and even when available, regulators may have difficulty interpreting it to determine its accuracy.[52] Furthermore, because of inadequate staffing, both on the federal and state level, universal enforcement is virtually impossible. Consequently, regulators often go after the most obvious and gross violators. This is a major problem in air pollution regulation as it is in environmental management generally. Undoubtedly, better enforcement of existing regulations would decrease air pollution significantly.

The EPA has a great deal of flexibility and discretion in administering the Clean Air Act. For example, when establishing new source performance standards, the agency is directed to require the best available control technology to be applied to new stationary sources of air pollution, taking into consideration the cost of a reduction along with health, environmental, and energy impacts.[53] The 1990 CAA required various levels of control depending on the pollutant and its source including, "reasonable available control technology," "lowest achievable emission rate," and the "maximum achievable control technology." What do these mean? In one extreme, they *could* be interpreted in some situations to mean "the best system of continuous emission reduction" or zero emissions. We do, after all, have the technical ability to reduce air pollution to close to zero. However, such reductions would be expensive and, because of the ability of the atmosphere to absorb some pollution without harm to humans, may be unnecessary. At the other extreme, related to the scientific uncertainty and the EPA's possible sympathy to hardship arguments of polluters, the agency might conclude that restrictions on new stationary sources in attainment areas should be minimal. The discretion lies in determining what limits need to be imposed between these two extremes.

Administrative discretion is, in and of itself, not a bad thing. In fact, given the complexity of air pollution and other regulatory problems, discretion is necessary. It is the exercise of regulatory discretion—in the implementation or formulation of environmental policy—that becomes a problem. Since much of air pollution regulation is implemented on the state level, industries that are influential on the state level or in a particular locality may be able to prevent meaningful pollution control.

This discretion has led to inadequate levels of air pollution control, according to some analysts. In their book *Air Pollution and Human Health*,

Lester Lave and Eugene Saskin conclude that the federal standards for particulate matter are too lax, and the standards approach in general, which assumes there is an acceptable level of exposure to air pollutants as determined by the EPA, ignores the negative health effects from exposure below the federal standard.[54] Even if there were no problems with the measurement of pollution or the willingness, or the lack thereof, of federal or state regulators to implement emission standards once established, there is still the problem of lack of certainty as to the harmful effects of air pollution:

> [The] scientific research into the harmfulness of air pollution has been much too little. . . .In short, there is a great deal we do not know about the hazardous effects of many air pollutants. Part of the problem is due to inadequate government research funding and the lack of any incentive, monetary or regulatory, on the part of industry to undertake air pollution impact research.[55]

As we saw earlier in the comments of a utility executive on acid rain, scientific uncertainty works to the advantage of those who argue for a go slow approach to pollution control.

Other major issues in air pollution control include the cost of emission controls, who should ultimately pay the costs that will be a burden to industry, and whether regulatory expectations in light of costs and benefits are realistic. In passing the Clean Air Act, Congress engaged in "technology forcing" by developing standards that were impossible to comply with, given the then existing technology. Congress assumed technological breakthroughs would lead to developments that would allow the standards to be met—forcing technology with little concern for cost. Technology forcing has occasionally been effective.[56]

The overall cost of air pollution control has always been a controversial issue. As we have seen, the auto industry first argued that automobiles are not a major source of air pollution. Then they argued pollution control is prohibitively expensive. Yet pollution control devices in use in 1990 have reduced the emissions of some pollutants in excess of 90 percent from 1970 levels. In the 1980s, the cost of air pollution control was estimated at $18 billion annually.[57]

Four air pollution problems have attracted a great deal of attention in recent years: acid rain, the greenhouse effect, the thinning of the ozone layer in the stratosphere, and toxic air pollution. Acid rain, ozone, and the greenhouse effect share international common pool management characteristics and problems and hence present special, perhaps insurmountable problems. All four of these problems are discussed in detail next.

Toxic Air Pollution

The terms *toxic* and *hazardous* are essentially synonymous and may be used interchangeably.[58] A chemical referred to as toxic in one statute may, and frequently is, referred to as hazardous in another. Typically, a toxic substance is something that causes serious human health problems even in very small amounts. While most of the discussion over toxic or hazardous waste problems center around water pollution, it has become increasingly apparent that toxic airborne pollutants pose a serious environmental threat.[59]

In the Clean Air Act, a hazardous air pollutant is defined as "[A]n air pollutant which no ambient air quality standard is applicable [to] which in the judgment of the administrator causes, or contributes to, air pollution which may reasonably be anticipated to result in an increase in mortality or an increase in serious irreversible, or incapacitating irreversible, illness."[60] Although the Clean Air Act has provisions for designating an air pollutant as hazardous and establishing an emission standard for that pollutant, the EPA has been slow to develop such standards. By 1990, nearly 20 years after the passage of the Clean Air Act, only seven substances had been regulated under the hazardous emission provision of the act.[61] The 1990 Clean Air Act amendments sought to overcome this problem. Title III of the 1990 CAAA, often referred to as the "air toxics" section, specifically listed 189 toxic pollutants, and set a schedule requiring EPA to develop standards for all major sources over a 10-year period. A major source is one that emits more than 10 tons per year of a single toxic or more that 25 tons per year of any combination of the 189 toxics listed.[62]

The EPA must further identify categories of the major sources and then develop "maximum achievable control technology" (MACT) for each category. These standards are to be based on technology that has already been proven to provide the best pollution control. Thus there are no technology-forcing aspects to this section. It is hoped the MACT standards will provide incentives for pollution prevention. By only setting standards for levels of toxic emission reductions, the act allows industry to substitute nontoxic substances for the current toxic chemicals. Also, sources that reduce emissions by 90 percent before MACT standards go into effect have six additional years to comply with the remaining 10 percent.

On July 16, 1992, EPA published an initial list of source categories for which it intends to establish national emission standards for hazardous air pollutants (NESHAPs). Of the 174 source categories, 166 are for major source categories and 8 are for area source categories.[63] These amendments set as an overall goal up to 90 percent reductions in the emissions of toxic air pollutants by 2003.[64]

These are admirable goals. Although it is too early to tell how successful the 1990 amendments will be, we can anticipate many of the regulatory problems that have come to be associated with command and control regulatory systems (see Chapter 3 for a discussion of regulatory systems), including the incentives of polluters to delay compliance.

There are a number of reasons why so few hazardous pollutants were identified for regulation by the EPA. The identification and verification process is long and complicated and made more so by the lack of monitoring equipment sophisticated enough to detect some pollutants. Furthermore, during the Reagan administration a combination of the decrease in the EPA's budget and a lack of enthusiasm among agency leadership for increasing regulation resulted in a situation that was not conducive to expanding hazardous air pollution regulation. Also, there is a lack of data on the human effects of pollutants. These studies take many years to complete and are very costly to conduct.

For example, asbestos, a hazardous air pollutant, has attracted attention of the EPA and state and local air pollution regulators. However, another air pollutant, lead, although not regulated under the hazardous air pollution regulations, is hazardous and has also attracted a great deal of attention. Humans may be exposed to lead through food or through exposure to lead-based paints, but exposure is most likely to occur from lead that is mixed in gasoline to improve octane ratings. Exposure to lead can lead to convulsions, anemia, and kidney and brain damage.[65] Use of lead has declined roughly 40 percent since the early 1970s, due to a ban on lead-based paints and restrictions on lead in all grades of gasoline. Fortunately, because of restrictions on leaded gasoline and the retiring of older automobiles that burned leaded gasoline, hazardous lead pollution in the air went down more than 70 percent from the early 1970s to the early 1990s.[66] The EPA estimated in the late 1970s that the average American's blood lead level was 50 percent higher than it would otherwise be without auto emissions.[67]

Asbestos is "one of the few substances with essentially irrefutable evidence demonstrating that it causes cancer in humans."[68] Although latency periods vary depending on the amount and duration of exposure, asbestos-induced cancer can occur after a relatively low dose and short latency period (the amount of time between the initial exposure to the cause of a disease, in this case airborne asbestos, and the actual onset of the disease).[69]

Asbestos is used in brake and clutch linings, some paper and plastic products, paint, cement, and roofing and flooring tiles. Today, the greatest asbestos exposure problem occurs in classrooms with deteriorating asbestos surfaces, particularly ceilings. Children are six times as likely as adults to develop cancer from exposure to asbestos. It was estimated in 1984 that one-third of all school classrooms in the United States had asbestos problems. In 1986 Congress required schools to inspect for asbestos-containing materials and develop a removal plan where necessary.[70] Congress did not, however, appropriate the funds necessary for effective asbestos removal, and many local governments, lacking the necessary funds, have been slow to act. The federal government's response to the problems of asbestos is typical of the environmental policy paradox. By recognizing a problem and subsequently passing legislation to deal with that problem, federal policymakers can take credit for having acted. To the extent the effort is not adequately funded, the credit may not be well deserved.

Toxic air pollution, especially carcinogenic substances, further illustrates the regulatory problems associated with risk assessment and economic trade-offs. In the case of asbestos, given the unusually strong evidence of a connection between even limited exposure and cancer, the risk question is not disputed. However, the economic issues are real and difficult. Asbestos is apparently the best material for use in clutch and brake linings.

Therefore, any risk to the mechanic who repairs automobiles has to be weighed against automobile safety concerns associated with using other materials. Of greater concern is the extensive use of asbestos in home heating and insulation, as well as in most other types of construction such as office and apartment buildings. The problem is what to substitute and when to replace these noxious materials. That type of balancing is troublesome at best.

It will cost billions of dollars to remove all asbestos from all schools, yet we know many children will develop cancer if the work is not completed. Delay in this situation is possible politically because the victims are unknown and the chance of any *individual* child developing cancer as a result of exposure to asbestos is very small. Yet, as a class of people, many children are at risk. This is the type of group that is unlikely to have influence in the policy process both because they are identified only as a class and because children as a class do not have the resources necessary for influencing the policy-making process.

Another group without the resources necessary to influence the policy process who have been victimized by a careless air pollution policy are the Native American miners on the Navajo reservation. For many years, the Navajo miners and their families have been exposed to inhalation of another acknowledged carcinogen, uranium, from open mines in the Arizona-New Mexico area. The danger was first recognized in 1949 when the U.S. Public Health Service conducted a study and decided not to tell the affected miners of the health dangers for fear many would quit and halt production, thus disrupting the nuclear armament program and posing an economic and a national security threat. These people were denied compensation in an unsuccessful suit against the U.S. government in 1979. "The Navajos are in a distinct position. The government not only didn't warn them, it was flagrant malpractice to do what they did," stated Stewart Udall, former secretary of the interior and the Navajo representative in the unsuccessful 1979 suit.[71] Only in the 1990s has this situation changed to some degree. The Radiation Exposure Compensation Act was brought before the 101st Congress in 1990 by Senator Orrin Hatch and Representative Wayne Owens to establish a $100 million trust fund to provide a $100,000 award to those miners who are victims of lung cancer and other diseases.[72]

This is an example of a weakness of normative pluralism. A group lacking the necessary resources to influence the policy process, the Navajo miners, did not have adequate influence early enough in the policy process.

Acid Rain

Many of the policy and regulatory problems that are associated with toxic air pollution are also present in acid rain concerns. Thanks to the popular press, nearly everyone has heard of acid rain, otherwise known as acid deposition because the acid and acid-forming substances that fall to the earth as a result of air pollution come not only in rain, but also snow, sleet, fog, dew, and even as dry particulate matter and gas. The term *acid rain* is used here, but you should remember it refers to acids deposited to the earth, regardless of their mode of transport.

Acid rain begins with emissions of sulfur and nitrogen oxide primarily from industrial plants and automobile exhaust. In the United States nitrogen oxides are emitted from utilities (33 percent) and automobiles (34 percent); most sulfur oxides are emitted from coal-burning power plants in the midwestern and eastern United States, and utilities and smelters in the western United States.[73] Sulfur dioxide and nitrogen oxides interact with water vapor and sunlight in the upper atmosphere to form acidic compounds. Over 80 percent of all sulfur dioxide emissions in the United States originate east of the Mississippi River with the heaviest concentrations coming from power plants in the Ohio River Valley.

Acidity is measured on the pH scale, which ranges from 0 to 14. A value of 7 on the scale is neutral; any grading below 7 is acidic. Readings above 7 are alkaline. Rainwater is normally acidic, primarily due to natural causes, measuring 5.6 on the pH scale. Although any pH reading below 5.6 is considered acid rain, damage to materials, plants, fish, and microorganisms in lakes and streams is associated with pH values of 5.0 and lower. The pH scale is logarithmic. For example, acid rain with a pH of 4.0 is 10 times as strong as acid rain with a pH of 5.0, and only one-tenth as strong as rain with a pH of 3.0, all other things being equal.

Acidity levels of rainwater between 4.2 pH and 4.8 pH are common throughout the eastern United States and Canada. Acid rain has been a problem on every continent. Serious damage has been reported in Brazil, Australia, Thailand, South Africa, and China.[74] An estimated 6 million acres of forest in nine European countries has been damaged, as have 18,000 lakes in Sweden and 2,600 lakes in Norway.

Rain with an acidity of 1.4 pH, which is more acidic than lemon juice, has been recorded in Wheeling, West Virginia. Rain of 2.4 pH, about the same acidity as vinegar, was recorded in Scotland in 1974. A pH reading of 3.0, which is extremely acidic and does extensive damage over time to buildings as well as the natural environment, is common.[75]

One problem inherent in developing policies to deal with acid rain is that there is not always a direct relationship between the reduction of emissions and the reduction of acid rain. Local soil conditions, along with prevailing wind patterns, create conditions in which the threshold level of acceptable pollutants (the level beyond the natural assimilative capacity of the affected ecosystem) varies from place to place.

The impacts of acid rain over the long term can be devastating. As wildlife ecologist Anne LaBastille described, "My log cabin looks out over a lake that is becoming increasingly clear in recent years, with a strange mat of algae spreading across the bottom. Native trout are now scarce, as are loons, osprey, and otters. Bullfrogs are all but silent. As much as a third of the virgin red spruce around the lake have died."[76] Thousands of lakes and streams throughout North America and Europe have become acidified to the point where they no longer support aquatic life. If air emissions continue at 1990s' rates, and there is every indication they will, many thousands of lakes, rivers, and streams worldwide will die, as will many millions of acres of forests.

In an effort to comply with U.S. air pollution emissions standards at ground level and decrease pollution in urban areas, tall smokestacks have been used on power plants so the emissions are discharged at altitudes high enough to pierce the thermal inversion layer and the pollution is carried to other regions or nations. For example, in the United States it is estimated that close to 40 percent of the acid rain deposited in the Northeast originates in the Midwest.[77]

Acid rain is a classic example of an international common pool management problem. Power plants in London belch fumes into the atmosphere that pollute and destroy forests, lakes, and streams in Scandinavia and Germany. More than three-fourths of the acid rain in Norway, Sweden, the Netherlands, Finland, Switzerland, and Austria is imported from other sections of Europe. Over half of the acid rain that falls on Canada comes from the United States.[78]

Projected increases in sulfur dioxide and nitrogen oxides in the former Soviet Union and Eastern Europe are particularly troubling.[79] Most of the region is a net exporter of the airborne pollutants that contribute to acid rain. In many of these countries, governments are under domestic pressure to increase production of consumer goods, and these governments will, understandably, be reluctant to restrain that activity and the pollution that results. Furthermore, since the region is a net exporter of airborne pollutants, the costs of these activities will not be fully felt by the nations emitting the pollutants.

Given the common pool nature of the acid rain problem, countries that are exporting their air pollutants have little incentive to restrict their polluting activities. International cooperation over acid rain has been limited, and even where attempted, has been ineffective. Indeed, there is no international organization that can provide the incentives through coercion or otherwise. In Europe, both the United Nations Economic Commission for Europe (ECE) and the 12-nation European Economic Community (EEC) have established guidelines for international cooperation in the control of acid rain. However, little progress has been made. The ECE sponsored a convention on Long-Range Trans-Boundary Air Pollution in Geneva in 1979, designed to address acid rain problems in both Eastern and Western Europe. The document produced contained language "so vague and general, and subjected to so many qualifications, that they do not impose on contracting parties any specific obligations with the respect to air pollution control policies."[80]

Since this initial agreement, there have been further attempts to strengthen it. In 1985 a protocol requiring SO_2 emission reductions of 30 percent from 1980 levels by 1993 was adopted without signature by the United States. Since then, legislation has been passed to reduce SO_2 emissions by 35 percent by 2000. A second protocol mandating a cap on NO_x emissions at 1987 levels was adopted in 1988. Additionally, in November 1991, 21 members of the ECE signed a protocol for a 30 percent reduction in VOC emissions by the year 2000. While these are positive steps, World Resources Institute editorializes, "There is little reason to believe that such reductions will cut acid deposition and ozone to the critical loads that ecosystems can tolerate."[81]

Independent sovereign states are not likely to restrict their polluting activities voluntarily when they see no benefit or perceived burdens. The fact that the Convention on Long-Range Trans-Boundary Air Pollution is perceived to be weak should not come as a surprise. We do not expect altruism in individual personal behavior; capitalist economies assume the opposite, in fact. The behavior of sovereign states is no different.

The midwestern United States, exporters of air pollution to the Northeast and Canada, are not likely out of self-interest to curtail their polluting activities voluntarily. Consequently, elimination of midwestern air pollution necessarily will have to be by action of the federal government. In 1980 the U.S. Congress approved the National Acid Precipitation Assessment Program. This is a research program, which as of the early 1990s had spent $500 million investigating the cause of acid rain. This research-only attitude was consistent with the position of the Reagan administration toward acid rain—more research is needed, better research is needed. Great Britain shares this attitude when accused of contributing to acidification in Scandinavia. Although scientists do not completely understand the dynamics of acid rain and the interactions that involve chemistry, meteorology, geology, biology, botany, soil science, and other sciences, there is overwhelming agreement on a strong connection between airborne pollutants from sulfur dioxide and nitrogen oxide and acid rain. As Arthur Johnson, a contributing author to the 1986 National Research Council report on chemical pollutants remarked, "There is no longer reasonable doubt" about the relationship between aquatic ecosystems and sulfur emissions.[82]

Title IV of the 1990 CAAA is the first law in the nation's history to attempt to deal comprehensively with acid rain. It requires that by the turn of the century, sulfur dioxide (SO_2) emissions be reduced approximately 40 percent from 1980 levels. In January 1993, the EPA issued its final rules to cut annual emissions of SO_2 in half, establishing a permanent national cap on utility emissions of just under a total of 9 million tons annually. Phase I begins in 1995 and Phase II begins in the year 2000 and will utilize a market-based allowance trading mechanism.[83]

Phase I will affect 110 of the largest coal-burning power plants. In 1991 the United States got more than 55 percent of its electricity from coal, consuming more than 750 million tons a year.[84] Sulfur dioxide, the most important contributor to acid rain, is produced when the sulfur in coal is released during combustion and reacts with oxygen in the air. The EPA, according to a formula based on the unit's average fuel consumption from 1985 to 1987, will issue allowances to emit sulfur dioxide to each of these plants. Each allowance will permit the plant to emit one ton of sulfur dioxide. If the utility is emitting more SO_2 than it has allowances, it has four choices. First, it can install pollution control equipment to reduce emissions. Second, it can try to buy allowances from other utilities nationwide. Third, it may choose to implement conservation measures to reduce both electric generation and emissions. The EPA will maintain a reserve of 300,000 special allowances for plants that develop qualifying renewable energy projects or use conservation measures. Finally, the plant can bid on a reserve of allowances (2.8 percent of the total each year) that EPA will put up for auction. Other than this, the EPA's role in allowance trading will be limited to tracking the trading.

Each plant will be required to install emissions-monitoring equipment and keep track of both emissions and allowance trading activity on an operating permit that includes all applicable requirements under the 1990 CAAA. These permits will not have to be amended each time there is trading.

Phase II for sulfur dioxide will begin in the year 2000 and will tighten emissions on these larger plants and will also affect the remaining 800 plants in the United States. Utilities that begin operation in 1996 or beyond will not be issued any allowances and will have to purchase them from other plants.

Title IV also calls for a reduction of nitrogen oxide emissions of 2 million tons by 2000 to be implemented in two phases.

Stratospheric Ozone

The second major international common pool resource problem associated with air pollution is depletion of the stratospheric ozone layer primarily through the release of chlorofluorocarbons (CFCs).[85]

Ozone in the stratosphere screens out more than 99 percent of the sun's ultraviolet radiation. Without this protection, the earth's atmosphere would not be conducive to supporting life as we know it.[86] CFCs have been used since 1955 in aerosol spray cans, refrigeration units, in industrial solvents and plastic foams for insulation, packing, furniture, and the plastic foam used in the manufacture of coffee cups and fast-food containers. Although CFCs in aerosol cans have been banned in the United States, Canada, and most Scandinavian countries since 1978, aerosol CFC production has increased overall in Western Europe as have worldwide non-aerosol CFCs.[87]

The increases in ultraviolet radiation due to ozone depletion have had a number of negative effects on humans. It is estimated that for every 1 percent decrease in ozone in the stratosphere, skin cancers increase by 5 to 10 percent. The EPA estimated that at 1991 rates of ozone depletion, skin cancer fatality rates in the United States could increase by 200,000 over the next 50 years.[88] In addition, the increase in ultraviolet light can have a negative impact on the ocean food chain by destroying microorganisms on the ocean surface. Crops on land may suffer decreased yields as well. Putting these percentages in perspective, it was estimated in 1988 that since 1969, ozone losses have averaged between 2 and 3 percent over North America and Europe and as high as 5 and 6 percent over parts of the Southern Hemisphere. Over the United States the hole in the ozone layer that was first found only in winter and spring has recently continued in summer. The EPA estimates there was a 4 to 5 percent loss of ozone between 1978 and 1991.[89] For the Southern Hemisphere, it is estimated that skin cancers in Australia and New Zealand will increase approximately 20 percent because of ozone depletion by the year 2010.[90]

The discovery of the relationship between CFCs and stratospheric ozone depletion provides valuable insight into the environmental policy process both locally and globally. It is also an excellent illustration of the problems associated with international common pool resource management. F. Sherwood Rowland, a chemist at the University of California at Irvine working with research associate Mario Molina, discovered the relationship of CFCs and ozone late in 1973.[91] Early in their research Rowland and Molina found it difficult to believe the scope of the implications of their findings. "Our immediate reaction," Rowland told an interviewer, was "we have made some huge error.[92] Rowland went home one evening and told his wife that his research "is going well, but it looks like the end of the world."[93] Rowland immediately set out to educate the public and policymakers and to urge that CFCs be banned. In the process of doing so, he alienated the $28 billion CFC industry and found he was branded by some as "some kind of a nut." CFC manufacturers, as represented by industry scientists and executives, labeled the ozone hypothesis "nonsense," going so far as to claim, as the president of an aerosol manufacturing firm did, that CFC criticism was "orchestrated by the ministers of disinformation of the KGB."[94]

In the face of industry opposition, as well as seeming indifference by policymakers, little happened on the ozone front through the mid to late 1970s. A classic combination of scientific uncertainty, no immediate crisis or a single easily identifiable interest group suffering harm, coupled with strong industry opposition and the lack of resources necessary to make opposition felt in a political system that favors maintaining the status quo, predictably led to no action. Then, in 1979 a team of British scientists discovered a hole in the ozone layer over Antarctica. This hole, covering an area larger in size than the United States, continued to show up annually in late September or early October, staying longer each year. In 1987 the hole did not break up until late December. The total depletion in the region was 50 percent below normal levels, causing alarm among atmospheric scientists and others worldwide.[95] Then, in 1989 a hole was discovered in the Arctic ozone layer, adding credence to the argument that ozone depletion was occurring worldwide. Scientists estimated that with the right weather conditions, concentrations of ozone could be depleted up to 1 percent per day in the Arctic region.[96]

The U.S. National Academy of Sciences studied the CFC-ozone link both in 1976 and 1979, essentially concluding that Rowland and Molina had been accurate in their estimates. The 1979 study estimated that ultimate ozone depletion would be somewhere between 15 and 18 percent.[97] The study had no major impact on policymakers, despite Rowland's five-year effort to urge a ban on CFC production. Even though studies had established a link between CFCs and ozone depletion, the U.S. congressional reaction was to ask for further study, in the form of National Aeronautics and Space Administration (NASA) reports every two years.[98]

As Rowland remarked of the period of the late 1970s, "That became the action item—to make a report rather than to have regulatory control."[99] The ozone problem is a classic example of the environmental policy paradox and problems associated with international common pool problems. Until the 1980s, despite strong evidence linking CFCs to ozone depletion and an understanding of the implications of that depletion, powerful interests—a $28 billion industry—had a stake in postponing action. A powerful lobby, coupled with the apparent noncritical, invisible nature of ozone depletion, made it easy for policymakers to defer action. In 1987 Secretary of the Interior Donald Hodel suggested the appropriate response to ozone depletion was to increase the use of a sunscreen and to wear head protection when out in the sun. (The proposal was labeled by conservationists as the "Ray-Ban Plan.") The interior secretary argued before the president's Domestic Policy Council that public awareness of ways to prevent skin cancer should be considered as an alternative to curbing CFC production. Although this is and was good advice, it clearly ignored or glossed over the more fundamental problem. Conservationists were outraged at the suggestion. A spokesperson for the NRDC charged that "[A]nimals, crops, fish and wildlife aren't going to wear hats and sunglasses."[100]

In 1985 NASA estimated that ozone depletion should be less than 1 percent over the United States, based on CFC production at 1980 levels. Total ozone depletion for the next century worldwide would be as much as 10 percent. Within two years, however, it was clear those estimates were much too low. Declines from 1969 through 1986 were estimated in 1987 to be an average of 2.3 percent in the Northern Hemisphere and, as we indicated, even higher in the Southern Hemisphere and over the United States.[101] A British discovery in 1979 led to a series of further tests of the Antarctic ozone and found the hole continually reappeared and was larger each time. A NASA ozone panel on March 15, 1988, confirmed that Antarctic ozone loss was attributable to CFCs and that ozone loss was detected at all latitudes. By then, worldwide attention had been focused on the ozone problem. Twenty-four nations signed what is known as the Montreal Protocol in September 1987. The protocol is designed to freeze production of five CFCs at 1986 levels and reduce total CFC production by 50 percent at the turn of the century. The U.S. Senate unanimously ratified the Montreal Protocol six months later. Shortly thereafter, Du Pont, the largest CFC producer in the United States, announced it had set a goal of "an orderly transition to the total phaseout of fully halogenated CFC production."[102] Du Pont was keeping a pledge it had made more than a decade earlier in full-page newspaper advertisements to phase out CFCs should they be found to be environmentally hazardous. Then, on March 2, 1989, environmental ministers from the European Economic Community agreed to a total phaseout of CFCs by the year 2000 and agreed to an 85 percent reduction in CFC production as soon as possible.[103] The next day President Bush called for a ban on CFC production by the year 2000, *provided* safe alternatives could be developed. This was a switch from the attitude of the Reagan administration. As the *Los Angeles Times* editorialized, "It is embarrassing for this country to be following someone else's lead on crucial environmental issues so much of the time, but Bush's reaction time was an improvement over the Reagan administration's response to such things. It probably would be calling for more study."[104]

The 1990 Clean Air Act amendments did, in fact, ban CFC production in the United States after the year 2000. In early 1993 the EPA proposed "speeded-up" phaseout dates for ozone-destroying chemicals. CFCs, carbon tetrachloride, and methyl chloroform production were listed for phaseout by January 1996, and halons production by January 1994.[105] Additionally, CFCs from car air conditioners, the biggest single source of ozone-destroying chemicals, must now be serviced using equipment that prevents release and recycles CFCs by the end of 1993. This applies to all service shops, not just to the larger shops that had been required to start using this special equipment in January 1993. Hydrochlorofluorocarbons (HCFCs), CFC substitutes, are scheduled to begin phaseout by 2003.[106] Finally, the Montreal Protocol was amended in 1990 to create a $160 million fund to compensate developing countries for following a CFC-free path. The funding would come from the largest CFC users.[107]

It is tempting to conclude that initial efforts at ozone control, through the Montreal Protocol, elimination of CFCs in aerosol sprays, and other measures, provide an example of how the system can work to deal with environmental problems when they are identified. And in a sense progress has been made. Within eight years, from the start of the Reagan administration when then-EPA administrator Anne Gorsuch Burford dismissed ozone depletion as another environmental scare, the U.S. president had called for a ban on CFC production.[108]

Surface appearances may not, however, provide a complete picture, particularly in the international arena. First, the Montreal Protocol was designed to cut CFC production by only 50 percent over 10 years. Even if successful the amount of CFCs still left in the atmosphere will have a significant impact on the environment—greatly increasing the incidence of skin cancer and damaging marine ecosystems. Furthermore, the Montreal Protocol allows lesser developed nations to increase CFC use for a decade and is, of course, dependent on the good faith of the signatory nations for enforcement.[109] Finally, the Montreal Protocol does not address emissions of carbon tetrachloride, a chemical banned in the United States but commonly used in other countries with even greater potential to damage the ozone layer than CFCs.[110] As Rowland commented on the Montreal Protocol, "[It] does little to protect the atmosphere. Very little for a decade and then not enough."[111] And, as a spokesperson for the Natural Resources Defense Council remarked, "[The] Montreal accord and the proposed EPA rules will cut CFCs by less than 50 percent over 10 years. The world has *already* suffered more ozone depletion than EPA predicted would occur under that level of cuts by the year 2050. Safeguarding the ozone layer requires a rapid and total CFC phaseout, not just a ten-year halfway measure."[112] Progress has undoubtedly been made. Many observers feel, however, that more needs to be done.

In a similar manner, the ban on CFCs in aerosol propellants would appear to be a victory, and in fact it was. The ready availability of substitutes in aerosol propellants, at roughly the same cost, undoubtedly made this environmental "victory" easier to achieve. Despite this success, many countries that did not sign the Montreal Protocol continue to produce CFCs. Those countries that did sign continue to produce, albeit at a reduced level. Thus the protective ozone layer will continue to be depleted.

The incentives operating in international common pool resource management are such that many nations will be slow to act. When the CFC-ozone link was first established, skeptics in Europe argued that the theory was developed by American manufacturers desiring to have a corner on the market for substitutes for CFCs. CFC manufacturers also questioned the motives of Rowland and others who argued for a ban of CFCs. Unfortunately, the production of CFCs has continued to increase in many countries in spite of the mounting evidence of the damage being done to the ozone layer. For example, in the United States, although CFCs are banned from aerosol sprays, an increase in CFC usage for other purposes has resulted in total CFC production at roughly the same levels as it was prior to the aerosol spray ban.[113] Under these circumstances, the outlook for the ban on CFC production, before extensive damage is done to the ozone layer and our environment, seems slim.[114]

The Greenhouse Effect

The gradual warming trend will likely go on.
And the green belts begin to slide closer to the poles.
The Plains States will be abandoned as giant dust bowls.
Greenland and Antarctica will join the new Great Powers . . .
Let them have their little time in the sun,
We'll say to ourselves as we begin to sway
To the strains of our native beach band,
Ignoring the hits from the Arctic on the radio.[115]

For over 100 years we have understood the possibility of atmospheric warming due to human carbon dioxide emissions. The greenhouse effect, which is a natural occurrence and has allowed the development of life on earth, is thought by many scientists to have been radically altered by humankind's impact on the composition of the atmosphere. The problem lies in humans' effects on the dynamic nature of the heat exchange process of the sun, earth, and black space. These alterations threaten to transform the global environment. As one observer wrote, "The year is 2035. In New York, palm trees line the Hudson River . . . Phoenix is in its third week of temperatures over 130 degrees . . . Holland is under water. Bangladesh has ceased to exist . . . In central Europe and in the American Midwest, decades of drought have turned once fertile agricultural lands into parched deserts."[116]

Problematic greenhouse gasses consist primarily of methane and carbon dioxide, according to recent studies. They also consist of water vapor and trace amounts of gasses including ozone, nitrous oxide, and CFCs. Greenhouse gasses prevent some of the sun's infrared radiation or heat from escaping the earth, similar to a greenhouse. As these gaseous levels in the atmosphere increase, greenhouse gasses trap more of the sun's heat in the earth's atmosphere, which has a number of effects on the earth's environment. Were it not for greenhouse gasses, most of the sun's energy would radiate back out into space, leaving the earth cold and lifeless with an average temperature of minus 18° C (0.4° F).[117]

To illustrate the problem, under normal conditions, which for our purposes we define as before people started to burn fossil fuels releasing carbon dioxide in the atmosphere, global levels of carbon dioxide were around 275 parts per million (ppm). Carbon dioxide levels increased from 275 ppm to 346 ppm, between 1860 and 1986, primarily due to the burning of fossil fuels and deforestation. By 1992 CO_2 concentrations had risen to 356 ppm and were estimated to be growing at 1.5 ppm each year.[118]

Plants convert carbon dioxide to oxygen and are one effective way to absorb carbon dioxide from the atmosphere. Deforestation has resulted in a reduction in the carbon dioxide to oxygen conversion. It is estimated that global levels of carbon dioxide in the atmosphere will reach 550 ppm sometime between 2040 and 2100; however, most analysts believe those levels will be reached closer to the middle of the twenty-first century.[119] Carbon dioxide levels of 550 ppm would raise average atmospheric temperatures approximately 4°C in the temperate regions, with temperatures rising two to three times this amount at the poles. Furthermore, increased temperatures would cause the expansion of seawater and the melting of ice in both polar regions, resulting in a rise in sea level, predicted by climatologists to be up to 1.5 meters (about 5 feet) by the year 2050.[120] This would devastate coastal areas around the world and cause hundreds of billions of dollars in damage. In 1987 the president of the Maldives, an island nation in the Indian Ocean, gave an impassioned plea to the United Nations to act on global warming. The estimated rising of the ocean due to global warming would completely submerge the low-lying Maldives Islands as well as most of the world's great seaports including New Orleans, Amsterdam, and Shanghai.[121]

The increase in temperatures would also result in a negative impact on agriculture in a number of regions. In the midwestern United States, where much of the land is dependent on irrigation from groundwater, which in most places is a finite resource, farming could become impractical. All over the world food production would become erratic, reflecting the changed weather patterns. The impact on agriculture would be particularly severe, since most food is grown in the middle or higher latitudes of the Northern Hemisphere where the greatest impact from the greenhouse effect would be felt. Climate changes would be the least felt in the areas near the equator, where relatively little food is grown. As climatic zones shift northward, animals, and particularly plants, will have a difficult time adapting to the change. This would lead to a significant loss in species variety and loss of genetic diversity.

An EPA report to Congress in 1988 reads, "[T]he landscape of North America will change in ways it cannot be fully predicted. The ultimate effects will last for centuries and will be irreversible. ... Strategies to reverse such impacts on natural ecosystems are not currently available."[122]

Although the scientific community is never unanimous given the nature of scientific inquiry to question and to test, there is, in the words of John Firor, the director of advanced studies at the National Center for Atmospheric Research in Boulder, Colorado, "a spectacular convergence of scientific opinion on global warming." Firor noted, "[T]here is just no disagreement that we're in for a rapid heating. The only question is how much."[123] Numerous reports from NASA, the EPA, and the Department of Energy have confirmed we are headed toward a warmer climate because of the greenhouse effect.

Deforestation of rain forests largely for agricultural development is related to the greenhouse effect in several important respects. Deforestation is occurring in many parts of the world and is particularly intense in the less developed countries. Reforestation is the primary means of effectively reducing carbon dioxide in the atmosphere. Worldwide rates of deforestation are about 10 times the rate of reforestation. According to the World Resources Institute, approximately 27 million acres a year of forests are being lost.

Much of this deforestation occurs in the less developed regions, notably Brazil, Indonesia, and Zaire, regions that rely on the forests for energy and increased agricultural production. Consequently the prospects for a dramatic end to deforestation are not encouraging.[124] Deforestation also has a dramatic effect on termite populations, increasing the number of termites by anywhere from three to ten times their predeforestation population. Termites give off methane gas. Increases in atmospheric methane, an important greenhouse gas, have been measured at between 1 and 2 percent each year, due in part, some scientists fear, to deforestation and the related increase in the termite population.[125]

The greenhouse problem is a classic example, and also one of the most frightening examples, of the environmental policy paradox. As an EPA policy analyst once wrote, "[G]lobal warming is an international problem that will require extensive and unprecedented cooperation . . . [N]o single country, acting alone, will be able decisively to affect the problem."[126] Another author described the policy environment surrounding the greenhouse effect as "the catch 22 of the greenhouse."[127] Since there is some scientific uncertainty about to the exact timing and nature of global warming and what impact it would have on a region-by-region basis, policymakers wait for additional research to be completed. Although there have been scientific conferences and international cooperation to study greenhouse gasses, the attitude of many governments has been one of "wait and see," and requests for further study. For example, the U.S. Congress passed the Global Climate Protection Act of 1987, which, despite its high-sounding title, basically called for a study and report on the greenhouse problem.[128] Some, limited, progress has been made internationally on the control of greenhouse gasses. At the 1992 UN Conference on Environment and Development in Rio de Janeiro (often referred to as the Rio Conference), 154 nations agreed to report each year on changes in their carbon emissions. Although this information will be useful, and may lead to further attempts to deal with global warming, this is only a reporting requirement and hence is what we might expect when dealing with sovereign states managing an international common pool problem.[129] Herein lies the paradox. When the uncertainties have been resolved, it may be too late to prevent or prepare for the negative impacts of global warming.[130]

The greenhouse effect also lends itself to incremental decision making. It is a long-term problem that does not have immediate identifiable effects on the public. Politicians are hesitant to ask for sacrifices now that will reap nonvisible present benefits and uncertain future benefits. Nevertheless, the scientific community is in agreement that we are headed for warming and the risks we take by ignoring the greenhouse effect are very great. Yet this is the policy of most governments—wait and see. What is needed is a crisis environment.

In the United States the summer of 1988, one of the hottest in recorded history, provided the crisis environment that is often necessary for policymakers to act.[131] Two bills were introduced to decrease fossil fuel use and in other ways deal with the generation of greenhouse gasses. In Congress, members were quick to sign up as cosponsors for the legislation. As one commentator noted, "[A]ll of this has politicians scurrying around to put themselves on record as firmly opposed to apocalypse."[132] The sponsor of one bill, Senator Patrick J. Leahy of Vermont, commented, "[T]here's too much at stake to let our normal cynicism—or realism—about congressional leadership hold sway. It is our job to worry about the long-term future of American agriculture and forestry. . . . Congress can't seem to make up its mind about whether it wants a two year budget, let alone focus on the effects of global warming, which may not occur for several decades."[133]

Although the United States is the largest producer of carbon emissions from fossil fuels, carbon plays a comparatively minor role in the total U.S. gross national product.[134] In many parts of the world notably China, Eastern Europe, India, and to a lesser extent Russia, fossil fuels are an extremely important part of the economy. Throughout Europe, coal is an important fuel, even more so since the Chernobyl disaster. Furthermore, carbon dioxide emissions in many parts of the world are a long-time and far-off threat, with many other problems such as food, sanitation, and health care more immediately pressing. As Lucas Reijnders of the Dutch Foundation for Nature and the Environment observed in Eastern Europe, "[T]here simply are much more pressing problems than carbon dioxide . . . and we all get a feeling that the USSR would not mind a warming up anyway. Awareness will come, but not for a time."[135]

A long-term problem, more pressing immediate economic and social needs, the common pool nature of the problem, and the lack of certainty or recognition of long-term effects all suggest global warming is a problem that will not go away any time soon. All these arguments support those that benefit from fossil fuel consumption, or those who fear the negative political fallout from limiting that consumption, to argue against taking corrective actions.

James Hansen, head of the NASA's Goddard Institute for Space Studies, told a U.S. Senate committee during the summer of 1988, "[It] is time to stop waffling so much and say that the evidence is pretty strong that the greenhouse effect is here."[136] After Hansen's Senate testimony, Joseph Mullan, a spokesman for the National Coal Association on environmental issues, told a *New York Times* reporter that perhaps there was no need to be concerned about the greenhouse effect because, Mr. Mullan explained, "[S]ince the earth faces another ice age within a thousand years or so one calamity might cancel out the other."[137]

Lester B. Lave from Carnegie-Mellon University, a strong supporter of using cost-benefit analysis in policy-making, argues that since the damage and the cost of global warming are at present impossible to determine, "there is no way to justify spending tens of billion dollars a year" to prevent the greenhouse effect.[138] However, the real or perceived lack of cost-benefit analysis data in global warming or any other environmental policy should not lead us to conclude, as Lave suggests, that protective measures which take costs into consideration should not be attempted. One can be against the use of cost-benefit analysis and still be in favor of cost-effective environmental policies. Cost effectiveness only means selecting the environmental policy that will clean up the environment for the least cost.

As serious as global warming is, the attention of many policymakers nationally and internationally seems to be best summarized by a 1989 Grammy award-winning song titled *Don't Worry, Be Happy*. On the bright side, the greenhouse effect may be such a catastrophic problem that nations would be willing to undertake measures they perceive not to be in their best short-term economic interest. An international conference on global warming sponsored by the United Nations Environmental Program and another UN body, the World Meteorological Organization, held in Geneva in late 1988 attracted representatives from 35 countries. The objectives of the group were to study scientific evidence and consequences of warming.

The United States was one of a few nations that insisted the conference examine the causes of global warming. The majority were convinced that enough was known about causes. Nevertheless, an American official in attendance, Frederick Bernthal, the assistant secretary of state for international environmental and scientific affairs, allowed that, "[We] know that greenhouse gasses are accumulating and in principle, they should lead to global warming."[139] It remains to be seen if this study effort will lead to corrective measures that will halt the pollution of the international commons due to global warming.

Air pollution, whether in the form of CFCs, greenhouse gasses, acid rain, or other forms of pollution provides numerous examples of the environmental policy paradox. We often understand the relationship between our polluting activities and the impacts these activities have on the environment. However, numerous factors operate to result in policies that do not fully address the problem.

There is a lot we can do as individuals to help clean the air. Carpooling, walking, bicycling, energy conservation, or anything that keeps fossil fuels from being burned is helpful. Rather than drive to that store which is only a block away, walk instead. Driving as a luxury is expensive both in terms of operating the car and costs in damage to our environment. Paradoxically most people know these things. Fortunately, we as individuals *can* control our own policy choices.

SUMMARY

This chapter provided an overview of air pollution, its components, health effects, laws and regulations, causes, and its effects locally, nationally, and internationally. In addition, we took a close look at toxic air pollution, acid rain, ozone depletion, and the greenhouse effect. Air pollution policy is, like much environmental policy, fraught with scientific uncertainty, particularly in regard to the lack of direct causal evidence of a relationship between particular airborne pollutants and human health. We do have strong evidence of human health impacts with some pollutants, but we have been slow to act. Congress debated amendments to the Clean Air Act through the 1980s, but regional and economic interests succeeded in preventing additional legislation to deal with air pollution. The 1990 Clean Air Act amendments may go a long way toward cleaning the nation's air, or they may not. Implementation will be the key. In any event, the failure to act throughout the 1980s, in light of the available evidence of air pollution damage, is a good example of the environmental policy paradox.

In the next chapter we examine U.S. water pollution policy and problems of water supply, use, and conservation. In water, as in air, uncertainties lead to policy paradoxes, and powerful vested interests make changing the status quo difficult.

NOTES

1. G. Tyler Miller, Jr., *Living in the Environment* (5th ed.) (Belmont, CA: Wadsworth, 1988), p. 424.
2. U.S. Environmental Protection Agency, *National Air Quality and Emissions Trends Report* (1984) pp. 3–24.
3. Conservation Foundation, *State of the Environment: A View Towards the 90's* (Washington, DC: Conservation Foundation, 1987), p. 67.
4. The U.S. Environmental Protection Agency, *National Air Quality and Emission Trends Report* (1984), pp. 3–12.
5. Sandra Postel, "Air Pollution, Acid Rain, and the Future of the Forest," *American Forests*, 90 (October 1984), p. 35.
6. Ibid.
7. Ibid.
8. U.S. Environmental Protection Agency, *National Air Quality Emission Trends Report* (1984), pp. 3–27.
9. John A. Paul, "Urban Air Quality: The Problem," *EPA Journal*, 17 (1) (1991), p. 24.
10. Ibid., p. 25.
11. Ibid., pp. 25–26.
12. Lester B. Lave and Eugene P. Seskin, *Air Pollution in Human Health* (Baltimore: Johns Hopkins University Press, 1987), pp. 235–237.
13. Miller, *Living in the Environment*, p. 432. See also Frederick G. Kappler and Gary L. Rutledge, "The Expenditures for Abating Portion of Emissions from Motor Vehicles, 1968–1984," *Survey of Current Business*, 65 (July 1985), p. 29. Some have estimated the number is well in excess of 50,000 in the United States.
14. Ibid., p. 433.
15. A thermal inversion is created when cool air is trapped within an air basin by overlying warm air.
16. Dean E. Painter, *Air Pollution Technology* (Reston, VA: Reston, 1975), p. 22. These numbers are subject to some dispute. The estimates are based on average numbers of deaths over the period compared to numbers of deaths during the period of the pollution. The London killer fog has been estimated by some to have led to more than 4,000 deaths.
17. Much is known, since each NAAQS has a "Criteria Document" that presents all known health data for that pollutant.
18. William K. Reilly, *EPA Journal*, 17 (1) (1991), p. 3.
19. John A. Paul, "Urban Air Quality: The Problem," *EPA Journal*, 17 (1) (1991).
20. *Environmental Protection*, 4 (1) (1993), p. 8.
21. Michael G. Renner, "Car Sick," *World Watch*, 1 (6) (November-December 1988), pp. 36, 38.
22. Miller, *Living in the Environment*, p. 433.
23. William H. Matthews, Frederick E. Smith, and Edward D. Goldberg, (eds.), *Man's Impact on Terrestrial and Oceanic Ecosystems* (Cambridge: Massachusetts Institute of Technology, 1971), p. 103.
24. National Acid Precipitation Assessment Program, *Interim Assessment: The Causes and Effects of Acid Deposition*, IV (Washington, DC: U.S. Government Printing Office, 1987). Cited in Lester R. Brown, "A New Era Unfolds," Lester R. Brown et al. (eds.), *State of the World* (New York: Norton, 1993), p. 13.
25. "Air Pollution," *Current History*, 59 (387) (July 1970), pp. 18–49.
26. Alvin W. Vogtle, Jr., "Investigate, Educate, Then Regulate: An Agenda for Dealing with Acid Rain," in Kent Gilbreath (ed.), *Business and the Environment Towards Common Ground* (2nd ed.) (Washington, DC: The Conservation Foundation, 1984), p. 245.
27. Richard D. Wilson, "Motor Vehicles and Fuels: The Strategy," *EPA Journal*, 17 (1) (1991), p. 15.
28. Renner, "Car Sick," p. 36.

29. Frederick G. Kappler and Gary L. Rutledge, "The Expenditures for Abating Portion of Emissions from Motor Vehicles, 1968–1984," *Survey of Current Business*, 65 (July 1985), p. 29.
30. Renner, "Car Sick," p. 36.
31. Ibid.
32. This is based on U.S. Department of Energy estimates of 1993 motor gasoline consumption of approximately 7.3 million barrels a day with 42 gallons in each barrel.
33. Robert Stobaugh and Daniel Yergin (eds.), *Energy Future* (3rd ed.) (New York: Vintage Books, 1983), p. 66.
34. "Environment: Victory for Clean Air," *Time* (October 5, 1970), p. 46.
35. "Detroit's Battle with Washington," *Business Week* (December 5, 1970), p. 28.
36. Walter A. Rosenbaum, *The Politics of Environmental Concern* (New York: Praeger, 1973), p. 153.
37. National Ambient Air Quality Standards, U.S. Environmental Protection Agency.

Primary (health-related)

Pollutant	Averaging Time	Concentration
Particulates	Annual geometric mean	75 µg/m3
	24-hour	260 µg/m3
Sulfur dioxide	24-hour	80 µg/m3 (0.14 ppm)
Carbon monoxide	8-hour	365 µg/m3 (9 ppm)
	1-hour	10 µg/m3 (35 ppm)
Nitrogen dioxide	Annual arithmetic mean	40 µg/m3 (0.053 ppm)
Ozone	Maximum daily	100 µg/m3 0.12 ppm
	1-hour average	(235 µg/m3)
Lead	average	1.5 µg/m3

Secondary (welfare-related)

Pollutant	Averaging Time	Concentration
Particulates	Annual geometric mean	60 µg/m3
	24-hour	150 µg/m3
	3-hour	1,300 µg/m3 (0.50 ppm)
Sulfur Dioxide	None	
Carbon monoxide	Same as primary	
Nitrogen dioxide	Same as primary	
Ozone	Same as primary	
Lead	Same as primary	

Special thanks to Richard Foust.

38. U.S. Code Title 42, Section 7409 (b) (1).
39. Painter, *Air Pollution Technology*, pp. 3–9.
40. U.S. Code Title 42, Section 7412 (a) (1).
41. See Margaret E. Kriz, "Dunning the Midwest," *National Journal*, 22 (15) (April 14, 1990), pp. 893–897.
42. Robert W. Hahn and Gordon L. Hester, "The Market for Bads: EPA's Experience with Emission's Trading," *Regulation*, 3–4 (1987), p. 48.
43. See Hahn and Hester, "The Market for Bads: EPA's Experience with Emission's Trading"; see also Robert E. Taylor, "EPA Is Expanding Its Bubble Policy for Air Pollution," *Wall Street Journal*, November 20, 1986, p. 18.
44. Robert W. Hahn, "Trade-Offs in Designing Markets with Multiple Objectives," *Journal of Environmental Economics and Management*, 13 (March 1986), pp. 1, 7.
45. Roger Rapoport, "Trading Dollars for Dirty Air," *Science 86*, 7 (July/August 1986), p. 75.
46. Ibid.
47. Ibid. Examples of ERC trades include the sale of hydrocarbon credits to General Motors by B.F. Goodrich in Louisville, Kentucky. Mobile Oil in Renton, Washington, reduced its hydrocarbon emissions and sold the credits to Reynolds Aluminum. Arundel Corporation reduced its total suspended particle emissions in Sparrows Point, Maryland, and sold its reductions to Atlantic Cement.
48. Phillip Shabecoff, "EPA Sets Rules on Air Pollution Allowances," *New York Times*, November 20, 1986, pp. 1, 22.
49. Ibid. The Natural Resources Defense Council unsuccessfully challenged the bubble concept as a violation of the Clean Air Act. The U.S. Supreme Court upheld the EPA's authority to create bubbles. "Supreme Court Upholds Bubble Pollution Concept," *The Oil Daily*, 174 (8) (June 26,1984), p. 1.
50. See, for example, the discussion of EPA bubble policy and the steel industry in Bill Schmitt, "Revised Bubble Policy Might Be Tougher," *American Metal Market*, 94 (March 13, 1986), p. 1.
51. That reportedly was the case in northern California when existing firms refused to sell pollution permits to a potential competitor. See W. David Slawson, "The Right to Protection from Air Pollution," *Southern California Law Review*, 59 (May 1986), pp. 672, 729.
52. W. David Slawson, "The Right to Protection from Air Pollution," *Southern California Law Review*, 59 (May 1986), p. 727.
53. U.S. Code Title 42, Section 7411 (a) (1) (c). The statute reads in pertinent part: "reflect the degree of emission reduction achievable through the application of the best system of continuous emission reduction which (taking into consideration the cost of achieving such emission reduction, and any non air quality health and environmental impact and energy requirements) the administrator determines has been adequately demonstrated for that category of sources."
54. Lave and Seskin, *Air Pollution in Human Health*, pp. 312–316.
55. Ibid., p. 693.
56. This point has been the subject of some controversy. In conversations with EPA air quality officials, the point was made that the catalytic converter was developed. Also, advances were achieved in coating technology. It is argued that technology-forcing rules have probably gained more than other traditional regulations.
57. Hahn and Hester, "The Market for Bads: EPA's Experience with Emission's Trading," p. 48.
58. All air pollutants are potentially hazardous to human health though the law does distinguish between conventional and hazardous pollutants.

59. Conservation Foundation, *State of the Environment*, p. 135.
60. U.S. Code Title 42 Section 7412 (A)(1). (Note: it takes a special talent to write a sentence like that.)
61. "On the Regulation of Toxic Air Pollutants: A Critical Review Discussion Papers," *Journal of the Air Pollution Control Association*, 36 (1989), p. 990.
62. 42 U.S.C.A. section 7412 (b) (1).
63. George Siple, "HON Rule Targets Specialty Chemicals," *Environmental Protection*, 4 (6) (1993), p. 44.
64. The figures on the 1990 Clean Air Act Amendments reported in this chapter were taken from Keith Schneider, "Lawmakers Reach an Accord on Reduction of Air Pollution," *New York Times*, October 23, 1990, pp. A1, A11.
65. Conservation Foundation, *State of the Environment*, p. 152.
66. Ibid.
67. Ibid. Also see "Deadly Lead," *Environmental Action*, 17 (5) (1986), p. 20.
68. Conservation Foundation, *State of the Environment*, p. 154.
69. Latency periods make it easy for those who oppose air pollution regulations to minimize the health dangers of air pollution. Long delays frequently occur between exposure to the toxic pollutant that then triggers the disease process leading to later manifestation of disease symptoms. These lengthy delays make it difficult to pin the cause to the resulting effect. Decision makers cannot know beyond a doubt that exposure to asbestos, for example, will cause a schoolchild to develop cancer. Thus they are open to persuasive arguments from lobbies concerned with the cost of implementing restrictive regulations.
70. Asbestos Hazard Emergency Response Act of 1986, P.L. 99–519.
71. Ibid.
72. Brenda Norrell, "500 Navajo Mine Victims Pack Hearing," *Arizona Daily Sun*, (March 14, 1990), p. 2. The act was passed and signed by President Bush in 1992. It provides for three levels of compensation: $50,000 for those downwind, $75,000 for those on site, and $100,000 for the miners themselves who satisfy damage criteria. The trust fund was not in the final version of the act but rather appropriations are being made on an annual basis. The first payouts began in 1992.
73. See U.S. Congress, Office of Technology Assessment, *Acid Rain and Transported Air Pollutants: Implications for Public Poly* (Washington, DC: U.S. Government Printing Office, 1984), p. 92; and U.S. General Accounting Office, *Air Pollution: Sulfur Dioxide Emissions from Non-Ferrous Smelters Have Been Reduced* (Washington, DC: U.S. Government Printing Office, 1986), pp. 9, 21.
74. Anne LaBastille, "The International Acid Test," Sierra (May-June 1986), p. 51.
75. Archie M. Kahan, *Acid Rain: Reign of Controversy* (Golden, CO: Fulcrum, 1986), p. 20.
76. LaBastille, "The International Acid Test," p. 51.
77. U.S. Office of Technology Assessment, *Acid Rain and Transported Air Pollutants*, pp. 71–73.
78. Miller, *Living in the Environment*, p. 432.
79. See Barbara Jancar-Webster, *Environmental Action in Eastern Europe* (Armonk, NY: M.E. Sharp, 1993).
80. Mark Pallemaerts, "The Politics of Acid Rain Control in Europe," *Environment* (March 1988), p. 42.
81. World Resources Institute, *World Resources 1992–1993* (New York: Oxford University Press, 1992), p. 199.
82. Conservation Foundation, *State of the Environment*, p. 77.
83. *Environmental Protection*, 4 (1) (1993), p. 10.
84. Ned Helme and Chris Neme, "Acid Rain: The Problem," *EPA Journal*, 17 (1) (1991), p. 19.

85. Other gasses are involved but the discussion here is limited to CFCs, being by far the largest contributor.

World Chlorofluorocarbon Production and Release 1971–1985 (millions of kilograms)

Year	Annual Production	Annual Release	Cumulative Release
1931	.0	.1	.1
1940	4.7	2.4	7.6
1950	41.2	35.0	163.5
1960	149.1	129.6	946.9
1970	559.2	506.5	4,066.5
1971	604.8	548.7	4,615.1
1972	686.8	605.7	5,220.8
1973	772.4	679.7	5,900.5
1974	812.5	740.0	6,640.5
1975	695.1	715.0	7,355.7
1976	750.5	707.1	8,062.7
1977	703.3	675.1	8,737.9
1978	681.0	624.9	9,362.8
1979	646.7	601.2	9,963.8
1980	639.8	583.3	10,574.2
1981	638.2	588.9	11,136.1
1982	599.4	576.9	11,713.0
1983	647.0	596.1	12,309.1
1984	694.5	630.5	12,939.7
1985	703.1	649.2	13,588.90

86 Another threat to the ozone layer may be presented by U.S. space shuttle flights. Experts in the former USSR claimed that every time the U.S. craft flies, it destroys massive amounts of atmospheric ozone. Calculations by Valeri Burdkov. one of the Soviet Union's leading geophysicists and Vyacheslav Filin, deputy chief designer at the S.P. Korolyev Design Bureau, show that in "one flight, the space shuttle destroys up to 10 million of the three billion tons of atmospheric ozone. Three hundred launches is enough to do away altogether with the thin ozone layer which is already holed." The solid fuel used in the Titan rockets burns to produce hydrogen chloride, one molecule of which is said to destroy 100,000 molecules of ozone. The rocket emits 187 tons of chlorine and chlorine compounds as well as ozone-depleting nitrogen compounds (7 tons), aluminum oxides (177 tons), and 378 tons of carbon oxidizers. However, NASA maintains the shuttle is ecologically sound. See Nick Nuttall, "Russians say US Shuttle Is Damaging Ozone Layer," *The Times* (London), December 20, 1989, p. 5.

87. Miller, *Living in the Environment*, p. 439.

88. William K. Reilly, "Statement on Ozone Depletion," U.S. Environmental Protection Agency, Washington, DC, April 4, 1991. Cited in Lester R. Brown, "A New Era Unfolds," Lester R. Brown et al. (eds.), *State of the World* (New York: Norton, 1993), p. 10.

89. See Thomas H. Maugh II, "Ozone Depletion Far Worse Than Expected," *Los Angeles Times*, March 16, 1988, Pt. I, p.1; and "Ozone Depletion Worsens, NRDC Leads Drive for Total CFC Phase Out," *Newsline* (Natural Resources

Defense Council), 6 (2) (May/June 1988), p. 1; and *The Plain English Guide to the Clean Air Act*, The EPA (April 1993), p. 16.

90. Maugh, "Ozone Depletion Far Worst Than Expected," p. 1.
91. Edward Edelson, "The Man Who Knew Too Much," *Popular Science* (January 1989), p. 60. See also Lanie Jones, "He Sounded, Paid Heavy Price," *Los Angeles Times*, July 14, 1988, Pt. 1, p. 1.
92. Jones, "He Sounded, Paid Heavy Price," p. 18.
93. Edelson, "The Man Who Knew Too Much," p. 63.
94. Jones, "He Sounded, Paid Heavy Price," p. 1.
95. Maugh, "Ozone Depletion Far Worst Than Expected," p. 19.
96. The discovery was made by a group of scientists representing Canada, the United States, the then USSR, and several European countries. As reported on Cable News Network, February 15, 1989.
97. Ibid.
98. Ibid.
99. Ibid.
100. Robert Gillette, "Hodel Proposal Irks Environmentalists," *Los Angeles Times*, May 30, 1989, Pt. I, p. 2. When asked about the proposal a spokesperson for Bausch & Lomb, the manufacturer of Ray-Ban sunglasses, remarked, "Sounds fine with us. . . . We'll be happy to set the Interior Secretary up as a distributor of Ray-Ban sunglasses." Ibid.
101. Maugh, "Ozone Depletion Far Worst Than Expected," p. 19.
102. Edelson, "The Man Who Knew Too Much," p. 102.
103. "EC Agrees to Ban All CFCs by 2000 in Surprise Move," *Wall Street Journal*, March 3, 1989, p. B2.
104. "Europe Takes Ozone Lead," *Los Angeles Times*, March 4,1989, Pt. 2, p. 8. See also Cathleen Decker and Larry Stammer, "Bush Asks Ban on CFC to Save Ozone," *Los Angeles Times*, March 4, 1989, Pt. 1, p. 1.
105. *Plain English Guide to the Clean Air Act*, The EPA (April 1993), p. 16.
106. Ibid., p. 16.
107. *World Resources Institute, World Resources 1992–1993* (New York: Oxford University Press, 1992), p. 152.
108. David D. Doniger, "Politics of the Ozone Layer," *Issues in Science and Technology*, 4 (Spring 1988), p. 86.
109. The agreement has provisions for trade sanctions against those who do not cooperate. The enforceability and utility of these sanctions is questionable, however.
110. "Ozone—Protection Plan May Have a Big Hole," *Honolulu Advertiser*, April 21,1989, Pt. D, p. 1.
111. Ibid.
112. "Ozone Depletion Worsens, NRDC Leads Drive for Total CFC Phase Out," *Newsline* (Natural Resources Defense Council), 6 (2) (May/June,1988) p. 1.
113. Jones, "He Sounded, Paid Heavy Price," p. 18.
114. A zero (0) indicates zero or less than one-half the unit of measure. Data are total of compounds F-11, which are about 94 percent of the chlorofluoromethanes produced. Chlorofluoromethanes are a group of carbon compounds. Data are available for the Chemical Manufacturers Association, which presents F-11 and F-12 separately. Data are composed of reports from 19 companies reporting to the Chemical Manufacturers Association's Fluorocarbon Research Program. Producers in USSR, Eastern Europe, and the People's Republic of China do not report data to the CMA-FPP, and are not included in this table.
Source: Chemical Manufacturers Association, Production, Sales, and Calculated Release of CFC-11 and CFC-12 through 1985 (Washington, DC, 1986).

115. Carl Dennis, "The Greenhouse Effect," *Poetry*, 146 (August 1985), p. 266.
116. Jeremy Rifkin, "The Doomsday Prognosis," *The Guardian*, August 21, 1988, p. 19.
117. Miller, *Living in the Environment*, p. 440.
118. Boyce Rensberger, "Taking the Earth's Temperature," *The Washington Post National Weekly Edition*, June 8–14, 1992, p. 7.
119. Rifkin, "The Doomsday Prognosis," p. 19; and Miller, *Living in the Environment*, p. 441.
120. Rifkin, "The Doomsday Prognosis," p. 19.
121. William H. Mansfield, III, "With a Global Focus," *EPA Journal*, 15 (1) (January/February), p. 37.
122. William Eaton, "Congress Urged to Fight Global warming," *Los Angeles Times*, December 2, 1988, Pt. 1, p. 41.
123. Lester R. Brown and John E. Young, "Growing Food in a Warmer World," *World Watch*, 1 (6) (November/December 1988), p. 32.
124. Rifkin, "The Doomsday Prognosis," p. 19.
125. David M. Schwartz, "The Termite Connection," *International Wildlife* (July/August 1987), p. 38.
126. Linda Fisher, "The Wheels Are Beginning to Turn," *EPA Journal*, 15 (1) (January/February), p. 42.
127. Stefi Weisburd, "Waiting for Warming: The Catch 22 of CO_2," *Science News* 128 (September 14,1985), p. 170.
128. Global Climate Protection Act of 1987.
129. Lester R. Brown, "A New Era Unfolds," Lester R. Brown et al. (eds.), *State of the World* (New York: Norton, 1993), p. 3.
130. Lewis M. Embler, Patricia L. Layman, Wil Lepkowski, and Pamela S. Zurer, "Social Economic Implications," *Chemical and Engineering News*, 64 (November 24, 1986), pp. 36, 39.
131. It should be noted that during the summer of 1988 many felt that the unusual temperature was related to the greenhouse effect. In fact there is little evidence this is the case.
132. "Shake or Bake," *The New Republic* (September 12, 1988), p. 5.
133. Eaton, "Congress Urged to Fight Global Warming," p. 41.
134. Christopher Flavin, "The Heat Is On," *World Watch*, 1 (6) (November/December 1988), p. 19.
135. Embler et al., "Social Economic Implications," p. 57.
136. "Notes and Comment," *The New Yorker* (August 29, 1988), p. 17.
137. Ibid., p. 18.
138. Ibid.
139. "35 Nation Conference Addresses Global Warming," *New York Times*, November 13, 1988, Pt. 1, p. 11.

chapter 6

Water Pollution

The earth has no shortage of water. Seventy-one percent of the world's surface is covered with it, and total annual global precipitation is estimated at around 126,000 cubic miles. However, 97 percent of the earth's water is in the form of salt water and of the 3 percent remaining freshwater only, 0.003 percent is available as freshwater for human use.[1]

In this chapter we explore the paradox of environmental water policy. We start with a discussion of types of pollution. Then we examine the health impacts of water pollution, laws and regulations governing water pollution policy, and summarize the particular problems of ocean pollution.

Water moves through a cycle, falling to earth and returning to the atmosphere. It falls to the earth in the form of rain or snow. On earth, most water percolates into the soil where it remains or moves into rivers, lakes, and eventually the ocean. Some water is held by plants, which eventually release the water back into the atmosphere through a process called evapotranspiration. Other waters at the surface, in rivers, lakes, or in the seas, evaporate into the atmosphere to complete the water cycle.

In the United States, roughly 75 percent of freshwater comes from surface sources; the balance originates from the ground. Groundwater, that water stored in underground reservoirs called aquifers, is the primary source of water for major sections of the arid western United States as well as large sections of northern and central Africa and other areas throughout the world. Since groundwater usually moves underground very slowly, it can take many years for water withdrawn to be naturally replenished and, as we see later, once polluted can be very costly to clean.

The source of water, surface or groundwater, and the way water is used is a function of the economy, level of development, and type of water resources available in an area. In more developed countries, large amounts of water are used for electric cooling and industry. For example, 38 percent of all water used in the United States is used for electrical cooling, whereas only 3 percent of the water used in India is used for that purpose.[2] Generally the less developed countries use more than 80 percent of their water for agriculture. Developed countries are also more intensive users of water for domestic purposes. In the United States per capita consumption of freshwater for domestic purposes is around 90 gallons (340 liters) a day. This is 15 to 20 times the amount of water used by people in the less developed countries for domestic purposes. It is estimated that between 30 and 50 percent of the water used in the United States is wasted unnecessarily.[3]

More than 2 billion people in the world, or approximately 86 percent of the world's rural population, do not have an adequate supply of clean water. Ninety-two percent of those living in rural areas lack facilities for proper disposal of human waste. The World Health Organization has estimated that it would cost $22 billion per year in capital investments to provide minimal sanitary disposal and freshwater needs. That is $10 billion more per year than the Third World now spends on water and wastewater facilities.[4]

In the United States many areas, most notably in the West, either are or will soon be suffering from water shortages; many others throughout the country are already experiencing serious water contamination problems.

SOURCES

When examining water pollution, the types of pollution are usually divided into point and nonpoint sources. Point sources of pollution are those that originate from some specific location such as a pipe, a sewer, or a ditch. Common point sources of water pollution would include factories, some sewage treatment plants, landfills, hazardous waste sites, and leakage from gasoline storage tanks. Common nonpoint sources of water pollution include runoff from irrigation containing salts and residue from pesticides, runoff from animal feedlots, salts from the salting of winter roads, and storm runoff from the streets of urban areas.

Until the late 1980s, the nation's water pollution abatement efforts focused on reducing pollution from point sources, primarily industrial and municipal sewage plants. An EPA administrator noted that the marked decline in point source pollution can be attributed to the $58 billion spent over the last 20 years to improve municipal sewage treatment plants.[5] The major problem areas in water pollution, however, according to most analysts, are nonpoint source pollution, particularly urban runoff and groundwater pollution. We examine both nonpoint and groundwater pollution in some detail later.

In some areas, such as Lake Erie and the Willamette River in Oregon, water pollution has improved considerably since the 1960s. Overall, however, water pollution is still a very serious problem in the United States. The EPA's 1991 Water Quality Inventory found that one-third of all surface waters do not meet water quality standards. Certain toxic metals such as arsenic, cadmium, and mercury as well as other contaminants including chlorides and nitrates are increasingly sources of pollution of surface waters in many areas.[6]

A major problem area in the United States, particularly in surface water pollution, is municipal wastewater. Many municipal wastewater treatment plants do not meet the standards established in 1972 in the Clean Water Act. Wastewaters are treated in accordance with one of three levels of purity. Primary treatment basically removes whatever floats to the top or sinks to the bottom of collected wastewater. Primary sewage treatment removes about 60 percent of suspended solids, 20 percent of nitrogen compounds, 30 percent of oxygen-demanding waste, and few, if any, chemical pollutants.[7] Secondary treatment aerates sewage that has received primary treatment, causing a biological process that neutralizes and allows the removal of additional pollutants. Secondary treatment removes up to 90 percent of oxygen-demanding waste, an additional 30 percent of suspended solids, as well as an additional 30 percent of nitrogen compounds, 30 percent of most toxic metal compounds, and most synthetic organic chemicals.[8] Tertiary treatment further treats sewage that has been through the secondary treatment method by additional chemical and physical processes, which, depending on the process and the pollutant, can bring water close to or in excess of drinking water standards. Tertiary treatment plants are four times as expensive to operate as secondary plants and twice as expensive to build. Hence tertiary treatment is used only when absolutely necessary. For example, in the community of Truckee, California, treated wastewater percolates into the ground and ultimately finds its way into the Truckee River and the water supply system for the city of Reno, Nevada. Tertiary treatment in Truckee is the only way to ensure the purity of Reno's water supply.

The Clean Water Act amendments in 1972 required that all municipal sewage treatment plants treat their sewage at the secondary level by 1977, with some extensions up to 1983. However, many municipal wastewater treatment plants have failed to meet these requirements and continue discharging wastewater that has only received primary treatment.

When asked why their surface water sources did not support designated uses, 19 state water officials identified municipal wastewater as the first reason, and officials representing 20 additional states ranked municipal wastewater as the second most important reason. Nonpoint sources of water pollution tied municipal wastewater as the primary cause of water pollution.[9]

Nonpoint Sources of Pollution

In the control on nonpoint sources of water pollution as well as groundwater, current laws have either been nonexistent or ineffectual. Nonpoint water pollution requires regulation of the land and its uses, specifically by the state and local governments. While Congress directed states to address the issue in 1985—particularly coastal states—most have yet to do so. A notable exception is the state of Nebraska, which has established 23 special districts around watershed boundaries that are authorized to tax and enforce controls if necessary.[10]

Agricultural runoff is the most widespread source of nonpoint water pollution. The U.S. Fish and Wildlife Service and the EPA found that nonpoint agricultural water pollution was primarily responsible for adverse impacts on fish communities in 30 percent of the nation's lakes and rivers. In 60 percent of all states, state water officials identified agriculture as the most common source of water pollution.[11] Dibromochloropropane (DBCP), for example, is a pesticide that was banned by the EPA in 1979 but continues to be found in municipal wells in rural areas. The city of Fresno was forced to close 25 of its wells that exceeded the DBCP standard and its plans over 70 filtering systems to address the problem—at an estimated cost of up to $1 million each.[12] In some areas, blatant violations from farming are treated as "point sources" under regulations normally designed for industrial and sewage plants.

Nonpoint water pollution from urban storm water is second to agricultural runoff as a source of water pollution. In many ways, urban runoff is more serious than agricultural water pollution primarily because the latter consists in large part of sediments whereas urban storm runoff contains many and diverse toxic substances as well as salts and oils. Urban runoff from streets, parking lots, and construction sites is estimated to affect 5 to 15 percent of surface waters and typically elevates temperatures (thermal pollution) in nearby streams, lakes, and reservoirs. Other nonpoint sources include projects such as dams that alter water flow patterns and sediment deposits; abandoned mines with their high acid concentrations and wastes; timber cutting and the soil erosion it encourages as well as debris from the logging roads that end up in nearby waters; construction of highways and other land development projects; and land disposal of wastes, including leaking septic tanks.[13]

Groundwater Pollution

Roughly half of the U.S. population relies on groundwater for drinking water, and in some areas groundwater provides close to or all of the domestic water supply.[14] Threats to groundwater quality come from a variety of sources including hazardous waste sites, landfills, wastewater disposal sites, leaking gasoline storage tanks, runoff from irrigation, salts from the salting of winter roads, seepage from septic tanks, and, on occasion, cemeteries. 20 percent of all public water systems relying on groundwater and 30 percent of such systems in urban areas show trace levels of man-made contaminants.[15]

EPA studies have found that synthetic organic chemicals have contaminated 45 percent of the larger public water systems in the United States served by groundwater sources. The EPA estimates that contaminated aquifers in urban areas affect between 5 million and 10 million people—and many feel these estimates are conservative. Rural households that rely on wells, which are not required to undergo any kind of testing, were found to have violated at least one of the federal health standards for drinking water in two-thirds of the households surveyed.[16]

Serious as existing groundwater pollution problems may be, the future promises to be worse. In 1986 the EPA identified 24,269 abandoned hazardous waste sites in the United States that have either caused or have the potential to cause contamination of drinking water sources. In addition, there are over 15,000 municipal landfills receiving hazardous and nonhazardous wastes that were both unlined and located near or above aquifers. Since groundwater moves slowly underground, it can take decades or centuries for water to be replenished. Groundwater pollution, consequently, may go undetected for years. That is why the number of hazardous wastes sites that have been abandoned and the number of municipal landfills that are unlined and continue to be used suggest a frightening prospect for water quality in the future. A study in Arizona, for example, a state heavily dependent on groundwater which in the past was lax in its regulation of the disposal of hazardous waste, identified 1,538 waste impoundment sites in the state. In examining these sites, the state of Arizona summarized what it termed "the average" surface impoundment and concluded that such an impoundment had a "strong potential to contaminate groundwater." The state described an average typical Arizona surface impoundment as

> unlined, and its purpose is to dispose of an unknown quantity of waste which is more hazardous to health than untreated sewage. Since the impoundment has no artificial barrier to prevent infiltration, the infiltration rate is controlled only by the vadose zone. It is located over . . . a high yielding aquifer that is used as a drinking water source with at least one well located within one mile of the impoundment . . . there is no groundwater monitoring at or near the impoundment to detect changes in groundwater chemical quality. . . .[17]

Although the numbers and the significance of pollution varies from region to region, the surface impoundment just described could be found anywhere in the United States.

Health Effects Of Water Pollution

The health effects of chemicals that are commonly found in drinking water are numerous and frightening. Cancer, liver, kidney, and nervous system damage, sterility in males, genetic mutations, fetal damage, and infant death are among the effects associated with consuming chemicals that are commonly found in drinking water.[18] These are the consequences of the chemicals that we know about and have some idea of how they impact the human body. However, only a fraction of the chemicals found in groundwater are routinely tested or covered by federal water quality standards. Most people have no idea what is in their drinking water or what effect it will have on their health and, remarkably, often neither do government officials. In some communities, public attention to the risks of the water supply system has led to the widespread use of bottled water. For example, in the city of San Jose, California, more than half the residents in some areas either buy bottled water or have installed home purification systems.[19]

Even for those substances for which U.S. drinking water quality standards have been established, the determination of acceptable exposure levels can be as much an art as a science. Problems of risk analysis and scientific uncertainty make establishing safe exposure levels to chemicals problematic. The effectiveness of any drinking water standard, however, depends on the strength and effectiveness of water pollution laws and the feasibility to purify water to meet standards for consumption.

WATER LAW AND REGULATION

Although active federal involvement in water pollution control can be traced as far back as the late 1960s and early 1970s, Congress addressed the issue of water pollution control much earlier. In 1886 Congress passed the first bill forbidding the discharge of anything that would impede navigation in New York harbor. Then, in 1889 Congress passed the Rivers and Harbor Act prohibiting such discharges into all navigable waters. In 1899 the Federal Refuse Act prohibited the discharge of "waste matter of any kind or description whatever" into a body of water without a permit from the Army Corp of Engineers.[20] From 1899 until passage of the Clean Water Act in 1972, 415 permits were issued by the Army Corp of Engineers under the Federal Refuse Act. Half of these permits expired and were never renewed; in 22 states *no* permits were ever issued.[21]

A variety of federal water pollution control acts were passed prior to the 1970s. Major federal laws impacting water pollution were passed in 1912, 1924, 1948, 1956, 1961, and 1966. Although all these laws increased the federal role in water pollution control somewhat, they left the design and implementation of water pollution control programs to state and local governments.[22]

The fragmentation and decentralization that characterizes environmental policy generally is quite pronounced in water policy. Although the federal role in water pollution control has expanded significantly, states and localities still have primary responsibility for implementation of water pollution policy. At least 27 federal agencies are involved in some capacity in water policy. There are over 59,000 water supply utilities as well as thousands of state and local governments and water districts, improvement districts, and other special districts involved in some capacity in water quality and supply delivery.[23]

The three major laws regulating water pollution in the United States are the Resource Conservation and Recovery Act (RCRA), the Clean Water Act (CWA), and the Safe Drinking Water Act (SDWA). The RCRA, although important in water pollution control, is dealt with in more detail in Chapter 8 on hazardous waste, the main concern of that act.

Clean Water Act   Under the Clean Water Act, any discharge of a pollutant from a point source is only allowed pursuant to a permit issued by the EPA or by a state agency after EPA approval of a state plan.[24] The CWA defines "point source" to mean

[A]ny discernable, confined and discreet conveyance, including but not limited to any pipe, ditch, channel, tunnel, conduit, well, discrete fissure, container, rolling stock, concentrated animal feeding operation, or vessel or floating craft from which pollutants are or may be discharged.[25]

Permits to pollute are issued under the Clean Water Act's National Pollution Discharge Elimination System (NPDES). Although more than 66,000 permits have been issued, the system has not lived up to its early promise. Budget cuts in the EPA, as well as in state environmental agencies, have forced officials to rely on industry for information necessary in establishing allowable discharges under the permit system. In addition, poor staffing has resulted in haphazard enforcement—pollution control agencies being forced to take action against the most visible permit violators while many other violators go undetected—and has led, particularly since the early 1980s, to the negotiated settlement with polluters that continue to violate their NPDES permits.

The Bethlehem Steel Sparrow's Point Plant on Chesapeake Bay provides an illustration of some of the problems with enforcement of the CWA. Between 1978 and 1983 Bethlehem Steel violated federal and state wastewater laws more than 700 times by pumping more pollutants into the Chesapeake Bay than its discharge permit allowed.[26] It is estimated that total discharges in excess of permit limits between 1979 and 1983 exceeded permit limitations in the amount of 4,500 tons. Daily discharges contained 11,860 pounds of oil and grease; 51,900 pounds of unspecified solids; 1,230 pounds of iron; and 990 pounds of zinc as well as other compounds.[27] Bethlehem Steel was able to circumvent the intent of the CWA by negotiating for implementation delays and using the courts to delay compliance. Furthermore, the numerous government agencies involved in the process added to the delay and confusion in efforts to seek compliance.

According to the National Resources Defense Council, "Bethlehem's flagrant violation of the law is not an isolated case. Violations are widespread and enforcement has been lax nationwide."[28] The U.S. General Accounting Office (GAO) issued a report in 1983 that substantially agreed with the National Resources Defense Council's position.[29] Since the GAO's study, EPA enforcement and federal laws have not changed significantly, hence it is reasonable to conclude the rate of compliance by industry with their NPDES permits has not changed either.

The Clean Water Act (CWA), which on the surface provides mechanisms necessary to protect the nation's water, has not done so due to difficulty in enforcement. The NRDC reports, "[T]he reason is that the law's case by case application and its reliance on self-monitoring make it highly flexible, especially in the absence of aggressive enforcement. . . . [A]t this point, the punch has been so thoroughly baked out of the Clean Water Act's Enforcement Program that goals the legislature once considered basic had been made to appear unattainable."[30]

Industry is not the only source, or even the major source, of water pollution in the United States today. The CWA required municipal wastewater treatment plants to provide secondary treatment by 1977 with extensions to 1983. Through its construction grant program, over $45 billion has been distributed to municipalities for upgrading wastewater treatment plants. Initially, the federal government paid 75 percent of the cost of building these plants. In 1981 this was reduced to 55 percent, and in 1987 the program was converted from a grant to a loan program. As of 1991 the full cost of sewage treatment construction is paid by local governments. While the federal government was generous by initially providing 75 percent of building costs for the CWA construction grant program, no money was provided for operation and maintenance. This led to the result, in the words of Helen Ingram and Dean Mann, that "[C]ities have built Cadillac projects without the funds or technically qualified operators to maintain them, and some plants operate substantially below design capacity."[31]

In 1989 the EPA estimated that over two-thirds of the nation's 15,600 wastewater treatment plants have "documented water quality or public health problems."[32] The bill for cleaning up the nation's waters will be enormous. According to the estimates by the Conservation Foundation, from 1972 until the mid-1980s government, business, and industry spent over $300 billion on water pollution control.[33] And even though between 60 and 70 percent of state and local spending for environmental programs is devoted to water pollution control, the future costs, particularly if storm waters are included, will be astronomical.[34]

In 1989 the EPA estimated the cost of bringing municipal wastewater treatment plants up to secondary treatment levels would be at least $83.5 billion.[35] Many municipalities, particularly large urban areas, have suffered from eroding tax bases as people and industry move to the suburbs leaving behind a deteriorating infrastructure and high social service costs. These municipalities, and they include parts of nearly every major metropolitan area in the United States, will be hard-pressed to find the funds necessary for improved municipal wastewater treatment.

Nonpoint sources of pollution are, for the most part, regulated by the states. Originally the CWA did not specifically address municipal runoff and storm water problems—two major sources of nonpoint water pollution.

Using the definition of point source in the CWA, the EPA found that "these definitions combine to drag storm water runoff into the permit program. There are pollutants and storm water. Storm water systems, curbs and parking lot burms all qualify as point sources."[36] The CWA amendments of 1987 limited this interpretation somewhat by not requiring permits for discharges composed entirely of storm water unless (1) a permit had already been issued; (2) a discharge was associated with an industrial activity; or (3) if the discharge was from a municipal storm sewer system serving a population of over 100,000.[37] If these provisions are vigorously enforced, a proposition that we explore in greater detail in the next section, the cost for local governments will run into the billions and billions of dollars.

The Reagan administration was hostile toward federal water pollution control regulations. Reagan vetoed the reauthorization of the Clean Water Act in 1986, arguing that water pollution regulations damaged the economy and gave too much control to the federal government. Reagan's veto was overridden by Congress early the next year. Contrary to the Reagan administration's position, many in the most polluting industries have supported the CWA. For example, in response to President Reagan's veto, a number of oil industry officials expressed disappointment. One official was quoted as saying, "[F]rom the standpoint of the programmatic part of the bill, it was a reasonable compromise among all the forces that play. It's the best we could have expected."[38]

Safe Drinking Water Act The Safe Drinking Water Act (SDWA) regulates drinking water produced by public water supply systems. Initially the 1974 act required the monitoring of and regulation of 22 different water contaminants. SDWA amendments in 1986 added 83 additional contaminants to those covered by the act as of 1991 and required public water systems to conduct a monitoring program for a variety of unregulated contaminants. An additional 25 contaminants are required to be added every three years. EPA regulations developed pursuant to the SDWA further specified criteria under which public water systems relying on surface water must install filtration equipment. Twenty of the nation's largest cities, including New York and Seattle, utilize some surface water supply systems that are unfiltered.[39]

Enforcement under the SDWA, as in the CWA, is a major problem. Recently, an important enforcement component of the SDWA and the Clean Water Act has been enacted which provides that citizens may bring suit to force compliance. Citizen suits allow any interested party to sue the polluter or even the EPA for failure to enforce the CWA. Although nearly every environmental statute passed or amended during the 1970s contains citizen suit provisions, most citizen suit activity has been focused on forcing compliance on polluters under the Clean Water Act.[40] In an effort to supplement enforcement efforts of the EPA, the CWA authorizes citizens to bring the action against persons or companies who are ". . . alleged to be in violation . . ." of their discharge permits.[41] Citizen suits are important for the opportunity they allow the average citizen to influence the implementation of environmental policy.

After a citizen suit is filed, the EPA has the option to enforce the CWA, or whatever other environmental regulation is in question, thereby ending the issue. Should the EPA not act, citizens have several remedies available, including seeking injunctive relief, which means the polluter is ordered by the court to do a specific act, like shut down operations until it can comply with permit limitations and/or seek civil penalties in the form of monetary damages.

One incentive a citizen or citizen group has to proceed with a citizen suit is that the CWA provides for an award for reasonable attorney fees and expert witness fees.[42] In an article addressed to municipal wastewater managers, a former EPA official wrote, "[T]he Clean Water Act allows citizens suits. In recent years, there has been a large increase in citizen suit activity. They have been very successful and they have talked about changing their focus from industry to municipalities."[43] In essence, if municipalities do not comply with the CWA, then the EPA would be forced, through citizen suits, into seeking compliance from them.

It is important in understanding any of these acts to keep in mind the fragmented nature of water pollution control in the United States and the governmental overlap that exists in the implementation of water pollution policy. For example, water that comes in contact with hazardous waste, regulated under the RCRA, may find its way into a municipal wastewater treatment plant regulated by the CWA, which after treatment is discharged into a river and picked up by another municipality for drinking water, hence then subject to the requirements of the SDWA. As an EPA official responsible for monitoring water quality said, "[T]here's lots of overlaps . . . different statutes have different deadlines. It's hard to coordinate our regulatory program."[44] In other instances the needed overlap is missing, such as the case of indoor radon gas, 1 to 5 percent of which is attributed to water in basements. The proposed drinking water standard for radon would only result in a 1 percent reduction in indoor air levels despite the extensive costs to achieve it. Meanwhile, no air pollution regulations address radon gas.[45]

Criticisms of Water Pollution Policy

Water pollution policy problems are both political and technical in nature. A criticism often leveled at water pollution policy, which is due to both political and technical concerns, is that we do not know the extent of the impact on humans of chemicals that find their way into our water supplies. Over 66,000 chemicals have been introduced in the environment since 1945, and only a few of these have been examined to determine their adverse health effects. As we have seen, the Safe Drinking Water Act only regulates 105 contaminants. Part of the problem, as former EPA official Arnold Kuzmack explained, is that, "[I]n many cases, there's not adequate toxicological data to determine the potential dangers of specific contaminants."[46] Even, however, when the potential dangers of the contaminant are known, they are not always regulated. For example, trichloroethylene (TCE) is a commonly used industrial solvent, which when ingested in humans can cause, among other problems, kidney damage. The EPA believes there is no safe level of exposure to TCE. Yet there are no *federal* rules prohibiting the consumption of water containing TCE, and in some communities, for example, Southern California and Nassau County, New York, TCE has been found in amounts far in excess of what the EPA *suggests* should be a maximum exposure level.[47] In addition, TCE was detected in one-half of the wells tested in the San Fernando Valley; one-quarter of the wells in the San Gabriel Valley, with 10 percent exceeding state levels, and 1 percent targeted for Superfund cleanup; 19 Superfund-targeted sites in Santa Clara County's "silicon valley" from underground storage tanks; municipal wells in the city of Burbank, all of which were forced to close; and in San Bernandino wells with levels of 3 ppb to 150 ppb (California's maximum contaminant level is set at 5 ppb).[48]

The solution, on the individual level, would seem to be to drink only bottle water. Bottle water, however, is subject to the same regulations, or lack thereof, as tap water and hence may or may not provide the desired level of protection.

A second criticism of water pollution policy concerns the role of state governments in pollution control, administration, and financing. When the Clean Water Act was debated in Congress in 1971, New York, California, as well as other states, and the Nixon administration, argued that the legislation vested too much power in the federal government.[49] Typically, state governments do not object to administering new programs, provided they are given the funds necessary for implementation with an appropriate amount of local discretion. In the case of water pollution policy, local discretion has always been limited, and, with changes in the construction grant program for municipal wastewater treatment plants, the so-called carrot of federal funding has disappeared as well. In a report issued by the Council of State Governments on state water quality planning, the authors noted "in adopting what has proven to be an unrealistic timetable for the National Clean Water's Program, the Congress seriously overestimated both federal and state technical, institutional and environmental management capacity. However, at least in the view of the states, the most serious flaw in the national strategy was the dominant role given the federal establishment."[50]

In the area of groundwater protection, the states have always had, and continue to have, primary responsibility for water pollution control. The Safe Drinking Water Act of 1986 required states to identify "well head protection areas" or areas around groundwater sources that could lead to the contamination of groundwater. States are required first to identify well head protection areas and then propose a program to keep contamination of surface areas around groundwater from polluting waters that are used for drinking purposes. As one commentator noted, "[The] states will have enormous discretion in determining what is an adequate program [under the statute]."[51] The EPA also has the authority to designate an area as a "sole-source aquifer" in areas where the population is dependent on one aquifer for its drinking water. After being so designated, the EPA may act to refuse funding for any federal program that threatens water quality, such as a dam or a highway, over or near the aquifer. This is authority the EPA has rarely exercised.

Ocean Pollution

For most of our history, the oceans have been considered a vast dumping ground that could receive our wastes with little or no apparent impact. With over 70 percent of the world's surface covered by the oceans, their assimilative capacity seems to be boundless. We have now come to recognize the ocean's limitations.

Ocean pollution is a problem worldwide. Japan's Inland Sea suffers some 200 red tides (poisonous blooms of algae) annually. One red tide in 1987 alone killed more than a million yellowtail tuna. Coastal areas from Mexico's Yucatán Peninsula to the islands of Hawaii are littered with plastics that have been dumped from ocean-crossing ships or deposited, as municipal waste, in the seas. The entryway to Rio de Janeiro, Guanabara Bay, as well as bays in estuaries worldwide including the Chesapeake and several areas along the Gulf of Mexico, suffer from sewage and industrial pollution entering the oceans via river systems.[52] An oil spill in Saudi Arabia damaged 375 miles of beaches and was not cleaned up. It is estimated it will require 40 years for the oil to wash away.[53]

There are many sources of ocean pollution. Wastewater from municipal treatment plants, municipal sludge, agricultural runoff, and oil are all major contributors to ocean pollution. In the United States, various urban areas including Los Angeles, New York, and Boston dispose of their municipal wastewater sludge in the ocean. Between 1977 and 1983, the amount of municipal wastewater sludge deposited in the oceans off the coast of United States increased by 60 percent.[54] Nonpoint sources of pollution including agricultural runoff, storm water runoff, and other types of urban runoff find their ways into surface water sources and eventually end up in the ocean. In addition, oil from the cleaning and unloading and loading of oil tankers, and accidents and blowouts of oil tankers contribute significant amounts of oil pollution to the ocean. Millions of tons of crude and refined oil is discharged annually, intentionally or accidentally, into the world's oceans from various sources. This oil kills hundreds of thousands of marine birds and mammals each year. In the North Sea and North Atlantic regions alone "it is estimated that . . . between 150,000 and 450,000 marine birds are killed each year by chronic oil pollution, mostly from routine tanker releases."[55]

One of the most serious and startling ocean pollution problems worldwide is pollution from nonbiodegradable plastics. Beverage containers, the plastic rings that hold together cans of soda, fishing nets, and other sources of plastic trash kill over 2 million seabirds and an excess of 100,000 marine mammals, including whales, seals, and dolphins, every year.[56]

In the United States, much of the near coastal ocean pollution could be prevented by the implementation of the Clean Water Act. As we have seen, for both political and financial reasons, the CWA does not live up to expectations. Near local coastal zones have suffered as a result. Globally, the problem is much more difficult to address. Pollution that occurs on the high seas is an example of a common pool environmental management problem. The effects of international ocean pollution are clear, and solutions are not difficult to understand. Given the common pool nature of the problem in international waters, it is likely that ocean pollution will be with us for some time to come. The inability of government to deal with international ocean pollution is an example of the environmental policy paradox. The paradox is also present in U.S. water pollution policy.

The Paradox in Water Pollution Policy

In the areas where the primary water problem is one of sufficient quantities of water, a water policy paradox becomes apparent where, in most instances, simple conservation measures would assure adequate supplies. Yet water conservation is not the norm. The managers of most water distribution systems, in the United States as well as elsewhere in the world, do not charge for water itself but rather charge for storing, transporting, and treating the water.[57] As a result, water is often quite inexpensive to the consumer. The simplest conservation method both for domestic and agricultural use is to raise costs. Researchers in Israel, Canada, Great Britain, and the United States have found that domestic water use drops by from 3 to 7 percent when prices increase 10 percent.[58] Furthermore, the true cost of developing water is often hidden and not reflected in the cost of water. In the United States municipalities often subsidize their water delivery systems through general taxes. Farmers, notably in the western United States, have water that is heavily subsidized by the federal government. For example, the U.S. Bureau of Reclamation supplies water to Arizona farmers for as little as $8 an "acre foot" (about 325,000 gallons), but municipalities developing water for distribution to residents in Arizona often find their cost to be in excess of $300 per acre foot. Agricultural subsidies of large western water projects are possible in part because the cost of developing the projects are spread across the nation as a whole. For example, a study of the Central Arizona Project by the Congressional Research Service found that the cost of the project would be about twice any anticipated benefits to the nation.[59] In another case, the Garrison Diversion Project in North Dakota, one analyst found that with a projected cost of more than $1 billion, "[I]ts most expensive feature is $674 million for irrigation of about 400 farms totalling 131,000 acres. That works out to an investment of about $1.7 million per farm compared with average annual net benefits per farm of only $23,597."[60] Due to federal budget constraints, the era of large federal water projects has likely come to an end. Existing contracts, however, ensure the federal subsidy for agricultural water in the West well into the future.

The situation in the United States is not unique. As one author concluded after an evaluation of global water supply and distribution, "Agencies often set water prices according to political expediency rather than in the cost of supplying it."[61]

Although manipulating cost is the easiest means of promoting conservation, few communities, as we noted, charge the full or true cost of water consumed. Some communities, such as Sacramento and Fresno, California, do not even meter water. Not metering water can lead to very wasteful water usage. A study in Boulder, Colorado, found that metering water caused water use for watering lawns to reduce by about half.[62]

The technology for increased water conservation is currently available. Flow reduction devices in showers, water-saving faucets and appliances as well as other means are available and are currently in use in water-short areas. Toilets that typically use 5 gallons with every flush can be built to only use 1.6 gallons or less.[63]

Agricultural conservation of water is also technologically feasible, although expensive. Drip irrigation, where water flows through a pipe directly to a plant's roots, can deliver over 90 percent of the water used directly to the plant. Center-pivot irrigation systems, which are large sprinkler systems that rotate in a circle, can deliver water with a 70 percent efficiency rate, that is, with 70 percent of the water being used by the plant. Flood irrigation, which is used widely throughout the less developed world as well as throughout the United States, even in the arid West, can waste an average of 70 percent of the water developed with the plant using 30 percent of the water supplied.[64]

The paradox, then, in water policy in terms of water scarcity is why conservation measures are not being practiced if they logically would work. Part of the answer has to do with artificially low pricing, which, for political reasons, is not likely to change in the near future. For example, when serious shortage situations are reached in the future, prices will increase for municipal users but not, ironically, for many agricultural users who are the largest users of water (because of federal subsidies to agriculture).

What is often referred to as a water supply problem is often, in fact, a water distribution problem. Existing contracts, accepted uses, and support for farming and the political clout farmers enjoy in the policy-making process often protect existing uses and limit possible incentives for conservation.

Groundwater use provides a good example of the environmental policy paradox and the politics that creates the paradox. Agriculture that relies on groundwater has often pumped the water at rates that exceed natural recharge. This practice is known as groundwater mining, and assures the resource will be depleted. Groundwater mining has already led to an end of irrigated agriculture in large parts of northern Texas and Oklahoma. If current practices continue, the loss of irrigated agriculture due to groundwater mining could result in serious disruptions in the Great Plains states. For example, it is estimated that Colorado could lose 40 percent of its wheat production by 2010.

In the United States, farmers and agricultural interests are still a potent political influence. U.S. farmers receive billions in subsidies. Although farmers enjoy an image of rugged individualism, working the land in relatively small family-owned farms, the reality has increasingly been one of agribusiness characterized by huge farm operations. The number of farms fell from 6.1 million in 1940 to 2.2 million in 1987, and at the same time the average size increased from 175 acres to 441 acres per farm.[65] Farmers are aided politically by other beneficiaries of the agricultural economy including pesticide and herbicide manufacturers, food packagers, exporters, and others. This combination of forces has allowed farmers to set their political agenda in some states and in the federal government, and assured a number of advantageous policies. These include liberal federal water rates, advantageous water rights laws, liberal regulation of pesticide use, and the ability to avoid policies that would force conservation measures designed to limit soil erosion, desertification, and the mining of groundwater basins. In each of these areas the problem is often that there is no policy in place.

Agricultural water subsidies make dubious economic sense. In California 1,000 acre feet of water is estimated to support eight farm jobs, 3,300 urban industry jobs, or 17,000 high-tech jobs.[66]

A discussion of water scarcity should also touch on questionable uses of water in urban areas. Desert cities such as Phoenix and Las Vegas maintain beautifully landscaped water-intensive golf courses and housing developments. In Las Vegas housing developments with names like Mirage, Desert Shores, and The Lakes defy the reality of a desert environment. And water is not in abundance in Las Vegas. As Bruce Babbitt, secretary of the interior, noted,

> Las Vegas is trying to take water at gunpoint from the rest of Nevada. The city's plan to tap water under the great underlying aquifer in central Nevada endangers vital water connections all over the region, perhaps even disrupting springs in Death Valley. It is the most environmentally destructive project in the history of the West.[67]

In contrast, in water quality policy a major problem is that we have good regulations which are poorly enforced. All levels of government in the United States lack the resources necessary to monitor and test water for impurities or to build the wastewater treatment plants that are necessary. Even when quality problems are obvious to all concerned, the decentralization in water management and fragmentation of water quality regulations makes solutions—even obvious solutions—difficult to come by.

For example, in 1981 TCE, or trichloroethylene, was discovered in wells serving the city of Tucson, Arizona, which prompted local remedial action. Recall the EPA believes there is no safe levels of exposure to TCE. Those involved in the Tucson situation included Hughes Aircraft Corporation, three federal agencies, the city water department, and two state agencies. Two and a half years after the discovery of the contamination, Tucson, frustrated by conflicts over determining who was responsible for well monitoring, decided to put in its own monitoring wells. Also there was some question as to which state department would administer a feasibility study, paid for with EPA funds, of the Tucson situation. When it was decided the Arizona Department of Water Resources would be responsible for the project, as Bruce Johnson, the chief hydrologist for Tucson Water states, "Then the Department of Water Resources found out that they didn't have the legal authority to contract with the EPA. The city funded the initial startup of the feasibility study while they went back to the state legislature to get the enabling act language amended for the Department of Water Resources, allowing them to contract with the EPA."[68]

One of the most frightening aspects of water pollution policy in the United States involves risk assessment. As we noted previously, trace amounts of many chemicals, whose effects on the human body we do not know, have been found in water supplies. Even with the known effects on people of some of the chemicals found in water, there has been an apparent trend among some water managers to think less in terms of risk assessment and more in terms of risk management. As Ted Smith of the Silicone Valley Toxics Coalition put it, "[T]here's a very serious effort to get people to accept contaminants in drinking water the way people have come to accept contaminants in air."[69]

Increasingly, industry and certain actors in the federal government encourage the weighing of certain levels of risk with the costs associated with cleaning the water source. For example, in 1986 the Office of Management and Budget asked the EPA to raise the maximum contaminant levels for drinking water because the costs of compliance was deemed to be too high.[70] As one author noted, "Risk management assumes that, after a certain level of effort to clean up the water, additional effort would not be worth the cost in jobs and profit."[71] Such a policy, when the effects of contaminants on your body is unknown, may be dangerous to your health.

On an individual level, water quantity problems can be addressed by decreasing consumption and use of water. A plastic bottle in your toilet tank, not bricks that can dissolve and cause other problems, will save between 3,000 and 5,000 gallons of water a year. Flow restrictors on showers and faucets can save an additional 5,000 gallons. With respect to quality problems, we present ways to test and treat waters you suspect of being contaminated by hazardous waste in the hazardous waste section of Chapter 8. For example, properly disposing of household wastes such as motor oil, cleaners, and solvents will help protect your community's water supply. Many service stations accept waste oil. For the location of disposal facilities for other toxic waste, contact your city or county department of public health or sanitation.

With respect to large polluters of water, there are citizen suit provisions in the Clean Water Act. You may not want to go to the trouble and expense of going to court to enforce a polluter to cease a discharge, but if you encounter what appears to be a source of serious water pollution, such as an obviously impure discharge into a river, contact your state or local environmental protection agency. If they will not or cannot do anything, contact one of the major environmental protection interest groups such as the Natural Resources Defense Council or the Sierra Club Legal Defense Fund.

SUMMARY

In this chapter we discussed types of pollution by source and location. In addition we examined the health impacts of water pollution, the laws and regulations governing water pollution policy, notably the Clean Water Act and the Safe Drinking Water Act, and summarized ocean pollution problems. The environmental policy paradox in water policy is, as we have seen, twofold. In international waters ocean pollution will be a problem for some time. The inability of government to deal with common pool international ocean pollution is an example of the environmental policy paradox. The paradox in water policy in terms of water scarcity is why conservation measures are not being practiced if they logically would work. Part of the answer has to do with the fact that water is cheap, artificially cheap because of government subsidies, which, for political reasons, are not likely to change in the near future.

In the next chapter we discuss the history of energy use and development and examine the pollution problems associated with different sources of energy.

NOTES

1. Peter Rogers, "Water: Not as Cheap as You'd Think," *Technology Review*, 89 (8) (Nov.-Dec., 1986), p. 32; and G. Tyler Miller, Jr., *Living in the Environment* (5th ed.) (Belmont, CA: Wadsworth, 1988), p. 208.
2. Miller, *Living in the Environment*, p. 213.
3. Ibid., pp. 213, 228.
4. Rogers, "Water," p. 41.
5. *Hydata News and Views*, 11 (4) (July 1992), p. 3. Reported by EPA Assistant Administrator for Water, LaJuana Wilcher, *Water Newsletter* 34(6).
6. Conservation Foundation, *State of the Environment: A View Towards the 90s* (Washington, DC: Conservation Foundation, 1987), p. xxv.
7. Miller, *Living in the Environment*, p. 478.
8. Ibid., p. 479.
9. Conservation Foundation, *State of the Environment*, p. 101.
10. Tom Arrandale, "The Pollution That Washes Off the Land," *Governing*, 5 (11) (August 1992), p. 69.

11. Conservation Foundation, *State of the Environment*, p. 105.
12. Sue McClurg, "Drinking Water Quality, Western Water." Published by the Water Education Foundation, Sacramento, California (July/August 1992), p. 10.
13. Robert Griffin, Jr., "Introducing NPS Water Pollution: We Can't Write Permits on Parking Lots," *EPA Journal*, 17 (5) (November/December 1991), p. 7.
14. See generally Zachary A. Smith, *Groundwater in the West* (New York: Academic Press, 1989).
15. Karen Fisher, "Rx. for Clean Water," *American City and County*, 101 (November 1986), p. 32.
16. Miller, *Living in the Environment*, p. 475.
17. Arizona, Department of Health Services, *Arizona Surface Impoundment Assessment—Draft* (December 1979), pp. i-1 and ii-2.
18. Substances known to cause cancer in humans (based primarily on tests with lab animals) which are commonly found in drinking water (and the effects on people in parentheses) include arsenic (cancer; liver, kidney, blood, and nervous system damage); cadmium (kidney damage, anemia, pulmonary problems, high blood pressure, possible fetal damage, and cancer); chromium (suspected cancer from some forms such as chromate); Lead (headaches, anemia, nerve disorders, birth defects, and cancer; metal retardation, learning disability, and partial hearing loss in children); mercury (nervous system and kidney damage; biologically amplified in food webs); nitrates (respiratory distress and possible death in infants, possible formation of carcinogenic nitrosoamines); Aldicarb (Temik) (high toxicity to nervous system); benzene (chromosomal damage, anemia, blood disorders, and leukemia); carbon tetrachloride (cancer, liver, kidney, lung, and central nervous system damage); chloroform (liver and kidney damage and suspected cancer); Dioxin (skin disorders, cancer, and genetic mutations); ethylene dibromide (EDB) (cancer and male sterility); polychlorinated biphenyls (PCBs) (liver, kidney, and pulmonary damage); trichloroethylene (TCE) (in high concentrations, liver and kidney damage, central nervous system depression, skin problems, and suspected cancer and mutations); Vinyl chloride (liver, kidney, and lung damage, pulmonary, cardiovascular, and gastrointestinal problems, cancer and suspected mutations). Adapted from Miller, *Living in the Environment*, p. 459.
19. Peter Steinhart, "Trusting Water," *Audubon*, 88 (November 1986), p. 11.
20. "Water Pollution," *New Republic*, 168 (March 27, 1971), p. 8.
21. Ibid. See also Harvey Lieber, "Water Pollution," *Current History* (July 1970), pp. 26–28.
22. Ibid.
23. Rogers, "Water," p. 33.
24. 33 U.S.C. Section 1342 (a) (b).
25. 33 U.S.C. Section 1362 (14).
26. This case study has been taken primarily from Todd Oppenheiner, "Humpty Dumpty," *The Amicus Journal* (Winter 1988), p. 14.
27. Ibid., p. 16.
28. Ibid.
29. Reported in ibid.
30. Ibid., p. 17.
31. Helen M. Ingram and Dean E. Mann, "Preserving the Clean Water Act: The Appearance of Environmental Victory," in Norman J. Vig and Michael E. Kraft (eds.), *Environmental Policy in the 1980s: Reagan's New Agenda* (Washington, DC: Congressional Quarterly Press, 1984), p. 256.
32. Douglas Jehl, "Clean Water Cost Put at $83.5 Billion," *Los Angeles Times*, February 15,1989, Pt. 1, p. 4.

33. As reported in Lyse Helsing, "Water Treatment: Solving the Second Generation of Environmental Problems," *Chemical Week*, 142 (May 18, 1988), p. 30.
34. Council on Environmental Equality, *Environmental Quality 1981* (Washington, DC: Government Printing Office, 1982), p. 308.
35. Jehl, "Clean Water," p. 4.
36. Bill Diamond, "How EPA plans to Move Ahead on Storm Water," *Nation's Cities Weekly*, 9 (December 15, 1986), p. 12.
37. 33 U.S.C. Section 1342 (p) (1) (2).
38. "Oil Officials Fear Stricter Water Act Provisions from New Congress," *Oilgram News*, 64 (218) (November 10, 1986), p. 2.
39. G. Wade Miller, John Cromwell, III, and Frank Dombrowski, "Drinking Water's New Guidelines," *The American City and County*, 101 (November 1986), p. 41.
40. Citizen suit provisions are found in the Federal Water Pollution Control Act, Section 505, 33 U.S.C. Section 1365; Clean Air Act Section 304, 42 U.S.C. Section 7604; Marine Protection, Research, and Sanctuaries Act Section 105(g), 33 U.S.C. Section 1415(g); Noise Control Act Section 12, 42 U.S.C. Section 4911; Endangered Species Act Section 11(g), 16 U.S.C. Section 1540(g); Deepwater Port Act Section 16, 33 U.S.C. Section 1515; Resource Conservation and Recovery Act Section 7002, 42 U.S.C. Section 6972; Toxic Substances Control Act Section 20, 15 U.S.C. Section 2619; Safe Drinking Water Act Section 1449, 42 U.S.C. Section 300j-8; Surface Mining Control and Reclamation Act of 1977 Section 520, 30 U.S.C. Section 1270; and Outer Continental Shelf Lands Act Section 23, 43 U.S.C. Section 1349(a).
41. 33 U.S.C. Section 1365 (a).
42. 33 U.S.C. Section 1365 (d).
43. Diamond, "How EPA Plans," p. 12.
44. Laurie A. Rich and Reginald Rhein, "How Water Is Regulated," *Chemical Week* (February 12, 1986), p. 45.
45. Sue McClurg, "Drinking Water Quality," pp. 5–6.
46. Barbara Quinn, "The Cost of Pure Water," *American City and County*, 101 (June 1986), p. 54.
47. Steinhart, "Twisting Water," 10.
48. Sue McClurg, "Drinking Water Quality," pp. 10–11.
49. "Pressure Against a Pollution Bill," *Business Week* (November 20, 1971), p. 70.
50. Council of State Governments, *State Water Quality Planning Issues* (Lexington, KY: Council of State Governments, 1982), p. 6.
51. John M. Winton et al., "Water Treatment: The State's Zero in on Groundwater Regulation," *Chemical Week*, 140 (February 11, 1987), p. 34.
52. Anastasia Toufexis, "The Dirty Seas," *Time* (August 1, 1988), p. 47.
53. *Hydata* (July 1992), p. 4, from *Water Newsletter* 34(8).
54. Conservation Foundation, *State of the Environment*, pp. 115, 415.
55. Miller, *Living in the Environment*, pp. 472–473.
56. Ibid., p. 469.
57. Rogers, "Water," p. 33.
58. Ibid., p. 40.
59. Cited in William Sander, "Shooting the Political Rapids of Western Water," *Wall Street Journal*, April 13, 1987, p. 26.
60. Ibid.
61. Rogers, "Water," p. 33.
62. Ibid., p. 40.
63. William S. Bergstrom, "Water, Profits Won't Go Down Drain of This Toilet," *The Arizona Republic*, April 30, 1989, p. E-2.
64. Rogers, "Water," p. 34–35.

65. U.S. Department of Agriculture, *Agricultural Statistics 1985–1987*, p. 372.

66. *Hydata* (July 1992), p. 5. Taken from an article by Carl Boronkay, general manager of the Metropolitan Water District of Southern California in *Focus* 2 (1992).

67 Frank Graham, Jr., "Gambling on Water, Las Vegas Raises the Stakes on Development in the West," *Audubon*, 94 (4), July-August 1992), pp. 65–69.

68. Quoted in Fisher, "Rx. for Clean Water," p. 38.

69. Steinhart, "Trusting Water," p. 11.

70. Ibid.

71. Ibid.

chapter 7

Energy

Energy makes life on earth possible. All energy, except nuclear and geothermal energy, is derived from the sun.[1] The fossil fuels the world has come to rely on were once ancient plants that depended on the sun's rays for photosynthesis. The food that plants produce is the fundamental energy source for all animals in the food chain. The sun's heat evaporates water causing rain and snow, which result in rivers that can be tapped for hydroelectric power. Uneven heating of the earth's atmosphere by the sun causes winds, another useful form of renewable energy. And the sun can be harnessed directly to produce heat and electricity using modern solar technology.

Humankind's ability to harness different forms of energy has played a large part in homo sapiens becoming the dominant species on the planet. The exploitation of fossil fuels has provided the means to support a rapidly expanding population. These fuels have also caused extensive pollution, which, as we have seen, threatens the world with catastrophic climatic changes.

Our dependence on nonrenewable fossil fuels has put us in a precarious position. Eventually fossil fuels will run out. The quality of life we will enjoy in the future is directly related to how carefully we manage our finite fossil fuels today. Energy experts are in agreement that a transition from fossil fuel dependence to renewable sources of energy is inevitable. Agreement notwithstanding, we seem, paradoxically, to be doing little to prepare for this eventuality.

In this chapter we discuss the history of energy use and development starting with fuelwood and coal. We also examine the pollution problems associated with different sources of energy. Finally, we look at the long-term implications of energy use and production and make suggestions for policy changes that will help ensure sustainable energy in the future.

The following section, history of energy development, draws heavily from the work of environmental historian Marvin Melosi. If you are interested in the history of energy use, be sure to read the extensive notes that accompany this chapter.

HISTORY OF ENERGY

When ancient humans discovered fire could be used for warmth, cooking, and heating, they adapted this form of energy to their purposes. Millions of years later, human ingenuity led to the harnessing of the wind and water to power sailing ships and to turn mills. However, fuelwood remained the most important source of energy for heating, cooking, and manufacturing in Europe and the United States until the dawn of the Industrial Revolution in the 1700s and 1800s. Huge tracts of land on continental Europe and over much of Great Britain were denuded for their fuelwood. In the lesser developed nations, fuelwood is still the primary source of energy—with similar environmental consequences.

Industrial Revolution

With the Industrial Revolution, techniques were developed for mining and transporting coal, an energy source that enabled people to undertake industrial projects which would not have been possible otherwise. The use of coke, a coal derivative, as a substitute for charcoal led to the mass production of high-quality iron and then steel. Coal was also convenient for stoking the boilers of steam locomotives and by 1880 accounted for 90 percent of locomotive fuel in the United States. In addition, coal was used to power steamboats and other machinery along with its use as a popular heating fuel.[2]

Coal utilization led to America's first major modern environmental crisis. The use of soft bituminous coal led to extensive smoke pollution in industrial cities, causing respiratory diseases, corroding marble statues, and depositing black soot on clothing, buildings, and streets. The toxic smoke compounded by overcrowded living conditions, traffic congestion, and inadequate sewage and solid waste disposal systems led to the first environmental protests and the realization that progress had its drawbacks.[3]

An alternate source of energy at this time was hydropower, which had been used since the 1800s for producing electricity.[4] But coal was the most important source of energy for industrializing the America of the 1800s, while oil was destined to become the premium fuel of the twentieth century. The petroleum industry grew rapidly after the first commercial oil rig hit black gold in Titusville, Pennsylvania, in 1859. Within a decade of the strike, oil production had increased tenfold.[5] The gigantic strikes in the Southwest and California in 1890 and 1901 transformed the nation west of the Mississippi by creating a new source of wealth. Unlike eastern oil, which was used mostly for a lubricant and illumination, this new oil was well suited for powering locomotives, steamships, and eventually automobiles. Thus it came into direct competition with coal.[6]

Oil and War

The era of oil began with World War I. The war effort was dependent on motorized transport, and oil played an essential role. In the words of Lord Nathaniel Curzon of the British War Cabinet, "The Allies floated to victory on a wave of oil."[7] The low cost of oil, well-financed and efficiently managed oil companies led by Standard Oil, and the ease of shipping gave oil an advantage over the cumbersome, financially weak, labor-intensive coal industry.[8]

After the war, the dismantling of the war bureaucracy caused confusion and a temporary shortage of oil in the United States. At the same time, overseas development of petroleum expanded significantly for the first time.

Fueled by oil and a maturing electrical industry, America experienced unprecedented prosperity after the war. Industrial output in the United States during the 1920s grew twice as fast as the population. Demand for oil more than doubled during the 1920s.[9] The temporary shortages experienced after World War I stimulated production and led to overproduction and intense competition as hundreds of producers entered the market.[10] The big producers began to recognize the dangers of indiscriminate drilling as prices and profits fell.[11]

During World War II oil was again the indispensable fuel for a successful Allied effort.[12] Access to oil and oil transport were essential strategic considerations for all warring nations. The naval vessels of all nations and 85 percent of merchant ships relied on oil for fuel.[13] The war prompted, after much controversy and delay, construction of two major transcontinental pipelines.[14]

The war demand for oil, gasoline, and lubricants for military vehicles and aircraft led to shortages in the United States and the development of synthetic fuels and synthetic rubber. The federal government, seeking to maximize production, introduced new subsidies, favorable tax provisions, and eased antitrust activity against energy companies. This general atmosphere of cooperation between the government, the military, and business would leave a legacy of economic advantages for the oil industry and establish a military-industrial complex as a major economic and political force in the nation.

Although Middle Eastern oil did not make a critical contribution to the Allied war effort, the importance of this region as an oil-producing area was recognized and firmly established during the war. The political, economic, and military interests of the United States had become clearly linked to the international oil market. The interests of American multinationals, which had exploited oil resources in Mexico, Latin America, and, to a lesser extent, the Middle East and Asia, became intimately connected and aligned with the foreign policy goals of the United States during World War II.[15]

The United States emerged from the war as the premier world power. The nation's abundant energy and material resources played a crucial role in this development. The war effort was a miracle of modern industrial achievement and fortified Americans' faith in capitalism, technology, and continued economic growth. The war utilized those resources that America would continue to be dependent on—electricity, coal, natural gas, petroleum, and its refined products; it also opened the door for the future development of nuclear power.[16]

Role of Personal Consumption

Just as the world wars had an impact on oil and energy policy in the United States, so did the development of personalized transit—the automobile. The emergence of the internal combustion driven automobile as a product for mass consumption began with Henry Ford's Model T in 1907. Before that time cars had largely been toys for the rich.[17]

The automobile industry was the most important segment of the manufacturing sector of the U.S. economy during the 1920s.[18] The automobile stimulated growth in all parts of the economy and was the major impetus to the petroleum industry in this century. And, as we have seen in other chapters, the widespread ownership of cars led to sprawling cities and suburbs and air pollution.

As people were buying cars they were also being introduced to the wonders of electricity—or more correctly, the wonders of electrical appliances and light bulbs. By the 1920s, electricity and electric appliances had become as important to the American people as the automobile. Mass communication facilitated advertising, which helped to create a mass consumer culture.

At the same time, giant utility companies came to dominate electrical generation, and the federal government gradually enlarged its role as regulator to curb abuses in the "power trust." The Security and Exchange Commission was formed in 1934 and provided with extensive authority to regulate the financing of utility holding companies and to break up monopolies formed by "tiering" one company on top of another. Utilities such as telephone companies were regarded as natural monopolies, and federal efforts were designed to protect the interests of the consumers while ensuring consistent and dependable service.

During the 1930s President Franklin Roosevelt promoted, in the face of heated opposition by private power generators, the concept of the public power ownership. Although public power holdings never approached the scale of those in the private sector, there were a few successes, notably the

Tennessee Valley Authority (TVA), a public corporation with the flexibility of a private enterprise.[19]

Some of the private purveyors of electricity also produced natural gas. Initially treated as a nuisance by early oil producers, natural gas became an important fuel in the 1930s.[20] Since the establishment of pipelines was very expensive, holding companies combined gas enterprises with electrical systems, creating new monopolies and new abuses. The Natural Gas Act of 1938 granted the Federal Power Commission (FPC) the authority to regulate the interstate flow of gas and to establish the place and pace of pipeline construction.

After World War II natural gas became an essential fuel.[21] Since 80 percent of the country's natural gas was being produced in only four states, distribution of natural gas presented problems. Under the Natural Gas Act of 1938 *intrastate* prices were determined by supply and demand and *interstate* prices were determined according to production costs. As long as there was little difference in the two there were no problems. However, in the 1970s, prices in the intrastate market rose.[22] Rising demand in the interstate market was not being accompanied by rising prices and this led to shortages. A day of reckoning was at hand as the country approached the oil "shock" of 1973.[23]

OPEC and the Oil Crises

By 1961 the Middle East had become the center of world oil production. Independents and host countries in the region were exerting increased control over their oil, and, in some instances, nationalizing oil industries. The Organization of Petroleum Exporting Countries (OPEC) was formed in 1960 largely because of dissatisfaction with price reductions by the major Western oil companies. Founding member countries were Saudi Arabia, Kuwait, Iran, and Iraq. Together they controlled 67 percent of the world's oil reserves, 38 percent of world production, and 90 percent of oil in international trade.[24]

The Yom Kippur War of 1973 provided the catalyst for OPEC's emergence as the undisputed world leader in crude oil pricing and production. When Egypt and Syria launched a surprise attack on Israel in October 1973, President Nixon fulfilled his promise to the Israeli state and airlifted weapons, tanks, and planes to its defense. The response was the Arab oil embargo of 1973. The days of cheap energy had passed.[25]

The Arab embargo lasted for six months, ending on March 18, 1974. The price increases and the shortage of fuel had shocked Americans. The past had suddenly collided with the future as the realization came that the days of cheap abundant energy were slipping away forever and with them the foundation on which industrial America had been built. America's dependence on foreign oil became painfully obvious.

Increased domestic production of oil and natural gas was not a solution—only a stop-gap measure. Oil started flowing through the Alaskan pipeline from the north slope oil fields to the port of Valdez in July 1977.

The crude created a temporary glut for California refineries and supported the illusion there was always more oil out there—all we had to do was find it. Americans failed to realize that several deposits the size of the North Sea and the Alaskan oil fields would have to be discovered each year to feed the voracious appetites of an energy-intensive society and to achieve energy independence.[26]

After the Arab oil embargo, President Nixon started "Project Independence," a program designed to decrease dependence on foreign sources of energy. Nixon emphasized the need to expand the nation's nuclear power generation, outer continental shelf development, and oil shale reserve leasing, but his message was largely unheeded. Nixon did eliminate oil import quotas in April 1973 and substituted fees, opening the door for more imports while making domestically produced oil more attractive.

Enmeshed in the Watergate scandal, the Nixon administration was unable to react effectively to the oil crisis. It engaged in crisis management by providing authority for gas rationing and maintaining price controls. Project Independence was a vague program that fell far short of its goal of eliminating America's dependence on foreign oil by 1980. In fact, by 1990 one-half of America's oil was imported.

President Ford entered office with an ambitious plan to bring about energy independence through the deregulation of oil prices. Yet politically the only way to legitimize deregulation to a skeptical public, in the face of large profits for oil companies, was the enactment of a windfall profits tax. Congress failed to pass a windfall profits tax bill; hence Ford's energy policy and oil deregulation, did not take place. Congress was likewise unable to pass legislation during the Ford administration that would have decontrolled natural gas.

The Carter administration created the Department of Energy (DOE). The DOE replaced ERDA, FPC, FEA, and the Energy Resources Council. The DOE was overwhelmed with the dual mission of formulating and implementing a national energy plan and organizing a new superagency when the Iranian revolution set off the second oil shock of the decade. Weekend and even weekday shutdowns of gas stations hit the big cities. For a time, 90 percent of New York gas stations were closed.[27] California was hit the hardest with gas lines extending for blocks. Fights broke out in lines and service station attendants were bribed as a panic psychology took hold. Shortages struck other populous states. The price of oil soared to $35 per barrel, bringing on a severe economic recession in the early 1980s. Gasoline prices approached $1 per gallon, which had been unheard of in the United States.[28]

The roller coaster energy ride was not over, however. As a result of rising prices, energy demand worldwide plummeted, which, ironically, produced an oil glut and declining prices beginning in 1982. OPEC was unable to maintain high oil prices and, as a result, the American economy benefited, bringing to an end the recession of the early 1980s.

When Ronald Reagan became president in 1980, he offered the public a panacea of "supply side" economics as a way out of the nation's economic woes. His vision was built on a faith that the productive capacity of the United States would resolve all energy crises. The potential for future shortages was dismissed, as some naively assumed the absence of a crisis meant the absence of a problem.

In August 1990 when Iraq invaded Kuwait and the United States sent troops into Saudi Arabia to prevent an invasion of that country (and to protect Western oil interests), the price of oil increased to $40 per barrel—as high as the price of oil had been during the peak of the Iranian oil crisis in 1979. President Bush responded, in part, by selling off part of the oil that was stored in the Strategic Petroleum Reserve, a 500-million-barrel supply in storage established in 1975 to protect the United States in the event of a national emergency. The sale of this oil had little, if any, impact on world oil prices.

Despite high prices during the Gulf War, after the war OPEC was unable to maintain production quotas. Production remains high, generating low prices. Cheap oil encourages unwise use of resources, a shift away from energy efficiency, and decreased domestic production.[29] U.S. dependence on oil imports is projected to increase from 41.3 percent in 1989 to 62 percent in 2010, and it is estimated OPEC will control 50 percent of the world's market share by the year 2000.[30]

Development of Nuclear Power

The development of nuclear power was thought by many to be the panacea for solving the energy crisis. Nuclear power started with the development and use of the atomic bomb during World War II.[31] As the joy over the end of the war mixed with feelings of horror at the power of the unleashed atom, astute politicians realized warfare and international relations would never be the same.

In the United States, the federal government granted itself a monopoly over nuclear power with the passage of the Atomic Energy Act in 1946. The Atomic Energy Commission (AEC) was established as well as the Joint Committee on Atomic Energy (JCAE) in Congress. The AEC was a unique federal agency. It had total control over nuclear energy development, including ownership of nuclear fuels. It was also entrusted with the sometimes conflicting role of nuclear power regulator.

The Atomic Energy Act of 1954 gave a boost to commercial production of nuclear power. Private firms would be allowed to own reactors while the government would continue to retain ownership of the nuclear fuels.

This was not sufficient incentive, however, for private enterprise to become involved in a technology with an uncertain future and huge potential liability problems in the event of an accident. In an effort to address the liability issue, Congress in 1957 passed the Price-Anderson Act, limiting the liability from a nuclear accident of an individual company, and provided governmental subsidies to cover damage above the liability limits. The Price-Anderson Amendments in 1988 raised the liability limits from $5 million per facility/per incident to $63 million per facility/per incident.[32] However, plant operators (or licensees) are not required to pay out more than $10 million in any one year in case of liability under the act.[33]

Although the Price-Anderson Act removed a major obstacle to commercial nuclear power, there were still inadequate incentives for the private sector to develop nuclear power. In 1963 Congress passed the Private Ownership of Special Nuclear Fuels Act, which would allow private ownership of nuclear materials for nonmilitary purposes. However, it was the environmental problems inherent in coal-fired plants and the great Northeast blackout of 1965 that gave an essential boost to nuclear power. It is ironic that environmental concerns helped to spawn an industry that would turn out to have environmental repercussions of frightening dimensions.[34]

The need for an alternative to polluting coal did not mean there were no organized environmental interest groups in opposition to nuclear power. In fact, the biggest threat to the vitality of the nuclear industry came from the new environmental movement, which recognized the potentially catastrophic impact of a major accident and the disposal problems of nuclear waste. Also nuclear power became associated in many minds with nuclear holocaust. The nuclear age had forced on the world the realization that humankind now had the power to destroy all life on earth.[35]

The 1973 energy crisis provided the nuclear power industry with an opportunity to promote their program as an alternative to oil and as protection from the whims of foreign oil exporting countries. By late 1974, orders for light water reactors (LWRs) reached a new peak. The market collapsed as quickly as it had risen as the demand for electricity dropped in reaction to the fivefold increase in the cost of oil.

By the late 1970s the future of nuclear power was uncertain. The energy crisis seemed over, thus eliminating one compelling reason to pursue the nuclear option, and cost overruns plagued the industry. In the late 1960s nuclear plants had cost twice what had been expected.[36] The year 1979 signaled the real decline of the nuclear power industry. That year the Three Mile Island (TMI) nuclear facility in Pennsylvania suffered a partial meltdown of one of its reactors. The accident made headlines worldwide and caused many to question the desirability of nuclear power generation.[37]

The accident at TMI was a turning point for the nuclear industry. Not a single nuclear power plant has been ordered since that fateful day, and 108 have been cancelled including all orders placed after 1974.[38] Business-oriented *Forbes* magazine has called the U.S. nuclear power program "the largest managerial disaster in United States business history," involving $100 billion in wasted investments, cost overruns, and unnecessarily high electricity costs.

Development of a National Energy Policy

From wood to coal to oil to nuclear, the history of U.S. energy development has been market driven—without any national energy policy. The Truman, Eisenhower, Kennedy, and Johnson administrations failed to develop comprehensive energy plans. The pattern was crisis management substituting for a well-thought-out long-term program. This is, of course, consistent with what we might expect, given what we know about the informal incentives that operate on policymakers. Sacrifice, interference in the market, especially when that market is very profitable to an influential economic interest group, and planning are just not things our system does well. The specter of future scarcities loomed large even then, but little was done to plan for the future. The 1967 Arab-Israeli war and the subsequent oil embargo were not regarded as serious omens of future developments. When oil crises occurred, even as late as 1990, there was no real energy policy.

The Ford administration's most significant energy achievement was the dissolution of the Atomic Energy Commission (AEC) and the creation of the Energy Research and Development Administration (ERDA), which took over the research and development of all energy forms, and the Nuclear Regulatory Commission (NRC), which assumed the AEC's regulatory function over the nuclear industry.

President Carter attempted to formulate a long-range, comprehensive energy program for the country. On April 18, 1977, Carter announced his National Energy Plan (NEP). Carter emphasized the serious nature of the energy crisis by calling it "the moral equivalent of war." The president did not belittle the situation with the usual political pep talk and empty promises of prosperity. Instead he warned Americans that ignoring the increasing scarcity of petroleum "would subject our people to an impending catastrophe."

Conservation was at the heart of Carter's message. It called for major improvements in energy efficiency for existing buildings and acceleration of the applications of solar technology. It asked for taxes and conservation incentives in information and transportation systems. It called for a reduction in average annual energy growth to less than 2 percent; reduction in natural gas consumption by 10 percent; and continued reductions in imported oil. This was a bold plan that called on Americans to make sacrifices.

Upon introduction in Congress, the NEP drew fire from all sides. Special interests attacked one of the most important parts of the bill—the Crude Oil and Equalization Tax (COET), which was designed to raise oil prices over the following three years to encourage the application of energy efficiency measures and thereby reduce demand. The revenues from the tax were to be diverted into several government programs. Without the price incentives, energy efficiency was much less likely to be recognized as an essential part of the national energy plan and its application was likely to be limited. Higher prices are necessary to spur consumers to conserve and engineers to develop better technologies.[39] The failure of the NEP to present a pricing strategy ensured only partial success of its goals.

The Natural Gas Act was one of the most controversial aspects of NEP. It eliminated the distinction between the inter- and intrastate markets with the government having a stronger, if only temporary, role.

The NEP also contained various conservation incentives, such as insulation credits, weatherization grants, energy audits, and loans for solar energy systems. It taxed gas-guzzling cars and prohibited the use of oil or gas in new electricity generation and new industrial plants and established voluntary electrical rate designs.

Members of Congress from virtually every region of the country attacked Carter's program. Northeastern representatives with constituents dependent on home heating oil, as well as westerners whose constituents used their automobile for extended travel, denounced various parts of the plan that would have increased the price of energy. The most ambitious aspects—those that would have led to the greatest energy savings—failed to pass Congress.

A major piece of legislation that passed during the Carter administration was the Public Utilities Regulatory Policies Act of 1978 (PURPA). PURPA has been best known for its requirement that utilities purchase electricity from independent power producers in order to encourage cogeneration and renewable resources for power production. Independent power producers were also exempted from state and federal regulations.

PURPA led to a number of interesting developments. First, cogeneration became a growth industry. When written, PURPA was meant to protect independent energy producers using small turbines in existing steam plants. PURPA encouraged energy production by forcing utilities to purchase energy produced as a by-product (cogenerated) of some industrial or manufacturing process. Many newer power plants, however, were much larger and devoted most of their resources into generating power rather than producing heat for the parent factory.[40]

Another unintended consequence of PURPA is exemplified by the construction of a power plant in Michigan. A nuclear power plant faced bankruptcy. To meet PURPA requirements of independence from utility company ownership, investors were gathered from among the plant builders, suppliers, and large potential private customers. Investors formed a 51 percent privately owned company that was not then subject to regulation by utility commissions. With the PURPA requirement that their electricity be purchased, bankruptcy was avoided; consumers, however, were forced to pay $1,700 per kilowatt hour for the power produced rather than the more typical rate of $600 per kilowatt hour.[41]

According to the Reagan administration, free markets would satisfy current and future energy needs as profit-motivated investors sought to reap the economic rewards promised by future energy demands. Federal government spending on research and development of alternative energy sources were cut dramatically or eliminated entirely during the Reagan years. Market forces were more pragmatic, however, and energy usage as a percentage of GNP declined as more energy efficiency measures were adopted.

On October 24, 1992, President Bush signed the Comprehensive National Energy Policy Act (CNEPA). Among a multitude of provisions,[42] CNEPA creates a director of climate protection to oversee greenhouse gas research and policymaking, foreign aid, and exploration of technology to combat global warming. CNEPA also targets a 30 percent increase in energy efficiency by 2010, a 75 percent increase in the use of renewable energy sources by 2005, and a decrease in oil consumption from 40 percent of total energy use to 35 percent by 2005.

The provisions for promoting renewable energy sources and energy efficiency are a positive change from our past mode of crisis management, market solutions, and short-term policies. Efficency standards, for example, are to be met by federal buildings and public housing. Standards will be established for lights, showers, toilets, faucets, small motors, and commercial heaters and air conditioners. The federal government will provide technical assistance with regional demonstrations of the latest technology. States are given incentives to update building codes to meet or exceed the new standards. The states will, for example, be eligible for utility grants to promote efficiency and conservation; and they have access to aid in establishing revolving funds to increase efficiency in state and local government buildings. Grants will also be available for industry to promote efficiency. Voluntary guidelines will be issued for homes along with a mortgage pilot program for energy-efficient homes and retrofitting.

There have been some criticisms of CNEPA, however. President Bush signed CNEPA in oil-producing Louisiana just before the election. Tax increases and gas mileage standards were absent from the legislation. CNEPA did include tax breaks to independent oil and gas drillers at an estimated cost of $1 billion over five years. Bush's eariler call for opening Alaska's Arctic National Wildlife Refuge for oil exploration was dropped from the final version of CNEPA.

Candidate Clinton raised hopes for environmental changes by choosing environmentalist Al Gore as his running mate. As of late 1994, however, the Clinton administration has not met environmentalists' expectations and has not developed what can be considered a comprehensive energy plan. While an additional gasoline tax of 4.3 cents a gallon was enacted into law, it was part of an economic stimulus package and is not expected to affect consumption to any siginificant degree. Similarly, President Clinton publicly endorsed fuel efficiency standards and reduction of greenhouse gas emissions early in his administration but also endorsed voluntary compliance to achieve them.

The Clinton administration appears to be taking a market-based approach to energy policy. The White House Office on Environmental

Policy (OEP) was created with an agenda to stress the economics of environmentalism, including creating jobs and new business opportunities for new technologies.[43] (See Chapter 4 for a discussion of environmental reorganization during the Clinton administration.)

NONRENEWABLE ENERGY SOURCES

Now let us examine the environmental consequences of different types of energy production. Although it all comes out of the wall socket the same way, sources of energy vary significantly in terms of their negative impacts on the environment. In the following two sections we examine the various types of energy sources used in the United States.[44]

As we have seen, America's environmental awareness grew significantly in the 1960s. Industrial expansion was causing environmental damage that could not be ignored or rationalized as the cost of progress. Fossil fuels and nonfuel by-products, such as petrochemicals, were choking America's waterways, soil, and air with toxins. Although fossil fuels are the dirtiest source of energy, in fact all energy, its exploration, production, and use, has an impact on the environment.

Coal

Of all fossil fuels, coal has the most harmful immediate and long-term effects on the environment and human health. People who lived in the industrial cities of the nineteenth century knew that coal produced annoying and debilitating smoke, but they could not comprehend the magnitude of coal's impact on the environment and the human body. Today we have scientific measurements that show the extent of the destruction. Air pollution, thermal pollution, land devastation, groundwater pollution, acidification of streams and rivers, erosion, subsidence of land caused by underground mines, hazards to miners, and, of course, global warming are all recognized as part and parcel of coal's utilization.

Coal is the most abundant fossil fuel in the United States. As petroleum and natural gas have become more expensive and scarce, coal development has accelerated.[45] Identified reserves in the United States are expected to last about 300 years at 1984 usage rates.[46] However, if all known reserves of coal were utilized, the consequences would be catastrophic for the environment by significantly contributing to global warming. Acid rain caused by coal-fired electrical generating plants has also had devastating effects on the environment. Acid rain is covered in detail in Chapter 5. Other environmental costs are associated with the mining of coal. These include loss of lives and health of miners during the extraction process, and the erosion and pollution of waterways.[47]

The Surface Mining Control and Reclamation Act of 1977 (SMCRA) could have protected valuable ecosystems from the ravages of strip mining if it had been strictly interpreted and enforced. However, legal confrontations have delayed action, and the Reagan administration cut back the federal inspection force by 70 percent, making enforcement virtually impossible.

A key provision of SMCRA is the requirement that land be reclaimed after mining operations cease. Enforcement was to include withholding of mining permits for those who did not restore past sites. In a lawsuit against the government for lack of enforcement, the court ordered the federal government to install a computer system to better track violators. The resultant $15 million "Applicant Violator System" was so flawed that half of the 660 permits in a six-month period were overturned by manual verification.[48] The Department of the Interior claims the system has been improved since its installation.

The SMCRA has had an impact, however. Even though enforcement is still spotty, some states have been much more aggressive in applying SMCRA than have others. For example, the state of Wyoming matches or exceeds SMCRA regulations for coal mining. Wyoming requires bonds up front that are returned only after revegetation is approved by the state Department of Environmental Quality (approximately a 10-year period in the arid West—if efforts succeed—as opposed to five years in the East). Reclamation costs in the West can range from $5,000 to $20,000 an acre.[49]

Demand for coal will remain strong into the foreseeable future. This is true for several reasons. First, it is projected that the use of coal to produce electricity domestically will increase; barriers to nuclear power (i.e., cost and waste disposal) make short term expansion of that source of power unlikely; worldwide demand for coal should be strong (especially in developing countries); President Clinton exempted coal exports from his Btu tax to ensure high production levels; and CNEPA promotes technological advances for "clean coal" promotion that can be exported along with the coal itself—all of which promise a bright future for coal.[50]

Oil

Oil causes many environmental problems. As we saw in Chapter 5, auto emissions contain nitrogen and sulfur oxides, carbon monoxide, hydrocarbons, ozone, nitrates, lead, and waste heat.[51] Carbon dioxide emissions contribute to the greenhouse effect. Oil also pollutes groundwater through the injection of brine solutions into aquifers.[52] All of these oil-related pollution problems are discussed elsewhere in the text. Although not as pervasive as air pollution from the burning of oil, one of the most attention-getting oil-related pollution problems is oil spills from tankers and ocean platforms.

While it was not the first major incident, the Santa Barbara oil spill in 1969 was a major environmental crisis and focused national and international attention on the devastating effects of large oil slicks. The leak released 235,000 gallons of crude from Union Oil's Well A-21 creating a slick 800 miles long.[53] Since the blowout occurred on federal lease land, Washington responded—with investigations and studies. Congress reacted by revising the Outer Continental Shelf Act to tighten regulations concerning federal leases and clarifying the responsibilities of oil producers to assume liability for any accidents. However, no amount of federal legislation can make up for industry neglect.

The Exxon Valdez oil tanker spill in 1989 reportedly occurred because of the negligence of Exxon employees. Ample federal regulatory procedures were in place to prevent such a spill, and, at least so we thought prior to the spill, to respond to and clean up after an accident. The Valdez released 10.1 to 12.6 million gallons of crude into Prince William Sound, Alaska, an area teeming with marine and bird life.[54] The largest oil spill in U.S. history spread out of control and covered 900 square miles within a week. Experts predicted that since the leak occurred in a closed body of water and there were no winds and waves to disperse the oil, particles would sink to the bottom of the bay to act as lethal time release capsules of toxic petroleum hydrocarbons, not only killing marine life but having the potential of destroying the local fishing industry.[55] For the thousands of waterfowl that use Prince William Sound as a summer nesting ground, the spill could not have come at a worse time. They returned in the summer of 1989 to find their home polluted and despoiled.

The Valdez spill provides several good examples of the paradoxical elements of environmental policy in the United States. Although what would have seemed to be adequate legislation was on the books, several things happened that theoretically should not have happened. First, the decentralized nature of the policy process was in evidence after the spill occurred. Several federal agencies as well as various Alaska state agencies were involved, but poor coordination hampered clean-up efforts. Furthermore, Congress was successful in getting the oil companies that would be shipping in Prince William Sound to give their assurances they would only sail double-hulled ships. Congress also established a fund to finance oil spills.

These actions provided the public with tangible evidence of congressional concern on an important, and popular, public policy issue. However, the clean-up fund was found to be inadequate and, due to the lack of follow-through and enforcement, double-hulled ships were not the norm in Prince William Sound.[56]

There is no doubt we can now see the bottom of the oil barrel.[57] The largest oil discoveries of the 1970s—in Alaska, the North Sea, and Mexico—have only been of moderate size. U.S. oil extraction will continue to be dominated by deposits in the Southwest (which have already been heavily exploited), the Gulf Coast states, and Alaska's North Slope.[58] In order to maintain the level of fossil-fuel-supported activity in the world today, several deposits of oil comparable in magnitude to the North Sea and Alaskan North Slope discoveries would have be found each year.[59]

Natural Gas

Natural gas is the most clean burning of any fossil fuel and relatively inexpensive. Carbon dioxide is given off as it burns but in lower amounts per unit of energy produced *when compared to other fossil fuels*. In its natural state, natural gas is easy to transport through pipelines. Natural gas may be converted to a concentrated form—liquid natural gas (LNG) for transportation by refrigerated tanker ship. Although this is an efficient means of moving natural gas, LNG is highly explosive. An explosion on board a tanker could create a massive fireball, causing fires and third-degree burns as far as 2 miles away.[60]

Geothermal Energy

One technology that has made impressive strides in recent years because of research and development (R&D) funding is geothermal power. With the possible exception of small amounts of wastewater and some unpleasant odors (when not properly controlled), geothermal energy is largely nonpolluting. In 1992 over 8 million megawatts of power were produced from geothermal sources by domestic utility companies. (Nonutility production figures are considered confidential due to the extremely competitive nature of the industry.)[61] Worldwide geothermal energy produces an estimated 1 percent of electricity produced.[62] Most geothermal resources are projected to last from 100 to 200 years.[63] Some geothermal resources such as those on the island of Hawaii in the state of Hawaii are perpetual and have the potential to supply large amounts of energy at a consistent rate.

Geothermal energy comes from the heat contained in underground rocks and fluids. About 10 percent of the world's landmass is suitable for developing this heat into usable energy. Currently there are about 20 countries that are exploiting geothermal deposits, supplying space heating for over 2 million homes in cold climates and enough electricity for 1.5 million homes.[64]

Most of the geothermal resources in the United States are located in the West. The Geysers steam field, the largest in the world,[65] located about 90 miles north of San Francisco, has been producing electricity since 1960.[66] It has been estimated that by the year 2000, this field could produce 25 percent of the state's electricity. In 1993, however, power output decreased to 1,400 megawatts out of a possible 3,000 megawatts, suggesting steam extraction at higher rates than groundwater inflow (see groundwater mining in Chapter 6).[67] The Geysers field is known as a dry steam deposit—the most rare but desirable type because of its ease of extraction. Wet steam and hot water geothermal deposits are more common but more difficult and expensive to convert to electricity.[68]

Nuclear Power

The direct environmental problems associated with nuclear power are from a nuclear meltdown, the mining and storage of nuclear fuels, and disposal of nuclear waste. The world witnessed the consequences of a nuclear meltdown in May 1986 when the Chernobyl nuclear power plant in the Russian Ukraine blew up, sending a lethal cloud of radioactivity across Europe.[69] Parts of Europe were badly contaminated and milk and other foodstuffs had to be thrown out. Sheep were quarantined in England. Reindeer were destroyed in Scandinavia. Thousands ultimately died from radiation poisoning.

Since the Three Mile Island (TMI) accident, there have been 30,000 mishaps at U.S. nuclear plants, some with the potential to have caused *more serious* disasters than that at TMI.[70] Although the potential for disaster from the production of nuclear-generated electricity is phenomenal, a realistic assessment of the true environmental costs of nuclear power must consider the entire nuclear fuel cycle from uranium mining at the "front end" of the industry to waste disposal at the "back end." These problems include radiation in mining, mine tailings or waste, and the potential for mishaps in the transportation and storage of radioactive materials. There are also potential security problems associated with the possibility that nuclear materials could find their way into the hands of terrorists.

RENEWABLE ENERGY

As we learned at the outset of this chapter, eventually all energy will be renewable energy. Finite resources, such as fossil fuels, by definition run out. After the world's first major oil shock, progress toward developing new sources of renewable energy have met with mixed success. The 1986 oil price collapse further set back renewable programs by lulling citizens, businesspeople, and politicians into a dangerous sense of complacency that was only temporarily shattered by the "Persian Gulf Crisis" brought on by the Iraqi invasion of Kuwait in August 1990.

In the United States, uneven allocation of federal subsidies favors fossil fuels and nuclear power over renewables.[71] Since development of new technologies entails certain financial risks and requires sustained research, experimentation, and demonstration projects, governments typically pay a large share of these costs, while private investment increases as the project nears commercialization. The widely fluctuating research support for renewable energy as experienced during the 1980s makes long-term programs difficult to plan and implement.[72]

Technologies with long-term potential that are in need of support by government monies include biochemical means of converting biomass feedstocks to energy, various solar thermal configurations, and systems that make use of the difference in temperature between surface and deep ocean waters. Development of an economical storage method that could stockpile electricity from solar and wind generators would be a great boon to those industries. In each case the private sector has not had adequate incentives to invest in the research and development necessary to make these sources of energy competitive with fossil fuels.[73] The 1992 CNEPA may provide some remedy. The act offers tax credits for wind and biomass energy production and generally promotes use of renewable energy sources. The real impact of CNEPA, however, is, at this writing, uncertain.

Hydropower

Historically, hydroelectric power has several advantages over other sources of power. U.S. hydroelectric power plants produce electricity cheaper than any other source. One reason for this is that most of the large dams used in generating electricity were constructed between 1930 and 1950 when costs were low. Also the resource that powers the plants—falling water—is free.[74] In addition to these benefits, hydroelectric plants last 2 to 10 times longer than nuclear and coal-fired plants.[75]

However, hydroelectric power is not without its drawbacks. The disadvantages to hydropower include the following:

- Reservoirs created by dams flood valuable forests, farmland, and sometimes uproot entire communities.
- The spawning grounds of fish, such as salmon, are often ruined by hydroelectric facilities.
- Impounding a river drastically changes the surrounding ecosystem. Instead of nutrient-bearing sediments being deposited on agricultural floodplains and providing food for fish, they build up behind dams and lessen the capacity and power output of the facility. This reduces the fertility of valuable farmlands at river mouths and decreases the amount of fish available for commerce, recreation, and survival.
- Hydroelectric dams can alter the oxygen and temperature of downstream waters, having a negative impact on aquatic species.
- In some instances, the water pressure behind large dams has triggered earthquakes, creating a severe hazard for communities downstream.
- Seepage from reservoirs can raise the water table, bringing salty deposits with it, and thereby damaging soil fertility.
- Utilities value hydroelectric plants because they can increase capacity quickly. However, this causes fluctuations in river levels and consequential disruption of aquatic life.
- Large reservoirs in tropical countries can become breeding grounds for carriers of malaria, river blindness, and schistosomiasis.

Since constructing dams on the few untouched rivers in the United States will most likely create a storm of protest, much smaller hydroelectric projects are being contemplated and constructed. Many small-scale hydro sites that were abandoned in the 1940s and 1950s because of cheap abundant fossil fuels could be made serviceable again. Small systems, where turbines are turned by the natural force of water, only have a perceptible effect on the immediate area of the hydro site.[76] Small-scale hydropower could be a benefit on a local basis, but its contribution to total U.S. hydro production would not be great.[77]

Hydropower has many advantages over coal or nuclear-generated power, since the resource is free, relatively nonpolluting, and the lifetime of the facility is longer. Hydropower produced 86,616 megawatts of electricity in 1985, far outstripping any other renewable resource.[78] According to the DOE, 1993 production levels may reach close to 300,000 megawatts in the United States alone; worldwide production in 1991 was estimated at 2,144.8

billion kilawatts.[79] However, in the United States, which has the largest installed hydroelectric capacity of any country, not one new large dam has been approved since 1976. This is due both to the lack of suitable sites and opposition from environmental groups. Any large new sources of hydroelectric power for the United States will come from Canada.[80]

Hydropower is an important source of energy in many less developed countries. In 1986 Venezuela completed the Guri Dam, the largest in the world at that time, with a generating capacity of 10,000 megawatts. Currently, the largest dam is Itaipu on the border of Brazil and Paraguay, with a capacity of 12,600 megawatts. China has just begun building an even larger one. In addition, thousands of small generators are being installed on remote rivers and streams in less developed countries. Most hydro projects larger than 1,000 megawatts are also being constructed in developing countries, since industrial countries have already tapped their most useful hydropower sites.

Dams proposed along the Danube River in Hungary and Czechoslovakia resulted in record-breaking protests by 40,000 people in Hungary and 60,000 in Slovakia.[81] Critics argued the dams would cause the flooding of communities, the loss of agricultural land, and, more importantly, the potential contamination of Europe's largest drinking water aquifer. Advocates of the projects could be found among environmentalists in nearby Austria, who hoped to use Hungary as an electric colony.[82]

Solar Power

There are several ways to take direct advantage of the perpetual and cost-free sunshine that falls on the earth. Passive solar designs capture sunlight directly within a structure and convert it to heat.[83] According to some experts, climate-sensitive passive solar cooling and natural ventilation should be able to replace air conditioning units within all but the largest buildings.

Active solar systems either collect, concentrate, or convert solar radiation into useful energy. The most basic method uses collectors to absorb relatively low-temperature heat and then transfer it to water or air. Solar hot water heaters are the most popular use for this type of solar energy exchange. The United States was the world's largest market for solar collectors in the early 1980s. However, the fall in gas and oil prices in 1986 and the elimination of the residential energy tax credit caused the bottom to fall out of the U.S. solar energy market.[84]

Somewhat more complicated are systems that concentrate the sun's energy and focus it on a central receiver to produce high temperatures for steam used to produce electricity. The Luz International Ltd. complex in California's Mojave Desert is the largest example of this type of facility. The Luz complex is the source of 90 percent of the world's electricity drawn from the sun's radiation.[85]

The third major category of solar technologies relies on the photovoltaic (PV) effect. This phenomenon causes electricity to be produced when sunlight strikes certain materials. First used to power spacecraft, the earthbound applications of this technology grew dramatically in the early 1980s.[86] Since then, the loss of tax credits, low energy prices, and slashed federal research funds led to a loss in sales in the United States while Japan took over as the world's largest solar cell producer.[87]

Half of the photovoltaics sold provide power to areas that are too remote to be hooked up to electric utility distribution lines. The communications industry accounts for a large segment of this stand-alone market. The second largest category of PV use is for consumer products such as solar calculators, solar toys, and backyard lighting systems. Widespread use of PV for producing electricity in centralized systems depends on reducing significantly the cost of producing PV cells.[88]

Although the negative environmental effects of solar technologies pale in comparison to coal and nuclear power, they do exist. Without effective controls, solar cell manufacture produces hazardous waste. Solar thermal plants require the use of large amounts of land, causing disruptions in natural ecosystems and preempting other uses.

Wind Power

Among all the renewable energy sources, none has grown as rapidly into an important industry as wind power. Since 1981, California has been the site for a boom in wind power as over a dozen companies began "farming" the wind on a massive scale.[89] Other small wind farms are catching on in other parts of the United States. Vermont, Hawaii, Oregon, Massachusetts, New York, and Montana boast small wind farm operations. Internationally, India has one of the most ambitious wind energy programs in the world. The Indian government wants to have 5,000 megawatts of wind power installed by the year 2000.

The total amount of energy in the wind has been estimated to be extremely large, ranging globally from 250 million to 2,500 million megawatts of average continuous power.[90] Even if only 1 percent of that energy was harnessed, the world could shut down all nuclear and coal-fired power plants. However, there are serious obstacles to utilizing the wind. The first is the lack of an economical means to store electricity from wind generation. Wind power also requires backup from a utility company when the wind dies down.

A second obstacle is finding suitable sites. Many feasible sites are already in use and wind turbines are precluded. Turbines in the heavily populated Northeast, along coastlines and visible mountain ranges, would cause visual pollution. Excessive noise and radio and TV interference are also problems with large turbines. In some areas, turbines would interfere with the flight pattern of migratory birds.

The cost of generating power from the wind has been brought into line with other traditional generating technologies in many markets. Costs are likely to be reduced further as Japanese firms begin to mass produce turbines.

Biomass

Biomass, the product of photosynthesis, is plant matter that acts as a versatile fuel capable of providing high-quality gaseous, liquid, and solid fuels as well as electricity. Forestry and wood products, crop residues, animal wastes, and energy crops are the most important sources of biomass-generated energy.

When assessing biomass systems, it is important to distinguish between those that convert waste products into energy, thereby increasing the efficiency of economic systems, and the type of biomass energy that requires the cultivation of special crops. The latter requires all the cost and effort involved in agriculture and/or silviculture.

Wood is by far the most widely used biomass energy source.[91] Over half the wood cut each year is burned to produce energy throughout the world.[92] Industrial uses of fuelwood are spread throughout the United States.[93] Each year the state of Virginia produces enough sawdust, logging residue, and unsalable low-quality trees to replace 42 percent of the oil and gas consumed in its industrial and commercial sectors in that state. Little of this potential has been exploited. However, as oil prices move upward, entrepreneurs are likely to take advantage of the opportunity.[94]

Crop residues can be a valuable source of energy when they are not being used for alternative purposes.[95] There are more than 70 developing countries that grow sugarcane whose residue (bagasse) can be used for power generation. Other crop residues that are and can be used extensively are rice hulls, coconut shells, cotton stalks and ginning waste, peanut and other nut hulls, fruit pits, coffee and seed hulls, and various kinds of straw and fiber. Alternative uses for these materials should be taken into account when assessing their relevance as energy sources. These materials are also useful for returning vitality to depleted soils. Robbing the land of life-giving nutrients is destructive; producing energy from a product that would be otherwise wasted is prudent and farsighted.

Some plants are grown specifically to produce energy. Fast-growing eucalyptus trees are being grown and harvested for this purpose in some parts of the world. The potential for fast-growing fuel plantations varies greatly among different countries. Use of marginal lands for this purpose makes the most sense.

The conversion of corn to ethanol is a beneficial use of biomass surpluses. Corn surpluses could replace 7 percent of the country's gasoline consumption.[96] More than 7 percent of the gasoline sold in the United States in 1987 was actually gasohol, a 1 to 9 blend of gasoline and ethanol.[97]

According to the DOE, by 1993 gasohol remained at approximately 8 percent of the nation's automobile fuel supply. Critics of ethanol, including the EPA, point to its increase in aldehyde emissions and ozone pollution without a significant decrease in imports. They attribute its passage into law to a coalition of Archer Daniels Midland (producer of 70 percent of domestic ethanol); Ralph Nader's Citizen Action; the Sierra Club; Natural Resources Defense Council; and help from corn-state senator Bob Dole.[98]

EPA's decision to endorse methyl tertiary butyl ether (MTBE) as the fuel additive of choice (rather than ethanol) was actually overturned by President Bush in October 1992.[99] Of particular concern to the Republican party was the state of Illinois, a corn state of crucial importance to Republican presidential hopefuls.[100] The Clinton campaign criticized the action, and the Clinton administration froze it and other last-minute orders from Bush.[101]

Brazil is proving that a biomass ethanol program can replace significant amounts of imported oil. In Brazil, sugarcane grown exclusively for fuel was converted into 10.5 billion liters of ethanol in 1986, providing about half of the nation's automotive fuel. The ethanol program in Brazil created about 475,000 full-time jobs in agriculture and industry and another 100,000 indirect jobs in commerce, services, and government. Cogeneration produced by the burning of bagasse powers mechanical cane crushers, produces electricity for on-site needs, and steam for alcohol distillation.

The Brazilian fuel program is not without problems, however. Runaway inflation and a large debt load has caused the Brazilian government to scale back its heavily subsidized fuel ethanol program, known as Proacool. The subsidies to the politically powerful sugar growers have allowed efficient producers to make huge profits and kept inefficient producers in business. Brazil's Institute of Technology recommends that subsidies be based on some minimum level of efficiency.[102] Furthermore, severe shortages of ethanol occurred in 1990 because of drought and higher prices on the world sugar market. Instead of being a gross exporter of ethanol, Brazil was forced to buy ethanol from the United States to alleviate this critical shortage.[103]

Due to protests against the resultant pollution in 1991 the Brazilian government decided to return to original mixtures of 22 percent alcohol and 78 percent gasoline rather than maintain the 12 percent alcohol levels of 1990. Brazil will need to import alcohol for the increased mixture levels. (Another problem facing Brazil is the bootlegging by sugarcane distillers of alcohol directly to the service stations, bypassing state control and taxes.)[104]

Nonetheless, if biomass fuel stocks are managed properly, they are a reliable and sustainable energy resource that can replace significant amounts of fossil fuels and assist in reducing carbon buildup in the atmosphere.

CONSERVATION AND ENERGY EFFICIENCY: SOME SUGGESTIONS FOR THE FUTURE

There are three energy strategies that need to be implemented in order to meet the impending shortfall of fossil fuels: subsidies to nonrenewable energy industries need to be removed, barriers to conservation need to be removed, and the price of energy should reflect its cost to society.[105]

First, institutional barriers prevent the rapid application of conservation and energy efficiency technologies. These barriers favor technologies

that are centralized, complex, glamorous, and backed by powerful constituencies. Solutions like conservation, which are mundane, simple, and
lead to a decentralized power structure, are subjected to a far more rigorous
set of economic tests and are left out of lavish subsidy giveaways to fend
for themselves.

Market forces have inevitably given conservation some attraction,
however. The oil crises of 1973 and 1979 forced the recognition of the ratio-
nality behind decreasing our dependence on all fuel sources simply by
needing and using less energy. Conservation tends to create images of
deprivation as people imagine having to turn down heaters in winter, turn
off air conditioners in summer, and drive less. However, energy efficiency
means continuing better or equal service with improved techniques and
technologies. For instance, it can mean encouraging the establishment of
mass transit facilities and building cars with maximum fuel efficiency.

There have been tremendous improvements in energy efficiency in
the United States since the early 1970s. These have come about through
subtle shifts in the economy as new technologies are implemented—not by
Americans driving tiny fuel-efficient cars or freezing in the winter.[106] Even
with these improvements, the United States has only just begun to reap the
benefits of energy efficiency.[107] Efficiency has become a key ingredient in
economic success. As a 1987 report of the International Energy Agency
stated, "Investment in energy conservation at the margin provides a better
return than investment in energy supply."[108] Most energy experts agree
that conservation can, and should, play a major role in our national energy
future. Fortunately, many such measures have been enacted into law
under CNEP. Types of conservation and obstacles to conservation are discussed next.

Conservation in Homes and Buildings

In 1985 the buildings in the industrial countries of the world used the
equivalent of 16.7 million barrels of oil per day, almost equal to the production of OPEC for the entire year.[109] The economic and environmental consequences of this level of energy consumption are staggering. The ever-grow-
ing number of buildings, however, have used an almost constant amount of
energy since the early 1970s.[110] Energy efficiency has filled the gap.[111]

Retrofitting, which means renovating to save energy, has proven to be
an excellent investment.[112] In over 40,000 retrofits that have been monitored
by U.S. utilities since the mid-1970s, energy use declined by 25 percent and
homeowners received a 23 percent return on their investment annually.[113]

Energy efficiency is cheapest when built in from the start and so the
efficiency potential in new buildings far exceeds those that must be retrofitted.[114] The key to these savings is superinsulation. This means doubling the
normal insulation and building an airtight liner into the walls. These houses
are so airtight that special ventilation systems must be installed to remove
indoor pollutants.[115]

The most efficient new buildings are "smart buildings," which utilize computers to monitor indoor and outdoor temperatures, sunlight, and the location of people within the building. The system sends heat, light, and cooled air only where they are needed.[116]

Windows are also critical to energy savings in buildings. As much energy leaks through American windows every year as flows through the Alaskan pipeline.[117] There are several technologies available for doubling the insulating potential of windows that insulate as well as ordinary walls.

Many other types of energy-saving measures could greatly decrease U.S. energy consumption. For example, planting trees is an effective, inexpensive way to cool buildings in hot weather. Furnaces, air conditioners, appliances, and lights are also candidates for energy savings.[118] New condensing furnaces cut fuel use by 28 percent while reducing air pollution.[119] Integrating heating and cooling equipment can increase energy savings dramatically. Refrigerators and air conditioners produce as much heat as cold air. Directing this heat to hot water tanks saves energy. Integrating furnaces and water heaters produces dramatic savings.[120]

Lighting, which accounts for 25 percent of U.S. electricity use, offers some of the most economical and easy to achieve energy savings now available. Arthur Rosenfeld of Lawrence Livermore Laboratory estimates that 40 large power plants could be retired by installing the latest cost-effective lighting technologies.[121]

The foregoing examples provide ample evidence that energy efficiency in the home or office is feasible and economical. Why, one might ask, are homeowners and others not adopting conservation measures in greater numbers? In part the answer has to do with the short-term economic incentives of energy conservation. Individuals, like government, often are attracted to options that have the lowest short term costs—ignoring possible long-term savings. Consequently, government intervention, in terms of economic incentives or otherwise, may be necessary if we are to enjoy the full benefits of conservation. Since building designs shaped energy policy for most of a century, strict efficiency standards could be made mandatory to ensure that maximum efficiency is built in from the ground up.

An alternative to regulating building efficiency codes would be to reward energy-wise buildings with cash bonuses from the utilities while fining energy gluttons. Consumer resistance to buying the most energy-efficient appliances and lights can be overcome somewhat through education and socialization and special energy-saving financing. Also, efficiency standards, such as those developed for refrigerators, can be developed and/or strengthened. The costs of retrofitting existing buildings might also be forwarded by providing special tax advantages. The market-oriented energy approach of both the Bush and Reagan administrations shunned government intervention to facilitate conservation. However, the mounting economic and environmental consequences of continued dependence on fossil fuels suggest further government intervention may be necessary.

Conservation in Transportation

Transportation is the largest single drain on world oil reserves. The United States burns 63 percent of its oil for transportation, much of it in the private automobile.[122]

The desire to own cars and trucks was not lessened by the oil crises of the 1970s. Buses, trains, and other mass transit systems, which require only 25 percent as much fuel to move each passenger the same distance, are avoided by many. People in American cities use more than twice as much gasoline as people in European cities and 10 times as much gasoline as people in Asian cities where walking is a popular way to get around.[123]

Part of the problem in convincing people to accept mass transit is that they often do not realize the true costs of private automobile use. There are both external costs that drivers do not pay (as discussed in the air pollution chapter) and also hidden subsidies that make private automobile ownership more attractive than it would otherwise be. The hidden costs of automobile ownership include road building and maintenance, traffic congestion, air pollution and environmental degradation, noise, and hazards to pedestrians. Elimination of the hidden subsidies of car ownership combined with the utilization of mandatory fuel efficiency standards that maximize fuel economy would be top priorities if we wanted to stem the flow of oil into transportation and out the tailpipe.[124]

Strict sets of new fuel standards and taxes to boost fuel efficiency would go a long way toward reducing air pollution and dependence on foreign oil. President Clinton's Btu tax on gasoline is a first step in raising taxes in fuel, but it is still not designed to impact consumption. Fuel standards, even on a voluntary basis, are also a small step toward progress.

Conservation in Industry

Industrial energy use in the United States was 17 percent lower in 1986 than in 1973, despite a 17 percent increase in productivity. About 45 percent of this energy savings is attributable to a shift in the economy toward more service industries and fewer energy-intensive products.[125] For example, production of steel and cement has fallen while electronics industries have proliferated. Some energy-intensive raw materials are now imported from newly industrializing countries. The other 55 percent of the improvement is attributable to the application of energy efficiency technologies and processes.[126] In many industries, the economic benefits of energy efficiency have been recognized and pursued. From 1986 to 1992, however, industrial energy consumption was estimated at just 6.4 percent less than 1973 levels—indicating that industrial conservation, perhaps due to low energy prices in the late 1980s and early 1900s, is tapering off.[127]

Most energy efficiency improvements in the United States have been in petroleum refining, chemicals, cement, paper, glass, and clay—energy-intensive industries. Less intensive industries now use a growing share of total industrial energy.[128]

One of the greatest opportunities for improving industrial energy efficiency is cogeneration, the combined production of heat and electricity. The waste heat of electricity generation is made available for industrial processes by installing a small boiler and electric generator within a plant.

Due to the Public Utilities Regulatory Policy Act of 1978, which allowed industry to sell power to utilities at fair market value, industrial cogeneration has grown explosively in the United States.[129] The cogeneration industry now includes 20 kilowatt units in fast-food restaurants and apartment complexes as well as 300,000 kilowatt units in petrochemical plants. Studies show that by using cogeneration many plants can raise their total energy efficiency from 50 percent to 70 percent. As previously discussed, electricity production is projected to grow under the CNEPA expansion to cogeneration plants without the requirement for private ownership.

Industry as a whole is on the path to substantially decreasing energy use. Most industrial countries are unlikely to use as much energy in the year 2000 as they did a quarter of a century earlier.[130] However, programs to improve energy efficiency in industrializing less developed countries are essential to prevent the repetition of the wasteful practices of the more developed world. Many less developed countries suffer from subsidized energy prices, limited access to energy-efficient technologies, and poor management. Policy changes and the transfer of relevant technologies are urgently needed. Enhanced energy efficiency is essential for economic success in a competitive world. Those countries that invest the most funds and education in energy efficiency now, and have the most developed system of renewable energy resources in the future, will be the world's economic leaders when we reach the bottom of the oil barrel.

Obstacles to Conservation

Instituting rational energy prices that reflect negative externalities and the cost of replacement of traditional energy sources with nonrenewable resources is necessary to discourage waste and create the conditions necessary for increased energy efficiency.

The chief obstacle to achieving sensible price controls and promoting energy efficiency is the instability of the price of oil. From 1973 until 1980, the price of oil increased sevenfold. Then real oil prices fell 75 percent between 1981 and 1986, hitting a low of about $12 a barrel before increasing again to $18 a barrel in 1987.[131] The higher oil prices of the 1970s encouraged production and gains in energy efficiency. From the early 1980s to 1990, and again after the Gulf War, the world oil market was dominated by overproduction, creating the oil glut and falling prices. Low prices and fluctuating markets both work against efficiency, since policymakers become hesitant to undertake programs during conditions of energy uncertainty.

Although unpopular with voters, taxes are an effective way to encourage conservation and prevent cheap imported oil from undermining efficiency gains. An environmental tax such as carbon tax on fossil fuels would bring the cost of energy closer to its real cost and reflect some of the hazard that burning those fuels represents. In Europe and Japan, fuel taxes are commonly used to raise revenues and discourage excessive driving. However, in the United States attempts to raise gasoline taxes have been defeated by the oil industry, consumer groups, and politicians reflecting constituent concerns.

AN ECOLOGICAL CONCLUSION

Before the invention of the steam engine and the discovery of coal, humankind had relied on energy resources that were recycled many times during a human lifetime. Humankind is now dependent on fossil fuel resources that have renewal times thousands to millions of times longer than the human life span. The discovery of fossil fuels and their utilization, compounded with breakthroughs in medical technology, have caused an unprecedented growth in population, furthering the strain on nonrenewable resources and hastening their ultimate depletion. Cultural and institutional inertia and obsolete myths about the limitlessness of finite resources have created an illusion of security and make the inevitable day of reckoning all the more certain and potentially traumatic.

The carrying capacity of an environment is only sustainable if a balance is achieved between renewable resources and the population that is dependent on them. Humankind could overshoot the earth's carrying capacity. Our reliance on fossil fuels has allowed us to develop an energy-intensive society. Abundant and inexpensive energy has permitted intensified agriculture, heavily populated metropolitan development, and unsurpassed material abundance. When fossil fuels run out, our energy needs will have to be met through renewable energy sources. The transition from finite to renewable energy may be slow and gradual, with substitutions made in a manner that does not disrupt our lifestyles, or the transition may be abrupt—causing social unrest and disruption. Although the former is the desired course, many alternative sources of energy require, as we have seen, market subsidy in order to ensure their development. Business does not seem to be interested in investments with long-term payoff periods. Policymakers, ever wary of increasing taxes, would rather put off tough decisions today and let tomorrow take care of itself. The general public is comfortable. Yet without development of alternative sources of energy, the transition to a steady state energy economy promises to be rough.

SUMMARY

In this chapter we summarized the history of energy use and development in the nation and world. The current mix of energy sources, renewable and nonrenewable, and the environmental problems associated with each were

also discussed. Finally, we examined the promises of and obstacles to conservation. Conservation is the cleanest, least expensive, and most technologically feasible future energy alternative. Yet we are slow to seriously
conserve. This is one of the paradoxes of environmental policy.

As we have seen, energy is not cheap. The by-products of energy production pose significant costs, or *negative externalities*, on society. We have
paid these costs as part of the price for many modern technological developments that today we take for granted. Technological developments, such
as new synthetic chemicals, have also generated significant negative environmental externalities in the form of toxic and hazardous wastes. That is
the subject of the next chapter.

NOTES

1. David E. Fisher, *Fire and Ice: The Greenhouse Effect, Ozone Depletion, and Nuclear Winter* (New York: Harper & Row, 1990), p. 186.
2. Marvin V. Melosi, *Coping with Abundance: Energy and Environment in Industrial America* 1820–1980 (New York: Newberry Awards Records, 1985), pp. 29–30.
3. By the 1920s more than 658 million tons of coal had been mined. At that time, coal represented more than 75 percent of the total energy consumption in the United States and exports exceeded 929,000 tons a year. Ibid., p. 33.
4. Electricity from hydropower peaked in 1946 while providing 35.1 percent of total generating capacity. Hydropower declined to 16.2 percent of total gener-ating capacity by 1970. In 1984 hydroelectric supplied 14 percent of electricity and 5 percent of total energy consumption—a little more than nuclear power at that time. The contribution of hydropower to overall power consumption in the United States is predicted to remain relatively flat—at around 14 percent. High construction costs and a lack of suitable large rivers for siting the facili-ties are the primary limiting factors in the growth of hydroelectricity. G. Tyler Miller, Jr., *Living in the Environment: An Introduction to Environmental Science* (Belmont, CA: Wadsworth, 1988), p. 403.
5. In 1890 total U.S. oil production for all years was 1 billion barrels. By 1929 U.S. production was 1 billion barrels annually.
6. Melosi, *Coping with Abundance: Energy and Environment in Industrial America*, p. 39.
7. Ibid., p. 97. During the war, 133 million barrels of oil were shipped to the Allies in Europe.
8. Ibid., p. 50. During the war the importance of oil as a military fuel gave oil producers leverage when dealing with elected officials. At the request of the industry in 1913, Congress granted the oil industry tax relief by approving an oil depletion allowance to increase production. This allowed producers to deduct 5 percent of the gross value of their oil and gas production against taxes. In 1916 the depletion allowance was changed so the 5 percent deduction could not exceed the annual costs of the discovery of oil. Then legislation was passed by Congress in 1918 that allowed producers "reasonable" deductions based on discovery costs or the fair market value of their properties. Since the market value of mineral properties greatly exceeded discovery costs, the oil industry became blessed with a major tax advantage that would last for decades. And this would not be the last time the oil industry would use the crisis of war to its economic advantage.
9. Ibid., p. 103.

10. The Great Depression beginning at the end of the 1920s could not have come at a worse time for the oil industry. Huge reserves in the East Texas fields were discovered in 1930 just as demand plummeted. The fact that the field was developed by small independents made it resistant to regulation. As production reached ridiculous heights, the Texas Railroad Commission (TRC) issued a prorationing order that attempted to limit production to expected demand. The Texas state legislature passed the Market Demand Act of 1932, which allowed the TRC to issue prorationing orders and thereby bring some stability to the industry. This kind of state initiative in Texas and later in Oklahoma preceded extensive involvement by the federal government in production controls. Oil had become essential to the economic well-being of the nation, and Congress limited its activity to antitrust legislation aimed at electrical utilities only. In a time of inexpensive energy, consumer protest was unknown and the oil industry emerged from the Depression on a firm financial footing.

11. Wasteful production and transportation practices were also causing pollution of rivers and coastal waters. Public attention led to congressional investigations into oil pollution problems and in 1924 Congress passed the Oil Pollution Act. Although inadequate enforcement procedures failed to halt the pollution caused from excess oil, this was the first attempt to deal with oil pollution at the federal level. It is interesting that this first federal effort at addressing oil pollution grew out of public response to a perceived crisis and resulted in congressional action and no enforcement. Thus federal policy makers were able to satisfy their constituents without alienating an important and influential economic interest group.

12. During the 1920s the coal industry had suffered from overproduction and low prices and had begun to limit production. Although coal was not the essential fuel for the war effort, it remained an important domestic fuel source and was needed for home heating, steel production, railroads, and electricity generation. Because of the war, the coal industry expanded and reached an all-time high output of 620 million net tons in 1944.

13. The U.S. Army Air Force alone consumed 14 times more gasoline during operations on the Western Front than were shipped to Europe between 1914 and 1918. Eight percent of the 7 billion barrels of crude oil used by the Allies between December 1941 and August 1945 was produced in the United States; hence long supply lines had to be maintained. By May 1942, 55 oil tankers that were servicing the eastern seaboard were sunk by German submarines. Ibid., p. 181.

14. The first pipeline dubbed "The Big Inch" carried crude 1,476 miles from the Southwest to Phoenix Junction, Pennsylvania. The second one was named "The Little Big Inch" and carried refined petroleum products 1,714 miles from Beaumont, Texas, to Linden, New York. Ibid., p. 184.

15. The conflict between domestic and imported oil flared up again after the Korean War with the ailing coal industry siding with the small domestic producers in demanding import quotas to stimulate sales of domestic energy. In the summer of 1956, imported oil was selling at $1.95 a barrel compared to domestic oil, which was selling for $2.75 a barrel. The vitality of the domestic market was at stake, and pressure was put on the Eisenhower administration to reverse its policy of no intervention in the oil market. Influenced by the national security threat represented by the Suez crisis and fearing that Congress would make the initial move in a way unfavorable to the administration, Eisenhower instituted mandatory controls in 1959.

The Mandatory Oil Import Program (MOIP) was no panacea. Although it protected the domestic oil industry from foreign competition, it also created an artificial environment in which oil prices did not respond to international realities. Prices rose and consumers footed the bill. Ultimately the MOIP had an impact on the ability of the United States to respond to the oil crisis of the 1970s.

16. A serious oil shortage occurred from 1945 to 1947 immediately after World War II. Until 1947 the United States had exported more than it imported. The year 1947 marked the transition of the United States as a net exporter to a net importer of oil. This created conflicts between domestic producers and the American multinationals, who were bringing in cheap foreign oil. Except during the Korean War, domestic oil supplies exceeded demand by a substantial margin. Small domestic producers called for quotas while the major companies, large independents, and the Truman administration supported voluntary controls. The preservation of the domestic oil industry was at cross-purposes with the administration's support of the multinationals and its reluctance to damage relations with Canada and Latin America by restricting imports. The Korean War and a booming domestic economy in the 1950s temporarily eased the tension as consumption rose to new levels. Consumption of oil increased by 80 percent between 1945 and 1959 and domestic production grew from 1.7 million barrels in 1945 to 2.6 million barrels in 1959. Ibid., p. 254.

17. The production of the Model T increased from 32,000 in 1910 to almost 735,000 in 1916. By 1921 the Ford Motor Company had reached the 1 million mark and by 1924 had produced 13 million cars. Ibid., p. 106.

18. In 1900 there had been only 4,200 cars in existence in the United States. By 1929 there were 5.6 million cars and trucks on the road. This was 1 car for every 5 Americans compared with 1 for every 43 British citizens, 1 for every 325 Italians, and 1 for every 7,000 Russians. Ibid., p. 108.

19. The TVA not only produces hydroelectric power but is also involved in flood control, fertilizer production, soil conservation, reforestation, inland waterway construction, and the promotion of regional growth. Ibid., p. 130. In 1936 Congress passed the Rural Electrification Act to establish nonprofit electrical cooperatives in those areas private utilities found uneconomical to service. The REA was a great success. In 1930 only 1 farm in 10 had electricity. By 1941 4 out of 10 had electricity and by 1950 9 out of 10 were receiving electrical power. Ibid., p. 136.

20. Much was wasted through flaring or burning it off.

21. Between 1945 and 1955 the number of households burning natural gas rose from 11 million to more than 21 million. Residential consumption increased from 607 billion to more than 2,000 billion cubic feet per year. Natural gas was clean burning and generated valuable consumer products such as solvents, films, plastics, adhesives, synthetic rubber, fiberglass, insecticides, gasoline additives, paints and drugs and was useful in the production of synthetic fibers such as nylon, orlon, and dacron. Ibid.

22. In 1971 90 percent of new gas production was going into the intrastate market representing 40 percent of total consumption.

23. World reserves of natural gas are estimated to last until 2033 at 1984 usage rates and to 2018 if usage increases by 2 percent per year. Miller, *Living in the Environment: An Introduction to Environmental Science*, p. 349.

24. Melosi, *Coping with Abundance: Energy and Environment in Industrial America*, p. 249.

25. By December of 1973, price per barrel rose 130 percent to $11.65. By 1974 Arab oil exported to the United States was $12.25 a barrel compared to $3.65 a year before. Ibid., pp. 280–281.

26. William R. Catton, Jr., *Overshoot* (Chicago: University of Illinois Press, 1982).

27. Melosi, *Coping with Abundance: Energy and Environment in Industrial America*, p. 292.

28. The groundwork was being laid for a future energy crisis. The high oil prices of the early 1980s had encouraged depletion of some of the world's most limited oil reserves all outside of the Middle East. The high price of oil made it economical to drill for oil in dozens of non-OPEC locations, many of which will soon reach a point of diminishing returns.

29. Oil production in North America, Europe, and the Soviet Union is likely to begin falling steeply during the next decade. Fifty-six percent of proven oil reserves are still found in the Middle East. Sometime in the 1990s the center of world production should again move to the Middle East. Christopher Flavin, "World Oil: Coping with the Dangers of Success," *Worldwatch Paper* 66 (July 1985).

30. Louis Bley, "OPEC's Best Friend," *Euromoney* (June 1990), p. E49; and Peter Morton, "OPEC will Soon Produce Half of World's Oil, CERI Predicts," *The Oil Daily*, October 7, 1992, p. 3.

31. On August 6, 1945, the Enola Gay dropped an atomic bomb named "Little Boy" on the city of Hiroshima. A blinding flash of white light was followed by searing heat as a huge fireball with temperatures of several million degrees Centigrade rose in the sky. Thousands of people were instantly vaporized as 13 square miles of the city were flattened or set aflame. Over 140,000 people were killed or doomed to a slow death of radiation sickness or wounds. Of the 76,000 buildings in Hiroshima, 48,000 were totally destroyed and 22,000 had been damaged. Two days later, on August 8, the hellish debacle was repeated as a plutonium bomb named "Fat Boy" was dropped on Nagasaki. Peter R. Beckman, Larry Campbell, Paul W. Crumlish, Michael N. Dobkowski, and Steven P. Lee, *The Nuclear Predicament* (Englewood Cliffs, NJ: Prentice Hall, 1989).

32. Price-Anderson Amendments Act of 1988 passed August 20, 1988 (P.L. 100-408) and extended coverage of the act to August 1, 1990. There are 114 reactors licensed to operate, with several operating reactors excluded, since the act only applies to reactors over 100 megawatts. Further, nine plants are in "deferred completion," with permits granted. An example is the Washington Public Power System where Units 4 and 5 were dropped with no construction being done after receiving licensing approval.

33. The Nuclear Regulatory Commission can, if loss is catastrophic according to certain criteria, assess a lesser amount than $10 million.

34. By the end of 1967, 75 nuclear power plants had been ordered. By the end of 1969, 97 nuclear plants were in operation, under construction, or under contract. However, by September 1968, only 14 plants were in operation. Melosi, *Coping with Abundance: Energy and Environment in Industrial America*, pp. 233, 239.

35. During the 1970s the conflict over nuclear power pitted expert against expert, creating a confusing amount of conflicting data and statistics about the safety of nuclear power generation. The battles were fought in the courts and in the streets as thousands joined in antinuclear demonstrations. In 12 states initiatives were introduced to block the expansion of nuclear power. Due in large part, no doubt, to the well-financed campaigns of the pronuclear forces, all but one failed. The successful initiative was passed in California, the voters there placing a moratorium on new nuclear plants until a solution was found for the nuclear waste problem.

36. Between 1971 and 1978 costs rose an additional 142 percent. Christopher Flavin, "Ten years of Fallout," *World Watch Institute* (March/April 1989).

37. Although there had been several serious nuclear accidents before Three Mile Island (TMI) and many mechanical mishaps at nuclear facilities, TMI came close to a complete core meltdown with potentially catastrophic consequences. In 1957 the AEC had conducted a study on the worse possible conse-

quences of a nuclear disaster. The report concluded that a meltdown of a light water reactor of 500 megawatt size located 30 miles from a major city would cause the immediate death of 3,400 people, injure 45,000, and cause $7 billion in property damage. A revised study by the AEC later concluded that it would be more accurate to predict that an accident of this magnitude would cause 45,000 fatalities and contaminate an area the size of the state of Pennsylvania. This is what could have happened at TMI. Paul R. Ehrlich, Anne H. Ehrlich, and John P. Holdren *Ecoscience: Population, Resources, Environment* (San Francisco: Freeman, 1977).

After several months of study a presidential commission appointed to study the TMI accident concluded that the plant could be made operational again at a cost of $466 million. Ten years later and after an expenditure of almost $1 billion the project is still not finished. Plans to reconstruct the TMI plant were abandoned. Tons of radioactive debris have been sent by rail to a "temporary" federal dump in Idaho. The lower reaches of the reactor vessel are still so highly radioactive that special remote control tools must be used to protect workers, and the reactor's owners are trying to get permission to seal the radioactive debris inside for decades. Flavin, "Ten Years of Fallout."

38. Christopher Flavin, "The Case Against Reviving Nuclear Power," *World Watch Institute* (July/August 1988).
39. Demand tracks price. Before the oil crisis of 1973, consumption had been rising by 7 percent per year. When prices rose dramatically, demand slid to less than half the annual rate. Peter S. Nivola, *The Politics of Energy Conservation* (Washington DC: The Brookings Institute, 1986).
40. Steve Wilhelm, "A Niche That Keeps Going: Cogeneration," *Puget Sound Business Journal*, 12(9) (July 15, 1991), p. 3.
41. David W. Tice, "Risky Venture: A Utility's Cogeneration Project Still Has Woes Aplenty," *Barron's*, 71(42) (October 21, 1991), p. 28.
42. This discussion is based on Holly Idelson, "National Energy Strategy Provisions," *Congressional Quarterly Weekly Report*, 50(47) (November 28, 1992), pp. 3722–3731.
43. C. C. Sullivan, "Economy and Ecology: A Powerful Coalition," *Buildings*, 87(5) (May 1993), p. 47.
44. Energy estimates are based, in part, on Chauncey Starr, Milton F. Searl, and Sy Alpet, "Energy Sources: A Realistic Outlook," *Science*, 256(5059) (May 15, 1992), p. 982. Some have predicted greater increases in the use of electricity with its relatively low prices, which would mean an increased demand for coal to fuel the plants; such a course would also coincide with CNEPA's loosening of regulations on PURPA's cogeneration facilities. See Helmut A. Merklein, "The Case for Electric," *Industrial Investor*, 24(13) (October 1990), pp. 504–505.
45. Some 10 trillion tons of coal—equal to more than 800 times the world's annual use of energy—are known to exist and may ultimately be recoverable. International Energy Agency, *World Energy Outlook* (Paris: Organization for Economic Cooperation and Development, 1982).
46. Miller, *Living in the Environment: An Introduction to Environmental Science*, p. 354. The world's estimated reserves would last about 900 years at 1984 usage rates and 149 years if usage increased by 2 percent per year.
47. Between 1900 and 1985 underground mining in the United States killed more than 100,000 miners, permanently disabled another 1 million, and created over 250,000 cases of black lung disease, a severe form of emphysema caused by inhalation of coal dust. Surface mining of coal has devastated over 1 million acres of land in the United States causing erosion, acid runoff, and lowered water tables. Ibid., pp. 352–353. Tens of thousands of miles of streams

have been polluted. Melosi, *Coping with Abundance: Energy and Environment in Industrial America*, p. 210.

48. Topper Sherwood, "Strip Search (Weak Enforcement of Surface Mining Control and Reclamation Act)," *Common Cause Magazine*, 15(3) (May–June 1989) p. 9.
49. This is on land that may have originally sold for $200 to $300 an acre. See Anna Maria Gillis, "Bringing Back the Land," *BioScience*, 41(2) (February 1991), p. 68.
50. Holly Idelson, "National Energy Strategy Provisions," pp. 3728–3730.
51. These chemicals can cause respiratory distress, destroy plants, rubber, textiles, and other materials. Residents of Southern California who vacation at Big Bear or Lake Arrowhead can see the dead pine trees by the side of the road. Ozone from Los Angeles smog has killed thousands of pine trees in the San Bernardino mountains. This is common throughout the United States. Lester R. Brown et al., *State of the World 1985* (New York: Norton, 1985).
52. Miller, *Living in the Environment: An Introduction to Environmental Science*, p. 346.
53. Ibid., p. 268.
54. George J. Church, "The Big Spill," *Time* (April 10, 1989), p. 38.
55. Ibid., p. 39.
56. Note the similarities between the Valdez oil spill and the circumstances surrounding the passage and implementation of the Oil Pollution Act of 1924. It is interesting that in both cases the federal effort grew out of public response to a perceived crisis (waste and pollution from oil and an earlier major ocean oil spill, respectively) and resulted in congressional action with poor enforcement. Thus federal policymakers were able to satisfy their constituents without alienating an important and influential economic interest group.
57. Global-proven oil reserves increased rapidly after World War II rising from 76 billion barrels in 1950 to 664 billion barrels in 1973. Since the mid-1970s global-proven reserves have only increased by 5 percent even though high oil prices have encouraged exploration and extraction. Total estimates of world oil resources ranged from 1,600 to 2,400 billion barrels. Of this amount, 554 billion barrels have been consumed and 700 billion barrels of proven reserve have been discovered. It is estimated that approximately 350 to 1,150 billion barrels of oil remain to be discovered. At the rate of world oil consumption in the early 1990s, ultimate depletion of the world's oil reserves is between 50 and 88 years away. Christopher Flavin, "World Oil: Coping with the Dangers of Success," *Worldwatch Paper* 66 (July 1985), pp. 23, 25.
58. Ibid., p. 29.
59. Catton, *Overshoot*, p. 247.
60. Miller, *Living in the Environment: An Introduction to Environmental Science*, pp. 348–349.
61. Telephone interview with DOE, October 25, 1993.
62. Hirokazu Hase, "Geothermal Programs Contributing to the Earth's Environment," *Japan 21st*, 38(3) (March 1993), p. 43.
63. Miller, *Living in the Environment: An Introduction to Environmental Science*, p. 361.
64. Ibid., p. 362. Almost all the homes, buildings, and food-producing greenhouses in Reykjavik, Iceland, a city with a population of 85,000, are heated by hot water drawn from deep hot water geothermal deposits. The hot salty brine pumped up from such deposits can be used to produce electricity in a binary-cycle system. The main problem is that the brine corrodes metal parts and clogs pipes.
65. Hirokazu Hase, "Geothermal Programs Contributing to the Earth's Environment," p. 43.

66. By 1987, it was producing 2 percent of California's electricity—enough to provide for a city the size of San Francisco at less than half the cost of a coal or nuclear power plant. Ibid., p. 362.
67. Ibid., p. 43.
68. Ibid., p. 364. The state of Hawaii has an aggressive plan to extract 500 megawatts of geothermal-generated electricity from hot brine on the island of Hawaii for export to the more populous islands of Maui and Oahu through an undersea cable. However, there has been well-organized protest against the project, since it would entail destroying a significant part of the only lowland rain forest in the United States, require extensive transmission lines through residential subdivisions, and be a potential source of air and groundwater pollution. Without adequate controls, there is moderate to high air pollution from hydrogen sulfide, ammonia, and radioactive materials as well as moderate to high water pollution from dissolved salts and runoff of various toxic elements such as boron and mercury.
69. "The Chernobyl Syndrome," *Newsweek* (May 12, 1986). Radiation levels in Poland were reported to be 500 times higher than normal.
70. Flavin, "Ten Years of Fallout."
71. In 1980 funding for research and development of renewable energy peaked in the United States at $900 million (in 1986 dollars), but since that time appropriations have been cut by 80 percent.
72. For example, energy tax credits that were available from 1978 to 1985 gave a strong financial incentive for the building of wind turbines, small hydropower facilities, geothermal projects, solar collectors, and photovoltaic industries. When the Reagan administration cut out these credits all at once instead of phasing them out gradually, the rug was pulled out from under many underfinanced renewable energy industries. Huge subsidies that are granted to the nuclear, oil, coal, and other conventional power industries should be removed. For example, in 1984 nuclear power supplied less than 5 percent of U.S. energy but received $15 billion in subsidies. Renewables, which produced 9.6 percent of total U.S. energy, received only $1.7 billion. "The Hidden Cost of Energy," *Sierra* (March/April 1986).
73. R&D monies are not the only means through which renewable technologies can be supported. The Public Utility Regulatory Policies Act (PURPA) of 1978 has had far-reaching consequences for renewable energy and could eventually and effectively end the traditional utility monopoly over public power. Among other things, PURPA mandated that utilities interconnect with independent power producers and pay them a fair market value for their electricity. It also exempted independent power producers from state and federal regulations. PURPA created a new spirit of entrepreneurialism in the utility industry. Since 1980, several hundred U.S. companies have entered the power generation business. Federal Energy Regulatory Commission, *Small Power Production and Cogeneration Facilities; Regulations Implementing Section 210 of PURPA of 1978* (Washington, DC: 1980); and, Christopher Flavin, *Worldwatch Institute Paper* 61 (1984).

In 1985 over 6,000 megawatts of renewable energy capacity had been built. By the fall of 1987, private developers had requested regulatory approval for an additional 16,335 megawatts of renewable energy projects. Biomass represented the largest share of this generating capacity followed by wind and small hydropower. 14 percent of the nation's electrical generating capacity relied on renewable technologies by 1985. In California where the act was most vigorously enforced, private developers aided by tax credits not only found it economical to build virtually all of the state's new generating capacity, they began to displace existing power plants as well. Cynthia Pollock Shea, *Worldwatch Institute Paper* 81, (1988), p. 46.

74. Hydroelectric efficiency is very high—80 percent to 95 percent—and plants produce power 95 percent of the time compared with 55 percent for nuclear and 65 percent for coal. Miller, *Living in the Environment: An Introduction to Environmental Science*, p. 403.

75. Ibid., p. 403.

76. Tim Palmer, "What Price Free Energy?" *Sierra* (July/August 1983).

77. For example, exploiting small hydro sites in water-rich New England would increase its total electrical generating capacity by about 7 percent. John Gever, Robert Kaufmann, David Skole, and Charles Vorosmarty, *Beyond Oil* (Cambridge, MA: Ballinger, 1986).

78. Shea, *Worldwatch Institute Paper* 81.

79. Telephone interview with DOE, October 15, 1993.

80. During the 1990s, New Englanders may receive 7 percent of their electricity from Quebec. Lester R. Brown et al., *State of the World 1988* (New York: Norton, 1988).

81. This discussion is based on James Ridgeway and Fred Pearce, "Watch on the Danube," *Audubon*, 94(4) (July-August 1992), pp. 46–54.

82. Environmentally the dams were a mixed blessing (or curse). The area is particularly poor and has a heavy reliance on lignite coal that is high in sulfur and titanium and produces an oil that is lethal when burned. Even if a hydroelectric facility was built, however, its electricity would be used to run the nearby petrochemical refinery that produces a horrible chemical smog and related birth defects, cancers, and chronic bronchial infections in the local children.

83. A well designed passive solar system can provide 50 percent to 100 percent of the space heating of a home or small building with an added construction cost of 5 percent to 10 percent. Miller, *Living in the Environment: An Introduction to Environmental Science*.

84. Sales volume dropped more than 70 percent from the 1984 level, and 28,000 out of the 30,000 people employed in the industry lost their jobs.

85. The Luz method is currently producing 194 megawatts by using long troughs of curved mirrors guided by computers to heat synthetic oil passing through vacuum-sealed tubes to 735 degrees Fahrenheit. The oil in turn heats water to produce steam and run an electric turbine. The company has built five new plants capable of tripling its generating capacity to 600 megawatts, enough to power a city the size of Washington, D.C. The new plants' larger size and certain technological improvements will enable the cost of the solar power to decrease to 8 cents per kilowatt hour—the lowest ever achieved by a solar technology. Company officials contend that their power costs would look even lower if governments compared the costs of solar with the environmental effects of air and water pollution and the devastating effects of uranium and coal mining that are inherent in the coal and nuclear power technologies. This is undoubtedly true. As we have seen, the cost of externalities associated with burning coal or oil are estimated to be two to three times the market price for these sources of energy. Building a solar plant is also much quicker than building either a coal or nuclear fired plant. The solar plant can come on line in 18 months; a coal or nuclear plant takes 5 to 10 years. Many experts feel the Luz project shows that solar power can become a vital supplement to more traditional energy sources, particularly during peak daytime hours in hot, dry climates. "A California Complex Finds Its Place in the Sun," *The Washington Post*, March 20–26, 1989.

86. Growth of 224 percent between 1980 and 1983 allowed production of 8.1 megawatts. Don Best, "Solar Cells: Still a Tough Sell," *Sierra* (May/June, 1988).

87. Ibid.

88. In 1976 the average price for a PV module was $44 per peak watt. Ten years later, costs were down eightfold (in constant 1986 dollars) to $5.25 per peak watt. Ibid., p. 31. Advances such as inexpensive automated methods of manufacturing PV cells of single-crystal silicon could reduce that to $1.50 per peak watt for the PV cell alone and perhaps $3 per peak watt for the complete system exclusive of storage. However even this would not bring the PV industry into a competitive balance with other means of producing electricity. It would produce electricity for 26 cents per kilowatt hour (kwh) while electricity in the late 1980s cost from 5 to 13 cents per kwh depending on location and source of power. The PV industry's dream of reducing costs to .60 cents per kwh, which would bring the cost to the consumer down to 5.2 cents per kwh, would make solar-generated electricity very attractive. Rose, Miller, and Agnew, "Reducing the Problem of Global Warming," *Technology Review* (May/June, 1984).

89. Shea, *Worldwatch Institute Paper* 81. More than 16,769 turbines have been erected, mainly in the mountain passes of Altamont, Tehachapi, and San Gorgonio. Together these machines have the capacity to produce 1,463 megawatts of power, enough to meet the needs of more than 400,000 households.

90. Paul Ehrlich, Anne Ehrlich, and John P. Holdren, *Ecoscience: Population, Resources, Environment* (San Francisco: Freeman, 1977).

91. Shea, *Worldwatch Institute Paper* 81, p. 19. In the United States, industrial utility and commercial applications account for two-thirds of the wood burned for energy. The remainder is used to heat homes.

92. Since 1983, four U.S. utilities have built wood-burning power plants, each able to generate 45 megawatts of electricity. According to a study by the California Energy Commission, wood-fired boilers can be installed for about $1,340 per kilowatt, which is 20 percent less than a coal-fired plant costs. Ibid., pp. 20, 22.

93. The largest market is in California where two dozen 10 to 50 megawatt wood energy projects are on-line as of 1988. Over 500 megawatts of power were under construction throughout the state that year. In Maine, there are over 250 megawatts of wood energy projects on-line worth over $500 million. Ibid.

94. Dean Mahin, "Wood-Fuel Users Report Cost Savings in Virginia," *Renewable Energy News* (October 1985).

95. In Hawaii, the sugar industry started selling electricity in the late 1970s and in 1985 supplied 58 percent of the power on Kauai and 33 percent on the island of Hawaii. Sugar companies have installed at least 150 megawatts of power based on the burning of bagasse, the sugarcane residue. Researchers at Princeton University estimate that globally some 50,000 megawatts of gas-turbine cogeneration units could be supported with the 1985 level of sugarcane production. The potential for South America alone is 18,000 megawatts. Shea, *Worldwatch Institute Paper* 81, p. 24.

96. Shea, *Worldwatch Institute Paper* 81, p. 26. The United States relied on surplus corn and other grains for 90 percent of the 3 billion liters of ethanol produced in 1987.

97. At 1988 consumption rates, converting 10 percent of U.S. cars to run on ethanol would reduce oil imports by 800,000 barrels per day. This is equal to what the United States imported from Iran, Iraq, and Saudi Arabia per day in 1986.

98. Brigid McManamin, "Political Greenmail," *Forbes*, 147(11) (May 27, 1991), p. 72.

99. David Ivanovich, "EPA Again Delays Plan to Push Ethanol-Gasoline," *The Journal of Commerce*, 395(27911) (February 9, 1993), p. 7B.

100. Paul Merrion, "Gasohol Stalls Bush Here," *Crain's Chicago Business*, 15(34) (August 24, 1992), p. 3.

101. The Clinton administration then decided to publish the order and then later put it on hold again. See David Ivanovich, "EPA Again Delays Plans to Push Ethanol-Gasoline," p. 7B.

102. Earl V. Anderson, "Brazil's Fuel Ethanol Program Comes Under Fire," *Chemical News Bureau*, March 20, 1989, pp. 11–12.
103. Earl Anderson, "Brazil's Fuel Ethanol Program Sputters," *Chemical and Engineering News*, January 15, 1990, p. 6.
104. "Brazilian Alcohol Bootlegging Fuels Alternative 'Gas' Market," *Platt's Oilgram News*, 69(156) (August 14, 1991), p. 2.
105. The price of energy should reflect the cost of replacing the dwindling supplies of depletable resources with renewable resources and alternative fuels. For example, if we know that replacing a $10 barrel of oil with synthetic fuel will cost $30 a barrel, and that the replacement technology will be needed so soon that we must start planning and constructing now, the option exists to either subsidize the synthetic fuel plant to bring it down to the $10 per barrel value, or to gradually raise the price of oil to reflect the value of its replacement, thereby making the replacement technology economically feasible. This would encourage efficient use and allow for an anticipated and gradual adjustment to increased costs of living instead of having to accept a sudden "price shock" at a later date.
106. In 1986 energy use by industry in the United States was actually 17 percent lower than in 1973, despite a 17 percent increase in production. The United States used 23 percent less energy in 1985 than was used in 1973. A new American office building, for example, has about the same lighting levels and temperatures as old ones but uses less than half as much electricity. Even large luxury cars built today get 20 to 25 miles to the gallon, which equals the mileage of much smaller cars built in the 1970s. Christopher Flavin and Alan Durning, "End of the Profligate Age?" *International Wildlife*, 18(3) (May/June 1988).
107. For example, it is possible to save 40 percent or more of the energy used in existing buildings through retrofitting and 70 percent in new ones. The United States spends 10 percent of its GNP to pay the national fuel bill compared to only 4 percent for Japan. This translates into a national fuel bill which is $200 billion higher than necessary, making the U.S. economy that much less competitive. Ibid., p. 13.
108. Alan B. Durning and Christopher Flavin, "Building on Success: The Age of Energy Efficiency," *Worldwatch Paper* 82 (March 1988).
109. Ibid., p. 13.
110. Commercial buildings—schools, hospitals, stores and office buildings—use substantially less energy today than they did in 1973. New U.S. office buildings, for example, which used a wasteful 5.7 million kilojoules per square meter of floor space per year in 1973, use 3.0 in 1988. Commercial buildings in Sweden now average less than 1.7. If all commercial buildings in the United States were that efficient, total U.S energy consumption would drop 9 percent. (These figures are for primary energy consumption. Electricity is counted in terms of energy content rather than the electricity itself.) Ibid., p. 17.
111. Ibid., p. 14. Buildings in these countries use 25 percent less energy per person than they did in 1973, which is more than the equivalent of 3.8 million barrels of oil per day—greater than the output of the rich North Sea discovery. Energy efficiency from U.S. homes and businesses combined is estimated to have increased 27.8 percent between 1973 and 1992, although total consumption still increased more than 22 percent. See "Fuels and Energy," *Air Conditioning, Heating, and Refrigeration News*, 188 (13) (March 29, 1993), p. 46.
112. Since average energy savings in retrofitted buildings run 24 percent, many of the technologies used in new commercial construction are worth installing in existing buildings. The Rocky Mountain Institute has estimated there are potential savings in commercial buildings of 1.8 billion kilowatt hours per

year or 73 percent of the buildings' current use. Although these figures seem incredible, they have been corroborated by an expert panel advising the Boston Edison Company. Rocky Mountain Institute, South Texas Project; *Boston Edison Review Panel*, Vol. 2, Appendix 6, (Boston: Boston Edison Company, 1987); and Durning and Flavin, "Building on Success: The Age of Energy Efficiency."

113. According to the Rocky Mountain Institute (RMI), founded by energy expert Amory Lovins, even more savings are technically feasible. RMI calculated that existing homes in Austin, Texas, could save 63 percent of their electricity use by employing specially designed and readily available technologies. These retrofits were estimated to cost between $1,700 and $2,400, an amount that could be repaid through energy savings in about three years. Durning and Flavin, "Building on Success: The Age of Energy Efficiency," p. 14.

114. For example, while average U.S. homes use 160 kilojoules of heating energy per square meter of floor space per degree day, Swedish homes use just 65. New superefficient homes in Minnesota use only 51 kilojoules; some individual units in Sweden use as low as 18 kilojoules. Ibid., p. 16.

115. Ibid., p. 16. As of the late 1980s there were more than 20,000 superinsulated homes in North America and 5,000 being built each year. However, this is not even 1 percent of new home construction. Superinsulation adds about five percent to the cost of new construction, which can be recaptured within 5 years through energy savings.

116 Analysts at Lawrence Livermore Laboratory of the University of California, Berkeley, calculated that homes in Los Angeles could cut their air conditioning bills in half by changing the controls on the conditioners to substitute ventilation for cooling when possible. Herb Brody, "Energy Wise Buildings," *High Technology* (February 1987).

117. Durning and Flavin, "Building on Success: The Age of Energy Efficiency."

118. The most energy-efficient new appliances have substantially lower energy requirements than the average appliances in U.S. homes. For example, the average American refrigerator uses 1,500 kilowatt hours of electricity every year. The average new model uses 1,100 and the most efficient model on the market—made by Whirlpool—uses only 750. This represents an energy savings of 32 percent from the average old model to the best available technology. Howard Geller estimates that placing a 750 kilowatt hour Whirlpool refrigerator in every home and apartment in the United States could shut down 12 1,000 megawatt coal-fired electricity plants. Other appliances also offer dramatic energy savings. The best air conditioner and the best water heater on the market use 75 percent less energy than the old average models. A new electric range uses 50 percent less energy than the old average model. New gas furnaces represent an energy savings of 59 percent. The best gas water heaters and gas ranges save 63 percent and 64 percent of energy usage; respectively. Howard S. Geller, "Energy-Efficient Residential Appliances: Performance Issues and Policy Options," *IEEE Technology and Society Magazine* (March 1986).

119. Electric heat pumps that heat in winter and cool in summer are replacing oil and gas. Since two-thirds of the energy needed to produce the electricity to run the heat pumps is lost at the power plant, the savings are not as spectacular as they might seem. However, heat pump clothes dryers are twice as efficient as conventional dryers. Howard Geller of the American Council for an Energy-Efficient Economy calculates that installing heat pump water heaters in American homes with conventional water heaters would eliminate the need for 15 large (1,000 megawatt) centralized power plants at a fraction of the cost. Howard S. Geller, "Energy-Efficient Residential Appliances: Performance Issues and Policy Options," *IEEE Technology and Society Magazine* (March

1986); and Durning and Flavin, "Building on Success: The Age of Energy Efficiency."

120. Gary Bosma, "A Realistic Approach to High Efficiency Gas, Water and Space Heating," in ACEEE, Proceedings from the 1986 ACEEE Summer Study on Energy Efficiency in Buildings, Vol. 1 (Appliances and Equipment) (Washington, DC: 1986); and, Durning and Flavin, "Building on Success: The Age of Energy Efficiency."

121. For example, one new screw-in 18-watt fluorescent bulb provides the light of a 75-watt incandescent bulb and lasts 10 times longer. In terms of energy savings this means that during their useful lives, an 18-watt fluorescent keeps 180 kilograms of coal in the ground and 130 kilograms of carbon out of the atmosphere.

Phillips has developed another light bulb called the "SL" which screws into a standard socket, provides excellent color, does not flicker, uses only one-quarter of the electricity of an ordinary 75-watt bulb and lasts 13 times longer. The high-priced SL bulb pays for itself two to three times over in electricity costs and replacement bulb costs.

Other energy-saving lighting technologies include high-frequency electronic ballasts, which cut energy use by 20 percent to 40 percent, and micro-electronic sensors, which automatically turn lights off and on according to the amount of sunlight in the room and people walking in and out. Substituting cool fluorescent bulbs for hot incandescent ones also lowers cooling bills. The California Energy Commission calculated that every 100-watt savings on lighting meant an additional 38-watt savings on air conditioning. Durning and Flavin, "Building on Success: The Age of Energy Efficiency," pp. 21, 22.

122. Ibid., p. 23.

123. Ibid.

124. The world's 400 million cars currently spew 547 million tons of carbon emissions into the atmosphere each year, which is 10 percent of the total from fossil fuels. If current trends continue, carbon emissions from cars would nearly double by the year 2010. However, if the number of cars was kept at no more than 500 million by 2010, through mass transit and greater use of bicycles and walking, and if all these cars were getting at least 50 mpg, carbon emissions would fall to 247 million tons per year, half of what they are today. Lester R. Brown, Christopher Flavin, and Sandra Postel, "Outlining a Global Action Plan," State of the World 1989 (New York: Norton, 1989).

125. Marc Ross, "Current Major Issues in Industrial Energy Use," Prepared for Office of Policy Integration, DOE, October 24, 1986; and Durning and Flavin, "Building on Success: The Age of Energy Efficiency."

126. Durning and Flavin, "Building on Success: The Age of Energy Efficiency," p. 31.

127. "Fuels and Energy," p. 46.

128. A few widely used technologies show great potential for energy savings. In the United States, 70 percent of industrial electricity goes for electromechanical drives, which can be improved in many ways. The use of electronic speed controls can cut power needs up to 50 percent. Sales of these drives have tripled since 1976. Durning and Flavin, "Building on Success: The Age of Energy Efficiency."

129. In 1985 13,000 megawatts were produced through cogeneration. More than 47,000 megawatts of planned cogeneration were registered with the Federal Energy Regulatory Commission (FERC) as of October 1, 1987. This is enough power to displace 47 large nuclear plants and has a market value of over $40 billion. Ibid., pp. 34–35.

130. Ibid., p. 36.
131. American Petroleum Institute, *Basic Petroleum Databook*, 5 (Washington, DC: 1985); and Durning and Flavin, "Building on Success: The Age of Energy Efficiency," p. 43.

chapter 8

Toxic
and Hazardous
Waste

Waste management is plagued by an "out of sight out of mind" public mentality. We are being slowly buried in our own garbage. Or, more accurately, the poor and racial minorities—being powerless to prevent it—are being buried.

As indicated in Chapter 1, one of the most dramatic examples of the environmental policy paradox may be found in the area of waste management. For example, for several decades we have understood and could have anticipated most of our solid waste problems. Based on available data from 31 states, the United States can continue to dispose of wastes in landfills for only 12.5 more years.[1] Policymakers, however, have been slow to act. The incremental nature of the policy process, the incentives operating on policymakers to adopt short-term low-cost policy options, and the lack of, until the late 1980s, any publicly perceived crisis, have all operated to produce waste policies that are not viable in the long run.

In this section we read about solid and hazardous waste management problems. We begin by summarizing the nature of our waste and the relationship between industrial development and waste generation. Due to their different composition and methods of disposal, the discussion is divided into two subsections, one on solid waste and one on hazardous waste.

SOLID WASTE

What Is Solid Waste?

In natural systems, waste products are broken down by decomposer organisms and converted to a form for use by other organisms within the ecosystem. Urbanization, agricultural specialization, and industrialization have produced inorganic by-products that have disrupted these natural systems. Today when an apple is produced on a farm and shipped to the city, organic material in the apple core is thrown in a trash can and eventually hauled to a landfill, thus taken out of the organic production cycle. Back on the farm, fertilizers are necessary to replace nutrients that have been depleted from the soil, some of which now lie—useless—in a landfill. Likewise, when waste was scattered across the surface of the land (i.e., agricultural waste, human or animal waste) it all became a part of natural ecological cycles. The concentration of wastes and the removal of wastes from the ecosystems in which they would naturally biodegrade has resulted in massive quantities of refuse, usually referred to as solid waste.

There is no precise definition of solid waste. The term is often applied to liquids as opposed to solids and to things that are not necessarily waste.[2] Here we limit our discussion to municipal waste, agricultural waste, and mining waste, paying particular attention to municipal waste and means of disposal of these wastes.

The difficulty in defining waste is reflected in the fragmented laws that are meant to deal with it. Of the nine major federal laws regulating some aspect of waste, some focus on where the waste is discharged (i.e., land, air, or water); where it comes from (e.g., a nuclear power plant); how it is disposed of; or the focus is on some characteristic of the waste, for example, if the waste is toxic or radioactive.[3]

Scope of the Problem

In the United States, per capita production of solid waste is estimated to be around 50,000 pounds every year. For the average family, if this waste was stacked out in the backyard, every year it would create a pile approximately 10 feet on each side and 28 feet high in the middle.[4] Most solid waste comes from mining or agriculture. It is estimated that from 1 to 2 trillion tons of solid waste each year (about 13,000 pounds per person in the United States) is generated from noncoal mining, and that most of these wastes are dumped on the ground near where they are generated. Likewise agricultural waste, which amounts to around 2 billion tons annually, is left in the fields—where it may accumulate or run off the land to pollute rivers and streams.

Municipal waste amounts to approximately 300 million tons a year in the United States. Although smaller in volume than agricultural or mining waste, municipal waste presents greater political and managerial problems, often having serious environmental impacts on land and water resources.

Although solid waste management problems are not unique to the United States, the country is rather singular in terms of the volume of municipal waste generated. On a per capita basis, the United States generates more than twice as much municipal waste as most of the more developed countries in the world.[5]

In 1990 67 percent of municipal solid waste was landfilled, 17 percent was recycled, and 16 percent was destroyed through incineration.[6] Meanwhile, the number of landfills in operation dropped from 8,000 in 1988 to 5,812 in 1991.[7] The decline is expected to continue as Resource Conservation and Recovery Act (RCRA) standards are tightened and landfills are closed rather than upgraded. A study undertaken in 1986 found that 75 percent of surveyed states had insufficient solid waste landfill capacity.[8] For example, in New Jersey, over 100 landfills that were handling as much as 90 percent of the state's waste in the late 1970s had been closed by 1987.[9] It was estimated in 1987 that 33 dumps being used by the city of Chicago would be full by the mid-1990s as would the dumps then in use by the city of Los Angeles.[10] Some New England towns that ran out of local dump space operate trucks on a 24-hour basis to carry waste to dump sites in Pennsylvania and Ohio. Towns on Long Island in New York ship their trash as far west as Michigan.[11]

Running out of space is only one of the problems associated with solid waste disposal. New York City's Fresh Kills landfill on Staten Island, a monstrosity approaching 200 feet which is expected to reach a peak of 500 feet when it closes in the late 1990s, leaks an estimated 4 million gallons a day of toxic fluids into nearby streams.[12] Improper disposal of solid waste can lead to a wide range of diseases including typhoid, dysentery, cholera, and infectious hepatitis.[13]

Disposal Methods

Adverse health effects, if any, depend on the methods used to dispose of solid waste. Disposal methods for municipal solid waste include open dumping, which is often accompanied by open burning, ocean dumping, and sanitary landfills. While open dumps and open burning are prohibited, and ocean dumping is limited by the Marine Protection, Research and Sanctuaries Act, all of these disposal methods are used by local governments throughout the United States. In theory, sanitary landfills provide a safe and effective means of disposal. Unfortunately, the theory of sanitary landfill operation oftentimes does not match the practice.

A sanitary landfill should be lined with some type of impervious barrier, either clay, granite, or some other natural material or some manufactured source. The sides of the landfill should slope, and polluted water that percolates through the landfill should be channeled off and disposed of properly. As waste is added to the landfill, it should be covered with 6 inches of fresh soil at the end of every day to prevent odor and the transmittal of disease by rats, flies, or other rodents and vermin. As noted in the example of the Fresh Kills landfill in New York City, many landfills do not, for a variety of reasons, meet this ideal. The primary problem is that landfills are often not constructed with satisfactory drainage capacity and the 6-inch daily cover of fresh soil may or may not adequately prevent exposure of the trash to the elements.

In the early 1990s, the fastest growing method of municipal waste disposal is the incineration of waste in conjunction with the sanitary landfill disposal of the resultant ash and noncombustible materials. This is the preferred method of disposal in several European countries and it has the advantage of producing electricity as a by-product. In Denmark in 1980, municipalities were using 60 percent of their waste to produce energy by burning the waste to produce steam. The Netherlands, Switzerland, and Sweden were processing close to 60 percent of their waste in this manner.[14] The United States is still far behind other countries in the use of solid waste to generate energy. EPA estimates that 16 percent of solid waste in the United States is incinerated.[15]

Most coastal cities have discontinued the dumping of municipal wastewater sludge in the ocean as a means of disposal. Wastewater sludge, what is left after the treatment of sewage, was still dumped into the ocean at a few major coastal cities including New York, Los Angeles, and Boston until a 1989 federal law ordered it stopped by 1991.[16]

Regulations

Although Congress, in 1965, passed the Solid Waste Disposal Act, this legislation is only advisory.[17] Solid waste disposal has traditionally been the responsibility of the state, and more importantly, the local government. In its findings when considering the Solid Waste Disposal Act, Congress stated "that while the collection and disposal of solid waste should continue to be primarily a function of state, regional, and local agencies" federal action was required through financial and technical assistance.[18]

The Resource Recovery Act of 1970 maintained a largely hands-off federal approach to local solid waste management by providing financial assistance for the construction of solid waste disposal facilities and funds for additional research.[19] It was not until passage of the Resource Conservation and Recovery Act of 1976 (RCRA) that the federal government got involved to any significant degree in the management of solid waste. Although most of the RCRA deals with the disposal of hazardous waste, it also created, for the first time, significant federal regulations for the management of municipal waste.

The RCRA required states to develop solid waste management plans, which, among other things, would stipulate the closing of all open dumps and either the recycling of wastes or the disposal of waste within sanitary landfills.[20] In 1993, 17 years after passage of the RCRA, opened dumps were still common in rural areas and many municipalities are either not practicing or inadequately practicing sanitary landfill methods.

As we have seen, some municipalities export their solid wastes into neighboring states. In the 1970s several states and localities, in an attempt to prevent the importation of waste into their areas, passed restrictions aimed at other states that prohibited the flow of waste to local disposal sites. In 1978 the U.S. Supreme Court found that such restrictions violated the commerce clause of the Constitution by restricting interstate commerce.[21]

Solutions

Solid waste management provides a good example of the environmental policy paradox in operation. The problem and its solutions have been well known to policymakers for decades. However, the best long-term solutions to municipal waste problems are expensive whereas short-term solutions seem to be cheap. Municipal solid waste management in many areas is reaching the crisis stage. Policymakers in some areas are being forced to take what they consider drastic measures that they might not otherwise be willing to consider. California, New York, New Jersey, and Connecticut have all implemented plans designed to recycle 25 percent of their solid waste and to incinerate much of the rest to produce energy.[22] California has targeted 50 percent recycling by the year 2000. Other localities have responded by requiring the separation of trash into recyclables and nonrecyclables, passing bottle bills (a universal deposit on returnable containers), and imposing litter or refuse taxes.

Recycling holds the most promise for the long-term reduction of solid waste. A great deal of the solid waste generated in the United States could be recycled. Roughly 37 percent of municipal solid waste is paper, 18 percent yard wastes, 10 percent metals, and 7 percent plastics—virtually all of which could be recycled.[23] However only 17 percent of solid waste was being recycled or reused in the United States in 1993.[24] Many communities in Japan and in parts of Europe recycle an excess of 50 percent of their solid waste. The major drawback to recycling is its cost and the requirement that individuals participate in the recycling process to attain maximum efficiency.

Unfortunately, the tax structure in the United States in a number of ways favors the use of virgin materials over recycled resources. For example, favoritism is shown through accelerated depreciation, depletion allowances, and special deductions for mineral exploration. As well, the U.S. rail freight rates discriminate against recycled materials, since railroads often charge a higher rate for recycled goods as opposed to virgin goods. Therefore many businesses find it profitable to avoid recycling.[25]

As of 1993, nine states had responded to the solid waste problem in part by the passage of traditional "bottle laws." In addition some states, such as California and Florida, have passed nontraditional incentive programs.[26] The first state to pass such a law was Oregon, which in 1971 began requiring a minimum 5 cent deposit on beer and soft drink containers. Bottle laws have significantly reduced roadside litter in Oregon and the other states in which they have been enacted. In addition, these laws have had some significant side benefits, including an increase in employment and a reduction of injuries suffered by children from broken glass in state parks. However, these laws encounter strong opposition from industry groups that manufacture beverage containers, supermarkets, and labor unions.

The success or failure of bottle bills in various states is indicative of the decentralization of environmental administration and problems that result therefrom. When local bottling or labor interests are influential in a state or locality, they may be successful in preventing implementation of waste management methods that they perceive to be against their interests, as bottling companies and labor unions were for many years in California.

A related problem is that a solid waste disposal site is a so-called LULU, or "locally unwanted land use." LULUs include power plants, airports, prisons, landfills, and low-income housing, to name a few. LULUs are often located in poor or economically disadvantaged areas. This should not be surprising, for it is in these areas where the inhabitants lack the political influence to prevent the siting of a LULU in their neighborhoods. The siting of a LULU in a poor neighborhood can often mean that such areas become even more disadvantaged.[27]

A sanitary landfill need not, however, be a LULU. The technology exists for the creation of landfills in conjunction with incineration and other disposal methods, making landfills an acceptable neighbor with no unsightly mountains of garbage or nasty smells.[28] However, the controls necessary to make a LULU an acceptable neighbor, and recycle or otherwise process our solid waste, can be expensive. Thus solid waste management is a good example of a policy problem that has short-term low-cost solutions that are inferior and long-term solutions that are superior yet require relatively high short-term expenditures. As we have seen, the incentives operating in the policy-making process in such situations motivate politicians to select the low-cost short-term solution. Here it is opening up or overloading a dump, or transporting waste into an adjacent state. Fortunately, or unfortunately depending on your perspective, solid waste management has reached crisis proportions in many regions, and consequently, policymakers no longer have the luxury of making the low-cost short-term decision. The low-cost decision has already been made in previous decades and now the bills must be paid.

Our dominant social paradigm plays an important role in the management of solid waste. The United States has become a throwaway society. Between 30 and 40 percent of all municipal waste in the United States consists of packaging materials; close to half of the cost of many consumer items is taken up in packaging.[29] We have become accustomed to the convenience of individual packaging, of disposable razors, bottles, and other consumer items. Only a generation ago, it was common for people to carry their own containers to the supermarket, to recycle milk and soft drink bottles, and to compost vegetable waste. The accepted convenience of a disposable society will be hard to break. Clearly, however, given the limitations on space for additional landfills, the break will be made. Changes have already occurred in some communities; for example, curbside recycling programs grew from 1,000 in 1988 to almost 4,000 by 1991.[30] The city of Los Angeles is planning to expand its program from its weekly pickup at 720,000 households to over 1 million households and to include yard trimmings, newspapers, corrugated cardboard, plastics, glass, food containers, steel, and aluminum cans.[31] The number of curbside recycling programs outnumbers the number of landfills in the Great Lakes and mid-Atlantic states. Not surprisingly, such programs have been least accepted in the more spacious Rocky Mountain and midwestern states.[32] In some states, at least, such measures will become the norm in the not too distant future.

HAZARDOUS WASTES

Toxic pollution affects you whether you know it or not. In the United States 8 out of 10 Americans, over 190 million people, live near a toxic waste dump or a source of toxic waste. Nearly half of all Americans live in counties containing toxic waste sites that have been identified by the Environmental Protection Agency as a priority site for cleanup.[33] Toxic pollutants are found throughout the earth's environment. Even polar bears living in the Arctic wilderness have been found to contain a wide variety of toxic chemicals including DDT and TCBs.[34] Although estimates vary, one study by the U.S. General Accounting Office found there may be as many as 425,389 toxic waste sites that are potential Superfund sites which may need corrective action.[35] Officials of the EPA have been quoted as calling the toxic waste problem "the most grave error in judgment we as a nation have ever made ... one of the most serious problems the nation has ever faced."[36]

Nature of the Problem

There are numerous sources of toxic pollutants. Toxic wastes are a by-product of energy development, agriculture, and most industrial activity. Toxic wastes are discussed throughout this book because they are found throughout the environment, in our air, water, and soil.

We do not know exactly how much toxic waste is produced in the United States or where that waste is disposed of with any great degree of certainty. As a study by the U.S. Office of Technology Assessment concluded, "There are major uncertainties on how much hazardous waste has been generated, the types and capacities of existing waste management facilities, the number of uncontrolled waste sites and their hazard levels, and on the health and environmental effects of hazardous waste releases."[37]

The largest 1 percent of hazardous waste generators produced 97 percent of hazardous wastes or close to 200 million tons in 1989. Medical (infectious) wastes produced in 1990 exceeded 465,000 tons.

Perhaps of even greater concern, however, are radioactive wastes. Commercial *low-level* waste is the term used for nuclear reactors that can deliver lethal doses of radiation in seconds.[38]

Rather than measuring volume, it is more informative to look at the amount of radioactivity, or curies. An uncontaminated area will register 5 to 20 disintegrations per *minute*; one curie is 37 billion disintegrations per *second*. In 1992 commercial disposal sites received over 1 million curies, 86 percent of which came from utilities.[39] These figures do not reflect the amount of waste generated, but only that shipped to licensed dumps. They also do not include radioactive wastes from weapons production; wastes from large reactor facilities that were decommissioned (at least four); wastes that have been deregulated and disposed of as hazardous only; or contaminated soils, described by the Nuclear Regulatory Commission's Nuclear Information and Resource Service as existing in "very large volumes."[40]

In addition to low-level wastes, there are commercial high-level wastes. One metric ton of light-water reactor irradiated fuel is estimated to contain over 177 million curies at discharge; irradiated fuel from nuclear plants is estimated to reach over 40,000 metric tons by the year 2000, or 6.8 trillion curies.

While exact figures of hazardous waste generation are not known, some estimate that only 10 percent of the hazardous waste generated in the United States is handled in a safe manner.[41] The EPA reports only 2 million tons of toxic wastes stored or disposed of on land, and 1 million tons incinerated. An additional 28 million tons are injected into wells.[42] Environmentalists challenge the use of injection wells and the validity of the models on which they are based, saying the models *assume* wastes will behave predictably but have never been tested.[43] While the EPA is tightening well injection regulations, producers report there are voluntary efforts underway to discontinue such practices by the year 2000.[44]

There is no question the many chemical substances that have been developed since World War II have contributed to the improvement of our quality of life. Chemicals have improved the control of disease, agricultural productivity, and production of goods and services in ways that we have come to take for granted. However, we do not know what price we have paid, or will pay in the future, for these benefits. The human effects of toxic contaminants are numerous and severe. Cancer, nervous system damage, kidney, liver, chromosomal, and lung damage as well as genetic mutations are some of the human impacts that may result from exposure to toxic pollutants. Perhaps even more frightening than this list of possible dangers is the fact that we know so little about the human impacts of toxins.

Over 7 million chemicals are known of which around 80,000 are in common use, with thousands more being discovered every year. Many of these chemicals are potentially hazardous. Globally, the production of chemicals has skyrocketed from 7 million tons a year in 1950, 63 million tons in 1970, to an estimated 250 million tons in 1985.[45] The National

Academy of Sciences published a report in 1984 on chemicals in the American environment and concluded "of tens of thousands of commercially important chemicals, only a few have been subjected to extensive toxicity testing, and most have scarcely been tested at all."[46]

In addition to a lack of knowledge, other problems are associated with the regulation of toxic substances. First, there are frequently latent effects on humans where the damage may not show up until decades after exposure to a toxic substance. Second, toxic substances can accumulate in plants and animals at higher dosage than in the surrounding environment and thus build up over time. This accumulation can be in your internal organs. Third, smaller dosages of toxic substances produce harmful effects on humans and plants and other animals than do conventional pollutants. Finally, many toxic substances resist biological breakdown.

The major regulatory problem with respect to toxic or hazardous waste disposal is finding the proper means, and policing those means, of the handling, storage, and disposal of hazardous waste.

Disposal Methods

It is estimated that between 80 and 90 percent of the hazardous waste produced each year is disposed of illegally or improperly. Roughly 60 percent of all hazardous and toxic waste in the United States is injected into deep wells, 35 percent is held in surface impoundments or holding tanks, and roughly 5 percent is deposited into landfills.[47] In addition to underground injection and land disposal, hazardous waste may be disposed of in the oceans, by incineration, through microbiotic breakdown, or the transport of waste—usually from more developed to less developed countries. Each of these options carries with them associated problems.

In theory, underground injection of hazardous waste provides a relatively cheap and safe method of disposal. A hole is drilled an average of 4,000 feet below the surface of the earth and an inner pipe, known as an injection tube, encased in steel and cement to prevent leaks into groundwater aquifers, is inserted. The waste is then pumped into the hole and, optimally, kept separate from freshwater aquifers. In fact, due to incorrect estimations of the interface between drinking water and hazardous injection sites, as well as leaks and spills and improperly functioning injection equipment, there have been numerous incidences of hazardous waste polluting drinking water.[48] According to the public interest law firm, the Legal Environmental Assistance Foundation (LEAF), at least 25 states have documented evidence of problems caused by underground injection of hazardous waste. As Suzie Ruhl, the executive director of LEAF stated,

> [I]t's a giant problem, but it's a stepchild within both the environmental movement and the regulatory system. I've been distraught over how little attention this has received. We can't show dead bodies right now. It's a classic out of sight, out of mind technology. I feel that underground injection is posing the greatest threat to our groundwater because of inadequate regula-

tions. They are just postponing our day of reckoning with the hazardous waste problem.[49]

The ocean dumping of hazardous waste is another serious dilemma— one suffering from the common pool property management problems that plague the oceans generally. An estimated 8 million tons of toxic waste are dumped annually into the coastal waters off the United States. Timothy Kao and Joseph Bishop, of the Catholic University Department of Civil Engineering and Oceanography, stated in a study of toxic pollutants in the ocean that "while major oil spills are highly visible and forced their attention on the public conscience, the dumping of toxic waste, on the other hand, is an idiocy and potentially more serious problem."[50] Many of these pollutants are nonbiodegradable and as Kao and Bishop note,

[W]hat is worse is that the toxic pollutant moves up in concentrates in the marine food chain. At the base of the marine food chain is phytoplankton, which may act as a primary concentrator of a pollutant. These are ingested by zooplankton, which in turn are fed on by crustaceans and fish. Contaminantly, the pollutant gets progressively more concentrated until it reaches lethal level for landbase species including humans.[51]

The incineration of hazardous waste may be the most promising long-term solution to the hazardous waste disposal problem. As the U.S. Office of Technology Assessment reported in 1983, "All land disposal methods will eventually fail."[52] Liners deteriorate, the ground shifts, it is only a question of when they will fail. Many toxic substances when heated to temperatures above 2,400°F are broken down. EPA tests of a mobile incinerator in Times Beach, Missouri, found that by heating soil polluted with dioxin to temperatures of up to 4,000°F, 99.99 percent of the dioxin was destroyed.[53]

The major obstacles to incineration of hazardous waste are political. As we see later, the public has generally opposed having disposal sites in their neighborhoods, and in the United States as well as abroad there has been vigorous opposition to building new incineration sites.[54]

As an alternative, incineration may be done on seagoing vessels. Various European countries have been incinerating at sea since 1969. The first officially sanctioned ocean incineration of hazardous waste in the United States occurred between October 1974 and January 1975 in the Gulf of Mexico. Intermittently since then, the EPA has tried to promote the incineration of hazardous waste at sea with varying success. The agency believed that much of the opposition to incineration on shore would not present itself if incineration was at sea. That has not been the case. Residents of coastal zone areas as well as environmental activists have been strongly opposed to the incineration of hazardous waste at sea.

In 1983 the EPA came close to issuing permits to the Chemical Waste Management Company to incinerate 80 million gallons of organic compounds in the Gulf of Mexico. In the face of public opposition the agency withheld the necessary permits. At the time, a spokesperson for the Office

of Technology Assessment said, "It's not at all clear if we will be incinerating anything at sea, at least in the near future. There's so much political
uproar even over research burns."[55]

Two years later when the EPA announced plans to issue permits for
experimental burnings of chemicals in the Atlantic Ocean, environmentalists were again in an uproar. As Eric Draper, the coordinator of the
National Campaign Against Toxic Hazards, stated at the time, "[I]t's a stupid decision. At this point, we are fighting for toxic source reduction. It's
not the time to start panacea solutions to toxic waste by taking it out in the
middle of the ocean and burning it."[56]

One of the problems with incineration at sea is the possibility of leaks
or spillage in the transportation of waste from land to the seas. As Peter
Carson, director of the Mid-Atlantic Cleanwater Action Project stated,
"[P]eople make mistakes, and when you make a mistake out in the ocean,
nobody is going to see it."[57]

One approach that some manufacturers and many of the more developed nations have taken for the disposal of hazardous waste has been
exporting that waste to other countries. With the current cost of disposal in
landfills estimated at $145 to $615 a drum for hazardous solids, and incineration costs that can range from $200 to $400 a drum,[58] many U.S. hazardous
waste generators try to avoid waste disposal in the United States. In part,
this has been done by corporations establishing manufacturing plants in
areas that have environmental protection requirements less restrictive than
the United States. For example, among major producers of chemicals in the
United States, the Dow Company has 59 manufacturing plants abroad, Du
Pont has 52, 3M has 41, and the Monsanto Corporation has 20.[59]

Attempts to export hazardous waste have, in many cases, created a
backlash among the people in the importing countries. For example, in
September 1988, in reaction to an Italian government order to let a toxic
waste carrier dock in the Italian port of Manfredonia, the city council
resigned en masse. The citizens of Manfredonia rioted for three days, setting fire to the town hall door and blocking entrances to the city.[60] In 1989
five ships carrying Italian hazardous waste were circling the globe in search
of a place to dispose of their cargo. In case after case where a hazardous
waste disposal destination was identified and the local population
informed of the importing agreements, such agreements to accept waste
have fallen through. For example, 15,000 tons of toxic ash from Philadelphia
municipal incinerators circled the globe for two years in the late 1980s trying to find a disposal site and being rejected by country after country.[61]

Those exporting hazardous waste have been able to find some willing
recipients among the less developed countries, however. It is not difficult to
understand the willingness of the leadership in some countries to accept the
hazardous waste of the more developed nations. The tiny nation of Guinea-
Bissau, which had a gross national product of $160 million in 1984, was
offered $40 a ton by a Swiss firm to bury drums of hazardous waste. The
deal did not go through. However, the $600 million that Guinea-Bissau

would have made over a five-year period was an attractive inducement for the poor nation.

Many less developed nations lack the technology or the sophistication necessary to handle the proper disposal of hazardous waste. Furthermore, many more developed countries have few if any restrictions on the exportation of hazardous waste.

In the United States hazardous waste exporters are required to give notice to the EPA prior to exporting waste and to receive the consent of the receiving country. Poor enforcement, due largely to inadequate staffing at the EPA, and loopholes in the law have hampered the effectiveness of the statute. Hundreds of tons of hazardous waste have been exported from the United States without proper notifications of intent to export filed with the EPA.[62]

Most less developed countries are opposed to transboundary shipments of hazardous wastes.[63] However, formal agreements and pronouncements are clearly inadequate to stem the tide of hazardous waste export. For example, Mexico and the United States have signed agreements governing the exportation of hazardous waste as well as the generation of hazardous waste by U.S. companies within Mexico. Nevertheless, Mexico has serious hazardous waste problems both from U.S. firms within its borders and from importation of waste from the United States. In 1986 three Americans and one Mexican were arrested in connection with the dumping of over 100,000 gallons of toxic waste in Mexico into "a few holes in the ground."[64] In 1993 the North American Free Trade Agreement (NAFTA) was approved by the United States. Although there have been various "side agreements"[65] dealing with environmental and pollution control measures, it is unclear what impact NAFTA will have on environmental quality in the United States or Mexico.

The disposal of hazardous waste is a particularly difficult problem for the more developed countries of Western Europe. Many Western European nations are generating two to four times the amount of waste they have the capacity to dispose of within their own countries. And, as with hazardous waste everywhere, a major problem is overcoming local opposition to the construction of hazardous waste disposal facilities. Great Britain, which still relies on land disposal for the bulk of its hazardous waste, has become a major European importer of hazardous waste. Hazardous waste traveling into the United Kingdom increased from 5,000 tons in 1983 to an excess of 350,000 tons in the early 1990s. The UK may be asking for problems both in the short and long term. Three-quarters of the local government authorities that have responsibility for hazardous waste control in the United Kingdom have no formal plan to deal with the waste.[66]

One possible solution for the management of hazardous and toxic waste is using microbes and enzymes to detoxify, deactivate, or otherwise degrade or break down complex chemicals. This method is particularly promising for pesticides and solvents; however, not all substances break down. Where appropriate this treatment may cost significantly less than other disposal alternatives and is much more environmentally acceptable.[67]

Federal Regulations

Toxic substances are regulated in the United States under a variety of federal acts. Chemicals used commercially are regulated under the Toxic Substances Control Act, the Federal Insecticide, Fungicide and Rodenticide Act, and the Food, Drug, and Cosmetics Act. These acts require that the manufacturers of chemicals conduct their own product safety tests and submit the results to the federal government. The regulatory agency involved then makes a decision on a case-by-case basis as to whether or not to ban the chemical, regulate its use, or leave it unregulated. The tests are also used to determine safe levels of exposure to chemical residues in drinking water, air, food, or the workplace. A major problem with these and other toxic substance control acts is the cost and number of substances that need to be tested. It is estimated that for each chemical, a good test can take from two to four years and cost from $40,000 to $1 million. As a result, critics have charged, only 1 percent of all commercial chemicals have been carefully tested.[68]

To regulate toxins that find their way into the environment through manufacturing and other industrial processes, Congress has passed the Clean Air Act, the Clean Water Act, the Occupational Safety and Health Act, and the Safe Drinking Water Act. Federal regulators undertake risk assessment to determine safe levels of exposure to regulated toxins under these laws and require that pollutants released into the air, water, or working environment do not exceed those standards. As we discuss in both the chapters on air pollution (Chapter 5) and water pollution (Chapter 6), many pollutants have not been evaluated to determine the "safe" level of exposure. And, as we discuss in Chapter 3, risk analysis is full of uncertainty. The two federal statutes that are most important in regulating the disposal of hazardous waste are the Resource Conservation and Recovery Act (RCRA) and the Comprehensive Environmental Response Compensation and Liability Act (also known as Superfund). The RCRA requires that anyone storing, treating, or disposing of hazardous waste do so under permit from the EPA. Permits are granted only to those firms that can demonstrate they have the financial capacity, the necessary insurance, and the expertise to know how to operate a landfill or disposal facility. The RCRA applies to any producer of hazardous waste generating at least 220 pounds of waste a month, an amount that fills a 55-gallon drum about halfway. The act provides the EPA with the authority to impose fines and hold individuals criminally liable for the improper disposal of waste. Because of their extreme toxicity, certain substances may not be disposed of in landfills or through underground injection.[69]

The Superfund established a fund jointly financed by the federal government and industry to finance the cleanup of hazardous waste sites that have been identified and placed on a hazardous waste site "priority list" by the EPA. The EPA may either clean up the site on its own using Superfund monies, require that the generator of the waste clean up the site, or sue those responsible for the waste and use the proceeds to clean the site. Those liable for cleanup cost include waste generators, waste handlers, waste site owners, or any middle person who arranged for disposal of the hazardous waste at the site. Furthermore, generators and handlers of toxic waste are liable for cleanup costs regardless of when the waste was generated or disposed of, even if the disposal was done in compliance with laws in effect at the time. The owners of hazardous waste sites are liable even if they had no knowledge that hazardous waste was being disposed there. In one case, for example, the Monsanto Chemical Corporation agreed to contribute $13 million to the cleaning up of a site where it had dumped acids more than 50 years previously.[70] State and local governments that have operated or are operating waste disposal sites, or allowed others to operate on the sites with governmental approval, are also liable under the act.[71]

Initially budgeted with $1.6 billion in 1980, $7 billion was added to the Superfund in 1986. Additional appropriations of $6.8 billion were made between 1990 and 1993. It is estimated, though, that the National Priority List (NPL) of Superfund sites will, as of 1992, require $16.4 billion alone to remedy. To help offset cleanup costs, a "potentially responsible party" program was instituted in 1986 wherein the EPA seeks reimbursement for cleanups from potentially liable parties. By the end of fiscal year 1992, $7.4 billion had been recouped.[72]

In terms of the number of sites, the EPA initially estimated there would be 400 NPL sites. Now the EPA projects as many as 4,800 sites may be eligible, though it may take 50 years to get them on the NPL. A University of Tennessee report estimates that by the year 2020 the cost of cleaning up NPL sites will be in the neighborhood of $200 billion a year. Currently there are 1,200 sites on the NPL, and although remedial action has begun on most of them, cleanup has only been completed on 55 sites since the program began.[73]

In some cases cleaning consisted of removing the waste from an unapproved site to an EPA-approved waste disposal facility. For example, in Greenville, Mississippi, 226 drums of toxic chemicals were moved to an approved landfill in Alabama, leading some to question the true extent of Superfund's "success."[74]

Both the RCRA and Superfund are plagued with budgetary, staffing, and enforcement problems. Close to 80 percent of the disposal sites licensed by RCRA are reportedly in violation of the law. The EPA has had to relax RCRA requirements because so few firms handling hazardous waste have been able to meet their requirements.[75] In the case of the Superfund, Congress was quick to pass legislation dealing with a visible environmental problem, but has been slow to appropriate funds necessary to deal with the problem—a good example of the environmental policy paradox. Policymakers were able to take credit for dealing with a problem that had come to the attention of the public but have not followed through with the resources necessary to complete the job.

Regulatory Problems

The formal requirements of any regulatory system tell only part of the story. Perhaps more important, and more interesting for what it teaches us about environmental policy, are the regulatory problems that have been encountered in implementing the RCRA.

Major regulatory problems involved in implementing the RCRA include public objections to toxic waste disposal facilities, insurance and liability concerns, the cost of disposal and related effects, and the lack of incentives in the legislation to reduce the generation of toxic substances.

Perhaps the greatest regulatory problem concerning toxic waste, a problem that makes everything the RCRA is attempting to do more difficult, is the position that industries and state regulators have taken toward the disposal of toxic waste in the past. The combination of an "out of sight out of mind" attitude as well as a misunderstanding of the cleansing capacity of the earth and the ability of toxic substances to move underground led, until the late 1960s and early 1970s, to very poor control over the disposal of toxic substances. Companies in the past have allowed waste to accumulate on their property in open lagoons or in drums that often leak with little concern or control over the long-term consequences of their actions. Furthermore, many state regulatory bodies have been lax in their regulatory efforts. For example, in California at the Stringfellow toxic dump site in Riverside County, a geologist hired by the state spent less than one hour investigating the site to determine whether or not the granite bedrock was impermeable and would be a safe repository for toxic waste. Stringfellow was a repository for toxic waste for 32 years and now threatens major sources of drinking water in the Los Angeles basin. It will cost an estimated $600 million to clean up Stringfellow.[76]

A major problem in the implementation of the RCRA and Superfund is the cost of cleaning waste disposal sites. The cost of cleaning up an average Superfund site in the early 1990s was $30 million. The U.S. Office of Technology Assessment estimated it could cost in excess of $100 billion, or $1,000 per household, for the cleanup of hazardous waste sites that have been identified in the United States.[77] Some think these cost estimates are conservative. Appropriations for Superfund had been a fraction of this amount. As we have seen under Superfund and the RCRA, the generators and transporters of hazardous waste as well as the owners of landfills have primary responsibility for disposing of waste properly and cleaning up improperly disposed waste. For a generator of toxic waste, this can be a significant sum. These costs have had two effects, one positive and one negative. On the one hand, the hazardous waste disposal business is booming as many legitimate operators are finding there is money to be made in the handling of hazardous waste. On the other hand, the incidence of "midnight dumping," or the illegal disposal of hazardous waste, has increased significantly.

The RCRA has a system for tracking hazardous waste, but as stated in a *Forbes* article, "[E]nvironmental protection agencies on both the state and federal level have set up elaborate tracking procedures to assure that hazardous wastes are disposed of properly, but circumventing them is easy. You just falsify the manifest."[78] A hazardous waste generator who ignores the EPA requirements by failing to notify the EPA of its existence and shipping the waste offsite without a manifest or disposing of its waste on its own premises without a permit is, according to an article in *Chemical and Engineering News*, "not likely to be found out. Neither is a transporter who forges a manifest stating that waste arrived at its proper destination when it didn't."[79]

A related problem has been the arrival of organized crime into the hazardous waste disposal business. Organized crime is already heavily involved, particularly on the East Coast, in the garbage collection and disposal business. According to a former teamster official, organized crime on the East Coast has utilized their control of the trash collection business to dispose of toxic waste illegally either by blending clean garbage with toxic waste and shipping it to landfills or by bribing dock operators to look the other way.[80] Waste is illegally disposed of by abandoning drums on deserted roads, opening tanker spigots and allowing the toxic liquids to flow onto highways, mixing toxic substances with fuel oil, burying tanker trucks, or pouring liquids into mine shafts, sewer systems, or along rivers and streams. All of these things happen with alarming regularity. For example, thousands of gallons of heating oil laced with dangerous chemicals were sold to Manhattan apartment owners before it was discovered the concoction was toxic. In this example the violators, connected to organized crime, profited from disposing of the hazardous waste and again from selling it in heating oil.[81]

A poll conducted for *Time* magazine in 1985 found that 79 percent of Americans felt not enough had been done to clean up toxic waste sites. When asked, "Would you be willing to pay higher state and local taxes to fund cleanup programs in your area?" 34 percent said no, 64 percent said yes, and only 2 percent were unsure.[82] Public support for cleaning up toxic and hazardous waste and public support for building a hazardous waste disposal facility, however, are two different things. A toxic waste disposal facility is a LULU of the greatest magnitude (or a lulu of a LULU, if you will). In 1980 the EPA estimated that between 50 and 125 new hazardous waste facilities, including treatment facilities, landfills, and incinerators, would be needed in the near future.[83] However, largely because of the public opposition, few new major hazardous waste facilities have been built in the United States since that time. When asked at what distance they would be comfortable having a variety of new industrial installations constructed from their homes, a hazardous waste disposal site was seen as the least desirable new neighbor.[84]

Given the nature of the policy-making process and the resources necessary for influencing public policy, where would you anticipate hazardous waste sites to be placed? Several studies have found that hazardous waste sites are most likely to be found in poor neighborhoods and neighborhoods with a large percentage of racial minorities. A U.S. General

Accounting Office study of hazardous waste landfills in the Southeast found that three out of four landfills were in areas that were predominantly black and poor. A United Church of Christ Commission on Racial Justice study in 1987 found that, in the words of the commission executive director Benjamin Chavis, "[T]he results of our research conclusively show that race has been the most discriminating factor of all those tested in the location of commercial hazardous waste facilities in the U.S."[85] In Houston, Texas, all of the city's five landfills and six of the city's eight municipal incinerators are located in predominantly black neighborhoods. The director of research for the Church of Christ racial justice study commented, "[T]he unwritten law governing corporate decision making about toxics seems to have been to do what you can get away with. It means that those communities which are poor, less informed, less organized, and less politically influential become more likely targets for abuse from polluters." Ecologist Barry Commoner put it another way. "[T]here is a functional link between racism, poverty and powerlessness, and the chemical industry's assault on the environment."[86]

Two related problems concerning the implementation of hazardous waste regulations are the inability of hazardous waste generators and handlers to secure liability insurance and bankruptcy. Amendments to the RCRA in 1984 required that all hazardous waste facility operators comply with certain financial liability standards by the end of 1985.[87] Failure to meet the standards meant the facilities would be required to close. When the deadline arrived, 48 land disposal facilities were unable to meet their financial liability requirements because they were unable to find insurance.[88] Superfund holds liable those transporting, storing, or producing hazardous waste, even if they were following government regulations in force at the time of their activity—that is, even if they were not doing anything wrong at the time of disposal and unanticipated problems develop later, referred to as strict liability. Estimating future liability for cleanup cost under such circumstances can be very difficult. Consequently, many insurance companies have pulled out of the pollution liability insurance market.[89] Even when insurance is available, the cost may be so great as to make insurance coverage impossible to afford for all but the largest operators. Yearly premiums on hazardous waste liability insurance policies can run as high as amount of coverage provided for the year.[90]

Faced with what can often be huge cleanup expenses, many companies chose bankruptcy as a way to avoid liability. In 1977 a solvent recovery firm in Massachusetts declared bankruptcy, leaving the state with about a million gallons of toxic waste to dispose of.[91] This problem was corrected, for the most part, in 1986 when the U.S. Supreme Court ruled that companies could not use the U.S. bankruptcy courts to abandon hazardous waste cleanup obligations mandated by federal or state laws.[92]

Major generators of hazardous wastes, such as oil companies, are self-insured and have the resources necessary to satisfy their cleanup obligations. However, in many cases, particularly for the thousands of smaller hazardous facility operators and waste generators, the combination of costly or unavailable insurance and the reality that a major cleanup could cost more than their total net assets, Supreme Court decisions notwithstanding, presents a major problem for long-term enforcement of Superfund in the future.

Another enforcement problem encountered in the regulation of hazardous waste disposal has been motivating some industries to take regulations seriously. Some polluters have taken the position that fines for failure to comply with hazardous waste rules and regulations are just another cost of doing business. In the 1980s the EPA established a Criminal Enforcement Division for prosecuting violators—company officials—with criminal charges. Thus EPA inspectors began carrying a gun in 1984. As an official of the EPA Criminal Enforcement Division was quoted as saying, "[A]dministrative fines are seen by some people as part of the cost of doing business, but going to jail and being a felon is not."[93] The president of Culligan Water Service in Los Angeles, the chairman of the board of Magnum Resources and Energy Company, as well as various chief executive officers, have been sentenced to short jail terms.[94] The policy seems to have had a positive result. To quote a Los Angeles pollution official, "[W]e want to make the message as loud as we can: penalties can result in CEOs spending time in the slammer. We're looking eye ball to eye ball with chairmen of the board and presidents of major companies. It's staggering to think that at this moment, three presidents or CEOs are in jail because of this."[95] However, as an article in *Fortune* magazine stated, "[M]ost corporate felons go to minimum security prisons, where they can play all the tennis or miniature golf they like as long as they do menial work and go to bed by eleven."[96]

The Policy Paradox
in Hazardous Waste Management

The EPA estimates that U.S. industries are capable of reducing their hazardous waste output 15 to 30 percent by the year 2010. Many environmentalists and the U.S. Office of Technology Assessment think these estimates are conservative. An Office of Technology Assessment study in 1986 estimated that companies generating hazardous waste could reduce their waste flows by close to 50 percent within a five-year period.[97] In fact, many waste reduction techniques are easily adaptable and would save industry money—yet they are not utilized. Hazardous waste source reduction techniques include pollution prevention, low- and nonwaste technology, source waste reduction, and waste minimization.[98] If reducing waste at the source could save waste generators money, and would avoid many of the waste disposal problems discussed in this chapter, why isn't there more source waste reduction?

Hazardous waste regulations in the United States are based on two assumptions: (1) Hazardous waste generation is an inevitable by-product of industrial production, and (2) the focus in hazardous waste management should be on the disposal of waste once generated.[99] Both the RCRA and Superfund focus on the management of hazardous waste after it has been produced. And in fact, according to one analyst, through policies developed for the RCRA, "[The EPA has] created disincentives for waste reduction. For example, EPA has kept the cost associated with land filling low, thereby not reflecting long-term cleanup cost . . . the true cost of disposal."[100]

If a waste generator has the choice between using a relatively low-cost landfill as opposed to higher cost alternatives such as incineration or modifying production methods, then naturally the low-cost option will be selected. Politically it is easier for state and federal regulators to pursue lower cost hazardous waste management practices, since the opposition from affected industries is less; hence we should not be surprised there has been little pressure on industry to adopt more expensive methods of hazardous waste disposal. This is a good example of the operation of informal incentives in the policy-making process. Landfill disposal of hazardous waste involves short-term relatively low costs and long-term high or unknown cost. Policymakers, when confronted with the choice between one policy that has low short-term costs and high long-term costs, and a competing policy that has a high short-term cost and low or unknown long-term costs, are likely to choose the former policy. Politically, given the concern about rising taxes today, it is the choice that elected officials prefer.

The true costs of hazardous wastes utilizing land disposal are eventually paid. They may be paid by future generations in terms of the unavailability of water or increased rates of cancer. But they are paid in some way. Although the public and politicians may benefit today by having less expensive goods and services, since the true cost of their production or delivery is not included in the market price, the public will eventually pay. As two hazardous waste policy analysts wrote in the *Los Angeles Times*,

> [E]very time government makes it cheaper for industry to casually discard hazardous waste—as the U.S. Environmental Protection Agency recently did by allowing the burial of liquid hazardous waste in landfills—the true cost of disposing that waste is shifted to the general public in the form of massive cleanup expenses, lost resources and spiraling rates of cancer, birth defects and disease.[101]

The longer we wait, or the longer we pursue inadequate disposal methods for our hazardous waste, the more it is going to cost society. However, these costs are easy for policymakers to ignore, since they are deferred and shifted to future generations.

The strict liability provisions of Superfund, specifically liability for the generator of hazardous waste regardless of who handles it or where it goes after it is passed on, is another interesting example of a policy paradox. On the surface, this would appear to be hard-line legislation to deal with a tough problem. In practice, what it has meant is that many hazardous waste generators who might otherwise recycle their hazardous waste by selling it or giving it to others have an incentive to hang on to it because they are, of course, liable for any damage caused by the waste. And this is liability that is easy to ascertain given the tracking and permit requirements of the RCRA.[102]

Even if environmental laws were perfectly written, there are implementation problems. As with many environmental regulations, the EPA has found full enforcement of Superfund and the RCRA virtually impossible. The EPA has had difficulty implementing many environmental regulations according to the timetables and deadlines established by federal statutes.[103] In the case of the RCRA and Superfund, not only have regulations been slow in coming from the EPA, but regulated industries are often not in compliance with those regulations in effect. For example, a study of leak detection systems, required under the RCRA to detect chemical leakage from hazardous waste disposal sites, found that close to 60 percent of the disposal facilities regulated under the RCRA lacked leak detection systems.[104] Moreover, not all disposal facilities are scrutinized. Perhaps thousands of these facilities have not come to the attention of the EPA.

As in other areas of environmental regulation, economics, politics, and risk analysis play an important role in hazardous waste regulation. Beginning during the Reagan administration, the Office of Management and Budget (OMB) has been given responsibility for weighing the cost and benefits of new federal regulations. Former president Ronald Reagan's first EPA administrator, Anne Gorsuch Burford, eliminated the Enforcement Division of the EPA by reassigning enforcement lawyers to other divisions. The agency also promoted voluntary compliance by industry and sought to limit the role of the federal government.[105] Furthermore, at various times during the Reagan administration, the OMB put pressure on the EPA to revise hazardous waste exposure requirements in a manner that would allow exposure levels greater than EPA officials thought were necessary to protect human health.[106] Ironically, lax enforcement of hazardous waste regulations was not what industry wanted. As an editorial in *Chemical Week* stated, "[A]n ineffective environmental protection agency is not what the chemical industry needs. What it needs and what it expects from the Reagan administration is an agency that will discharge intelligently its responsibility to the American people. ... [A] management attitude that turns off hundreds of confident and dedicated professionals—and EPA has them—is not good."[107]

What can you do if you are worried about exposure to toxic waste? You can have your water supplies tested by state and local officials or, better yet, an independent testing laboratory. For a free directory of independent laboratories, write to the American Council of Independent Laboratories, 1629 K Street N.W., Washington, DC 20006 (phone: 202-887-5872). If you suspect serious water quality problems may already be impacting the health of your community, you might attempt to conduct an epidemiological study. Activists in San Jose, California, Willow Springs, Louisiana, and Lowell, Massachusetts, as well as other areas, have conducted such studies on their own and the results have prompted local officials to require the removal of toxic and hazardous waste.[108] The Johns Hopkins University Press has published a guide for citizens to conduct such surveys of their communities titled *The Health Detective's Handbook*. This book explains proper study design, means of community organization, types of data analysis, and provides a sample questionnaire. As in other areas of environmental regulation, citizen suit provisions are available that allow you to force industries that are not complying with federal regulations into compliance.[109]

An interesting case study of self-help in dealing with water contaminated by toxic pollutants occurred in Southern California in the late 1980s. Two small water companies, the Hemlock Mutual Water Company with 240 customers, and the Richwood Mutual Water Company with 217, both located in the San Gabriel Valley, found their groundwater wells were polluted by industrial solvents. The Hemlock Water Company, after heavy pressure from the EPA and its contractor in the area, the CH2M Company, decided to reject federal help. Over a three-day weekend, the president of Hemlock Water, with the assistance of an electrical contractor and a plumber, put in a filtration system costing $40,000. Neighboring Richwood Mutual Water Company decided to follow the consultant's and EPA's advice and accept federal assistance. Three years after the Hemlock system was in operation, Richwood's $1.5 million purification system, with operating costs of $100,000 a year, was still not functioning.[110]

SUMMARY

We began this chapter by summarizing the nature of our waste and exploring the relationship between industrial development and waste generation. The management of solid waste provides one of the most dramatic examples of the paradox of environmental policy. Although for several decades we have understood and could have anticipated most of our solid waste problems, as we have seen more than half of the cities in the United States will have exhausted their landfill capacity and are without acceptable new sites.[111]

In the next chapter we discuss land-use problems. Specifically we look at local land-use planning and how money and politics operate to determine how our neighborhoods look. Then we examine three things that threaten U.S. and global agricultural production: farmland conversion, desertification, and soil erosion. Finally we discuss federal land management issues including harvesting trees on federal lands, multiple-use management, wilderness designation and protection, and endangered species.

NOTES

1. Jim Glen, "The State of Garbage," *BioCycle* (April 1992), p. 48.
2. Conservation Foundation, *State of the Environment: A View Towards the Nineties* (Washington, DC: Conservation Foundation, 1987), p. 106.

3. Ibid., p. 411. The nine major federal laws are the Clean Water Act, the Marine Protection Research and Sanctuaries Act, the Safe Drinking Water Act, the Clean Air Act, the Resource Conservation and Recovery Act, the Comprehensive Environmental Response, Compensation, and Liability Act, the Surface Mining Control and Reclamation Act, the Nuclear Waste Policy Act, Low Level Radioactive Waste Policy Act, the Uranium Mill Tailings Radiation Control Act, and the Toxic Substances Control Act.

4. Ibid., p. 407. These figures assume a waste density of 40 to 60 pounds per cubic foot and an average household of 2.7 persons.

5. Council on Environmental Quality, *Environmental Quality: The Sixteenth Annual Report of the Council of Environmental Quality* (Washington, DC: U.S. Government Documents, 1985), p. 421. Per capita municipal waste generation in the United States was reported as 703 kilograms. Figures for a few other countries were as follows: Canada, 526; Austria, 208; France, 289; Federal Republic of Germany, 338; Norway, 415; Spain, 215; Sweden, 301; Switzerland, 337; United Kingdom, 282; Japan, 334; and Australia, 681.

6. Jim Glen, "The State of Garbage," p. 46.

7. Ibid., p. 47.

8. Conservation Foundation, p. 111.

9. Joseph F. Sullivan, "States Are Making Recycling a Must," *New York Times*, January 11, 1987, p. 9.

10. "Tons and Tons of Trash and No Place to Put It," *U.S. News and World Report* (December 14, 1987), p. 58.

11. Ibid. In response, however, newer landfills opening up have greater capacities—buying some states additional time.

12. Ibid.

13. Other diseases include myiasis, onchocerciasis, Ozyard's, filariasis, leishmaniasis, African sleeping sickness, yaws, tularemia, bartonellosis, catarrhal sandfly fever, conjunctivitis, salmonellosis, poliomyelitis, entamoebiasis, fish, beef, and pork tapeworms, roundworms (whipworms), hookworms, and many others. See Brian J. L. Berry et al., *Land Use, Urban Reform and Environmental Quality* (Chicago: University of Chicago, 1974), p. 194.

14. Jonathan Turk, *Environmental Studies* (2nd ed.) (Philadelphia: Saunders, 1985), p. 295.

15. These are 1990 figures—the most recent available as of this writing. Telephone interview with EPA representative, November 1993.

16. Ibid., and Conservation Foundation, *State of the Environment*, p. 115.

17. Public Law No. 89-272, *Title Two* (1965).

18. Ibid., Section 202(a) (2,6).

19. Public Law No. 91-604 (1970).

20. 42 U.S.C.A. Sections 6943 (a) (2).

21. *City of Philadelphia v. New Jersey*, 437 U.S. 617 (1978).

22. Sullivan, "States Are Making Recycling a Must."

23. Ibid., p. 419. These estimates vary; for example, some put the paper percentage at 50 percent, food at 12 percent, wood and garden refuse at 10 percent, glass at 9 percent, and metal at 9 percent; see Turk, *Environmental Studies*, p. 291.

24. Telephone interview with EPA representative, November 1993.

25. Turk, *Environmental Studies*, p. 300.

26. Such programs typically provide economic incentives to recycle.

27. Frank J. Popper, "The Environmentalist and the LULU," *Environment*, 28 (March 1985), p. 6.

28. Bill Paul, "New Environmental Controls Improved Outlooks for Dumps," *Wall Street Journal*, October 2, 1987, p. 17.

29. Turk, *Environmental Studies*, p. 291.

30. Jim Glen, "The State of Garbage," p. 46.
31. Telephone interview with the City of Los Angeles Recycling Office, November 1993.
32. Jim Glen, "The State of Garbage," p. 46.
33. John E. Anderson, "The Toxic Danger," *American Demographics*, 9 (January 1987), p. 45; and "Toxic Territories," *American Demographics*, 8 (September 1986), p. 67.
34. "Urban Toxic Pollutants Found in Polar Bears," *The Columbus Dispatch*, May 21, 1986, p. 2.
35. U. S. General Accounting Office, *Hazardous Waste: Corrective Action Cleanups Will Take Years to Complete* (Washington, DC: U.S. Government Printing Office, 1988); see also Ed Magnuson, "A Problem That Cannot Be Buried," *Time* (October 14, 1985), p. 76.
36. Louis Regenstein, "The Poisoning of America: How Deadly Chemicals Are Destroying Our Country," *U.S.A. Today* (magazine) (September 1983), p. 18.
37. U.S. Office of Technology Assessment, "Technologies and Management Strategies for Hazardous Waste Control" (Washington, DC: U.S. Government Printing Office, 1983), p. 13.
38. This discussion is based on data from the EPA and the Nuclear Information and Resource Service, November 1993.
39. Ronald Fuchs and Samuel D. McDonald, "1992 State-by-State Assessment of Low-Level Wastes Received at Commercial Disposal Sites." Department of Energy Publication DOE/LLW-181, September 1993.
40. Telephone interview and written communication with the Nuclear Regulatory Commission, Nuclear Information and Resource Service, November 1993.
41. Peter A. Berle, "The Toxic Tornado," *Audubon*, 87 (November 1985), p. 4.
42. Telephone interview with EPA representative, November 1993.
43. Ken Sternberg, "HazWaste Well Accepted—for Now," *Chemical Week*, 146(20) (May 23, 1990), p. 6.
44. Elizabeth Kirschner, "An Anxious Industry Sees New Limits to Its Options," *Chemical Week*, 153(6) (August 18, 1993), p. 23.
45. "Hazardous Chemicals," United Nations Environment Program, UNEP Environment Brief Number 4 (no date), p. 2.
46. Keith Schneider, "The Data Gap: What We Don't Know About Chemicals," *The Amicus Journal* (Winter 1985), p. 15.
47. Timothy Aeppel, "Halting Hazardous Waste at the Source," *Christian Science Monitor*, April 30, 1987, p. 20; Bruce Piaseckin and Jerry Gravander, "The Missing Links: Restructuring Hazardous Waste Controls in America," *Technology Review*, 88 (October 1985), p. 43.
48. For a discussion of problems associated with the underground injection of hazardous waste, see Michael Brown, "The Lower Depths," *The Amicus Journal* (Winter 1986), p. 14.
49. Ibid., p. 18.
50. Timothy Kao and Joseph Bishop, "Coastal Ocean Toxic Waste Pollution: Where Are We and Where Do We Go?," *U.S.A. Today* (magazine), 114 (July 1985), p. 21.
51. Ibid.
52. G. Tyler Miller, Jr., *Living in the Environment* (5th ed.) (Belmont, CA: Wadsworth, 1988), p. 507.
53. Peter Stoler, "Turning to New Technologies," *Time*, (October 14, 1985), p. 90.
54. Laurie A. Rich, "Burning of Toxics Faces Rising Protest Worldwide," *Chemical Week*, 136 (May 22, 1986), p. 18.
55. Pamela S. Zurer, "In an Incineration of Hazardous Waste at Sea: Going Nowhere Fast," *Chemical and Engineering News*, 63 (December 9, 1985), p. 24.
56. Maura Dolan, "EPA to Permit Burning of Toxic Waste at Sea as Test," *Los Angeles Times*, November 27, 1985, Pt. 1, p. 1.

57. Ibid.
58. Telephone interview with an EPA representative, November 1993; and Eli Kirschner, "An Anxious Industry Sees New Limits to Its Options," pp. 23–24.
59. "Beyond Our Borders: How U.S. Multinationals Handle Hazardous Waste Abroad," *Conservation Exchange* (National Wildlife Federation), 6(3) (Fall 1988), p. 1.
60. Tyler Marshall, "Western Europe Has Its Fill of Toxic Waste," *Los Angeles Times*, Pt. 1, p. 1.
61. Dermota O. Sullivan, "Program Targets Issue of Hazardous Waste Exports," *Chemical and Engineering News* (September 26, 1988), p. 24.
62. "Waste Exports Open Door for Crisis," *Conservation Exchange* (National Wildlife Federation), 6(3) (Fall 1988), p. 7.
63. "Report of the Ad Hoc Working Group on the Work of Its Third Session— Transboundary Movements of Hazardous Waste," United Nations Environment Program, November 16, 1988.
64. "Deadly Gunk from El Norte," *Time* (May 5, 1986), p. 27.
65. These are agreements that have been negotiated between the United States and Mexico which are not part of the formal NAFTA accords.
66. Carol Cirulli, "Toxic Boomerang," *The Amicus Journal* (Winter 1989), p. 9; and Marshall, "Western Europe," p. 10.
67. Judy R. Berlfein, "A Natural Response to Toxic Waste," *Los Angeles Times*, July 11, 1988, Pt. 2, p. 4; "Enzymes: Alternative for Waste Detoxification," *The Journal of Commerce*, 361 (August 30, 1984), p. 228; and "Bugs Have Big Future in Cleanup of Waste," *European Chemical News*, 44 (June 3, 1985), p. 14.
68. Carl Pope, "An Immodest Proposal," *Sierra* (September-October 1985), p. 43.
69. Gordon F. Bloom, "The Hidden Liability of Hazardous Waste Cleanup," *Technology Review*, 89 (February-March, 1986), p. 58.
70. Ibid., p. 61.
71. The Superfund Amendments and Reauthorization Act, 100 Stat. 1613, P.L. 99-499, 1986. Upheld by the U.S. Supreme Court in *Pennsylvania v. Union Gas*, 1989 LEXIS 2970 (June 15, 1989).
72. Seventy percent of which was since 1989. Telephone interview with an EPA representative, November 1993.
73. Telephone interview with an EPA representative, November 1993.
74. Magnuson, "A Problem That Cannot Be Buried," p. 78.
75. Bloom, "The Hidden Liability of Hazardous Waste Cleanup," p. 60.
76. Kim Murphy, "State Held Liable for Stringfellow Toxic Dump Site," *Los Angeles Times*, June 3, 1989, Pt. 1, p. 1.
77. Magnuson, "A Problem That Cannot Be Buried," p. 76.
78. James Cook, "Risky Business," *Forbes*, 134 (December 2, 1985), p. 112.
79. Janice Long, "Illegal Hazardous Waste Disposal Probed," *Chemical and Engineering News* (April 22, 1985), p. 22.
80. "Witness Says Crime Figures Rule Disposal of Toxic Waste," *New York Times*, September 20, 1984, p. B10.
81. J. Miller and M. Miller, "The Midnight Dumpers," *U.S.A. Today*, (magazine) (March 1985), pp. 60–64.
82. Magnuson, "A Problem That Cannot Be Buried," p. 77.
83. Robert Cameron Mitchell and Richard T. Carson, "Citing of Hazardous Facilities: Property Rights, Protest, and the Citing of Hazardous Waste Facilities," *American Economic Review*, 76 (May 1986), p. 285.
84. Frank J. Popper, "The Environmentalist and the LULU," *Environment*, 27 (March 1985). The other installations measured were for a nuclear power plant, coal-fired power plant, a large factory, and a ten-story office building.
85. Timothy Aeppel, "Civil Rights Group Links Race with Citing of Toxic Waste Dumps," *The Christian Science Monitor*, 16 (April 1987), p. 5. See also Dick Russell "Environmental Racism," *The Amicus Journal* (Spring 1989), p. 22.

86. Russell, "Environmental Racism," p. 25.
87. 42 U.C.S. Section 6925.
88. Bruce J. Parker, "The Insurance Crisis and Environmental Protection," *Environment*, 28 (April 1986), p. 14.
89. "Some Technical, But Meaningful Facts About Pollution Liability Insurance," *Journal of American Insurance*, 62 (Spring 1986), p. 11; see also U.S. General Accounting Office, *Hazardous Waste Insurance Availability* (Washington, DC: U.S. Government Printing Office, 1988).
90. Linda M. Watkins, "Chemical Firms Battle Insurers on Policy," *The Wall Street Journal*, August 28, 1986, p. 6. Liability insurance is available even though it is costly. In a phone call to the EPA Superfund hotline on June 21, 1989, the author was supplied with the names of eight companies willing to write hazardous waste liability policies.
91. Eleanor Smith, "Angry Housewives," *Omni*, 9 (December 1986), p. 22.
92. For a discussion, see "Bankrupt Firms Liable for Toxic Cleanup," *Oilgram News*, 64(19) (January 28, 1986), p. 2.
93. "Don't Pass Go, Go Directly to Jail," *Fortune*, 114 (December 8, 1986), p. 9.
94. See, for example, Eleanor Smith, "Midnight Dumping," *Omni*, 6 (March 1984), p. 21; and Steve Taravella, "L.A. Jails Company Officers for Breaking Pollution Laws," *Business Insurance*, 18 (April 2, 1984), p. 2.
95. Travella, "L.A. Jails Company Officers for Breaking Pollution Laws," p. 3.
96. "Don't Pass Go, Go Directly to Jail," p. 10.
97. Robert E. Taylor, "EPA Offers Aid for Firms to Cut Hazardous Waste," *Wall Street Journal*, October 31, 1986, p. 48.
98. Larry Martin, "The Case for Stopping Waste with Their Source," *Environment*, 28 (April 1986), p. 35.
99. Roberta G. Gordon, "Legal Incentives for Reduction, Reuse, and Recycling: A New Approach to Hazardous Waste Management," *Yale Law Journal*, 95 (March 1986), p. 810.
100. Ibid., p. 813.
101. James Louis and Katherine Durso-Hughes, "Hazardous Waste: The Public Will Pay," *Los Angeles Times*, March 17, 1982, Pt. 2, p. 7.
102. Gordon, "Legal Incentives," p. 813.
103. Bradford W. Wyche, "The Regulation of Toxic Pollutants Under the Clean Water Act: EPA's Ten Year Rule Making Nears Completion," *Natural Resources Lawyer*, 15 (1983), p. 511.
104. "Many Waste Sites Lack Leak Detection Systems," *Chemical and Engineering News*, 63 (May 13, 1985), p. 16.
105. Robert Cahn, "EPA Under Reagan," *Audubon* (January 1982), p. 16.
106. These efforts were not always successful. See, for example, "EPA Worse Case Guideline Assessing Hazards," *Wall Street Journal*, August 26, 1986, p. 6.
107. Cahn, "EPA Under Reagan," p. 14.
108. John Carey and Susan Katz, "How to Track Down Toxins," *Newsweek* (May 6, 1985), p. 81.
109. See Toxic Substances Control Act, Section 20, 15 U.S.C., Section 2619; The Safe Drinking Water Act, Section 1449, 42 U.S.C., Section 300J-8; and The Resource Conservation and Recovery Act, Section 7002, 42 U.S.C., Section 6972.
110. Michael Ward, "Tiny Suppliers Water Cleanup Is Faster, Cheaper Without EPA Aid," *Los Angeles Times*, June 5, 1989, Pt. 1, p. 3.
111. Miller, *Living in the Environment*, pp. 491–495.

chapter 9

Land Management Issues

In this chapter we look at land-use problems—broadly defined. First local land-use planning and the role of money and politics in neighborhood growth and planning is discussed. Then we examine soil erosion, farmland conversion, and desertification, which all threaten long-term, sustainable food production. Finally we discuss federal land management issues including timber harvesting, multiple-use management, wilderness lands designation, and the loss of endangered species.

Local land-use planning and the incentives that operate on policymakers have shaped urban development. There is no mystery why our cities look the way they do. With apologies to "Pogo," we have "seen the enemy and they is us"—they are the systems we have created to manage urban development.

LOCAL LAND-USE PLANNING

In the United States, freedom to do as one pleases with one's property is considered sacrosanct—a very important part of our dominant social paradigm (DSP). Consequently, planning, or land-use control, is contrary to our dominant social paradigm. In fact, in some communities, such as Houston, Texas, land-use planning by government is nonexistent.[1]

Most major metropolitan areas in the United States have grown without careful land-use planning. Since World War II, cities such as Los Angeles, Chicago, and New York and their suburbs have grown miles in every direction. This growth has been fueled by subsidized mortgages, which for the first time allowed the middle class to enjoy home ownership, and a freeway system that permitted workers to commute from the suburbs to jobs in the city.

Most of you are familiar with metropolitan traffic problems. In some cities, freeway traffic is bumper to bumper during most of the day. Traffic congestion can cause physiological and psychological stress, and can be expensive. Even ignoring damage to our minds and bodies, traffic congestion makes automobiles more expensive to operate. It is estimated that traffic jams add an additional $800 a year to the cost of operating an automobile.[2] Anyone familiar with the transformation of the San Jose or Orange County areas in California or Long Island in New York has to wonder what forces dictate land-use patterns. As we see later, a combination of our DSP and the informal incentives in the political process are what influence land-use decisions in the United States. Therefore, chances are we may not end up with the metropolitan areas we desire, but given the reality of the policy-making process, they are often the only kind of development the system will produce.

Typically, local governments develop "comprehensive plans" designed to provide a blueprint for land use and development in future years. Zoning and subdivision regulations are designed to carry out the plans. Usually comprehensive plans are revised every five or ten years. More important than these revisions, however, is the issuance of variances, or exceptions to the zoning guidelines that are laid out in plans. In some states, jurisdiction over large projects that have an areawide impact, such as the location of a power plant or a prison, have been "kicked upstairs" to state or regional boards. Florida, for example, has state and regional boards that review "developments of regional impact." In Maryland, power plant location is a responsibility of state government.[3] This assertion of state control over large projects has been referred to as the "quiet revolution" in land-use planning.[4] Nevertheless, most planning is still done on the local level.

Local government authority for land-use planning was affirmed by the U.S. Supreme Court in 1926.[5] The Court found that zoning ordinances were presumed to be valid as long as they were reasonably related to public health, safety, morals, or the general welfare of citizens.

Guy Benveniste has identified four basic types of planning: trivial, utopian, imperative, and intentional.[6] The trivial plan is little more than a statement of what will take place. It projects the future but makes no attempt to influence that future. The utopian plan shares with the trivial plan the characteristic that it will have no impact on the status quo but for a different reason. The utopian plan describes the future that no one expects will occur—hence no one takes it seriously. The "ideal type" of planning is referred to as imperative planning. Imperative planning is what most people think of when they think of land-use planning. Under imperative types of land-use planning, development plans are mandatory, made well in advance and enforced. However, as Richard Foster and Lawson Veasey point out, "Ideally, the plan is a guide, implemented by law and applied to specific situations by rational people operating in a nonpolitical environment. . . . [T]his ideal type of imperative planning conforms with the reality only occasionally. . . . [L]ocal land use decisions are both intense and political in nature."[7]

Finally, intentional planning is planning in which the means of implementation for the plan are unavailable or insufficient and hence the realization of the plan is dependent on factors external to the planning process. For example, planning may be dependent on the agreements of private parties, or individual action.

Planning is an inherently political process. The political nature of planning and zoning was described by Richard Babcock in his book *The Zoning Game* as "part of the political technique through which the use of private land is regulated. When zoning is thought of as part of the governmental process, it is obvious it can have no inherent principles separate from the goals which each person chooses to subscribe to the political process as a whole."[8]

The politics of zoning are best demonstrated in the issuance of a variance or a request for land use that is inconsistent with the overall plan. For example, to put a convenience store in a residential neighborhood or a subdivision on previously designated agricultural land requires a variance permit that involves a special process. As Neil Carn describes it, "[W]hen such a request is made, it is likely to be approved only if a proper strategy can be found that fulfills the legal, technical, and political concerns of the zoning officials."[9] In most cases the technical and legal considerations are easy to meet—particularly if the political concerns of zoning officials are also met.

The decisions made in planning are reinforced through zoning ordinances that establish zoning districts, which both identify current usage and establish future uses. Urban planning is carried out with four major types of urban designations: residential, commercial, industrial, and special-use areas. Within these four categories are a number of subcategories. For example, within a commercial zone, there may be large or small commercial areas, industrial heavy or light. Within the residential category may be single-family homes, multiple-family dwellings, or combination of both. Typically, the intent behind comprehensive land-use planning is to segregate those activities that have negative side effects and to preserve the quality of life by maintaining open space, or the residential character of a neighborhood, or by determining the suitability of land for particular uses. Despite attempts to segregate land use by activities and characteristics, some mixing is unavoidable. For example, due to traffic problems, the community of Fort Collins, Colorado, no longer rigidly separates industrial and

residential areas. By allowing the clustering of residences with new industry, traffic problems can be minimized.[10]

Zoning decisions are made by planning commissions, or zoning
boards who are elected or appointed and usually have no formal training in
planning or government. Oftentimes, the planning commission or zoning
board is the same body that governs a city or county. Consequently, the
same forces that influence decision making in local legislative bodies, such
as the desire for reelection, the need for campaign contributions, and the
disproportionate influence of economic interest groups, influence the planning and zoning process.

The stakes in zoning can be very high. From the perspective of a
developer, it can mean increased wealth or the opportunity to stay in business; from the perspective of those attempting to prevent development, it
can mean the loss of the neighborhood, an open space, or an agricultural
preserve. As one student of land-use planning wrote, variance decisions
"bring out all the chumminess, informality, and deal making qualities of
local government."[11]

To summarize, land-use decisions are made by politicians dependent
on campaign contribution for reelection. Those contributions come disproportionately from those who propose to develop the land over which the
elected officials have jurisdiction. Hence we should not be surprised at the
rate at which agricultural land is being converted to urban use or at the lack
of green open space in most metropolitan areas.[12] This is particularly true in
a political environment that assumes individuals should have an unrestric-
tive right to do as they please with their private property. Given the nature
of the land-use decision-making system and the incentives operating on
political actors, it would be surprising indeed if metropolitan areas in the
United States had developed any other way.

The past does not bind us to the future. Local politicians are responsive to political pressures. The business-as-usual relationship between local
policymakers and land developers is upset when citizens become organized
and vocal. Land-use and zoning decisions provide the entry point for many
citizens into environmental politics. The potential that a new subdivision
will be put in one's neighborhood, or that old Victorian house on the corner
will be torn down to be replaced by a gas station, provides an impetus for
many individuals to become involved in the policy-making process who
would otherwise be uninvolved in environmental politics. By watching for
notices and attending public planning hearings, writing letters to the editor,
and joining with others who are concerned, people can have an impact on
how their community develops. If we don't watch out for and protect our
interests, someone else will define those interests for us.

Soil Erosion

Although less visible than the new shopping center down the street,
soil erosion and the loss of agricultural productivity is no less a threat to

many communities and, ultimately, to all of us. Every year, slowly but surely, the United States loses potential future agricultural productivity. Agricultural productivity is dependent on the quality and quantity of soil and the availability of water—all of which are in short supply. Many problems facing farmers today are similar regardless of where they occur. Soil erosion presents a threat to future agricultural productivity worldwide.

Soil erosion is the movement of soil, either by wind or water, off farmlands and into lakes, rivers, streams, or the oceans. Soil erosion is a good example of an environmental problem that develops slowly and seemingly has little impact. It lacks the "crisis" qualities that are sometimes necessary to motivate policymakers to act. Consequently, due to the dynamics of the policy process, it is difficult to mobilize policymakers or the public to take corrective action to prevent soil erosion. Nevertheless, further loss of valuable cropland will surely lead to crisis.

In the United States, close to 6 billion tons of topsoil are lost each year. Historically, about one-third of the topsoil, originally on U.S. croplands, has been lost.[13] It is estimated that the total loss of U.S. topsoil to erosion in the next 50 years will amount to between 25 and 62 million acres.[14] Internationally, topsoil losses amount to some 25.4 billion tons per year. This represents approximately 7 percent loss of topsoil from cropland every 10 years.

Some people point to huge increases in agricultural productivity since World War II as evidence that additional corrective measures are not necessary to prevent soil erosion. For instance, U.S. exports of soybeans, wheat, and corn nearly tripled from 1965 to 1985. However, the increased use of fertilizer, and the farming of marginal cropland, have masked the impacts of soil erosion. Between 1950 and 1985 there was a ninefold increase in the use of fertilizer worldwide and a near tripling of the amount of land put into production.[15]

In the United States, the Soil Conservation Service within the Department of Agriculture has primary authority over soil erosion. Although the service provides technical assistance and produces useful data, they have no authority to require agricultural practices that prevent erosion. Internationally, the United Nations provides expertise; however, the advice is often ignored.

U.S. lawmakers did take a major step toward preventing erosion on previously undeveloped farmland in 1985. In the passage of the 1985 farm bill, a "sod-buster" provision denied federal farm benefits for crops grown on newly plowed grasslands vulnerable to erosion. Although this was a positive measure, the long-term projections are for continued and even accelerated soil erosion. What land is not blown or washed away, furthermore, is being converted to nonagricultural uses at an alarming rate. Farmland conversion, although a national and international problem, most often must be dealt with on the local level—through planning and zoning procedures.

Farmland Conversion

Farmland conversion is a worldwide problem. Oftentimes the best farmland is adjacent to a metropolitan area. As that area grows, the land becomes covered with homes, roads, and other improvements that take it out of agricultural production. Each year 2.5 million acres of agricultural land is converted to nonagricultural uses in the United States.[16]

Our dominant social paradigm plays an important role in agricultural land conversion. The primacy of markets and individual enterprise in the management of private property can be an insurmountable barrier to attempts to regulate the conversion of agricultural lands. The efficient thing to do with land is to develop and to increase its value.

Some economists argue that when the value of agricultural land is high enough, buildings and pavement will be moved and the land put back into production. This is unlikely from a practical standpoint and perhaps impossible from an ecological standpoint, since the land would no longer be suitable for farming. As Paul and Anne Ehrlich explain,

> [A]fter all, shopping malls and high rise buildings are considered more valuable today than cornfields. If the value of corn should rise enough to change all that in ten or a hundred years . . . presumably . . . an economical way would be invented by scientists to peel cities off the land. Sadly, however, if that were possible, the bared land would not be prime farmland but wasteland, since the process of first disturbing and then covering it would destroy the physical and biological characteristics that make the soil productive.[17]

In the United States, government efforts to limit the conversion of agricultural land to urban use have met with limited success. Most measures, such as the Williamson Act in California, provide property tax relief for farmers that agree to keep their land in agricultural production. These have turned out to be temporary measures postponing conversion until the agricultural land adjacent to urban areas is at a premium. As such, they sometimes work as little more than tax breaks for farmers—or, in the case of California, the major corporations that dominate California agriculture. Soil quality also has a major impact on agricultural production and when quality deteriorates to the extent that the land is no longer good for farming, no one wins.

Desertification

Desertification, the process of turning productive land into wasteland, is occurring at an alarming pace. In semiarid areas, such as the American Southwest, grasses and other vegetation secure the soil and retain moisture. If the plants die, through overgrazing, trampling, or harvesting for fuel, the moisture retention capacity of the ground is lost and the land is slowly converted to desert. In the United States, desertification is impacting an estimated 225 million acres, primarily in the Southwest. Like soil erosion, desertification is not a problem with a simple solution. The slow and gradual nature of desertification does not lend itself to crisis management.

Although a serious problem in the United States, desertification is even more troublesome internationally—particularly in the less developed world where productive farmland and the capacity to develop sustainable agriculture are disappearing swiftly. International desertification problems are discussed further in Chapter 10.

Farmers are understandably reluctant to support any measures, regardless of how environmentally sound, that threaten their livelihood. With investments in equipment and machinery subject to substantial debt, farmers, for practical purposes, may believe they have no other alternative but to increase their productivity through the use of fertilizer and pesticides, as well as the use of marginal lands for planting.

The conditions just described threaten our future ability to produce food for those parts of the world that have become dependent on our agricultural production, and may, ultimately, challenge our ability to feed ourselves. One group studying domestic agricultural production found that by the year 2000 the "unavoidable implication is that food prices will go up and that Americans will have to change their eating habits to demand less, per capita, of the land. That will probably include eating less meat, growing more food in backyard gardens, and turning to locally grown produce."[18]

Although opinions vary on the severity of the domestic farm/food problem, there is strong evidence that a significant shift to organic farming would increase farm income and reduce soil erosion and nutrient depletion while meeting domestic food needs and reducing oil imports.[19] For a variety of political and institutional reasons, even when the scientific community is in substantial agreement on what needs to be done, we are often unable to pursue those policy ends. Therefore, regardless of the potential benefits of organic farming, and the obvious problems associated with soil erosion, desertification, and other problems, the incentives operating on policymakers in the policy-making process, including the localized strength of agricultural interests, make it very unlikely that any significant changes will be made in the foreseeable future in U.S. farm policy. That is the paradox.

FEDERAL LAND MANAGEMENT

The management of federal land holdings in the United States is of major importance to the economies of the western states. Federal lands make up approximately one-third of the continental United States (some 700 million acres) and contain roughly one-quarter of the nation's coal, four-fifths of our shale oil deposits, and half of U.S. uranium, oil, and gas deposits. Half of the nation's inventory of softwood timber is under federal management. Eighty percent of western public lands are leased to ranchers at relatively low rates for grazing what amounts to only 2 percent of cattle produced in the United States.[20] (This is, in effect, a subsidy to western interests. In 1991 federal leases charged $1.97 per animal per month; the Forest Service required $3.88 to cover its costs. Private rates averaged $9.22.[21]) The major federal land management agencies are the Bureau of Land Management (BLM), the U.S. Forest Service, the National Park Service, and the U.S. Fish and Wildlife Service.[22] Later, we examine land-use management problems that have confronted them together and independently.

The land management policies of federal agencies reflect the bargaining, compromise, and power struggles that are characteristic of pluralistic democratic systems. Land management policies and goals in the federal bureaucracy reflect the changes over time of constituencies in the political environment of a particular agency. The land management issues we examine here include multiple-use management, timber management, wilderness management, and endangered species management.

Multiple use   *Multiple use*, as the term suggests, means various activities can be carried out simultaneously on federal lands. It has been a policy of some federal land management efforts since the turn of the century. You may recall that Gifford Pinchot was an early proponent of the idea of multiple use on federal lands during the conservation movement. Only recently, however, has multiple use been given explicit legislative sanction. The U.S. Forest Service Multiple Use Sustained Yield Act of 1960, the Bureau of Land Management's Classification and Multiple Use Act of 1964, and the Federal Land Management and Policy Act of 1976 provide the statutory basis for multiple-use land management in the BLM and Forest Service.[23]

Under multiple-use management, permitting a variety of activities such as forestry, mining, or grazing along with hiking, camping, or to a certain extent, wilderness preservation, are all goals of federal land management. The difficulties in reconciling these competing uses have led some to question whether or not multiple-use management is possible or desirable. As Marion Clawson wrote, "Multiple uses applied to national forest, other public forest, and private forests are more a slogan than a blueprint for actual management."[24]

Critics of multiple-use management argue that the discretion allowed administrators to choose among a number of competing uses for the land results in management which reflects the historical institutional bias of the Forest Service and the Bureau of Land Management. We should not be surprised, these critics maintain, that multiple-use plans currently in existence place a great deal of emphasis on economic uses of federal lands.[25]

There is evidence of a shift in the clientele base of the BLM and the Forest Service. Both agencies have significantly decreased the amount of grazing allowed on their lands. In the case of the BLM, the decrease is roughly 50 percent.[26]

Timber Management   A major controversy in multiple-use management concerns the management of timber. Providing for multiple use in one area often results in conflicting management policies. For example, while the selective cutting of old growth timber in an area may be consistent with recreational use, clear-cutting usually is not. Other timber management issues include the cost of federal forest management and allowable harvest in the preservation of wilderness areas.

A recurring criticism of federal forest management, particularly Forest Service management, is that timber sales generate less income than it costs the government to manage the forest. Essentially this amounts to a subsidy from taxpayers to the wood products industry. A study done by Bob Wolf, a former employee of the Forest Service, the Bureau of Land Management, the Bureau of the Budget, as well as other government agencies, found that the Forest Service timber sales showed a deficit of $1.6 billion for the 10-year period between 1973 and 1983. Idaho, Colorado, Utah, and Alaska were the states that most consistently showed negative cash flows. California, Oregon, and Washington were the most profitable states for the Forest Service. Forest Service costs associated with timber sales included administrative overhead and, most importantly, the cost of building roads into the forests so the logs may be removed.[27] The General Accounting Office in 1983 released a report titled, "Congress Needs Better Information on Forest Service Below Cost Timber Sales" that studied 3,244 timber sales between 1981 and 1982 and found that in 1982, 42 percent of the sales did not generate revenues sufficient to cover Forest Service costs associated with the sale.[28] Economists have argued that deficit timber sales represent a hidden subsidy to the timber industry and artificially lower the cost of wood products. Environmentalists have argued that the development of roads to allow for timber sales, in addition to being costly, prevents those areas from being used for some recreational and wilderness purposes. As former Interior Secretary Cecil Andrus puts it, "If you would statutorily outlaw deficit timber sales, you would resolve the wilderness issue."[29]

Related to deficit timber sales is the definition of sustained yield, or harvesting of forestry resources in the manner that will ensure the long-term availability of wood. Although the United States imports over 30 percent of its softwood lumber, primarily from Canada, estimates of timber growth in the United States suggest that wood growth is adequate to meet domestic needs.[30] However, these growth figures do not take other forest uses into consideration. The elimination or the disruption of a forest also has an impact on wildlife habitat, recreational opportunities, watershed protection, and wilderness preservation. Generalizations about overharvesting in the United States are difficult to make inasmuch as conditions vary from forest to forest.

The Endangered Species Act has been an important variable in reducing timber sales from some federal lands. For example, the spotted owl, listed as endangered in 1990, is a major factor in the decrease in timber sales in the Pacific Northwest. Timber sales went from a high in 1986 of 6 billion board feet to a low in 1992 of 560 million board feet in the forests the spotted owl inhabits.[31]

Some analysts have argued that privatization of the national forest system would lead to more efficiency and better management. In Canada, private forest lands are much more productive than federally owned lands in the United States. This has led some critics to question federal ownership and management of forest lands.[32]

A controversial forest management practice in the National Park Service is the "let it burn" policy for fires that are started from natural causes. In the summer of 1988 a series of lightning-caused fires led to extensive destruction that burned close to one-half of Yellowstone National Park's 2.2 million acres. The National Park Service came under heavy criticism for its "let it burn" policy. President Reagan, who previously was unaware any such policy existed, ordered the policy suspended until the end of the season.

For the Park Service, a "let it burn" policy is consistent with its mission of managing its forests in a natural state. During the Yellowstone fires of 1988, Park Service employees were determined to let fires burn themselves out in accordance with Park Service policy. A memo written by a Park Service fire specialist surfaced during congressional hearings on Park Service policy that said Yellowstone staff members were bemoaning the fact that new (fire) starts, as mandated by the secretary of the interior, "had to be suspended."[33] Because of many years of forest protection when all fires were extinguished, undergrowth in the national parks has been allowed to accumulate to an unnatural and hazardous depth. Under such conditions when fires are started through natural or other causes, the heat generated is so intense it kills all growth. Under natural conditions, wildfires would have cleared out the brush and subsequent fires would not have generated as devastating a heat problem.

Wilderness   The designation of lands for wilderness areas has been one of the most controversial federal land-use issues in the second half of the twentieth century. As Paul Culhane put it, "[W]ilderness issues evoke more passion among public lands interest groups than any other issue."[34] The designation of an area as wilderness precludes the use of that land for any other purpose. Hence, unlike the conflict that goes on between users of Forest Service lands that are managed under multiple-use principles, the designation of an area as a wilderness area takes it out of multiple-use management. It is for this reason that the designation of land as a wilderness area has been a hotly contested issue between environmentalists and those that would prefer wilderness areas be left open for other uses.

The Wilderness Act of 1964 provides that an area may be designated as wilderness if it has the following attributes:

> [It is] an area of undeveloped land retaining its primeval character and influence, without permanent improvements or human habitation, which is protected and managed so as to preserve its natural conditions and which (1) generally appears to have been affected primarily by the forces of nature, with the impact of man's works substantially unnoticeable; (2) has outstanding opportunities for solitude or primitive and unconfined type of recreation; (3) has at least 5,000 acres of land or is of sufficient size as to make practicable its preservation in use and in an unimpaired condition; and (4) may also contain ecological, geological, or other features of scientific, educational, scenic, or historic value.[35]

Since September 3, 1964, when the Wilderness Act was signed into law, over 96 million acres have been designated as wilderness area in accordance with the act's provisions. If enacted, the California Desert Protection Act will add another 6 to 7 million acres to the system. This would be the largest land act passed in the United States since the designation of Alaskan lands in 1980. Prior to the creation of wilderness areas through the Wilderness Act, the U.S. Forest Service had designated certain areas as "primitive areas," meaning they were removed from regular multiple-use management. At the time of the creation of the Wilderness Act, the Forest Service had some 14 million acres of "primitive areas." The National Park Service was also effectively managing many of its holdings as wilderness areas.

It is an interesting part of natural resource bureaucratic history that the U.S. Forest Service adopted wilderness preservation in some areas largely as a means to protect itself from having its lands removed from its jurisdiction and added to the National Park System. Since the 1920s, the Forest Service has been under pressure to release lands for Park Service protection, and as Craig Allin explains, "If the Forest Service could portray itself as the champion of wilderness, the case would dissolve for transferring to the Parks Service those lands most suited for preservation."[36] The strategy was largely successful. By designating areas adjacent to Yosemite National Park as primitive areas, the total acreage of which exceeded the 2.2 million acres of Yosemite National Park itself, the Forest Service prevented moves to expand the park onto Forest Service lands.

Shortly after the Wilderness Act became law, the Forest Service adopted the position that wilderness status should only be granted to lands that were "pure wilderness," defined in part as those lands that were not within the sight or sounds of roads or any other development.[37] Such a designation would have severely limited wilderness areas. Congress was not persuaded by the Forest Service's logic and in 1987 passed the Endangered American Wilderness Act, which established wilderness areas in many areas that the Forest Service had found as not worthy of wilderness protection.

In an attempt to determine what Forest Service holdings should be designated wilderness, the service has undergone three reviews of Forest Service lands, otherwise known as the Roadless Area Review and Evaluation (RARE) plans. The first RARE study, referred to as Rare-1, involved 55.9 million acres. Rare-1 recommended that 12 million acres should be designated as additional wilderness. Conservationists criticized Rare-1 as being a "rocks and ice" plan which designated only those areas that were inaccessible for timber or mining purposes. The Sierra Club challenged the Forest Service's Rare-1 study in U.S. District Court in San Francisco. The suit was settled out of court in 1972 when the Forest Service agreed to follow the EIS requirements of NEPA before permitting any developments within roadless areas.

The Forest Service continued to come under attack for the slowness of its wilderness planning. In 1977, President Carter's first year in office, the Forest Service began Rare-2, the second inventory of Forest Service lands to determine those that should be designated as wilderness. Rare-2, completed in 1978, recommended that Congress designate 15.4 million acres immediately as wilderness, and that 10.6 million acres of potential wilderness be given further study. Rare-2 also recommended that 36 million acres be released for timber harvesting and other multiple-use purposes.[38] During Carter's term, the wilderness preservation system in the continental United States grew by some 12.4 million acres. An additional 56 million acres were set aside in Alaska under the Alaska National Interest Lands Conservation Act passed in 1980.

In 1983 the Ninth Circuit Court of Appeals ruled the Forest Service had not followed NEPA EIS requirements in the California Rare-2 study. On February 1, 1983, the Reagan administration announced it would begin Rare-3 and would throw out the Rare-2 recommendations. The Forest Service wilderness designation process has been completed largely through congressional action on a state-by-state basis.

The Wilderness Act of 1964 had a provision that allowed the establishment of new mining claims in wilderness areas until December 31, 1983. Claims made on that date could be mined, provided the development was "substantially unnoticeable."[39] By tradition, although not by law, the secretary of the interior had not allowed mining within wilderness areas, that is, until James Watt became the secretary of the interior during the Reagan administration. Although exploration and development drilling had taken place in wilderness areas, Secretary Watt was the first to approve large-scale mineral developments, beginning with development in Death Valley National Monument in California. Public and congressional reaction forestalled further mineral development in wilderness areas. However, there are still numerous mining claims in wilderness areas that have not been developed. This promises to become an issue at some point in the future.[40]

Mining and the wilderness is potentially a decisive issue for the Bureau of Land Management. The Federal Land Management Policy Act of 1976 required the BLM to inventory its lands to determine which should be designated wilderness areas, and to report in 1991 which BLM lands shall be so designated.

The BLM has often been criticized for poor management of its western rangeland. In 1979 the agency conceded that 135 million of its 170 million acres of Western rangeland were in only fair condition or worse. By 1992, when the BLM completed its wilderness review, 38 percent of its rangelands were rated to be in good to excellent condition—more than double the amount so rated in 1936. The percentage of lands rated in poor condition was cut by more than half, down to 13 percent, when compared with 1936.[41]

Although the focus of the BLM has shifted significantly since the days when it was referred to as a bureau of livestock and mining, many within the agency adhere to traditional values. As Richard Miller wrote, "[W]ilderness is a value that is not tightly focused within the agency and is also typically at odds with our uses that have effective proponents at the local level where day to day planning decisions are made."[42]

The first phase of the BLM's wilderness classification process was completed in November 1980 when it was found that of the 172 million acres under BLM jurisdiction, only 24 million warrant further consideration as wilderness. The BLM is required under federal law to maintain lands under consideration for wilderness designation in a wilderness state until a determination has been made. However, the BLM has been criticized for not adequately protecting lands that were under consideration for wilderness designation. For example, Exxon Corporation assembled and operated a drilling rig inside the Mt. Ellen Wilderness Study Area in southern Utah. The BLM had approved Exxon's application, which included the bulldozing of the new road and a drilling pad the size of two football fields.[43] In its defense, BLM receives approximately 10 cents per acre to manage wilderness study areas in contrast to the National Park Service, which receives $10 per acre to manage its lands.[44]

In many areas the National Park Service, consistent with its mandate to "preserve and protect" its lands, adopted a hands-off policy toward land management and let systems develop as they would naturally. Although seemingly consistent with maintaining land in its present state and the preservation of wilderness, its policy has been criticized for ignoring past human intervention into park ecosystems and not taking into consideration that the parks themselves are not closed ecosystems. In fact, park ecosystems are part of a much larger system over which the Park Service does not have control but for which park management must compensate.

For example, one significant management problem the National Park Service encounters is encroachment, usually through development, onto park lands. In 1980 the Park Service released a report titled *State of the Parks—1980* that listed 4,325 specific threats to the 320 park units that were listed.[45] Over 50 percent of these reported threats were from sources or activities that were occurring outside of the park boundaries. Threats included dam construction, sewage and chemical runoff, oil, gas, uranium mining, and power plant developments. All of these threaten the ability of the Park Service to manage its lands in a manner that will prevent degradation.

In addition, the National Parks have been faced with budget cutbacks and increased numbers of visitors leading to overcrowding, noise, and air pollution.[46] While the Park Service operating budget dropped below prior years in 1986 and 1990, the budgets since 1991 have grown steadily. In contrast to the 1990 low of $767.8 million, $976.5 million was allocated in 1992 and $1.16 billion was requested in 1993.[47]

Politics within the Park Service has also impacted the management of Park Service lands. Compared to other resource agencies the National Park Service has enjoyed very little controversy. Most Park Service directors have come from within the ranks of the service or have shared the philosophy of the Park Service to preserve and protect park lands—much in the manner of wilderness even in those areas within the parks that have been kept out of wilderness designation. For example, the Park Service director for the last four years of the Reagan administration, William Mott, was an outspoken proponent of park acquisition and endangered species protection. His appointment was greeted with enthusiasm by environmentalists.[48] Mott was not given a free rein in the administration of the National Park Service, however. The director's ideas frequently met with a cool reception higher up in the Reagan administration. In 1986 Mott circulated a memorandum within the Park Service that had been written in the office of assistant interior secretary for Fish, Wildlife and Parks, William E. Horn, that proposed a radical change in management of the parks. The memo indicated that a park be judged in good condition, the highest ranking, if 80 percent of its resource space was undamaged. "For example," the memo read, "the esthetics of Yosemite Valley are obviously essential to the park, whereas the health of the mule deer herd is not."[49] This policy was not carried out.

In short, designation as a national park may or may not protect land in the same manner as wilderness (in those areas in the parks that have not been designated wilderness) depending, as always, on contemporary political considerations. Since Congress must approve any wilderness designation, the politics of wilderness designation is often played out in that arena. With the exception of well-publicized national wilderness battles, such as that over the Bob Marshall Wilderness in Montana, wilderness disputes are fought out on a state-by-state basis—the main actors being resource users, such as timber companies, and environmental groups, organized on the state or local level.

In the future, in established wilderness areas, there promises to be conflict over appropriate management policies to protect the wilderness. The issue of water rights in and from wilderness areas has already played a role in wilderness politics. (Wilderness can be managed in a manner that increases water runoff.) In addition, the demands of hikers on wilderness cannot be accommodated in many areas if fragile wilderness ecosystems are to be protected. Often those ecosystems support endangered species.

Endangered Species   Endangered species, the ultimate loss of plants and animals, is a federal land management problem and it is also an important global environmental problem. We first examine the global aspects of species loss, and then look at efforts that have been made to protect species on federal lands in the United States.

It is estimated there are somewhere between 5 million and 30 million plant and animal species on the earth, the largest number being insects. Each day on the average, one of these species becomes extinct. Species preservation is very important for the future health and development of humankind. Approximately 40 percent of prescription and nonprescription drugs used by humans have active ingredients that have been extracted from plants and animals. Of the millions of estimated total number of species, only 1.7 million species have been identified, and less than 1 percent of those identified plant species have been thoroughly studied to determine their possible usefulness to humans. Plants that provide 90 percent of the world's food supply today were developed from previously wild plants

growing primarily in the tropics. We have no idea what contributions existing species may make to food, medicine, or other necessities or luxuries.[50]
Although certain well-known and loved species such as the bald eagle or
gray whale are protected for cultural, political, or other reasons, many other
lesser known plant and animal species are not so fortunate.

Given ecosystem interdependence and our inability to predict the
impact that tinkering with natural systems will have on those systems in
the long run, the elimination of species may be permanently impairing the
natural balance of the world in a way we do not understand or perhaps will
not understand until it is too late. As G. Tyler Miller wrote in a widely used
environmental science text, "The millions of species inhabiting the earth
depend on one another for a number of services. Because of this complex,
little understood web of interdependence, the most important contributions
of wild species may be their roles in maintaining the health and integrity of
the world ecosystems."[51]

Species endangerment primarily results from hunting and habitat
destruction. Extinction rates of mammal and bird species have increased
with the increase in the sophistication of hunting techniques. From the period 8000 B.C. to A.D. 1600, approximately one species was lost every 1,000
years. Yet from the period 1600 to 1900, one species was lost every four
years, while from 1900 into the mid-1990s, one mammal and bird species
was lost every year.[52] Extinction of plant species is most closely related to
habitat destruction and the various activities that we discuss throughout
this book including deforestation, desertification, and air and water pollution. Thus by 1975 the estimated annual extinction rate for all species was
100 a year. In the 10-year period between 1975 and 1985, this rate increased
ten-fold to 1,000 a year and it was estimated that it would increase ten-fold
again in the five-year period between 1985 and 1990 to 10,000, doubling
again by the year 2000 for an estimated annual extinction rate of all species
in the year 2000 of 20,000 species per year.[53] Even if these estimates are high,
an average extinction rate of 1,000 species a year by the end of the century
would still equal the greatest mass extinctions in world history.

Internationally, species endangerment provides a classic example of
common pool resource problems. Ocean fish and mammals in international
waters that are not owned by anyone may be harvested by everyone.
Several species of whales have been hunted to the brink of extinction, and
many commercial fish have been overfished to the point of commercial
extinction, meaning it is no longer profitable to harvest them.

The most significant treaty protecting endangered species at the international level is the Convention of International Trade in Endangered
Species and Wild Fauna and Flora. This treaty was developed by the
International Union for the Conservation of Nature and Wildlife Resources
and is administered by the United Nations Environment Program. The
treaty is signed by 87 countries and prohibits the hunting or capturing of
700 species.[54] This and other international treaties to which the United
States is a signatory have been incorporated into the U.S. Endangered
Species Act as part of U.S. federal law.[55] Nevertheless, although internation-

al treaties have helped reduce pressures on some species, enforcement is imbalanced among the nations.

Wildlife biologists that study international species management have argued that at least 10 percent of a global land area in selected regions should be set aside for ecosystem preservation, thereby preserving plant and animal species habitats that would ensure their protection. There *are* over 3,500 protected areas throughout the world, but with 1.6 million square miles (or 4.3 million square kilometers), this area represents less than 3 percent of the earth's land.[56]

The United States took the lead in the protection of endangered species with the passage of the Endangered Species Act of 1973.[57] The U.S. Supreme Court lauded the act as "the most comprehensive legislation for the preservation of endangered species ever enacted by any nation."[58]

Federal intervention in the protection of endangered species in the United States began around the turn of the century.[59] However, federal legislation prior to the Endangered Species Act of 1973 usually contained qualifying language or lacked necessary sanctions to carry out its provisions. Nonetheless, the act itself was a strong statement and a big step toward species preservation, and although it has been weakened somewhat, the act's passage is an example of nonincremental policy making in Washington, D.C.

The Endangered Species Act authorizes the National Marine Fishery Service, an agency within the Department of Commerce, to identify endangered and threatened marine species. The U.S. Fish and Wildlife Service, within the Department of the Interior, is authorized to identify and list other animal and plant species that are endangered or threatened in the United States and abroad. For a species to be endangered, there must be so few individuals surviving that the existence of the species is threatened. For a species to be threatened, they may still be abundant but declining in numbers such that if existing trends continue, they will be endangered in the future.

In 1993, 1,349 species were identified and included in the endangered and threatened species list pursuant to the Endangered Species Act, 818 of these species in the United States alone.[60] Significantly, and in contrast to administrative procedures in most environmental policy areas in the United States, the determination of endangerment or threatened status is based on biological grounds alone without economic considerations. The 1982 reauthorization of the Endangered Species Act passed both the House and the Senate without opposition and was accepted by both industry and environmentalists.[61] In the early 1990s, however, the Endangered Species Act came under criticism. Some interests criticized the act for unnecessarily interfering with land development or resource utilization (e.g., timber harvesting). In addition, many environmentalists as well as the U.S. Fish and Wildlife biologists, feel the act is too narrow and rather than focusing on particular species should be designed to protect ecosystems.

Pursuant to the Endangered Species Act, once a species is listed as endangered, no one may buy or sell the species even if it was acquired lawfully. The act further forbids killing, harming, and the harassing of endangered species with few exceptions.[62] One of the more controversial aspects of the Endangered Species Act has been the impact the act has had on federal land use and development. Perhaps the most controversial case involved the Tellico Dam on the Little Tennessee River in Tennessee. After construction of the dam had begun, the snail darter, a 3-inch-long minnow, was placed on the endangered species list. It was found that completion of the dam would result in the destruction of the only known breeding habitat of the snail darter. In 1975, although the dam was 90 percent complete and in excess of $100 million had been spent on the $137 million project, construction was halted pursuant to court order. In 1979 Congress passed special legislation that exempted the Tellico Dam from the act. And in 1978, partially in response to the Tellico situation, Congress amended the Endangered Species Act and established a seven-person review committee called the Endangered Species Committee that was empowered to grant exemptions from the requirements of the act.[63]

The snail darter case and subsequent congressional reaction illustrates conflict between environmental values and economic values. Congress clearly wanted to protect species but did not anticipate the consequences of an absolute ban on federal activity. Environmentalists at the time were concerned a congressional backlash might lead to a wholesale weakening of the Endangered Species Act, and were relieved at the compromise that resulted in establishment of the Endangered Species Committee. Fortunately for the snail darter, additional populations were found in several remote tributaries of the Little Tennessee River in 1981, and in 1983 the fish was downgraded by the Fish and Wildlife Service from an endangered to a threatened species.[64]

In his dissent in the snail darter case, U.S. Supreme Court Justice Powell wrote, "The Court today holds that Section 7 of the Endangered Species Act requires a federal court, for the purposes of protecting an endangered species or its habitat, to enjoin permanently the operation of any federal project, whether completed or substantially completed. This decision cast a long shadow over the operation of even the most important project. . . ."[65]

The Endangered Species Act has delayed or halted construction of a number of projects that either were using federal funding or required federal approval. These include the Columbia Dam on the Dock River in Tennessee, which threatened mussels and snails; a hydropower facility in Wyoming that threatened to impact a stopover area for migrating whooping cranes; oil and gas leases in Alaska for fear of damage to whales; the Dickey-Lincoln water project in Maine that threatened to inundate the only known habitat of the Furbish lousewort, a variety of snapdragon; and other projects all over the United States.[66]

Other federal laws, such as the Fishery Conservation and Management Act which attempts to prevent overharvesting of fish, and specific laws to protect wild horses, burros, bald eagles, and golden eagles, contribute to the protection of endangered species in the United States. The National Wildlife Refuge System has primary responsibility, mostly through the management of wetlands, for endangered species protection in the United States. Wildlife refuges are the responsibility of the U.S. Fish and Wildlife Service. Most of the species in the United States that are on the endangered list have habitats within the national wildlife refuge system.

There has been some controversy over Fish and Wildlife Service management of the national wildlife system. Unlike the Forest Service or the BLM, Congress has not yet established clear guidelines such as multiple use for the National Wildlife Refuge System. Consequently, many wildlife refuges allow hunting, trapping, timber cutting, farming, grazing, and mineral development as well as recreational activity.[67] The Reagan and Bush administrations encouraged resource development in National Wildlife Refuges just as it did on all federal lands. The Fish and Wildlife Service has been operating, since 1962, under a "compatible use" doctrine. Implementation of the compatible use doctrine has been challenged by environmentalists' lawsuits, the Clinton administration, and proposed legislation in Congress. Although, as of this writing, the suits have been settled out of court, the Fish and Wildlife Service is now required to identify all potential compatible uses and eliminate all incompatible uses on refuges. Although not enacted into law, the service also operates under a "dominant use" doctrine wherein wildlife is viewed by the service as the primary concern of refuge management, and wildlife-oriented public use is seen as a secondary concern. Studies of secondary uses by the GAO in 1989 and the Fish and Wildlife Service in 1990 have led to review of not only blatant threats to wildlife, such as grazing, but more subtle ones such as hiking.[68]

The National Wildlife Refuge System has experienced both water and air quality problems. In 1983 a Fish and Wildlife Service survey found that 86 percent of federal refuges had water quality problems, and 67 percent had air quality problems including visibility problems.[69]

The state of Hawaii deserves special mention in any discussion of endangered or threatened species. Ninety-nine percent of the known animal species, and 95 percent of flowering plants in the Hawaiian Islands, are found nowhere else in the world. Extensive deforestation and urbanization have caused tremendous loss of species in Hawaii. Nearly half the birds classified as endangered in the United States and half of the 300 extinctions of plants and animals in the United States since 1950 are attributable to the loss of native Hawaiian plant and animal species.[70]

SUMMARY

In this chapter we looked at land-use problems—broadly defined. Local land-use planning started out the chapter with a discussion of how money and politics operate to determine how our neighborhoods evolve. Then we examined farmland conversion, desertification, and soil erosion, which threaten U.S. and global agricultural production. Finally we discussed the federal land management issues of timber harvesting, multiple-use management, wilderness designation, and endangered species.

Species loss at a global level is, as we have indicated, a good example of an international common pool problem and the environmental policy paradox. In the chapter that follows, the obstacles to efficient, or even effective, international environmental management are explored in greater detail. The prospects, as we will see, do not look promising.

NOTES

1. As of this writing, Houston is considering adopting limited zoning regulations.
2. Richard Wolkomir, "A High Tact Attack on Traffic Jams Helps Motorists Go with the Flow," *Smithsonian* (April 1986), p. 44.
3. Carol M. Rose, "New Models for Local Land Use Decisions," *Northwestern University Law Review*, 79 (5 & 6) (1984–85), p. 1156.
4. U.S. Council on Environmental Quality, *The Quiet Revolution in Land Use Control* (Washington, DC: U.S. Government Printing Office, 1971).
5. *Village of Euclid v. Ambler Realty Co.*, 272 U.S. 365 (1926).
6. Guy Benveniste, *The Politics of Expertise* (Berkeley: Gelndessary Press, 1972), pp. 106–116.
7. Richard H. Foster and R. Lawson Veasey, "Shootout at Blackrock. The Politics of Land Use Planning," *Natural Resource and Environmental Administration* (American Society for Public Administration), 5(6) (Spring 1982), p. 2.
8. Richard F. Babcock, *The Zoning Game: Municipal Practices in Policies* (Madison: University of Wisconsin Press, 1966), pp. 124–125.
9. Neil G. Carne, "Is Highest and Best Use a Justification for Zoning?" *The Appraisal Journal*, 52 (April 1984), p. 180.
10. Wolkomir, "A High Tact Attack on Traffic Jams Helps Motorists Go with the Flow," p. 45.
11. Rose, "New Models for Local Land Use Decisions," p. 1171.
12. For discussion of greenbelts and open space, see Judith Kunofsky and Larry Orman, "Greenbelts and the Well Planned City," *Sierra* (November-December 1985), p. 42.
13. G. Tyler Miller, Jr., *Living in the Environment* (5th ed.) (Belmont, CA: Wadsworth, 1988), p. 198.
14. R. Neil Sampson, "Saving Agricultural Land," in Nannem Blackburn (ed.), *Pieces of the Global Puzzle: International Approaches to Environmental Concerns* (Golden, CO: Fulcrum, 1986), p. 67.
15. Miller, *Living in the Environment*, p. 197.
16. Roger Swain, "Losing Ground," *Horticulture: The Magazine of American Gardening* 70(7) (August-September 1992), p. 15.
17. Paul and Anne Ehrlich, "Space Age Cargo Cult," in Kent Gilbreath (ed.), *Business and the Environment: Toward Common Ground* (Washington, DC: Conservation Foundation, 1984), p. 177.
18. Maryla Webb and Judith Jacobsen, *U.S. Carrying Capacity: An Introduction* (Washington DC: Carrying Capacity, 1982), p. 33.
19. Miller, *Living in the Environment*, p. 259.
20. Rennicke, "Sacred Cows?" *Backpacker*, 20(5) (August 1992), pp. 47–58.
21. Ibid., p. 48.

22. Lands controlled by the Department of Defense are not included in this analysis.
23. See, for example, Multiple Use Sustain Yield Act of 1960, 16th Space U.S.C. Section 528–531 (1974); and Federal Land Policy and Management Act, 43 U.S.C. Section 1710-1784 (Supp. 1984).
24. Marian Clawson, "The Concept of Multiple Use Forestry," *Environmental Law*, 8(2) (1978), p. 281.
25. Charles Davis and Sandra Davis, "Wilderness Protection at What Price? An Empirical Assessment," in Phillip Foss (ed.), *Federal Lands Policy* (New York: Greenwood Press, 1987), p. 113.
26. Noel Rosetta, "Herds, Herds on the Range," *Sierra* (March/April 1985), p. 74; see also V. Alaric Sample, Jr., *Below Cost Timber Sales in the National Forests* (Washington, DC: The Wilderness Society, 1984); and Dennis C. LeMaster, Berry R. Flamm, and John C. Hendee (eds.), *Below Cost Timber Sales: A Conference on the Economics of National Forest Timber Sales*, Proceedings of a Conference, Spokane, Washington, February 17–19, 1986 (Washington, DC: The Wilderness Society, 1986), p. 2.
27. Steve Forrester, "Forest Service at a Loss," *Sierra* (November/December 1984), p. 22.
28. Ibid.
29. Ibid., p. 23.
30. The Conservation Foundation, *State of the Environment: A View Towards the Nineties* (Washington, DC: The Conservation Foundation, 1987), pp. 128–129.
31. Telephone interview with U.S. Forest Service representative, November 1993.
32. Jane O'Hara, "Canada's Vanishing Forest," *Maclean's* (January 14, 1985), p. 36.
33. Susan Schauer, "Let-it-Burn Policy Assailed in Hearings," *Arizona Daily Sun*, February 6, 1989, p. 2.
34. Paul J. Culhane, "Sagebrush Rebels in Office," in Norman J. Vig and Michael E. Kraft (eds.), *Environmental Policy in the 1980s* (Washington, DC: Congressional Quarterly, 1984), pp. 293–318.
35. The Wilderness Act, *Public Law* 88-571: 78-stat.-890.
36. Craig W. Allin, "Wilderness Preservation as a Bureaucratic Tool," in Foss, *Federal Lands Policy*, p. 132.
37. Douglas W. Scott, "Securing the Wilderness," *Sierra* (May/June 1984), p. 42.
38. Hoyt Gimlin, (ed.), *Earth's Threatened Resources* (Washington, DC: *Congressional Quarterly*, 1986), pp. 65–68.
39. The Wilderness Act, 16 U.S.C. Section 1131(c) (1982).
40. See Olen Paul Matthews, Amy Haak, and Kathryn Toffenetti, "Mining and Wilderness: Incompatible Uses or Justifiable Compromise," *Environment*, 27 (April 1985), p. 12.
41. Telephone interview with BLM representative, November 1993.
42. Richard O. Miller, "Multiple Use in the Bureau of Land Management: The Biases of Pluralism Revisited," in Foss, *Federal Lands Policy*, p. 57.
43. Ibid. Other violations include Red Cloud Peak Wilderness Study Area in Colorado and Little Book Cliffs Wilderness Study Area in Colorado, New Mexico's West Portrillo Mountains Wilderness Study Area, Big and Little Jacks Creek Wilderness Study Area in southwestern Idaho, the Owyhee River Canyon Lands in Oregon, Panamint Dunes in Southern California, and the Soda Mountains Wilderness Study Area in Southern California.
44. Richard Conniff and David Muench, "Once the Secret Domain of Miners and Ranchers, the BLM Is Going Public," *Smithsonian*, 21(6) (September 1990), p. 41.
45. National Parks Service, U.S. Department of the Interior, *State of the Parks— 1980*, A Report to Congress (1980).
46. Maura Doland, "National Parks Beset by Mounting Pressures," *Los Angeles Times*, May 25, 1986, p. 1.

47. Telephone interview with National Park Service representative, November 1993.
48. Nancy Shute, "Howling at the Moon," *The Amicus Journal* (Winter 1987), p. 39.
49. Ibid., p. 43.
50. G. Tyler Miller, Jr., *Living in the Environment* (5th ed.) (Belmont, CA: Wadsworth, 1988), pp. 292–293.
51. Ibid., p. 293.
52. Ibid., p. 295.
53. Ibid. These estimates were developed from Edward O. Wilson, *Biophilia* (Cambridge, MA: Harvard University Press, 1984); and Norman Myers, *A Wealth of Wild Species: Store House for Human Welfare* (Boulder, CO: Westview Press, 1983).
54. See also "Promise and Peril: A New Look at the Endangered Species Act of 1973," *St. Louis University Law Journal*, 27 (November 1983), p. 959.
55. Ibid.
56. Miller, *Living in the Environment*, p.306.
57. 16 U.S.C. Section 1531–1543 (1981). The Endangered Species Act was amended in 1976, 1978, 1979, 1982, and 1987.
58. *TVA v. Hill*, 437 U.S. 153, 180 (1978).
59. In 1900 Congress passed the Lacey Act, ch. 553, 31 Stat., which banned interstate traffic in illegally killed wildlife and was designed primarily to protect birds that were being killed for their plumes.
60. Telephone interview with U.S. Fish and Wildlife Service, November 1993.
61. "House, Senate Passed Endangered Species Bills," *Congressional Quarterly*, 40 (1982), p. 1403.
62. Exceptions include Alaskan natives who are not subject to the prohibitions of the act if a species is taken for subsistence purposes or, at the discretion of the secretary of the interior, those who have entered into contracts involving endangered species prior to the notice of the species protection appearance in the federal register may be exempted by the secretary of the interior if the act would cause a person to suffer undue economic hardship. See Endangered Species Act, 16 U.S.C. Section 1539 (1987).
63. The Tellico Dam Case. *Tennessee Valley Authority v. Hill*, 4378 U.S. 153 (1978).
64. Miller, *Living in the Environment*, p. 305.
65. *TVA v. Hill*, 437 U.S. 153, 195 (1978).
66. See George Cameron Coggins and Irma S. Russell, "Beyond Shooting Snail Darters in Forth Barrels: Endangered Species and Land Use America," *The Georgetown Law Journal*, 70 (August 1982), pp. 1433–1434.
67. Miller, *Living in the Environment*, p. 304. As of 1985, 250 refuges allowed hunting.
68. Telephone interview with U.S. Fish and Wildlife Service, November 1993.
69. Miller, Living in the Environment, p. 305.
70. Ibid., p. 296.

chapter 10

∂℮

International
Environmental Issues

The international environmental crisis is more pervasive and in some ways more frightening than any of the other environmental problems we have studied in this book. International pollution transcends ideological and political boundaries. Furthermore, our technical ability to manipulate and exploit the global environment may have surpassed our ability to manage the negative impacts of those actions. Damage that has been done to the environment, particularly stratospheric ozone depletion and the buildup of global warming gasses, and damage that can be anticipated if current trends continue, threaten worldwide disaster.[1] As Mostafa K. Tolba, the executive director of the United Nations Environment Program said, "[U]nless all nations (mount) a massive and sustained effort into safeguarding their shared living resources, we will face a catastrophe on a scale rivaled only by nuclear war."[2]

In this chapter we examine the international environmental problems that impact all others—overpopulation, food production and, relatedly, desertification. In addition we summarize four global common pool pollution problems: destruction of the ozone layer due to the production of chlorofluorocarbons (CFCs); the warming of the earth's environment due to the release of gasses, or the greenhouse effect; and, briefly, deforestation and ocean pollution. Finally we examine some of the unique problems facing the less developed countries of the world and the relationship of international environmental issues to global security.

The leadership of all political parties in the Western democracies agree the world has serious food and population problems. Some argue that population problems are not environmental problems in the same way as, for example, air pollution is. However, all environmental problems—including overpopulation—are related. The press of an expanding population impacts forests, soil erosion, energy needs, and many other environmental problems.

POPULATION AND FOOD PRODUCTION

The carrying capacity of an environment, that is, the population an ecosystem can sustain over a long-term period, is only sustainable if a balance is achieved between renewable resources and the population dependent on them. When the population of one species, rabbits for example, grows to the point where the renewability of its food source is put in jeopardy, the species is threatened with extinction as food runs out. This die-off in turn impacts other species. Using the example of rabbits, when the rabbit population grows, so do the populations of the rabbits' natural predators—perhaps mountain lions. As the grass, which is the rabbits' food supply, is destroyed, the rabbits die and so do the lions who became dependent on an abundant rabbit population. This explosion–die-off sequence is common in nature.

Humankind has overshot the earth's historical carrying capacity. Through reliance on fossil fuels—stored energy—we have been able to develop intensified agriculture, concentrated housing, and labor saving that has resulted in a population far in excess of what we thought sustainable two centuries ago. We are in a crisis situation. As a U.S. National Academy of Sciences and Royal Society of London study reported, "If current predictions of population growth prove accurate and patterns of human activity on the planet remain unchanged, science and technology may not be able to prevent either irreversible degradation of the environment or continued poverty for much of the world.[3]

The food and population problem is not new. Throughout recorded history world food supply and demand have never been in close balance.[4] However, never before in the world's history have we seen population rates increase as dramatically as they have in the nineteenth and twentieth centuries.

In 1994 world population is about 5.5 billion, an increase from 4.5 million in 1980. In 1980 it was estimated the population of the developed countries would increase by 12 percent between 1980 and the year 2000 and the population of the less developed countries would grow 50 percent during the same period. Africa was estimated to have the largest increase at 76 percent followed by Latin America at 65 percent.[5] Studies conducted by the

United Nations in the early 1980s projected world population would total 6.1 billion in the year 2000 and 8.1 billion in 2025.[6] Most of this projected growth will occur in less developed countries. It is interesting to note that in 1950 roughly one-third of the world's population resided in more developed countries, yet by the year 2025 only 17 percent of the world's population will reside in more developed countries.[7]

By examining fertility rates one can determine if a given country is headed toward a stable, declining, or growing population. A fertility rate of 2.1 births per woman is considered the replacement level fertility rate and results in a stable population size. Fertility rates in excess of 6.0 are common in Africa. Kenya has a fertility rate of 8.0; Tanzania, 7.1; Zambia, 7.0; Nigeria, 6.6; just to mention a few.[8]

Fertility rates and the projections of world population become an important concern when we consider the carrying capacity of the world. The Earth's carrying capacity, meaning that human population the world can sustain over a long term, is extremely difficult to measure globally. However, a 1982 United Nations study examined the population-sustaining capacity in 117 developing countries and concluded that by the year 2000, 65 of the countries studied, with the combined population of 1.1 billion people, would be unable to provide their inhabitants with even minimum levels of nutrition. Lester Brown observed, "[In these 65 countries] population would overshoot the numbers who could be sustained by 440 million, implying a heavy dependence on imported food, widespread starvation, or more likely, both."[9]

Worldwide food production has declined in per capita terms each year since 1984. From 1951 to 1984 the production of grain, for example, increased at a rate of 3 percent a year. Between 1984 and 1992 grain production grew by less than 1 percent a year. When measured against population growth, this represents a 6 percent decline in grain production.[10] In the two areas with the greatest population growth—Africa and Latin America—food production has declined significantly over the last few decades. In Africa, per capita production has declined 27 percent since 1967. In Latin America, food production has declined roughly 10 percent since 1981. Latin America was a net exporter of grain up until the early 1970s. Africa, while not a grain exporter, did supply most of its needs up to the 1970s.[11] These decreasing food yields are due primarily to the environmental problems discussed throughout this book: deforestation, dwindling water supplies, and soil erosion.

What exactly is the world's carrying capacity? Estimates vary from as low as 6 million to as high as 24 billion, and some have argued there are no practical limits. William Ophuls, after studying the issue and citing numerous scholars, argued a realistic limit is one person for each acre of arable land. Ophuls concludes that the maximum population the world could sustain would appear to be 8 billion people, there being at most 8 billion acres of potentially arable land. These numbers assume we would all be vegetarians, thereby saving the energy lost by converting plant proteins to animal proteins for human consumption.[12] About one-third of the world's grain is fed to animals for the production of meat, milk, and eggs.

The United Nations has estimated world population will exceed 8.5 billion by the year 2025.[13] Others have estimated the 8 billion mark will be reached by the year 2010, with populations surpassing 15 billion by the year 2045.[14] If fertility levels were reduced worldwide to a replacement rate by the year 2000, demographers estimate the world's population would increase to 5.9 billion and eventually stabilize at 8.5 billion.[15] This, of course, is a very big assumption. As the figures have demonstrated, we are very far from replacement fertility rates in virtually all of the less developed world.

What do all these figures mean? For some analysts, not very much. For example, Julian Simon, an economics professor at the University of Illinois, has argued that greater numbers of people will mean an enhanced quality of life for everyone. Using aggregate population and economic figures, Simon finds that, "[T]he bigger the population of the country, the greater the number of scientists and the larger the amount of scientific knowledge produced. ... This argues that faster population growth—which causes faster growing industries—leads to faster growth of productivity."[16] Simon's ideas, although provocative, are very much in the minority. Noted biologists Paul and Anne Ehrlich, in a critique of Simon's work, found little or no causal relationship between the variables examined and the conclusions of Simon's research. After examining an article Simon wrote arguing that market forces and other resources would operate to provide an abundance of whatever materials are needed by humans, the Ehrlichs conclude, "Simon's weird ideas are not, by any means, restricted to physics. He treats us to mathematical amusements as well. ... [O]ne might be tempted simply to write off Simon's views as being unworthy of consideration by any educated person."[17] The problem is, the Ehrlichs point out, Simon is taken seriously by many and is commonly published in otherwise high-minded publications, hence giving added credence to his claims.

A great deal depends on what numbers one examines and how they are interpreted. For example, Simon measures pollution in one study by plotting life expectancy over time and concludes that increased life expectancy is evidence of decreased pollution. Some might argue there are better ways of measuring pollution, since many other factors enter in to confound the pollution/life expectancy relationship.

Few scholars that study ecology agree with Simon and the other optimists. A combination of environmental stresses, including a rising population and decreasing agricultural productivity, suggest, to most observers, that the world is in for a rocky future unless mitigation measures are taken soon.[18] Absent some change or unforeseen developments, we are headed in this or the next generation toward widespread starvation that will make the famine in northern Africa in the early 1980s seem mild by comparison. Furthermore, the United States is not likely to be in a position to provide much food assistance far beyond the year 2000.[19]

Food and population presents perhaps the greatest environmental policy paradox of all. We have a fairly good idea of the steps that need to be taken to mitigate widespread starvation and disruption. We have been slow to take these steps. This is due in part to something called the "demographic trap" or the "demographic transition."

In 1945 demographer Frank Notestein outlined a theory of demographic change known as the demographic transition. Notestein essentially classifies societies as being in one of three stages. During the first stage, both birth and death rates are very high and population grows very slowly, if at all. This first stage characterizes premodern societies. In the second stage, health measures improve living conditions causing death rates to decline while birthrates remain high and population grows rapidly. In the third stage, birthrates level off to a replacement rate as families, enjoying economic security and lower infant mortality rates, are smaller. In the third stage, births roughly equal deaths.[20] Most of the industrialized world has undergone the transition from the second to the third stage as is reflected by the fact that fertility rates are at or below that necessary for replacement. Unfortunately, much of the less developed world may never get out of the second stage. Lester Brown refers to this as the demographic trap. Once incomes begin to rise and birthrates begin declining,

> [T]he process feeds on itself and countries can quickly move to the equilibrium of the demographic transition's third stage.... Once a population expands to the point where their demands begin to exceed the sustainable yield of local forest, grasslands, croplands, or water supplies, they begin directly or indirectly to consume the resource base itself... not only have they failed to complete the demographic transition, but the deteriorating relationship between people and ecological support systems that is lowering living standards may prevent them from ever doing so.[21]

Leaders of the less developed countries may not notice they are headed for the demographic trap. The relatively slow pace of desertification, soil erosion, deforestation mitigated by imported food, borrowed money, and the development of marginal farmland can mask the slide of a country into perpetual poverty and eventual starvation.

The DSP of many less developed nations also contributes to the slide into the demographic trap. We discussed the impact of religion on environmental management in Part One. Here it is worth noting that two major religions in the less developed world, Roman Catholicism and Islam, promote fertility and, directly or indirectly, large families.

The leaders of many less developed countries are understandably reluctant to limit their population growth rates or to undertake other measures proposed by the more developed countries. Suggestions from the United States that less developed countries limit their resource demands sound like, "I got mine, too bad for you."

Assistance from more developed countries to less developed countries has typically placed emphasis on nonrenewable development, like road building, mineral extraction, and large-scale hydropower projects, instead of sustainable development, such as agriculture or renewable forestry.[22] Assistance has also taken the form of food transfers to the starving.

The policy of shipping reserves of food to those that have showed little inclination to control their population growth may only be prolonging the inevitable. Such policies keep more people alive to be even hungrier when the next shortage occurs. Clearly, food alone is not enough unless it is accompanied by the means for people to become self-sufficient. Unfortunately, because of the demographic trap, the capital necessary (in terms of natural resources) for self-sufficiency may be exhausted before self-sufficiency is achieved. Alofchie and Commines wrote in *The Futurist*, "[I]f the resources in human energy allotted to food aid programs could be channeled towards improving the countries' own systems of economic management, transportation, storage and distribution, this would undoubtedly do more to alleviate hunger on a long-term basis than any quantity of external food assistance."[23]

Humanity will survive the population explosion. After a crash, as in the rabbit example, most systems reach a steady state. Preparing for a sustainable global population today could prevent a human population crash. As Paul and Anne Ehrlich put it, "[N]ature may end the population explosion for us—in very unpleasant ways—well before 10 billion is reached. . . . We should not delude ourselves: the population explosion will come to an end before very long."[24]

Perhaps the greatest environmental policy paradox, therefore, is in the area of food and population policy. The consequences of a future of unrestricted growth are clear. Yet, again quoting the Ehrlichs, who have been studying population biology for over 35 years, "[O]ne of the toughest things for a population biologist to reconcile is the contrast between his or her recognition that civilization is in imminent serious jeopardy and the modest level of concern that population issues generate among the public and even among elected officials."[25]

Sustainable agriculture, instead of transfers of food, is what is needed over the long term.

What can we do as individuals to address the world food situation? You and I can contribute to the world food balance in a small way by eating nonprocessed food such as whole oats, rice, or wheat, and low-processed foods such as bread and tortillas. Also, since it is much more efficient to eat grain proteins directly rather than getting protein in the form of animals, becoming vegetarian would contribute to the available food supply. When grain is fed to beef, only about 10 percent of the calories in the grain is delivered to people eating the beef. If vegetarianism is a bit more than you are willing to sacrifice, eat less beef and more chicken or fish grown through aquaculture. Both chicken and fish grown for harvest are much more efficient converters of grain to animal proteins than beef, hogs, or sheep.[26]

DESERTIFICATION AND FOOD PRODUCTION

Closely related to food and population problems are the food production problems caused by desertification. Desertification, the process of turning productive land into wasteland, is occurring at an alarming pace—particularly in countries in the less developed world. In semiarid areas, grasses and other vegetation secure the soil and retain moisture. When plants die, through overgrazing, trampling, or harvesting for fuel, the moisture retention capacity of the ground is lost and the land is slowly converted to desert. An estimated 30 percent of the world's land surface containing one-sixth of the world's population is threatened by desertification.

All continents are suffering from some desertification. Areas with high or very high desertification potential include most of the southern part of South America, southern Africa, most of central Asia, the west and southwestern United States, parts of the Canadian midwest, and nearly all of Australia.[27] The greatest impacts have been felt in Africa. The Sahara Desert expanded 100 kilometers eastward between 1958 and 1975.[28] In the North African countries where desertification has been particularly severe, per capita food production declined 40 percent between 1950 and 1980.[29]

Desertification involves many social, cultural, and political as well as ecological problems. Forests are stripped for fuel or burned off so land may be planted. However, the benefit is only short term, as eventually desertification sets in.

Desertification is a difficult problem. The slow and gradual nature of desertification does not lend itself to crisis management, and in many countries the activities that lead to desertification—overgrazing and harvesting fuel, for example—are seen as essential to maintain life. Desertification is part of a cycle in the struggle for existence in these countries. As it continues, nations fall further and further into the demographic trap.

GLOBAL POLLUTION

As discomforting as the long-term population and food problems the world faces may be, global pollution problems are no less frightening. Like overpopulation and desertification, we understand much about the causes of and solutions to global pollution problems. Yet paradoxically, because of the nature of global pollution and the international institutions and incentive systems operating on international actors, it is quite possible that timely solutions to global environmental problems, including overpopulation, will not be found.

Many global pollution issues have been discussed in previous chapters. Here we review and summarize some of the major global pollution problems that are clearly common pool in nature and hence whose solutions will require international cooperation.

Although there are many international environmental problems that may require international solutions, four: the ozone layer, the greenhouse, deforestation, and ocean pollution, have been the focus of the most attention by the public and policymakers.

The Ozone Layer

As we saw in Chapter 5, ozone in the stratosphere protects us from the sun's ultraviolet radiation. Without this protection, the earth's atmosphere would be uninhabitable. CFCs have been used since 1955 in aerosol spray cans, refrigeration units, industrial solvents, and in plastic foams for insulation, packing, furniture, and the plastic foam used in the manufacture of some coffee cups and fast-food containers.[30] CFCs in aerosol cans have been banned in the United States, Canada, and most Scandinavian countries since 1978. Still CFC production has increased globally since the 1970s and although international agreements have been reached that will stem, somewhat, the increase in global CFC production in the future, total production will continue at rates that threaten the ozone layer.[31] (Reread Chapter 5 if you don't remember the international environmental paradox problems associated with CFC production.)

For every single percentage decrease in ozone in the stratosphere, skin cancers increase by an estimated 5 to 10 percent. The increase in ultraviolet light can have a negative impact on the ocean food chain by destroying microorganisms on the ocean surface and causing crops on land to suffer decreased yields. It is estimated that since 1969, ozone losses have averaged between 2 and 3 percent over North America and Europe and as high as 5 and 6 percent over parts of the Southern Hemisphere.[32]

CFC production causes global pollution problems that necessitate international cooperation if they are to be addressed before serious damage is done to the atmosphere. Fortunately, as we saw in Chapter 5, some steps have been taken in the international political arena to deal with the CFC problem. No such measures have been taken to deal with greenhouse gasses and, given the world's dependence on fossil fuels, future prospects for international cooperation in time to avert serious environmental problems seems remote.

The Greenhouse

For over 100 years we have understood the possibility of atmospheric warming due to human carbon dioxide emissions. According to many scientists, the greenhouse effect has seriously been altered by humankind's impact on the composition of the atmosphere. It is estimated that global levels of carbon dioxide in the atmosphere will reach 550 ppm sometime between 2040 and 2100, however *most* analysts feel those levels will be reached closer to the middle of the twenty-first century.[33] Carbon dioxide levels of 550 ppm would raise average atmospheric temperatures approximately 4°C in the temperate regions with temperatures rising two to three times this amount at the poles. These increased temperatures would cause the expansion of seawater and the melting of ice in both polar regions, resulting in a rise in sea level, predicted by climatologists to be up to 1.5 meters (about 5 feet) by the year 2050.[34] The result will be worldwide coastal flooding, including the inundation of significant portions of the coastal United States in what are now heavily populated areas.

All over the world, food production will become erratic. The impact on agriculture would be particularly severe in the United States, since most food is grown in the middle or higher latitudes of the Northern Hemisphere where the greatest impact from the greenhouse effect will be felt. As climatic zones shift northward, animals, and particularly plants, will have a difficult time adapting to the change. This will lead to a significant loss in species variety and loss of genetic diversity. As the EPA has reported, "The landscape of North America will change in ways that cannot be fully predicted. The ultimate effects will last for centuries and will be irreversible. ... Strategies to reverse such impacts on natural ecosystems are not currently available."[35] As with CFC production, this is clearly a global problem requiring global solutions.

Deforestation

Deforestation of rain forests largely for agricultural development is related to the greenhouse effect in several important respects. Although not an international common pool problem per se, deforestation has serious impacts on common pool air resources.

Deforestation is occurring in many parts of the world and is particularly intense in the less developed countries. Reforestation is the primary means of effectively reducing carbon dioxide in the atmosphere. Worldwide rates of deforestation are about 10 times the rate of reforestation. According to the World Resources Institute, approximately 27 million acres a year of forests are being lost. The World Wildlife Fund has estimated that close to half of the world's original tropical rain forests have been destroyed or degraded.[36]

Much of this deforestation occurs in the less developed areas, notably Brazil, Indonesia, and Zaire, regions that rely on the forests for energy and increased agricultural production. Consequently the prospects for a dramatic end to deforestation are not encouraging.[37] Deforestation also has a dramatic effect on termite populations—increasing the number of termites by anywhere from three to ten times their predeforestation population. Termites give off methane gas. Increases in atmospheric methane, an important greenhouse gas, have been measured at between 1 and 2 percent each year, due in part, some scientists fear, to deforestation and the related increase in the termite population.[38]

Ocean Pollution

Pollution that occurs on the high seas is the fourth example of an international common pool environmental management problem we review here. (Ocean pollution is covered in greater detail in Chapter 6.) The effects of international ocean pollution are clear and solutions are not difficult to understand—but many of the causes of ocean pollution will require international cooperation and action. Given the common pool nature of the problem, in international waters, it is likely ocean pollution will be with us for some time to come.

Ocean pollution is a problem worldwide. Coastal areas on all continents suffer from sewage and industrial pollution entering the oceans via river systems.[39]

The sources of ocean pollution include wastewater from municipal treatment plants, municipal sludge, agricultural runoff, and, one of the most important international pollution problems, oil pollution.[40]

Oil from the cleaning, unloading, and loading of oil tankers, and accidents and blowouts of oil tankers contribute significant amounts of oil pollution to the ocean. In 1985 approximately 3.6 million tons of crude and refined oil were discharged, intentionally or accidentally, into the world's oceans from various sources, killing hundreds of thousands of marine birds and mammals. The inability of government to deal with international ocean pollution—when the causes and solutions are so clear—is an example of the environmental policy paradox.

The international environmental problems discussed so far in this chapter often involve conflicting interests of one group of countries against another group or the rest of the world. Often the interests and concerns of the more developed world, primarily Western democracies, are at odds with the interests and concerns of less developed countries. These conflicts and their implications for a healthy global ecosystem, as well as a stable global political system in the future, are the subject of the rest of this chapter. In Chapter 11 we examine political and institutional relationships that impact environmental management globally and discuss institutions that may need to be created to deal with international environmental problems.

LESS DEVELOPED COUNTRIES: NORTH VS. SOUTH

Less developed countries of the world, the poorer nations concentrated in the Southern Hemisphere, play a vital role in global environmental management. As many of these countries rush headlong into industrialization, they encounter serious environmental problems. Carbon dioxide concentrations in the earth's atmosphere are reduced by tropical forests. Deforestation of tropical rain forests, primarily in Africa, southern Asia, and South America, promises to speed global warming and the greenhouse effect worldwide. As we have seen, these forests, which contain one-half of the world's species of plants and animals, are being destroyed at a rate of approximately 27 million acres a year. Forests are cleared for fuel, to open grazing land, and to allow cultivation and settlement. Even the most stable less developed countries, firmly committed to environmental protection, experience difficulties controlling environmental degradation due to deforestation.[41] Already close to half of the world's original tropical rain forests have been destroyed or degraded.[42] This is a major global environmental problem that threatens both long-term sustainable agricultural productivity in less developed countries and air quality in the more developed world.

Yet it is difficult to fault less developed countries for the destruction of their tropical rain forests. Often deforestation is vital to survival. In many less developed countries, in excess of 40 percent of the population lack incomes sufficient to provide the necessities for sustaining life. It is not unusual, in some countries, for half of the workday to be taken up by the collection of fuelwood to provide energy. To expect countries with populations struggling to meet basic living requirements to forgo deforestation so more developed nations can continue to burn fossil fuels strikes many as bizarre.

Even when it is not a question of survival, economic incentive systems provided by international markets make deforestation very attractive to less developed countries and their political leaders. For example, the market for beef has induced South American ranchers to clear vast areas of rain forest (an estimated 55 square feet of forest must be cleared to produce a quarter pound of beef) to supply international markets.[43]

There is no small amount of irony in the fact that many less developed countries find themselves saddled with environmental problems that are a direct outgrowth of interaction with the more developed world. The African colonizers, like colonizers throughout the world, had policies that undermined the delicate balance between humans and nature and set in motion the disruption and decimation of social, political, economic, cultural, and environmental systems in the lands they colonized.[44]

The colonizing nations of Europe used their advanced technology to exploit their colonies' resources. This exploitation has not ended. Even though colonial systems are less prevalent today, America's toxic waste, as we saw in Chapter 8, finds its way into many less developed countries. Also, pesticides and other goods banned in the United States are used in agriculture in less developed countries, often without regard to precautions necessary to protect worker health. That food often finds its way back into U.S. markets.[45]

Although done in the name of self-determination and with the best intentions, the activities of developed countries in the less developed world have—paradoxically—often had negative impacts on the environment. The model of development set for the less developed world has proven to be detrimental to the ecosystems of those nations. Much of the money borrowed from the World Bank and other international lenders goes to development projects that are not ecologically sound.[46] Instead of supporting sustainable development, such as agriculture or renewable forestry, the emphasis has been on road building, mineral extraction, large-scale hydropower, and agricultural exports.[47]

For example, World Bank and African Development Bank financing paid for a huge dam on the Awash River in Ethiopia. The Awash Dam resulted in the displacement of thousands of people, many of whom became the Ethiopian famine victims of the early 1980s. In the lead paragraph of an article discussing the Ethiopian famine, the author wrote, "[L]ittle did the world know it was helping to rescue victims of earlier aid efforts."[48] Yet the need to improve living conditions through development spurs countries to act for short-term developmental gains without regard for the long-term environmental costs. Only in the late 1980s, largely in response to the demands of environmental organizations, did some international lending institutions begin to take environmental degradation into consideration when making loans. There is no evidence, however, that these institutions have any inclination to move away from large-scale intensive development projects and toward ecologically sustainable development.

The foregoing discussion of the environmental problems facing the less developed world and the relationship between the environmental problems of the less developed world and the more developed world suggest a potential for conflict in the future. Many feel that is what the future holds.

INTERNATIONAL CONFLICT

The pollution, population, and other environmental problems facing the less developed world threaten the survival of everyone. As Richard Tobin wrote,

> The population, development, and environmental problems of the Third World dwarf those of the developed world and are not amenable to immediate resolution, but immediate action is imperative. To meet their daily needs for food and fuel, millions of people are steadily destroying their biological and environmental support systems at unprecedented rates. ... Whether this situation will change depends on the ability of Third World residents, not only to reap the benefits of sustained economic growth, but also to meet the demands of current populations while using their natural resources in a way that accommodates the needs of future generations. Unless the developing nations are able to do so soon, their future will determine ours as well.[49]

It may not seem like an environmental issue, but there is a growing consensus among environmental and international relations analysts that environmental degradation and resource scarcity will have an impact on global security and world peace in the future.

At the United Nations Conference on the Human Environment in 1972 (known as the Stockholm Conference), a major disagreement arose between less and more developed nations over the impact environmental controls would have on future economic growth and development. Similar to the concerns of unions and representatives of the urban poor in the United States who were, and to a lesser extent remain, skeptical of environmental regulations for fear they slow economic development, the leadership of many less developed countries fear the road to prosperity, or out of poverty, may necessarily involve increased industrial pollution.

When the leaders of less developed countries reflect on the history of industrial development in the United States, they find it is replete with resource exploitation. The destruction of Eastern forests, pollution of urban air and water, and the continued use of renewable resources at rates that are in excess of natural rates of return all suggest the United States is prescribing an austerity medicine for other nations after our own prosperity has been assured, medicine we have been reluctant to take ourselves—or to take in sufficiently high doses.

Since the Stockholm Conference, most less developed countries have accepted that the environment needs to be protected. Only nine nations had environmental ministries in 1972. Ten years later over 100 had established some kind of environmental protection organization. Although often poorly staffed or ineffective, this is, at least, evidence of global recognition of the need for environmental protection.

Nevertheless, conflict between rich and poor nations will be a big part of international environmental administration in the future. The finite resources the more developed world has used to fuel economic expansion and a comfortable lifestyle will not be available for a repeat performance for future, or even present, generations in the less developed world.

In fact, citizens of more developed countries can count on lifestyle changes that reflect resource scarcity. In the last 20 years, for example, young Americans have had to accept that they may never own a single-family detached home, a second home, or an array of high-powered recreational vehicles—certainly not necessities, but common among the middle class in America a generation ago and less so today. The day may not be long off when automobile travel, beef consumption, the pleasure of a household pet, or a room heated to 72°F in the winter will be luxuries only a few can afford. As resource scarcity begets other lifestyle changes for middle-class Americans, we can anticipate that pressure will be put on politicians to find political solutions to domestic scarcity problems. This may lead to conflict and the exploitation of the poor by the rich. As Daniel Henning and William Mangun put it, "[T]he less developed countries face the additional threat of technological and resource exploitation by the developed countries themselves experiencing resource scarcity as they attempt to maintain high consumption levels."[50]

During the 1980s several well-written and widely received books and reports examined the relationship between international environmental problems and global peace and security.[51] One, *Our Common Future* (the Brundtland commission report to the United Nations), reported,

> The deepening and widening environmental crisis presents a threat to national security—and even survival—that may be greater than well-armed ill-disposed neighbors and unfriendly alliances. ... Environmental stress is both a cause and an effect of political tension and military conflict. Nations have

often fought to assert or resist control over raw materials, energy supplies . . . and other key environmental resources. Such conflicts are likely to increase as these resources become scarcer and the competition for them increases.[52]

In light of the consequences of ignoring global environmental problems and watching as the less developed world slides deeper and deeper into irreversible capital resource loss, it would seem, as Robert Paehlke put it, that "[R]eal security . . . requires a transfer of funds from military expenditure to sustainable development."[53] The funds are there. By returning military spending to the same percentage of the world's GNP that it was just prior to 1960, $225 billion could be made available on an annual basis.[54]

Unfortunately, international policy formation, like domestic policy formation, often requires a crisis situation before policymakers act. Most environmental policy analysts and other environmental specialists agree we are in a crisis situation. Yet for political and institutional reasons little happens—another environmental policy paradox.

SUMMARY

The picture this chapter paints is not pleasant. Most of the less developed world finds itself with growing populations, a deteriorating resource base, and an unhealthy environment. Furthermore, the continuing scarcity of world resources, the future necessity of sacrifice, and less material abundance (or the prospect, for many countries, of never becoming more developed and enjoying the privileges the more developed world takes for granted) have turned environmental problems into national security problems.

Solving the international environmental problems discussed in the chapter—overpopulation and its related effects, ozone depletion, global warming, deforestation, and ocean pollution—as well as the other environmental problems we have discussed throughout the book, will require money and organization. The World Resources Institute has estimated it will take $20 to $50 billion a year to save the environment in the developing world. In contrast, the budget at the beginning of the 1990s of the United Nations Environment Program is less than $30 *million* a year.[55] Yet, as we have seen with our summary of defense expenditures, the money is there. What is lacking is the will or the incentives and the institutional framework. In the next chapter we examine international environmental management and the prerequisites to successful global pollution control.

NOTES

1. Peter Borrelli, "Debt or Equity?" *The Amicus Journal* (Fall 1988), p. 47.
2. Larry B. Stammer, "Saving the Earth: Who Sacrifices?" *Los Angeles Times*, March 13, 1989, Pt. 1, p. 16.

3. Royal Society of London and the U.S. National Academy of Sciences, *Population Growth, Resource Consumption, and a Sustainable World* (London and Washington, DC: 1992). Cited in Lester R. Brown, "A New Era Unfolds," in Lester R. Brown et al. (eds.), *State of the World* (New York: Norton, 1993), p. 3.
4. S. Wortman and R. Cummings, Jr., *To Feed This World: The Challenge and the Strategy* (Baltimore: Johns Hopkins University Press, 1979), p. 83.
5. Jonathan Turk, *Introduction to Environmental Studies* (2nd ed.) (Philadelphia: Saunders, 1985), p. 90.
6. United Nations, Department of International Economic and Social Affairs, Population Studies No. 85, *The World Population Situation in 1983*, p. 49.
7. Ibid.
8. Population Reference Bureau, *1987 World Population Data Sheet* (Washington, DC: 1987). Other countries with high levels of fertility include Afghanistan, 7.6; Jordan, 7.4; Saudi Arabia, 6.9; Ethiopia, 6.7; Senegal, 6.7; Pakistan, 6.6; Sudan, 6.5; Zimbabwe, 6.5; Iran, 6.3; Bangladesh, 6.2; and Zaire, 6.1.
9. Lester Brown (ed.), *State of the World*, 1977, manuscript, pp. 2–8.
10. Lester R. Brown, "A New Era Unfolds," pp. 5, 11.
11. Lester R. Brown, "Reexamining the World Food Prospect," in Lester R. Brown et al., *State of the World: 1989* (New York: Norton, 1989), pp. 43, 55.
12. William Ophuls, *Ecology and the Politics of Scarcity* (San Francisco: Freeman, 1977), p. 55.
13. The World Resources Institute, The United Nations Environment Programme and The United Nations Development Programme, *World Resources: 1992–93* (New York: Oxford University Press, 1992), p. 76.
14. Ibid., p. 48.
15. Turk, *Introduction to Environmental Studies*, p. 90.
16. Julian L. Simon, "The Case for More People," in Kent Gilbreath (ed.), *Business and the Environment: Toward Common Ground* (2nd ed.) (Washington, DC: Conservation Foundation, 1984), p. 169.
17. Paul and Anne Ehrlich, "Space Age Cargo Cult," in Gilbreath, *Business and the Environment*, p. 174.
18. Although total food outputs are high, world capital food production is not increasing at the same rates as it has in the past. Production rose 15 percent from 1950 to 1960, 7 percent in the decade from 1960 to 1970, and then only 4 percent from 1970 to 1980. "Supply Side Ideas Challenge Old Population Theory," in Gilbreath, *Business and the Environment*, p. 184.
19. Maryla Webb and Judith Jacobson, *U.S. Carrying Capacity: An Introduction* (Washington, DC: Carrying Capacity, 1982), p. 33.
20. For summary, see Lester R. Brown, "Analyzing the Demographic Trap," *State of the World 1977* (New York: Norton, 1987).
21. Ibid.
22. Borrelli, "Debt or Equity?" p. 48.
23. M. Alofchie and S. Commines, "Famines and Africa," *The Futurist* (April 1985), pp. 71–72.
24. Paul R. Ehrlich and Anne H. Ehrlich, "The Population Explosion," *The Amicus Journal*, (Winter 1990), pp. 24–25.
25. Ibid., p. 22.
26. Fish harvested from the sea by trawlers require large amounts of energy. Hence, even though fish caught in the sea are very efficient converters of protein, the energy required to harvest makes this a resource-intensive food. See Albert Sasson, "Aquaculture: Realities, Difficulties and Outlook," in Jacques G. Richardson (ed.), *Managing the Ocean: Resources, Research, Law* (Mount Airy, MD: Lomond, 1985), pp. 61–72.
27. Edward A. Keller, *Environmental Geology* (4th ed.) (Columbus, OH: Merrill, 1985), p. 454.

28. Turk, *Introduction to Environmental Studies*, p. 184.
29. Ibid.
30. Another threat to the ozone layer may be presented by U.S. space shuttle flights. Soviet experts claim that every time the U.S. craft flies, it destroys massive amounts of atmospheric ozone. Calculations by Valeri Burdkov, one of the Soviet Union's leading geophysicists and Vyacheslav Filin, deputy chief designer at the S.P. Korolyev Design Bureau, show that in "one flight, the space shuttle destroys up to 10 million of the three billion tons of atmospheric ozone. Three hundred launches is enough to do away altogether with the thin ozone layer which is already holed." The solid fuel used in the Titan rockets burns to produce hydrogen chloride, one molecule of which is said to destroy 100,000 molecules of ozone. The rocket emits 187 tons of chlorine and chlorine compounds as well as ozone-depleting nitrogen compounds (7 tons), aluminum oxides (177 tons), and 378 tons of carbon oxidizers. However, NASA maintains the shuttle is ecologically sound. See Nick Nuttall, "Russians say US Shuttle Is Damaging Ozone Layer," *The Times* (London), December 20, 1989, p. 5.
31. G. Tyler Miller, *Living in the Environment* (5th ed.) (Belmont, CA: Wadsworth, 1988), p. 439.
32. See Thomas H. Maugh II, "Ozone Depletion Far Worse Than Expected," *Los Angeles Times*, March 16, 1988, Pt. 1, p. 1; and "Ozone Depletion Worsens, NRDC Leads Drive for Total CFC Phase Out," *Newsline* (Natural Resources Defense Council), 6(2) (May/June 1988), p. 1.
33. Jeremy Rifkin, "The Doomsday Prognosis," *The Guardian*, August 21, 1988, p. 19; and Miller, *Living in the Environment*, p. 441.
34. Rifkin, "The Doomsday Prognosis," p. 19.
35. William Eaton, "Congress Urged to Fight Global Warming," *The Los Angeles Times*, December 2, 1988, Pt. 1, p. 41.
36. Daniel H. Henning and William R. Mangun, *Managing the Environmental Crisis* (Durham, NC: Duke University Press, 1989), p. 281.
37. Rifkin, "The Doomsday Prognosis," p. 19.
38. David M. Schwartz, "The Termite Connection," *International Wildlife* (July/August 1987), p. 38.
39. Anastasia Toufexis, "The Dirty Seas," *Time* (August 1, 1988), p. 47.
40. Conservation Foundation, *State of the Environment* (Washington, DC: Conservation Foundation, 1987), pp. 115, 415.
41. For example, the Central American nation of Costa Rica, perhaps the most democratic and stable government of Latin America, has a rate of deforestation that is inconsistent with its expressed commitment to conservation. Experts predict that despite its commitments, logging will proceed and the country will have virtually depleted its hardwood stocks by 1995. See Borrelli, "Debt or Equity?" p. 47.
42. Henning and Mangun, *Managing the Environmental Crisis*, p. 281.
43. Arnold J. Heidenheimer, Hugh Heclo, and Carolyn Teich Adams, *Comparative Public Policy* (New York: St. Martin's Press, 1990), p. 331.
44. Christine H. Russell, "Squandering Eden," *The Amicus Journal* (Fall 1988), p. 50.
45. Perhaps there is justice.
46. Borrelli, "Debt or Equity?" p. 48.
47. Ibid.
48. Patricia Adams, "All in the Name of Aid," *Sierra* (January/February 1987), p. 45.
49. Richard J. Tobin, "Environment, Population and Development in the Third World," in Norman J. Vig and Michael E. Kraft (eds.), *Environmental Policy in the 1990s* (Washington, DC: Congressional Quarterly Press, 1990), p. 298.

50. Henning and Mangun, *Managing the Environmental Crisis*, p. 299.
51. See, for example, International Union for Conservation of Nature and Natural Resources, *World Conservation Strategy* (Gland, Switzerland: International Union for Conservation of Nature and Natural Resources, 1980); Independent Commission on Disarmament and Security Issues, *Common Security: A Blueprint for Survival* (New York: Simon & Schuster, 1982); and Willy Brandt, *World Armament and World Hunger* (London: Victor Gollanez, 1986).
52. World Commission on Environment and Development, *Our Common Future* (New York: Oxford University Press, 1987), pp. 6–7, 290. Cited in Robert Paehlke, "Environmental Values and Democracy: The Challenge of the Next Century," in Norman J. Vig and Michael E. Kraft (eds.), *Environmental Policy in the 1990s* (Washington, DC: Congressional Quarterly Press, 1990), pp. 349–367.
53. Paehlke, "Environmental Values and Democracy: The Challenge of the Next Century," pp. 359–360.
54. Ibid., p. 360.
55. Vig and Kraft, *Environmental Policy in the 1990s*, p. 380.

chapter 11

International Environmental Management

Because of the nature of current global environmental problems and the international institutions and incentive systems operating on international actors, it is quite possible timely solutions to many of the problems discussed in the previous chapter and throughout this book will not be found. In this chapter we discuss the nature of international environmental cooperation—specifically the elements necessary for any satisfactory international solution to global pollution problems—and the prerequisites and prospects for responsible international environmental administration. In addition, we compare the environmental records of communist and capitalist countries and examine the conditions necessary for the creation of international organizations that will have the authority necessary to deal with those problems. As Norman Vig and Michael Kraft have written, "Governments are ill equipped to resolve many long-term and severe problems in the global environment; hence, institutional reforms and new methods of decision making will be critical to success in such cases."[1] We examine obstacles to the creation of such new methods of decision making.

Environmentalism is becoming a dominant political force in nations all over the globe. For example, in the former Soviet Union, "[O]nce the province of an elite cadre of writers and scientists, environmentalism has, in the space of just a few years, moved into the Soviet mainstream."[2] In many countries environmental concern has manifested itself in the development of "green movements" and "green" political parties. Beginning in the late 1970s, first in West Germany, new environmentally oriented political parties emerged to challenge the ecological management policies of established parties. Spokespersons for green parties argued that established political parties could not deal with the world's problems, because opposition "to this dominant world view cannot possibly be articulated through any of the major parties, for they and their ideologies are part of the problem."[3] Although the ideology of green parties varies from country to country, they usually include beliefs in "ecological wisdom, grassroots democracy, personal and social responsibility, nonviolence, decentralization, community based economics, postpatriarchal values, respect for diversity, global responsibility, and future focus."[4] These general beliefs manifest themselves in a variety of policy proposals including non-nuclear defense, feminism, local control, recycling, mass transit, self-reliance, renewable energy, and requiring that one's work be personally satisfying.[5] Green parties have been formed all over the world including Brazil, Costa Rica, Japan, Canada, and the United States (where Barry Commoner's Citizens' Party—active in the 1980 election—is most often cited as the American green party), and candidates from green parties have been elected to national parliaments in Switzerland (first in 1979); Belgium (1981); Finland, Portugal, and West Germany (1983); Luxembourg (1984); Austria (1986); Italy (1987); Sweden (1988); and the Netherlands (1989).[6]

The environmental policies of other nations, communist or capitalist, are remarkably similar both in terms of their objectives and their implementation problems. To varying degrees, environmental management in the industrialized countries is decentralized. Even in countries where central authorities were responsible for overseeing environmental management, such as the former Soviet Union, bargaining and negotiation between authorities in different ministries at various levels was the norm.[7]

In industrial democracies, approaches to environmental enforcement vary from the standards and enforcement approach of the United States (with standards set, usually nationwide, enforced by fines or punishment) to a consultation, negotiation approach characteristic of Great Britain (where pollution requirements are negotiated on an industry-by-industry basis, taking into consideration the situation at individual plants).[8] Most industrial democracies fall somewhere in between these extremes, using a combination of bargaining and standardized regulations.[9]

As you may have noticed in earlier chapters, I have been rather critical of the policy-making process in the United States and the environmental policies that system has produced. Due to the formal and informal incentives operating on policymakers, I am not optimistic about future environmental policies the system, in the United States as well as internationally, will produce. Although I have tried to suggest throughout the book ways in which you can have an impact on environmental policy formation, you might conclude at this point that the policy-making system in the United States and democracy itself is fundamentally flawed. Indeed, some of the best known observers of the environmental policy-making process and of environmental problems have concluded that existing governmental arrangements will fail and should be replaced by oligarchic governments staffed by environmental experts with the power to enforce sound environmental policy.[10] I don't agree. To paraphrase Winston Churchill, democracy is the worst form of government—except for all the others.

Even though the trend in the world is clearly away from communism and toward democratic capitalism, it is not unusual for commentators to blame capitalism and the private enterprise system for the woes of the environment. Because of this fact I think it is important we look at alternative political systems and see what kind of a job they have done in protecting the environment.

ALTERNATIVE POLITICAL SYSTEMS

The main doctrines of political systems focus on the scope of political freedom accorded to the individual, including personal freedom to interact, organize, and dissent. Vast differences exist between the doctrines of democratic and communist systems. How societies based on these doctrines actually work is equally diverse.

Industrialization brings the same environmental problems to developed and developing nations—communist or capitalist. Neither societies with high degrees of political freedom nor those with little political freedom have fared demonstrably better at ecologically sound management.

In practice, many nations combine free market and collective socialist activities within one "mixed economy," combining predominantly private initiative and property with public responsibility for social welfare. For example, Great Britain has state (collective or public) ownership of critical industries and services, such as health care, but privatization of previously state-owned industry advanced under Margaret Thatcher's Conservative government during the 1980s. So although most nations do not engage exclusively in one economic system or another, *those states advocating public ownership of the means of production with a centrally planned economy are here termed collective ownership systems* and include socialist as well as communist states; *states that protect private ownership and competition of the free market economy are called capitalist*. The system of government within which an economy operates is an important factor, but only one among many that affect a country's economic activity and the resultant pollution.

Market-Based Economies

Capitalist nations, where private ownership of industry is the rule, are driven by the profit motive in a free-market economy. Under communist governments the whole economy is planned, but in the comparatively unregulated operation of the free-market economy, supply and demand by consumers drives production. The incentive is to make money by selling a manufactured good at a profit. Industrialists in general and capitalists in particular traditionally have been unconcerned or unable to internalize the true environmental costs of their goods. Internalizing environmental costs, or eliminating externalities, means reduced profits or decreased output.[11]

Capitalism, in Western industrial societies, means that ownership and control of the means of production, for example factories and equipment, are, with some exceptions, generally held by individuals, not by the government.

According to its critics, one problem with democratic capitalism is that corporation managers wield far-reaching power over stockholders and employees and make decisions that affect the public without any clearly defined responsibility to the people. In addition, they wield power over politicians and public policy by virtue of their ability to make campaign contributions in greater amounts than groups representing environmental organizations. As corporations continue to grow, they take on the unhealthy characteristics of big bureaucracy, which is the same problem that large-scale socialized enterprise faces. As Denis Healey, prominent spokesman for the socialist cause in Britain stated, "Industrial power in every large, developed economy now rests with a managerial class which is responsible to no one. The form of ownership is irrelevant. State control over nationalized industries is as difficult as share-holder control over private firms."[12]

The environmental problems and societal responses within a democracy have been detailed throughout this book. How much better have communist systems fared?

Collective Ownership Systems

Central planning in the communist command economy determines how, for what purposes, and in what relative proportions available capital resources and labor are to be allocated. In practice this has meant the state not only controls what is produced but how it is produced, and with what materials. With public ownership, production is said to be limited only by scarce resources and incomplete knowledge, not by social institutions, such as the private profit motive.[13]

Under communist systems, the state owns the means of production and sets an overall goal of what is to be produced and how available resources of labor, land, and capital are to be employed. The freedom of the consumer, worker, and producer (what to produce, where to work, live, travel) is replaced by the orders of the state. Since the communist state possesses widespread power, it can work to turn the plan into reality. It is the collective control and planning function of communist systems that have led some to conclude those systems provide the means necessary for effective environmental management. In theory perhaps these people are correct. A centralized economic system could internalize pollution externalities, develop renewable resources, and in other ways establish sustainable economic and agricultural activities. In practice, however, the environmental policies and records of the two largest collective systems, China and the former Soviet Union, illustrate some of the problems collectivist societies have had in dealing with environmental problems.

Eastern Europe and the Former Soviet Union

As of this writing the political systems of the states that made up what was the Soviet Union and Eastern Europe are in flux. The summary of environmental problems in these former communist countries, and the conditions that lead to these problems, illustrate, nonetheless, the utility of alternative political systems (in this case, communist systems) for providing wise environmental management.

Since Stalin, communist leaders have placed a high priority on transforming their nations into industrial powers. This rapid modernization was accomplished with only minimal attention to pollution controls and with industrial processes that inefficiently consumed copious amounts of polluting fossil fuels.[14] For example, in the former Soviet Union the leadership took the view

> that nature is simply a source of raw materials which can be exploited to permit nearly unlimited growth for man's benefit. The environmental damage that results from such exploitation is either ignored or seen as a temporary problem that can be overcome without affecting development. This is the primary reason for many of the Soviet Union's severe pollution problems.[15]

In general, the former Soviet Union did not suffer from a shortage of environmental laws. What was lacking was enforcement. (Does that sound familiar?)

The environmental record of the communist systems in the former Soviet Union and Eastern Europe is very poor. When faced with trade-offs between economic growth and pollution control, the former usually won out over the latter.

The political reforms that swept across Eastern Europe in 1989 and 1990 opened up those societies and brought to international public attention some of the worst pollution problems imaginable. Scientists believe that up to 10 percent of the deaths in Eastern Europe are due to pollution. Before it became a part of a united Germany, air pollution in East Germany was 13 times as high as air pollution in West Germany. In a number of East European cities, the air is so polluted that cars turn on their headlights in the middle of the day to improve visibility and avoid running into each other. Doing laundry can be difficult under such conditions. As a Czechoslovakian housewife put it, "You cannot hang your clothes outside. If you do, they will be filthy before they are dry."[16]

And it is not only a problem of air pollution. In Poland, 65 percent of the rivers are so polluted that factories do not use the water for industrial purposes for fear the water will damage their pipes. The water quality situation is similar throughout Eastern Europe.[17]

Eastern European pollution problems are aggravated by the geography of the region. The countries lie in a narrow corridor without a large landmass to spread the pollution, like in the United States and China. According to a UN study, "The industrial regions of Central Europe are so choked by pollution that the health of children is impaired and the lives of adults shortened."[18]

Why did these countries fail to prevent resource depletion and pollution? In theory, collective systems would protect the environment, since "state ownership of the means of production would remove the motives for pollution because there was no reason for the state to contaminate itself and reduce its own wealth."[19] In practice, factory managers were pressured to meet production goals and had little incentive to prevent pollution. Managers were often paid bonuses for increasing production and faced few if any penalties for depleting resources or polluting the environment. In many communist countries there were systems of fines for pollution, but these were poorly enforced.[20]

China

In the People's Republic of China, traditional Chinese values have emphasized the necessity of harmony between humans and nature.[21] This is in contrast to Judeo-Christian Western belief systems that have emphasized the conquest of humans over nature. Yet the Chinese respect for nature must exist only in the abstract. As with other communist countries, economic pressures have created priorities of their own, and pollution of the Chinese environment is the result.

As in the former Soviet Union, a factory manager's performance in China is judged either by the amount he or she is able to increase productivity or by their political consciousness. "Since pollution control equipment would have meant the nonproductive divergence of labor, capital and material, no manager would have undertaken to install such devices unless mandated by party policy."[22] Since none of the frequent shifts in economic policy that occurred from 1949 to 1979 contained any industrial pollution control policy, no pollution control equipment was installed in China during this period. The result is that the Chinese now are forced not only to deal with the physical effects of years of industrial pollution, but they must also overcome the reluctance of officials and factory managers to take the consequences of pollution seriously.[23]

Since the adoption of the "Forestry Act" and the "Law on Environmental Protection" in China in 1979, there has been a new attitude and approach toward environmental problems in China. Articles, conferences, and other activities sanctioned by the government suggest there is now serious concern about threats to the environment.[24]

The Chinese face a number of obstacles in attempting to deal with pollution problems. First, China is a large country, both geographically and in numbers of citizens. And, as in the West, compliance with requirements that existing factories correct their pollution problems is expensive and does not contribute to a primary domestic goal—increasing productivity. Yet another problem stems from the government's land-use policies. Part of the industrial pollution problem is the location of factories—there is very little of what we would call zoning in China. Furthermore, peasants have been encouraged to plow up pastureland and forests, and to terrace mountains to plant grain. Serious erosion problems exist where the land has been cleared.[25] Since 1979, the goals of reducing industrial pollution, better land use, and the protection of national relics and historical sites have forced the Chinese to choose among government policies and have met with mixed results.

The Chinese have taken a positive approach toward cleaning up their environment. In addition to the aforementioned laws, the Chinese have moved to adopt a formal legal system better suited to enforcing environmental policies. As Bruce Ottley and Charles Valauskas have written, "[T]hese new policies, however, have been formulated at the same time that the Chinese have embarked on a program of 'four modernizations' with its emphasis on rapid economic growth."[26]

Like other communist nations, China lacks the technology and financial ability to introduce sophisticated pollution control devices in its factories. Damage from burning coal is a particularly difficult problem. This energy, necessary for continued industrial expansion, produces extensive air pollution. The northern part of the country is blanketed with high levels of both sulfur dioxide and suspended particulate matter; the southern half is feeling the effects of acidification, damaging soils and buildings.[27]

Product and profit orientation, regardless of the system, drives nations in ways not conducive to sound long-term ecological management. Collectivist societies with public ownership of agriculture and industry in a centrally planned society have not fared better in their management and prevention of pollution.[28] As "state capitalists," socialist states and capitalist private managers have a similar concern for profits.[29] The environmental problems of planned economies, such as those in the former Soviet Union and today in China, can be traced to the fact that they are state monopolies. A monopoly and the resulting concentration of economic and political power in a capitalist democracy can be opposed by the political power of the state. But "When the monopolist is the state itself, who will protect the citizen against the state?"[30] The environmental problem of a state monopoly has been exacerbated by the changes that have occurred over the years in communist countries. Industrial policy has concentrated on maximum production capacity with little concern for environmental consequences.

It is becoming increasingly obvious in advanced economies that perpetual growth is causing enormous environmental problems. Great rivers in industrialized countries worldwide, regardless of political system, have been turned into sewer lines. In Russia, the Volga River is polluted by publicly owned factories; in the United States the Mississippi is just as polluted by waste and refuse from privately owned plants. It makes little difference to the environment if the polluter is a privately or publicly owned enterprise. Both systems have equally materialistic production and consumption values, pay little heed to environmental degradation, and ignore externalities. "In our own day, the experience of communist economic change teaches again that the principal issue is not whether the government owns the means of production, but who owns the government."[31]

INTERNATIONAL ENVIRONMENTAL MANAGEMENT

Lynton K. Caldwell, a recognized expert on international environmental management who has been studying environmental policy for over 35 years wrote,

> [P]lanetary environmental developments occurring beyond America's borders are now perceived, or anticipated, to be beyond national control. The concept of national sovereignty is of declining significance in a world that increasingly faces environmental problems affecting people everywhere. The fates of the first, second, and third worlds are interlinked through the biosphere.[32]

In 1972 representatives from 113 nations met in Stockholm for a Conference on the Human Environment. At the time only nine countries had internal administrative organizations set up to deal with environmental problems. Since then, numerous treaties, programs, organizations, and international regimes have been created to deal with environmental problems. The United Nations Environment Program, created at the Stockholm conference to provide environmental education and training, is one of the more visible organizations. Yet global environmental problems are worse now than they were in 1972. What happened?

Common Pool Resources

Common pool property problems are very much a part of global environmental management. Air is an example of a common pool resource. Individual manufacturers polluting the air have no incentive to limit their polluting activities assuming there are no restrictions. The cost of air pollution in this instance is not borne by the polluter but rather by everyone. Each individual polluter has no incentive to protect the common pool resource of clean air, and, in fact, the individual has every incentive to continue polluting.

As we have seen, two major international common pool resource problems that are associated with air pollution are depletion of the stratospheric ozone layer through the release of chlorofluorocarbons (CFCs) and the warming of the earth's atmosphere from the accumulation of greenhouse gasses.[33] These long-term problems with pressing *immediate* economic and health needs, in addition to the common pool nature of the problems and the lack of certainty as to long-term effects even in the face of certainty of *some* negative effects, make global warming and ozone depletion issues that will not go away any time soon. All of these uncertainties allow those that benefit from fossil fuel consumption and CFC production, or those who fear the negative political fallout from limiting that consumption, to argue against taking corrective actions.

Given the common pool nature of global pollution problems and the incentives, or lack thereof, operating on governments to restrict production of CFCs and greenhouse-producing gasses, it would seem that some type of international government organization (IGO) is necessary for dealing with these problems. By way of analogy, the farmers in Garret Hardin's common pasture are nations. Unless these nations are willing to give up low-lying coastal areas and live with disruptions in agricultural production as well as significantly increased skin cancer rates, the community of nations that makes up the global commons will have to restrict access to global common pool air resources. This means an IGO, either in existence or created for the purpose, will be necessary.[34] As we have seen, the common pool nature of international environmental problems makes cooperation—which may involve sacrifice—difficult. For example, the 1992 Rio Conference did result in carbon emission reporting agreements (154 countries, including the United States, signed a climate treaty requiring reporting), but the conference failed to agree on goals and timetables for restricting carbon emissions, largely because of the opposition of the United States.

A threshold issue for international environmental management must be, therefore, under what conditions and constraints can a successful IGO be created.

Creation of an IGO

An international government organization is an international or multinational organization established "with the objective of structuring communication and cooperation between member states on a continuing basis."[35] The Rhine River Commission, created in 1815 to regulate traffic on the Rhine, was the first modern IGO.[36] Although estimates vary, the number of IGOs is in excess of 600.[37]

An IGO is created when there is the perception of an existing or pending crisis by two or more governmental actors. This first step is relatively easy to make. Conferences have been held on the environment generally (Stockholm, 1972); on food (Rome, 1974); population (Bucharest, 1974, and Mexico City, 1984); desertification (Nairobi, 1977); and biological diversity (Rio de Janeiro, 1992) among others. Global conferences on the atmosphere were held in 1987 (the Montreal Protocol) and 1989 (in London). Once a group of nations decides to cooperate on a problem by forming an IGO, participants must decide on the appropriate procedures and decision-making rules the IGO will follow. Participants must also agree on the means of detecting compliance with any agreements and enforcement of agreements. Enforcement is a particularly difficult task if, as in the case of the production of greenhouse gasses, there is strong disagreement over the nature of, and responsibility for, the problem.

The problem with an IGO approach to managing international environmental problems is that the creation of an IGO, as well as the agreement on appropriate procedures and enforcement mechanisms, requires the mutual consent of all parties involved. However, as Marvin Soroos has pointed out, "[P]roblems are in the eyes of the beholder, for to refer to any actual or potential condition as being problematical presumes a certain interpretation."[38]

Decisions within IGOs are either by consensus or through some decision-making rule such as the will of the majority or plurality. Obviously, decisions reached by consensus are preferred, since problems of compliance are likely to be minimized—all the participants agree on the policy. Unfortunately, with ozone and greenhouse gasses in international environmental common pool management, consensus decision making is unlikely. As *Los Angeles Times* environmental writer Larry Stammer wrote, "Will China deny citizens the chance to own a refrigerator? Will Brazil go deeper in debt by cutting back logging on its lush rain forest? . . . In short, will the nations of the world—rich and poor alike—make huge sacrifices in an effort to spare the global environment from further destruction?"[39] The answer depends on the perception of a crisis situation that needs to be addressed and perceptions of national self-interest.

The sacrifices some countries will need to make will be great. This suggests there will be compliance problems. Noncompliance with agreed upon environmental controls is an example of a common pool free-rider problem. A nation that continues to produce CFCs or greenhouse gasses reaps the benefits of less atmospheric pollution globally at no cost to itself. The free-rider problem necessitates some means of enforcement.

The first problem of enforcement is to identify violators. This raises certain sovereignty questions and questions of whether or not access will be available to check on compliance. The International Atomic Energy Commission (IAEA) has a great deal of experience in this regard. Founded in 1957, the Vienna-based IAEA is an international organization comprised of more than 100 nations. The IAEA is credited with being the major international actor responsible for preventing the proliferation of nuclear weapons. Nevertheless, the activities of the IAEA are limited by national sovereignty questions. As Leonard Spector wrote, "[I]f a country does not openly display its nuclear capacities or break IAEA rules, it may approach and actually cross the nuclear weapons threshold with virtual impunity."[40]

Once identification problems have been solved, then the question becomes one of enforcement. An IGO and member nations may decide to use negative or positive sanctions. Negative sanctions would include economic sanctions such as boycotts or embargoes, which are rarely effective as the experience of Rhodesia and South Africa have shown, or military negative sanctions up to and including going to war. Positive sanctions could include cash transfers, debt relief, or the delivery of expertise or other positive inducements to persuade noncomplying nations to agree with policies that have been established by the IGO.

Equity considerations would seem to require that positive sanctions be used for enforcement of IGO air pollution regulations. By far, the greatest percentage of buildup of ozone in the stratosphere and of greenhouse gasses has been due to the activities of the more developed countries. An estimated 90 percent of the world's CFCs are produced and consumed in the industrialized countries.[41]

In a sense, the atmosphere has been used, much the way water is drawn from a nonrecharging well, to assist in the economic development of the more developed countries since the beginning of the Industrial Revolution. Because there is no effective means of "cleansing" the atmospheric environment so we might start with a fresh slate of a valuable stock of global resources, our protective air cover, which has been depleted by one group of nations, is no longer available for the use of the rest.

Is it equitable for the United States and Western Europe, which together produce 4 times as many CFCs as Asia and 20 times as many CFCs as Latin America, to call for a ban on production? The more developed world already has in place the refrigeration units, automobiles, and other consumer goods for which the world has paid with its protective ozone layer. Is it fair, for example, to tell China, which built 12 CFC plants during the 1980s to provide refrigerators for its population (fewer than 10 percent of whom owned refrigerators in 1989), that it must now close those plants?[42] India has similar concerns, and both China and India let it be known at the 1989 London CFC conference that it would be difficult for them to agree to limit CFC production without financial and technological assistance.[43] As Joan Martin Brown, the United Nations Environment Program liaison to the United States put it, "The Third World says you're telling us not to do what you did to achieve your high standard of living. What are you going to do for us? Do you want to rent the trees from us? You know you can rent them for $1 billion a year in hard currency and we won't cut them down."[44]

Fortunately, the world may not need to rely on perceptions of equity. It is in the self-interest of the more developed countries to begin *now* with transfer payments and technological assistance to less developed countries to stem CFC production and the growth of greenhouse gasses. The cost to the more developed countries of mitigating damages due to global warming and increased solar irradiation will be much greater in the future and for decades to come than will the short-term cost of protecting the earth's atmosphere. The question is, will the leadership of the more developed countries see it as being in their best interest to begin transfers now rather than waiting for a crisis? Given the incentives operating on politicians to think in short-term cycles and the propensity of politicians as well as people generally to discount the future, the answer would appear to be no.

Each step in the process of environmental common pool management through an IGO requires the perception on the part of the actors involved that there is a crisis which needs to be addressed. Furthermore, the perception of crisis must be greater at each stage of the process. The overriding question for international pollution management becomes, then, whether the crisis situation necessary to facilitate IGO organization and action will be so bad that by the time action is taken much of the damage to the environment will have been done.

As Soroos pointed out, perceptions of problems differ. In less developed countries, illiteracy, poverty, as well as other internal factors, may limit domestic perceptions of, or pressure to respond to, any crisis. This further increases the level of damage (or perception of crisis) necessary for the leaders of those countries to act. For example, Brazil, Indonesia, and Zaire, countries suffering from illiteracy as well as a host of other internal problems, are also suffering deforestation problems. The more developed world has an interest in protecting the forests in these countries. By the time the leaders of these and other less developed countries move deforestation to the top of their political agendas, significant global environmental damage may have already been done.

The time for a multinational effort to protect the earth's atmosphere is upon us. As Maurice Strong put it, "[P]eople have learned to enlarge the circles of their allegiance and their loyalty, as well as the institutions through which they are governed, from the family to the tribe to the village to the town to the city to the nation state. We are now called upon to make the next and final step, at least on this planet, to the global level."[45]

By the time appropriate perceptions of crisis are reached to facilitate the necessary intergovernmental cooperation and action, much damage will have been done and the cost of mitigating that damage will be much higher than would have otherwise been the case.

Although it would be less costly for developed nations to recognize the hazard now—and not wait for a crisis situation—and to begin transfers of technology and other resources to assist in the transfer to a CFC- and fossil-fuel-free global commons, the incentives operating on international policymakers make this unlikely—another paradox of environmental policy.

SUMMARY

One might think that different political systems would produce different environmental outcomes. As we have seen, that is not the case. Differences in government forms do not matter much in pollution control outcomes.[46] Some problems are universal. For example, studies have shown that regardless of the political system, a municipality, or other local authority that is powerful, is likely to hinder rather than help in the implementation of a pollution control program.[47] Even when a plan exists to solve environmental problems, and even when it is well executed, it will frequently not have the desired outcome—regardless of the political system in place.[48]

Furthermore, we have seen that some international environmental problems will require global cooperation and international organizations and the obstacles to creating such organizations are great. It may be that international actions are only taken after serious damage has been done to the environment. On the brighter side, in the 1980s and 1990s there have been a number of international environmental meetings and agreements, and "green parties" have sprung up everywhere. In the concluding chapter we speculate on the future ability of democratic societies to deal with the environmental policy paradox.

NOTES

1. Norman J. Vig and Michael E. Kraft (eds.), *Environmental Policy in the 1990s* (Washington, DC: Congressional Quarterly Press, 1990), p. 4.
2. Hilary F. French, "The Greening of the Soviet Union," *World Watch* (May/June 1989), p. 26.
3. Petra Kelly, quoted in Jonathon Porritt, *Seeing Green: The Politics of Ecology Explained* (New York: Blackwell, 1985), p. x.
4. Raymond Dominick, "The Roots of the Green Movement in the United States and West Germany," *Environmental Review*, 12(3) (Fall 1988), p. 4.
5. See Jonathon Porritt, *Seeing Green: The Politics of Ecology Explained* (New York: Blackwell, 1985), Ch. 10.
6. Michael G. Renner, "Europe's Green Tide," *World Watch*, 3(1) (January/February 1990), p. 25. The ability of a green party to win seats in any national government is a function of the electoral system used in the country. Most European governments have some form of proportional representation wherein parties are given seats in the national legislature that approximate their popularity with the voters. For example, the West German green party, *Die Grunen*, won about 5.6 percent of the national vote in 1983. In the districts where *Die Grunen* ran the strongest, the party only polled approximately 10 percent of the vote. Yet they were rewarded with 27 of the 518 seats in the lower house of the national legislature. In the United States, representatives are elected to Congress and state legislatures on a single-member plurality basis—the person with the most votes represents the district. For an American green party to win a legislative seat, their candidate would have to get 50 percent of the vote in a given district, a difficult task given the propensity of voters in the United States to stick with one of the two established parties. Many European green parties have the advantage that their governments will pay the campaign expenses of minor parties even if they are not successful. In 1980 the West German greens polled only 1.5 percent of the national vote, far below the 5 percent minimum necessary to win seats in the national legislature but enough to receive one million German marks from the federal government. (See Dominick, "The Roots of the Green Movement," p. 21.) Successful minor political parties often find the more established parties adopt the issues that led to the creation of the minor party in the first place. When this happens, the minor party may disappear. We then say that the issue has been coopted by the major party. In the United States, both major political parties have adopted environmentalism—to varying degrees—as part of their national platforms. In other nations, green parties have been coopted or have joined in coalitions with the more dominant parties. Although green parties have played an important role in bringing environmental issues to the attention of the public in many countries, they are not likely to play a major role in governing any of the countries where they have emerged.

7. Joan de Bardelaben, *The Environment and Marxist-Leninism: The Soviet and East German Experience* (Boulder, CO: Westview Press, 1985).

8. David Vogel, *National Styles of Regulation: Environmental Policy in Great Britain and the United States* (Ithaca, NY: Cornell University Press, 1986).

9. Arnold J. Heidenheimer, Hugh Heclo, and Carolyn Teich Adams, *Comparative Public Policy* (New York: St. Martin's Press, 1990), pp. 323–325.

10. See, for example, William Ophuls, *Ecology and the Politics of Scarcity* (San Francisco: Freeman, 1977), Ch. 4; and Garrett Hardin, "The Tragedy of the Commons," *Science*, 162 (1968) pp. 1243–1248. Robert L. Heilbroner, *An Inquiry into the Human Prospect* (New York: Norton, 1974); and Ted Robert Gurr, "On the Political Consequences of Scarcity and Economic Decline," *International Studies Quarterly*, 29 (1985), pp. 51–75.

11. William Ebenstein and Edwin Fogelman, *Today's Isms:Communism, Fascism, Capitalism, Socialism* (8th ed.) (Englewood Cliffs, NJ: Prentice-Hall, 1980), p. 152.

12. Denis Healey, *The New Leader* (August 17, 1957), quoted in Ebenstein and Fogelman, *Today's Isms* p. 239.

13. William Echikson, "Dissident Groups Defy Government to Aid Environment," *Los Angeles Times*, January 17, 1988, p. 2.

14. Hilary F. French, "The Greening of the Soviet Union," *World Watch* (May/June 1989), p. 22.

15. Bruce L. Ottley and Charles C. Valauskas, "China's Developing Environmental Law: Policies, Practices and Legislation," *Boston College International and Comparative Law Review*, 4(1) (1983), p. 91.

16. All these examples were taken from Mark M. Nelson, "As Shroud of Secrecy Lifts in East Europe, Smog Shroud Emerges," *Wall Street Journal*, CXXII, (42) (March 1, 1990), p. A1.

17. Larry Tye, "Pollution a Nightmare Behind the Iron Curtain," *Arizona Republic*, February 25, 1990, p. C1.

18. The World Resources Institute, The United Nations Environment Programme and The United Nations Development Programme, *World Resources: 1992–93* (New York: Oxford University Press, 1992), p. 57.

19. Ibid., p. 60.

20. Ibid.

21. Ottley and Valauskas, "China's Developing Environmental Law: Policies, Practices and Legislation," p. 84.

22. Ibid., p. 108.

23. Ibid., pp. 108–109.

24. Ibid., p. 121.

25. Ibid., pp. 125–127.

26. Ibid., p. 130.

27. Don Hinrichsen, "Like First World, Like Third World," *The Amicus Journal* (Winter 1988), p. 7.

28. William A. Echikson, "Pollution Seeps to the Forefront of Eastern Bloc's Consciousness," *Los Angeles Times*, Jan. 17, 1988, p. 2.

29. Stanley J. Kabala, "Poland: Facing the Hidden Costs of Development," *Environment*, 27 (November 1985), p. 39.

30. Ebenstein and Fogelman, *Today's Isms*, p. 235.

31. Ibid., p. 42.

32. Lynton K. Caldwell, "International Environmental Politics: America's Response to Global Imperatives," in Norman J. Vig and Michael E. Kraft (eds.), *Environmental Policy in the 1990s* (Washington, DC: Congressional Quarterly Press, 1990), p. 301.

33. Other gasses are involved, but the discussion here is limited to CFCs, being by far the largest contributor. See Thomas H. Maugh II, "Ozone Depletion Far

Worse Than Expected," *Los Angeles Times*, March 16, 1988, Pt. 1, p. 1; and "Ozone Depletion Worsens, NRDC Leads Drive for Total CFC Phase Out," *Newsline* (Natural Resources Defense Council), 6(2) (May/June 1988), p. 1; Christopher Flavin, "The Heat Is On," *World Watch*, 1(6) (November/December 1988), p. 19.

34. The creation of an IGO is not necessary for dealing with all international environmental problems. For example, international agreements for international coordination of responses to nuclear accidents might be arranged on a contractual basis without the creation of an IGO. However, in international common pool situations where there are clear winners and losers, where no individual nation has an incentive to restrict its activities, and hence where some enforcement mechanism may be necessary to ensure compliance with rules designed to protect the commons, an IGO likely is necessary, most analysts have concluded. See Oran R. Young, *International Cooperation: Building Regimes for Natural Resources and the Environment* (Ithaca, NY: Cornell University Press, 1989).

35. Marvin S. Soroos, *Beyond the Sovereignty: The Challenge of Global Policy* (Columbia: University of South Carolina Press, 1986), pp. 81–82.

36. Ibid., p. 83.

37. Harold K. Jacobson, *Networks of Interdependence: International Organizations and the Global Political System* (2nd ed.) (New York: Knopf, 1984), p. 9.

38. Soroos, *Beyond the Sovereignty: The Challenge of Global Policy*, p. 34.

39. Larry B. Stammer, "Saving the Earth: Who Sacrifices?" *Los Angeles Times*, March 13, 1989, Pt. 1, p. 1.

40. Leonard S. Spector, "Silent Spread," *Foreign Policy*, 58 (Spring 1985), p. 56.

41. Stammer, "Saving the Earth: Who Sacrifices?" p. 16.

42. Larry B. Stammer, "Global Talks on Ozone Described as Successful," *Los Angeles Times*, March 8, 1989, Pt. 1, p. 6; CFC production in the United States in 1986 was estimated at 1,070 million pounds; for Western Europe, 1,100; for Asia and the Pacific, 550; the Eastern bloc, 250; and in Latin America, 100.

43. Stammer, "Saving the Earth: Who Sacrifices?" 1989, p. 16.

44. Ibid.

45. Maurice F. Strong, presented to the International Development Conference, Washington, DC, March 19, 1987. Reprinted in Lester R. Brown, Christopher Flavin, and Sandra Postel, "A World at Risk," in Lester R. Brown et al. (eds.), *State of the World: 1989* (New York: Norton, 1989), p. 20.

46. Paul B. Downing and Kenneth Hanf (eds.), "Cross-National Comparisons in Environmental Protection: A Symposium," *Policy Studies Journal* (September 1982), p. 38; see also Paul B. Downing, "Cross-National Comparisons in Environmental Protection: Introduction to the Issues," *Policy Studies Journal* (September 1982), p. 184.

47. See Bruno Dente and Rudy Lewanski, "Administrative Networks and Implementation Effectiveness: Industrial Air Pollution Control Policy in Italy," *Policy Studies Journal*, 11 (1982), p. 129; Robert F. Durant, *When Government Regulates Itself: EPA, TVA, and Pollution Control in the 1970s* (Knoxville: University of Tennessee Press, 1985); and David Vogel, *National Styles of Regulation: Environmental Policy in Great Britain and the United States* (Ithaca, NY: Cornell University Press, 1986).

48. See, for example, Downing, "Cross-National Comparisons in Environmental Protection: Introduction to the Issues," p. 186.

Conclusion

We have examined environmental policy in America within the context of a paradox: Policymakers often seem to know what to do but for a variety of reasons, it doesn't get done. In air pollution, for example, its causes and the long-term environmental consequences of burning fossil fuels are relatively clear. However, political and economic realities seem to guarantee we will continue our dependence on fossil fuels for the foreseeable future. Also, in solid waste management, we have known for many decades the consequences of a policy of ever-expanding landfill operations. Yet it has not been until the 1990s that most municipalities have seriously considered alternatives to landfill disposal of solid waste.

Although the environmental policy paradox concept is useful for understanding problems in environmental policy, it does not apply to all situations equally well. In some areas of environmental policy, the problem is an *uncertainty* of knowledge often coupled with a lack of agreement over values, trade-offs, and the appropriate course of action. Or the scientific community may not be in agreement on the nature of the problem or the appropriate solution.

The paradox of environmental policy is very useful, however, for understanding some aspects of the policy-making process, such as informal incentive systems that operate on policymakers. Such systems, discussed in Part One, promise that long-term solutions to environmental problems with high immediate costs are unlikely to be pursued. In some cases, this is unfortunate. Deferring action on serious environmental problems is very much like accumulating debt. Eventually the debt must be paid off. When it becomes clear the environmental deficit needs to be retired—renewable energy must be developed, the burning of fossil fuels must be cut back, the flow of solid waste must be drastically reduced—the cost of retiring that deficit will be very high.

Students of the environmental policy process often question the ability of democratic political systems to cope with environmental problems. Given what you have learned in this book, do you think an ecological government is possible? If such a government is possible, how can it develop or rule, given the political and institutional obstacles that create the paradox of environmental policy?

Some of the best known observers of the environmental policy-making process and of environmental problems have concluded that existing governmental arrangements will fail. It has been argued by some of the most respected environmental policy analysts that democratic systems need to be replaced by oligarchic governments staffed by environmental experts with the power to enforce sound environmental policy.[1] It is also not unusual for commentators to blame the private enterprise system for our environmental problems. But as we saw in the last chapter, state-controlled economies are no more likely to protect the environment than are market-based/capitalist economies.

Some have concluded there is a fundamental conflict between democratic systems and the sacrifice, decisiveness, and speed with which environmental policy needs to be developed and implemented if it is to be effective. For example, William Ophuls has argued that some type of oligarchy run by technological elites may be necessary. In contrast, others, such as Dean Mann, have argued that "[T]he environmental program in the United States remains of sufficient vitality that it will continue to mitigate, in halting but meaningful ways, the current and foreseeable threats to ecological systems and the quality of the environment."[2]

I think the truth lies somewhere between these two positions. Basically, the policy-making process in our American democracy will work reasonably well in some cases, but it will not work well at all in others. The system does respond to crisis situations and those controversies that attract a great deal of public attention. The amount of media attention and the nature of the problem itself will determine whether or not the system responds well and in a timely manner to an environmental problem. The attention, in the early 1990s, that is being focused on solid waste and recycling provides an example. Even though many communities have run out of landfill space, there are practical, if not particularly desirable, solutions to our long-term solid waste problems. Other environmental problems, such as global warming and the depletion of the ozone layer, may not lend themselves to satisfactory solutions given the constraints in the policy-making process. Simply put, by the time we reach a crisis situation in the global environment and action is taken both in the United States and internationally, the damage will be severe—and irreversible.

Surrendering democratic power to a central governmental authority with the power to deal with environmental problems in a timely and comprehensive manner has certain attractions, and promises quick solutions to our environmental problems. However, the cost for many, myself included, is too great.

Oligarchic governments established to deal with environmental problems would bring other problems. Who will rule the rulers? Nevertheless, an argument can be made that oligarchic political systems are both necessary and inevitable. The environmental crisis, unless mitigated, could lead to the establishment of a fascist or some other oligarchic system in the United States. The editors of *State of the World* wrote, "[A]s the world enters the twenty-first century, the community of nations either will have rallied and turned back the threatening trends, or environmental deterioration and social disintegration will be feeding on each other."[3]

Extremism that polarizes blocks of people within a society can force the people into choosing between anarchy and repression. Such a polarizing force as terrorism, racism, or a rapidly deteriorating environment that disrupts a society and accepted standards of living could force the choice. And as former U.S. Senator Margaret Chase Smith cautioned, "[M]ake no mistake about it, if that narrow choice has to be made, the American people, even with reluctance and misgiving, will choose repression."[4]

The 1990s will be a crucial decade in our battle for the environment. Many of the environmental problems discussed in this book will reach a critical stage during the decade. Unfortunately, in some cases, environmental problems that are manageable in the early part of the 1990s, such as global warming, ozone depletion, or overdependence on fossil fuels, will be much worse—given current trends—at the turn of the century. As assistant secretary for external affairs at the Smithsonian Institution and biologist Thomas Lovejoy, stated, "I am utterly convinced that most of the great environmental struggles will either be won or lost in the 1990s. And that by the next century it will be too late."[5] Or as Eduard Shevardnadze, the foreign minister of the former Soviet Union stated to the United Nations General Assembly, "[W]e have too little [time] and problems are piling up faster than they are solved."[6] The decade of the 1990s must be the turnaround decade. Otherwise, it is only a question of what will collapse first—the environmental foundation on which we stand or the fossil fuel intensive, environmentally insensitive economic support system from which we hang.

What the world will look like in the future is an open question. Throughout this book I have tried to address ways that we, as individuals, can have an impact on the quality of our environment. Over the long term, a shift must be made in our dominant social paradigm. Lester Milbrath's work suggests a paradigm shift may be in process. It remains to be seen if the environmentalists, the "vanguard for a new society" as Milbrath calls them, will become a majority or remain a minority. But, as Milbrath concludes, "In modern society, we have developed a socio-technical-economic system that can dominate and destroy nature. Alongside it, we have retained a normative and ethical system based on 2000-year-old religions. The lack of congruence between these two systems threatens the continued existence of our civilization."[7]

On an individual level, you can work to live a less energy-intensive life. Switching to fluorescent light bulbs, walking or cycling instead of driving, insulating your home, shunning disposable products, recycling, conserving water, and eating less meat are all things you can do that will help the environment. There are several books available that provide extensive suggestions on how you can live a less environmentally destructive life.[8]

More than anything else, it takes getting involved. Politically involved—in city council meetings, following events in the Congress and your state legislatures, attending agency hearings, and writing letters to the editor of your local newspaper. The informal incentives that operate in the policy-making process, particularly the importance of special interest money, political action committees, and the natural tendency of politicians to avoid tough decisions, can be derailed if enough people become interested and involved in the policy making process. It is up to each of us. It is our future.

NOTES

1. See, for example, William Ophuls, *Ecology and the Politics of Scarcity* (San Francisco: Freeman, 1977), Ch. 4; and Garrett Hardin, "The Tragedy of the Commons," *Science*, 162 (1968), pp. 1243–1248.

2. Dean E. Mann, "Democratic Politics and Environmental Policy," in Sheldon Kamieniecki, Robert O'Brien, and Michael Clarke (eds.), *Controversies in Environmental Policy* (Albany: State University of New York Press, 1986), p. 32.

3. Lester R. Brown, Christopher Flavin, and Sandra Postel, "Outlining a Global Action Plan," in Lester R. Brown et. al. (eds.), *State of the World: 1989* (New York: Norton, 1989), p. 194.

4. Quoted in William Ebenstein and Edwin Fogelman, *Today's Isms: Communism, Fascism, Capitalism, Socialism* (8th ed.) (Englewood Cliffs, NJ: Prentice-Hall, 1980), p. 131.

5. Brown, Flavin, and Postel, "Outlining a Global Action Plan," p. 192.

6. Brown, Flavin, and Postel, "Outlining a Global Action Plan," p. 192. Statement before the Forty-third Session of the UN General Assembly, New York, September 27, 1988.

7. Lester W. Milbrath, *Environmentalists: Vanguard for a New Society* (Albany: State University of New York Press, 1984), p. 101.

8. See, for example, Ruth Caplan, *Our Earth, Ourselves* (New York: Bantam Books, 1990); John Elkington, Julia Hailes, and Joel Makower, *The Green Consumer* (New York: Penguin Books, 1990); Diane MacEachern, *Save Our Planet: 750 Everyday Ways You Can Help Clean Up the Earth* (New York: Dell, 1990); and Earth Works Group, *50 Simple Things You Can Do to Save the Earth* (Berkeley, CA: Earthworks Press, 1989).

Index

A

Acid rain (*see* Air pollution)
Aerojet General Corporation, 56
Africa, 213–214, 216, 218
Africa Development Bank, 221
Agenda setting, 38–40 (*see also* Policy making process)
Agriculture:
conservation of water, 118
land conversion, 194–195
organic farming, xii, 195
productivity, 216
runoff, 106, 113, 117
and solid waste, 165
Air pollution, 49, 68–97, 128, 137, 234
acid rain, 49, 68–69, 71, 84–88, 136, 233
National Acid Precipitation Assessment Program, 87
Air Quality Control Regions (AQCRs), 74
Alaska National Interest Lands Conservation Act, 61–62
asbestos, 83–84
banking, 78
bubbles, 30, 78
Clean Air Act, 54, 75–88, 91
Convention on Long Range Trans-Boundary Air Pollution, 91

costs:
of air pollution control and acid rain, 84
of motor vehicle emission abatement, 72
crop loss, 71
Emission Reduction Credits (ERC), 78–80
emission-trading, 78
global warming and the green-house effect, 3, 49, 68, 84, 92–97, 133, 210, 217–218, 235, 236
termites and methane gas, 94
hazardous air pollutants, 81–84
law, regulations, and enforcement, 73–81
lead, 83
motor vehicles, 72–73
National Ambient Air Quality Standards (NAAQS), 75
netting, 78
offsets, 78
particulate matter, 68–70
primary standards, 75
scientific uncertainty, 72, 81, 89
secondary standards, 75
sulfur oxides, 68–70, 85, 138
toxic air pollution, 81
(*see also* Ozone layer)
Alaska, 138, 197, 206
Allin, Craig, 199

ABOUT THE AUTHOR

Zachary A. Smith received his B.A. from California State University, Fullerton, and his M.A. and Ph.D. from the University of California, Santa Barbara. He has taught at Northern Arizona University, the Hilo branch of the University of Hawaii, Ohio University, and the University of California, at Santa Barbara; and has served as the Wayne Aspinall Visiting Professor of political science, public affairs, and history at Mesa State College in Grand Junction, Colorado. A consultant both nationally and internationally on environmental matters, he is the author or editor of nine books and many articles on environmental and policy topics. He currently teaches environmental and natural resources policy and administration in the public policy Ph.D. program in the Political Science Department at Northern Arizona University in Flagstaff.